WOMEN AND POLITICS IN ANCIENT ROME

Richard A. Bauman

London and New York

First published 1992
by Routledge
11 New Fetter Lane, London EC4P 4EE

First published in paperback 1994
by Routledge

Simultaneously published in the USA and Canada
by Routledge
29 West 35th Street, New York, NY 10001

© 1992, 1994 Richard A. Bauman

Typeset in 10 on 12 point Garamond by
Intype, London
Printed in Great Britain by
T J Press (Padstow) Ltd, Padstow, Cornwall

British Library Cataloguing in Publication Data
Bauman, Richard A.
Women and politics in Ancient Rome.
I. Title
937.05

Library of Congress Cataloging in Publication Data
Bauman, Richard, A.
Women and politics in ancient Rome / Richard A. Bauman.
p. cm.
Includes bibliographical references and index.
1. Women–Rome. 2. Women in politics–Rome. I. Title
HQ1136.B38 1992 91–45088
305.42′0937′6–dc20

ISBN 0–415–05777–9

To my granddaughter Ella Kate
and
her grandmother Sheila

CONTENTS

vii

CONTENTS

PREFACE

Some thirty years ago a writer on Roman women was able to claim that 'Intriguing as ancient Roman women may have been, they are the subject of no single work of deep and learned scholarship in English or in any other language' (Balsdon 1962). Since then the explosion in women's studies has produced many works 'of deep and learned scholarship', a substantial proportion of which deals with the role of women in Roman history, politics and law. In terms of size there has been nothing to compare with Balsdon's coverage – the history of women from Romulus to Constantine, plus a large section on what he calls 'their habits' – but what later works lack in length they more than make up for in depth. One need only glance at the works listed in our bibliography. For the republican period those works do not include any overall study since Balsdon's assessment, though Herrmann (1964), if used with caution, partly discharges that function. The tendency has been to focus on special aspects. A number of writers have concentrated on women and the law: one notes the pioneering work of Peppe, the in-depth studies of A. J. Marshall, and the paper by Dixon. Others have examined the laws applicable to women: Corbett's basic book on marriage is supplemented by the works of Watson and J. F. Gardner, and a particular law is discussed by Culham. (I have not seen S. M. Treggiari, *Roman Marriage*, 1991). Studies of individual women include Deroux, Dorey, McDermott, Ramage and Skinner on Clodia; Babcock on Fulvia; Singer on Octavia; and Horsfall and Instinsky on Cornelia's letter. Specific problems affecting women are discussed by Boyce, Hinard (in part), E. Rawson and Reinach. The Vestals have been explored from several important points of view by Beard, Cornell, Koch and Münzer. There is a special study of protest by Gallini, and studies of cults by Festugière, Gagé, Rousselle and Scheid.

The early Principate has generated a number of overall studies. Ferrero's work is still useful, despite his habit of making *ex cathedra* pronouncements without any documentation. Since then overviews have been furnished by Carcopino, Hoffsten, Malcovati, Meise and Sirago. There has been a proliferation of works on special aspects. Studies of women and the law have emanated from A. J. Marshall and (for the later Principate) Beaucamp. Augustus' legislation on marriage and morals has inspired works by Badian, Besnier, Brunt, Cantarella, Csillag, Della Corte, Des Bouvrie, Galinsky, Jörs, Last, Raditsa, Thomas and Villers. Studies of individual women include Leon on Scribonia; Groag and Sattler on Julia; Purcell and Ritter on Livia; Kaplan and Rogers on the elder Agrippina; Herz on Drusilla; Ehrhardt, Guarino and Robleda on Messalina; and Melmoux on the younger Agrippina. One early study that tends to refute Balsdon's dismissal of his predecessors is Ollendorf's on Livia. Particular problems bearing on the role of women have been addressed by Colin, Fanizza, Norwood, Raepsaet-Charlier, Thibault and Wiseman.

Works of great interest, but not readily assignable to any of the above categories, have been produced by Cantarella, De Riencourt, Finley, Hallett, Pomeroy and Zinserling. Studies of individual emperors that help to fill out the picture include Kornemann, Levick, Marsh and Seager on Tiberius; Barrett and Nony on Caligula; Levick and Scramuzza on Claudius; and Cizek, Griffin, Warmington and Walter on Nero. There is no completely adequate book on Augustus. Syme's account in his 1939 work is still the best, but is badly in need of updating; his 1986 work does not fully meet that need. My own works relating to our subject are listed in the bibliography.

The writer, having spent many years teaching and writing about both Roman history and Roman law, attempts in the present work to apply that accumulated experience to the role of Roman women in the business of politics, government, law, and public affairs in general. The theme offers both a special view of Roman history and a special view of Roman women. Although never allowed to hold office or to vote, Roman women played an important, and often – in spite of determined resistance – decisive role in public affairs. The work covers a longer time span than has been adopted in recent years. The discussion runs from c. 350 BC to AD 68, from the middle years of the Republic to the end of the Julio-Claudian dynasty which presided over the first hundred years of the Principate. The story of Roman women over the period is one of cohesion and continuity, of the steady expansion of women's historic role in public affairs. That steady expansion, and the various means by which it was achieved, provide the basic framework of the study. Within that framework are offered a number of solutions to old problems, as well as solutions to problems that have not been addressed before. The book has been written with two classes of reader in mind – the specialist in Roman history, politics or law, and the non-specialist. In the interests of the latter technical discussion is confined to the notes.

The work is cast in chronological form. Desirable as a thematic approach might be, it would not offer sufficient compensation for the loss of sequential development. In any case the thematic approach has not been abandoned entirely. Themes are developed within each chronological period, and the highlights of the entire period are drawn together in thematic form in the final chapter.

My sincere thanks are due to Professor Edwin Judge of Macquarie University, Sydney, and to Mr Richard Stoneman, Senior Editor at Routledge, who read a first draft of the work. Their judicious comments and suggestions have substantially assisted the final organization of the work. I acknowledge with thanks the contributions to seeing the work through the press made by Virginia Myers, Desk Editor at Routledge, Alison Stanford, Copy Editor and Heather McCallum, Editorial Assistant. I also wish to thank the librarians and staffs of Fisher Library, University of Sydney, the Law Library of the University of New South Wales, and Macquarie University Library, for their unfailing courtesy and co-operation.

Sydney, February 1992   R. A. B.

LIST OF ABBREVIATIONS

Except where otherwise indicated, abbreviations of the names of periodicals, classical authors and their works are as listed in *L'Année Philologique* and/or the *Oxford Latin Dictionary* and/or Liddell and Scott, *A Greek-English Lexicon*.

AA	Ovid, *Ars Amatoria*
AC	*Acta Classica*
AE	*L'Année Epigraphique*
AG	Aulus Gellius, *Noctes Atticae*
AJP	*American Journal of Philology*
ANRW	H. Temporini and W. Haase (eds), *Aufstieg und Niedergang der römischen Welt*, Berlin/New York 1972–
AP	*L'Année Philologique*
BMC	H. A. Gruener, *Coins of the Roman Republic in the British Museum*
CD	Cassius Dio
CG	Plutarch, *Life of Gaius Gracchus*
CIL	*Corpus Inscriptionum Latinarum*
Coll.	*Mosaicarum et Romanarum Legum Collatio*
Coll. Lat.	*Collection Latomus*
CP	*Classical Philology*
CQ	*Classical Quarterly*
D	*Digesta Justiniani*
DH	Dionysius of Halicarnassus
EJ	V. Ehrenberg and A. H. M. Jones (eds), *Documents Illustrating the Reigns of Augustus and Tiberius*, 2nd edn, Oxford 1955
FIRA	S. Riccobono *et al.* (eds), *Fontes Iuris Romani Anteiustiniani*, 3 vols, 2nd edn, Florence 1942–3
Furneaux	H. Furneaux, *The Annals of Tacitus*, 2 vols, 2nd edn, Oxford 1896, 1907
Gai.	*Gai Institutionum Commentarii Quattuor*
Hist.	*Historia*

LIST OF ABBREVIATIONS

HSCP	*Harvard Studies in Classical Philology*
ILS	H. Dessau, *Inscriptiones Latinae Selectae*
J.Inst	*Institutiones Justiniani*
Kl.P	K. Ziegler and W. Sontheimer (eds), *Der Kleine Pauly: Lexikon der Antike*, 5 vols, Stuttgart 1964–75
Koestermann	E. Koestermann, *Cornelius Tacitus: Annalen*, 4 vols, Heidelberg 1963–8
L	Livy
Lat.	*Latomus*
Lex. Tac.	A. Gerber and A. Greef, *Lexicon Taciteum*, Leipzig 1903
L Per.	Livy, *Periochae*
MRR	T. R. S. Broughton, *The Magistrates of the Roman Republic*, 3 vols, New York 1951–86
OCD	*Oxford Classical Dictionary*, 2nd edn, Oxford 1970
OGIS	W. Dittenberger (ed.), *Orientis Graeci Inscriptiones Selectae*, Leipzig 1903–5
OLD	*Oxford Latin Dictionary*
ORF	H. Malcovati (ed.), *Oratorum Romanorum Fragmenta*, 2nd edn, 1955
P	Ovid, *Epistulae ex Ponto*
PE	Pliny, *Epistulae*
PIR	A. Stein and L. Petersen (eds) *Prosopographia Imperii Romani*, Part IV, 2nd edn, Berlin 1952–66
PNH	Pliny, *Naturalis Historia*
QIO	Quintilian, *Institutio Oratoria*
RE	A. Pauly *et al.* (eds), *Real-Encyclopädie der classischen Altertumswissenchaft*, Stuttgart, 1894–1978
RG	*Res Gestae Divi Augusti*
RhM	*Rheinisches Museum*
RIDA	*Revue Internationale des Droits de l'Antiquité*
SA	Suetonius, *Augustus*
SC	Suetonius, *Claudius*
Schol. Bob. St.	*Scholia Bobiensia* ed. T. Stangl
SDHI	*Studia et Documenta Historiae et Iuris*
SG	Suetonius, *Gaius (Caligula)*
SJ	Suetonius, *Julius (Caesar)*
SMW	E. Mary Smallwood (ed.), *Documents Illustrating the Principates of Gaius Claudius and Nero*, Cambridge 1967
SN	Suetonius, *Nero*
ST	Suetonius, *Tiberius*
SZ	*Zeitschrift der Savigny-Stiftung für Rechtsgeschichte (Romanistische Abteilung)*
T	Ovid, *Tristia*
TA	Tacitus, *Annales*
TAPA	*Transactions of the American Philological Association*
TG	Plutarch, *Life of Tiberius Gracchus*
TH	Tacitus, *Historiae*
TLL	*Thesaurus Linguae Latinae*

VM	Valerius Maximus
VP	Valleius Paterculus
ZPE	*Zeitschrift für Papyrologie und Epigrafik*

1

INTRODUCTION

No offices, no priesthoods, no triumphs, no spoils of war.
Elegance, adornment, finery – these are a woman's insignia,
these are what our forefathers called the woman's world.

(The tribune L. Valerius, 195 BC)

Must we accept laws from a secession of women? Our ancestors would not have a woman transact even private business
without a guardian, but we allow them to visit the Forum
and the Assembly, to support a bill, to canvass for the repeal
of a law. Let them succeed in this, and what limit to their
ambitions will there be?

(Cato the Censor, 195 BC)

Women are barred from all civil and public functions. They
may not be judges or jurors, or hold magistracies, or appear
in court or intercede for others, or be agents.

(The jurist Ulpian, c. AD 200)

Why should we pay taxes when we have no part in the
sovereignty, the offices, the campaigns, the policy-making
for which you contend against each other with such perni-
cious results?

(The matron Hortensia, 42 BC)

POLITICS IS NOT ONLY ABOUT VOTES

The above passages reflect the situation of Roman women from
the strictly constitutional point of view.[1] Although enjoying
considerable social mobility under the influence of Etruscan and
Hellenistic ideas, and gradually achieving a large measure of

1

independence under the private law, women were at a permanent disadvantage in the public sector. They were rigorously excluded from all official participation in public affairs, whether as voters, senators or magistrates; the only exception was priesthoods, to which they were admitted as Vestal Virgins and in a few other cases. So had it been since time immemorial, and so it continued to be. The public position of women was so unfavourable that it has even been doubted whether they were Roman citizens. The doubts are unfounded, but the general disadvantages are clear.[2]

What, then, can we hope to uncover in regard to the participation of Roman women in politics and public life? Or, to put it another way, what exactly might the political involvement of Roman women mean? The usual answer is not an encouraging one. It is supposed that it was only through men that women could exert any influence in the public sector; whether by counsel, cajolement, manipulation or promise, a woman could only operate behind the scenes.[3] Even Tanaquil, the legendary prototype of the woman of character and determination who leaves an indelible mark on the political scene, could do no more than make her husband the first (recorded) Etruscan king of Rome, and her protégé, Servius Tullius, his successor; and even that degree of interference by a woman was frowned on by later generations.[4] But indirect influence is only part of the story. There were, in an ongoing process of steady expansion, a number of avenues that gave women access to a more direct public role. Uncovering the more important of these is one of the principal purposes of this book.

Our investigation spans some four hundred years, from the mid-fourth century to AD 68. It was a period of profound change, when a city-state in central Italy gradually advanced to domination of the Mediterranean world, and slowly, and with much travail, adapted its institutions to the demands of its new status. The period witnessed major changes in the situation of women in the private sector, and concomitantly with that women's public role gradually expanded. Purely for the purpose of outlining our coverage of that expansion, the period can be notionally divided into five phases. They are offered purely as abstractions; they do not (except for the fifth) coincide with any of the usual divisions of the period. But they help to trace the gradual evolution of a feminine presence in Roman public life. They are intended to do no more than that. They are therefore only mentioned in this introductory chapter; they are not used either as headings or discussion points in the main body of the work.

The first notional phase runs from the mid-fourth to the end of the third century BC. That is the period which is covered in Chapters 2 and 3. If anything epitomizes this phase, it is the examples, sporadic but significant, of campaigns of direct action mounted by women. The goals were limited, since the participants at no time demanded the vote (despite Cato's forebodings), but the activities were undeniably political. Some of the protests had specifically feminist goals. Thus, when they campaigned against their disadvantaged status in marriage, they were challenging a system that condemned them to inferiority. At other times they addressed concerns of the community at large, as when they demonstrated against wartime casualty rates, or made their own special contribution to the conflict of the orders, or set up an organization to handle their contributions to the war effort, or exerted significant influence on mainstream politics by promoting new cults.

The second phase covers the first half of the second century BC. It is dealt with in Chapter 4. A feature of the period is that the names of individual women occur more frequently, and more credibly.[5] That is precisely what one would expect, for the sources are simply reflecting the changed realities. Rome's conquest of the western Mediterranean was, except for a later postscript, complete, and a similar felicitous result in the east was in the making. In that propitious climate the Great Man makes his appearance, and he is soon joined by *La Grande Dame*.[6] She owes her début to changed conditions, for the turn of the third century is precisely when serious inroads into the legal and social disabilities of Roman women began to be made. No longer tied down by childbearing, spinning and weaving quite as rigidly as they had been, many upper class women were able to acquire more than a smattering of education,[7] and with familiarity with philosophy, rhetoric and literature came questions about society and women's role therein. A reassessment of the *res publica* had begun exercising the more progressive minds in male society as well, and the tensions building up on such issues as popular sovereignty spilled over into the area of women's rights. There was another current of equal importance. The aftermath of the great wars saw mounting social and economic dislocation, and in the rising tide of campaigns for social justice women were, if anything, more prominent than men.

In a very real sense the politics of protest, which is the hallmark of the period, was a feminine phenomenon.

By about 150 BC the second phase merges into the third. The latter covers the later Republic down to the death of Caesar, and is discussed in Chapters 5 and 6. Ideological and social tensions intensified, and exploded into the Gracchan period. Women's public role expanded accordingly. Names of individual women are now linked to more adequate source material. The politically conscious matron reaches maturity, and by the second half of the first century she is every bit as credible as her descendants, *les grandes dames* of the triumviral period and the Principate, will be in their turn.

The educated matron of the later Republic subjected the problems of society in general, and of women in particular, to more searching scrutiny than her predecessors had done, and in the hands of small, specialized groups women's involvement in public affairs took on new, and more sophisticated, dimensions. Three such groups are identified in the Gracchan period. One group, headed by Cornelia, mother of the Gracchi, is of paramount importance. A second group consists of women who possess some degree of legal knowledge. They make their mark in two ways. One or two women developed skills as legal theorists, and successfully challenged constitutional conventions. Others set up as court practitioners, thus encroaching on the preserve of legal expertise and court oratory which male politicians had always regarded as an important route to electoral success. The third group is the Vestals. Long treated as sacrificial victims and scapegoats by benighted priests and unscrupulous politicians, the Vestals in the Gracchan period rose up against the taboos of a society which had conquered the world but had not learnt how to rid itself of superstition.

By the mid-first century some great republican matrons had come to exert so much indirect influence that it virtually became a form of direct control. Women like Clodia and Servilia, and perhaps Praecia before them, were politicians in their own right. Theoretically they were no nearer to the franchise and office than they had ever been, but their highly organized networks which gave them access to senators and magistrates could no longer be dismissed as mere counselling or cajolery. These women foreshadowed, and in some ways even surpassed, the women of the early Principate. A Servilia, for example, had to be able to pick her way through a veritable minefield of warring elements, none of which could claim undisputed supremacy over the others. The women of the Principate were at least able to gear their activities to a single source of power.

The fourth phase spans the triumviral period, that bridge between the late Republic and the Principate which runs from Caesar's death to Octavian's triumph over Antony. It is covered in two chapters. Chapter 7 deals with women other than Octavian's sister, Octavia, and his wife Livia. One of the women discussed in this chapter, Fulvia, almost pre-empted Livia's role as the first empress. Chapter 8 deals with Octavia and Livia in the first stage of their careers, that is, in the triumviral period. The history of these two women in the 40s and 30s is a vital element in the formation of that most important institution of the Principate, the Domus Caesarum or House of the Caesars. The material in these chapters could no doubt be distributed differently, with part being added to the late Republic and part to the Principate, but the transitional character of the period is as meaningful for women in public life as it is for anything else.

The fifth phase is co-extensive with a generally accepted period of Roman history. It covers the early Principate from its foundation by Augustus in 27 BC to the death of Nero in AD 68, and is dealt with in Chapters 9 to 13. The introduction of what was, for all practical purposes, a radical departure from the republican system of government, had a profound impact on all aspects of Roman life. In one sense, albeit a negative one, the new system was advantageous to women. This is because the entire basis of male politics changed under one-man rule. The senate remained nominally important, but was seldom much more than a shadow. Office was increasingly dependent on the emperor's fiat rather than on the alliances and coalitions of the Republic. And the popular assembly, never much more than a rubber-stamp except in brief and troubled interludes, soon lost even its formal role in the process of government.[8] The decreased importance of the popular assembly is the crucial factor, for it made the denial of the franchise to women less relevant; it meant that something that had been refused to women, though available to all men, no longer mattered. Other inequalities, such as exclusion from the senate and magistracies, remained, but women were no worse off than the great bulk of men belonging to the middle class and the plebs, who were theoretically eligible for preferment but were, apart from the fortunate few, unlikely to achieve it.[9]

In a more positive sense feminine politics underwent a transformation in the Principate because of the innate nature of the new institution. Over the entire period 27 BC to AD 68 the head of state was chosen repeatedly from a single family (or combination of two families), and the throne was seen as a hereditary possession.[10] The family acquired a new status (originating in the triumviral period) as the Domus Caesarum, the House of the Caesars, and the women of the Domus shared in that status to the full. Nor was it simply a matter of honorific titles and privileges, for to some extent the position of imperial women was officially recognized and they became constitutional entities.

What must be accounted one of the most important political roles of imperial women, if only because of its prominence in the history of the period, is the problem of the succession. There had never been a succession problem in the Republic. When a particular family held a series of consulships, it did so by means of electoral alliances. But the emperor was not elected, nor did he have the power to appoint his successor. The most that he could do was to indicate his preference, by dynastic marriage and adoption, and to confer on the candidate of his choice the essential powers that he would need if acclaimed as emperor when the time came. It was in influencing the emperor's choice of a candidate that imperial women played one of their major roles.

A strong-minded woman was also able to influence general aspects of the emperor's policy. Sometimes she held his policies in contempt and sought to undermine them. At least one member of the Domus went so far as to form a colourable facsimile of a political party in order to oppose the emperor. Once or twice women came close to a co-regency. In a sense all this was simply a function of the Principate itself. Once the ground rules of government had changed, the political horizons of women could not fail to expand in the light of new conditions and new opportunities.

Our chosen segment of the Principate sees women's involvement in politics and public life at a peak. Perhaps because of the novelty of having the palace replace the forum, the women of the Domus rose to a higher, and more spectacular, position than any of their republican forebears. In a very real sense the domestic history of the period is the history of those women. Their targets were less diversified than in the Republic. The wide range of activities open to women in the later Republic was a reflection of the rich potential of the Roman Republic as a whole; but as the choices open to men narrowed in the Principate, so did those open to women. But what the Principate loses in variety it makes up for in intrinsic interest. The politics of the imperial women sheds instructive light on the new order as a whole.

An interesting by-product of the Principate, symptomatic of their greater access to public affairs, was the change in women's names. In the Republic a woman had only one name, her father's *nomen gentilicium*, or family name, with a feminine ending: Julius–Julia. Sisters were distinguished by numbers or priority adjectives: 'the first Julia', 'the elder Julia'. But in the Principate women acquired a second name, a *cognomen* – thus Julia Agrippina and her sister Julia Drusilla, for which modern investigators are truly grateful.

SOURCES AND SCOPE

The above general outline can now be supplemented in a number of respects. First, the coverage. This is determined partly by the relative importance of the events, but also by the availability of source material. For the Republic we depend largely on Livy and Cicero, supported by other sources. For the triumvirate, Appian and Dio are the mainstays, assisted by Plutarch. For the Principate we rely on Tacitus, with substantial support from Suetonius, Dio and others. Legal evidence is available right across the board, in both juristic and literary texts.[11] But epigraphic and numismatic material is confined to the triumviral period and the Principate.

In a certain sense the material is the message. When the full Livy is available the coverage is correspondingly ample. Late Republican topics owe an even greater debt to Cicero. When those resources fail, time and circumstance have usually preserved reasonable substitutes. But if any single author is indispensable it is Tacitus. One need only compare what can be pieced together for Livia in the triumviral and Augustan periods with the fully rounded Tiberian figure of *Annales*. We can hardly guess how differently Caligula's sisters would present if what Tacitus did say about them had come down to us. But let us be grateful for what we have. At least we do not have to use scissors-and-paste after

Livia, for the two Agrippinas and Messalina are fully documented by the greatest Roman historian.

A word about the book's title. First, what is meant by 'politics'? All definitions are dangerous,* and this word is no exception. One can only define it by giving examples. The examples are in the book. They relate mainly, but not exclusively, to politics, government, law and public affairs in general. Second, what is meant by women? Our primary concern is with upper-class matrons, married women belonging to senatorial or equestrian families. This is not an inflexible rule, however, for unmarried women (especially Vestals) are prominent. So, when the sources authorize it, are one or two plebeian women, apart from the many anonymous players. But on the whole participation in public affairs is no better attested for sub-equestrian women than it is for sub-equestrian men.

The discussion is largely built around individual names, and with good reason. The Roman sources were as much addicted to name dropping as the modern media are, and they were not mistaken. Events were linked to names in the public perception, and the writing of history through concepts rather than personalities was seldom practised.[12] That the prosopographical method has weaknesses if taken to extremes the writer would be the first to admit,[13] but it would be perverse to deny its general relevance to the writing of Roman history.

Although names are prominent, they are far from being reeled off as mere narrative. Rather, they are grouped in topics and concepts. The choice of names is consequently a selective process. It does not encompass every woman about whom some scrap of information can be uncovered, but only those who contribute to our theme of women's steadily expanding direct participation in public affairs.

No account of what the book contains would be complete without some mention of what it does not contain. The chosen period, it may be thought, begins too late and ends too early.

---

* The jurist Iavolenus, *D* 50.17.202. Cf. S. I. Hayakawa, *Language in Thought and Action*, London 1952: 172–3: 'People often believe, having defined a word, that some kind of understanding has been established, ignoring the fact that the words in the definition often conceal even more serious confusions and ambiguities than the word defined. If we try to remedy matters by defining words, and then . . . go on to define the words in the definitions of the defining words, we quickly find ourselves in a hopeless snarl. The only way to avoid this snarl . . . is [by] giving specific examples of what we are talking about.'

There is admittedly a vigorous tradition for early Rome in which women in political settings are prominent. The tradition is important for the light that it sheds on later institutions and on the manipulations of early history by propagandists. Tanaquil the kingmaker, Lucretia the paradigm of virtue, Verginia and the XII Tables, the Maid of Ardea and intermarriage – not all the information is legendary, but the residues of genuine fact do not support the elaborate roles assigned to the participants. One would especially like to be able to exploit the story of Coriolanus' mother, Veturia, who led a deputation of women to her son's camp to beg him not to attack Rome. Writers of the late Republic and Principate disclose the existence of an acute controversy as to whether the women acted with official authority or on their own initiative.[14] It is thus clear that at some point much later than 488 BC the story was used by supporters and opponents of women's movements, but it is not possible to pinpoint the occasion. So much, then, for the very early period. Our focus is on the activities of historically credible women in credible situations. The mid-fourth century provides the first outlines, sometimes dotted but still discernible, of what we want. From then on the Republic is an integral and essential part of the work. Without it the women of the early Principate would have neither antecedents nor ancestry.

At the other end of the period it may be asked why the discussion does not continue down to, say, the Severan period, thus extending the time-span by 150 years. The source material is quite good, and there is much of interest in the story of the post-Julio-Claudian imperial women. But apart from considerations of space, there are sound reasons against their inclusion. The death of Nero in AD 68 ended what may for the purpose of convenience be called the Julio-Claudian dynasty (cf. Chapter 11, n. 22), and ushered in what was seen as the second foundation of the Principate. The more stable basis then established is reflected in the role of the women. Pyrotechnical displays are at a premium and, even more to the point, there are no movements to match the Party of Agrippina, which was so important in Tiberius' reign. Nor is there any clarion call to match the divine blood of Augustus. All in all, where the Republic and the Julio-Claudian period in tandem ensure continuity, the later period would require an entirely new set of parameters.

Finally, a word about aspects of the work for which originality can perhaps be claimed. The theme of women's direct, and expanding, involvement in public affairs provides a certain unity and cohesion. That quality is, however, exploited without losing sight of the individual parts that make up the whole, and the work may offer a new perspective on the great historical issue of change in the role of Roman women.

Specific innovations, in the sense of matters which have either not been raised before, or not in the form in which they are presented here, are about equally divided between the Republic and the Principate. For the Republic such matters include the following: attacks on inequalities in marriage; Verginia and the conflict of the orders; changing attitudes on barbaric forms of expiation; women as both protesters and collaborators in the Second Punic War; Aemilia and women's rights; the importation of the Great Mother; the repeal of the *lex Oppia*; the Bacchanalian suppression and its aftermath; the specialized groups of Cornelia, women lawyers and the Vestals; eulogies; the first 'fixers'; the trial of Caelius; the loyalties of Servilia.

For the triumviral period there are the diplomacy of Mucia; Hortensia and the *ordo matronarum*; the achievements of Fulvia; the sacrosanctity of Octavia and Livia; the diplomacy of Octavia.

For the Principate the most important innovation is the Party of Agrippina. The ongoing theme of the divine Julian blood is of comparable significance. Other items are Octavia, Livia and the succession; Livia and moral rearmament; the changing politics of protest; Livia and the courts; Ovid's banishment; aspects of Caligula's relations with his sisters; Messalina and the new politics; the younger Agrippina's political machine; her decline and fall; Poppaea and the destruction of Octavia.

'THE CHEEK OF IT!'

We conclude this introduction with some important aspects of bias in the sources. Patriarchal Roman society did not like women's involvement in politics. The sources are unanimous about this. The keynote is struck early in the piece, in Livy's account of the regal period. Tullia, daughter of Servius Tullius, despises her sister for failing to display *muliebris audacia*, 'feminine cheek'. And Sallust credits his contemporary, Sempronia, with *virilis audacia*, 'a man's boldness'. The sources are not being complimentary. Livy expresses surprise at the fact that Tullia was 'the first to call

Tarquin king' when so many men were present. He also criticizes Tanaquil, a foreign woman who twice conferred the royal power. It was not for a woman to usurp the king-making function of the Roman assembly.[15]

Criticism is retrojected to the early Republic. When Coriolanus' mother, Veturia, leads a group of matrons to his camp to plead with him not to attack Rome, Livy complains that he is unable to find out whether the *démarche* was the result of public policy or women's anxieties (*muliebris timor*). A later age was clearly critical of this delegation that had been organized by women on their own initiative. Plutarch has the women declare that 'We have come as women, not under a decree of the senate or the consuls'. Dionysius strongly disapproves of the women 'who laid aside the proper custom of keeping to their homes'. A few years later, when Verginia is destroyed by Ap. Claudius, and the matrons give public expression to their grief, Livy dismisses their plaints as 'women's anguish (*muliebris dolor*) reinforced by their lack of self-control'.[16] Political pressure by women had become a crisis point in the late Republic.

Livy is less forthcoming on meritorious acts by women, for he says nothing about the matrons who handed over their gold and gave their hair for bowstrings when the Gauls attacked Rome in 390 BC; despite the long and boring speech that Livy writes for Camillus, we have to look to other sources for the women's role.[17] But Livy returns to active duty with the great poisoning trials of 331, when the city is afflicted by *muliebris fraus*, 'feminine treachery' (L 8.18.6). Many years later Tacitus has Germanicus succumb to *muliebris fraus* instead of dying in honourable combat (*TA* 2.71.4). The demonstration against the Oppian law in 195 is *consternatio muliebris*, 'a feminine riot', which produces a display of *impotentia muliebris*, that 'womanish lack of self-control that destroyed our freedom' (L 34.2.2, 6). Tacitus is constantly worried by *impotentia muliebris* in the Principate (*TA* 1.4.5, 4.57.4, 12.57.5). When Fulvia left Italy after a courageous stand against Octavian, it was not just a departure but *muliebris fuga*, 'womanish flight' (VP 2.76.2). The emperor's Domus was plagued by *muliebres offensiones*, 'womanish spite' (*TA* 1.33.5, 12.64.5). Otho's negotiations with Vitellius were tainted by 'womanish flattery' (*muliebribus blandimentis*) (*TH* 1.73). There is no need to labour the point. *Muliebris* is so consistently pejorative that it is not used for any laudable acts, such as the heroic deaths of Calpurnia, Servilia and Arria (VP 2.36.3, 88.3; *PE* 3.16).

Bias was also expressed in other ways. The sexual motif is especially prominent. The prime example is Juvenal's sixth satire, but the phenomenon is general. That *impudicitia*, unchastity, dominates the trials of Vestals is understandable, for that is what Vestal misconduct was all about. But secular politics is exposed to the same theme. Time and again a woman who is proving to be a political embarrassment is charged with adultery or *stuprum* – illicit intercourse by, respectively, a married woman of good repute (*matrona*) and a widow or unmarried girl. Closely linked to this were charges of poisoning; there was a presumption that an adulteress was a poisoner and a poisoner was an adulteress, and wine was believed to encourage immorality.[18] This battery of misdemeanours provided a political woman's enemies with more than enough ammunition to counteract her popular appeal, but there was an even more important reason for the use of charges of immorality. The standard tactic against a political opponent was to charge him with treason, but that weapon could not easily be used against a woman, because women could not be charged with aspiring to supreme power (*TA* 6.10.1) – logically enough, given their ineligibility for any sort of power. Other forms of treason came to be charged against women, but aspiring to supreme power was not one of them. This reason for the prevalence of the sexual motif has not been noticed before, but it should be constantly borne in mind.

The matters discussed in this chapter are, then, our guidelines. The relative weight of the issues involved, and the interactions between them, will be worked out in the investigations that lie ahead.

2

WOMEN IN THE CONFLICT OF THE ORDERS

INTRODUCTION

In this first segment of our discussion of the Republic, organized protests by women were, to a large extent, built around the long-running conflict of the orders, the plebeian struggle for parity with the patricians.[1] The particular aspect of that conflict with which we are here concerned centres on 331–295 BC. The issues were women's disabilities in both the private and public sectors. Two questions of private law were prominent: the inferior status of women in *manus* marriages, in which the wife was 'as a daughter to her husband';[2] and the disadvantaged position of women in the matter of divorce. Although belonging to the private sector, these questions generated organized action which can quite properly be described as political. This chapter also adverts significantly to intermarriage between patricians and plebeians, an issue which was unequivocally political.

THE POISONING TRIALS OF 331 BC

The year 331 brought the first great poisoning trials at Rome. It was, says Livy, a terrible year, with many leading citizens dying of a mysterious illness which was due to poison rather than pestilence. A slave woman (*ancilla*) approached the curule aedile, Q. Fabius Maximus, and offered to reveal the cause of the mischief if she were indemnified against prosecution. The indemnity having been given, she disclosed that the city was assailed by feminine wickedness (*muliebris fraus*). She led Fabius to where some matrons were brewing noxious concoctions; other such substances were found in their houses. Some twenty matrons, in whose

13

houses substances had been found, were summoned to the forum. Two of them, Cornelia and Sergia, both patricians, claimed that the substances had curative properties. The informer challenged them to drink the draughts in order to prove the charges false in the sight of all. After waiting for the crowd to disperse, the women agreed. All drank, and all were killed by their own wickedness. A large number of matrons were then prosecuted on information disclosed by their associates, and some 170 were found guilty and punished. This, says Livy, was the first trial for poisoning at Rome. The affair was seen as a prodigy, though one dictated by insanity rather than by criminal intent. A return to sanity was secured by nominating a dictator to drive in a nail.[3]

The twenty matrons involved in the first phase of the official reaction were perhaps subjected to trial by ordeal, but the 170 were tried by a more sophisticated procedure, a special commission established by the senate and presided over by the curule aedile, Q. Fabius Maximus Rullianus.[4] The women were thus dealt with under the public criminal law, instead of by family courts as one might have expected. That departure from tradition was needed because the interests of the entire community were involved. The women were seen to have generated the prodigy as a group, and had to be tried as a group.

What was behind the mass poisonings? There had been many pestilences and prodigies, and many poisoning epidemics, but it had never come to a mass trial – or to any public trial, for family courts had dealt with such matters behind closed doors. What was there about this particular episode that brought it into the public domain? An attempt to find a political explanation is made by Herrmann (1964: 48). She postulates a group of patrician women who were seeking equality of civil and political rights, even by crime. Herrmann does not develop her theory, but she presumably draws an inference from the patrician status of the two named women, Cornelia and Sergia. Such an inference is perfectly possible,[5] for there is evidence to suggest that women belonging to the more progressive wing of the patrician order[6] were influenced by the current climate to such an extent that they staged a conflict of the orders in reverse, even resorting to violence in imitation of plebeian models. For the validation of this idea we must turn to the next section of this chapter.

THE CULTS OF PATRICIAN AND PLEBEIAN CHASTITY

Pudicitia (Chastity), the goddess who personified feminine virtue, was the centre of an intense struggle between patrician and plebeian women over the years following the trials of 331. Fabius Rullianus, still in office as curule aedile, founded a shrine of Patrician Chastity (Pudicitia Patricia) in the Forum Boarium.[7] The right to worship at the shrine was confined to women of patrician birth who had been married (to patrician husbands) only once.[8] In 296 the shrine was the centre of a crisis. Verginia, a patrician woman married to the plebeian careerist, Lucius Volumnius Flamma, was denied access to the shrine because she had married out of the patriciate. She retaliated by founding an altar of Plebeian Chastity (Pudicitia Plebeia) in her house in the Vicus Longus. She urged plebeian matrons to compete in modesty as men competed in valour; let them cultivate the new altar even more reverently than its patrician counterpart. Admission was restricted to women of proven chastity who had been married only once, but in the course of time, says Livy, the cult was defiled by the admission of degraded women and eventually disappeared (L 10.23.1–10).

In its essentials the story rings true. It discloses the existence of a lively issue on *conubium*, intermarriage between patricians and plebeians. Legend had that issue generate much heat in the mid-fifth century, and it was still shrouded in legend in 377, when Fabia, a daughter of the patrician Fabius Ambustus but married to a plebeian, Licinius Stolo, complained about her inferior status compared with her sister who was the wife of a patrician; her father promised to raise her to her sister's status. The story is fictitious, but it does identify a burning issue in the fourth century, and *a fortiori* in 296.[9]

Equally important, Verginia is linked to one of the private law questions to which we attach political overtones. Of the three methods by which a husband could acquire *manus* over a wife,[10] the informal method of 'possessing' the wife for a year (*usus*) could be defeated by *trinoctium*: if the patrician wife of a plebeian absented herself from the marriage-bed for three consecutive nights, *manus* could not come into existence in that year. Verginia's husband, Volumnius, was a close ally of Appius Claudius Caecus, a progressive patrician and the leading lawyer of the day. Appius wrote a monograph on 'Interruptions' in which he discussed *trinoctium*.[11] That Verginia availed herself of that exposition by her husband's political ally is certain. Livy describes her as *Auli filia*, 'daughter of Aulus [Verginius]' (10.23.4), but if she had been under Volumnius' *manus* she would have been in the position of a daughter to him and would have been *Lucii filia*.[12]

We now have *conubium* in place as an important issue at the turn of the fourth century. We also have Verginia as a progressive patrician contributing to the achievement of parity between the orders – at the upper-class level, for there are no champions of social justice for the underprivileged at this time. But there is yet another piece to be incorporated in the picture and it is to that that we now turn.

THE *STUPRUM* TRIALS OF 295 BC

One of the curule aediles in 295 was Fabius Gurges, son of Fabius Rullianus who had been curule aedile in 331. The year was marked by pestilence and prodigies as 331 had been, and Gurges consulted the Sibylline Books. Acting on the advice therein contained, he brought a number of matrons to trial on charges of *stuprum*. Again the trials were conducted by a magistrate under the public law, not by the family courts which traditionally exercised jurisdiction over women.[13] Gurges collected substantial fines from the defendants (there is no sign of capital penalties),[14] and with the money built a temple to Venus Obsequens, 'Obedient Venus' (L 10.31.8–9). That the fines sufficed for a project of that size suggests that a large number of women were involved. As *stuprum* here means systematic fornication rather than occasional adulteries, the matrons were trading as prostitutes. That brought it within the jurisdiction of the curule aediles, for as market masters they were responsible for brothels.[15]

It has been plausibly argued by Palmer (1974: 122–3, 134) that the defendants of 295 were patricians, as we know those of 331 were; as Rullianus founded the shrine of Patrician Chastity in 331 to atone for the poisoners' crimes, so Gurges enshrined Obedient Venus to atone for the second wave of patrician misconduct. So far so good, but what has this got to do with our politics of protest? Here Palmer suggests that Gurges was reacting to the challenge thrown out by Verginia the previous year; Verginia having emphasized the superior probity of plebeian women, Gurges, a member of a family bitterly opposed to Appius Claudius

Caecus and his allies,[16] moved to redress the balance by punishing the patrician offenders.[17] This confirms the women's role in the ongoing struggle of the orders, but it does not explain why the matrons of 331 killed their husbands *en masse*, nor why those of 295 became prostitutes. In order to draw the threads together we must inspect the general ambience in which these events took place.

THE CLIMATE OF PROTEST

The poisonings of 331 followed closely on the heels of a most distressing occurrence in 337, when the Vestal Minucia was convicted of adultery and subjected to the traditional punishment of being buried alive. As a member of a family once patrician but later of plebeian status, Minucia was the first plebeian woman to be made a Vestal. Equally important, she was the first Vestal to receive such barbaric punishment for at least 150 years, and perhaps at all.[18] The diehards amongst the patricians had expressed their opposition to the admission of a plebeian to the Vestal order in the most brutal fashion.[19] But many of the people who witnessed the interment conducted by the Pontifex Maximus were left with an indelible memory, a lasting dislike of some of the more unpleasant features of patriarchal society.

In the yeast-charged atmosphere of the time, with intermarriage and plebeian Vestals prominent in people's thinking, some patrician women began to re-examine their own situation. And their thinking turned inevitably to *manus* marriages. The avoidance of that inferior status by *trinoctium* was not available to patrician women who married patrician men; it was only in a mixed marriage that the question of a year's *usus* and its interruption by *trinoctium* could arise.[20] The more forward-looking patrician women of the later fourth century felt strongly about the need for some improvement in their matrimonial situation. The story of Fabia, daughter of Ambustus, reflects the depth of feeling, even if the details are fictitious.

For good and sufficient reasons, then, many women felt the need to apply pressure in order to secure matrimonial reform. But because they were barred from all constitutional forms of protest, they had to resort to the extra-constitutional, to direct action. That action took the form of a criminal conspiracy directed not

17

only at their husbands but at public figures in general; Livy says that the *primores civitatis*, the leading citizens, were dying of the mystery disease (8.18.4). There would be other women's movements over the years to which the word 'conspiracy' would be applied. It would almost invariably signify a protest of some sort. As already observed, women could not be charged criminally with plotting to take over the state, and 'conspiracy' accordingly has a more general meaning (see Chapter 1, p. 12).

The last word belongs to Verginia, the first woman to take an active part in Roman politics. She was the lineal descendant of the patrician women of 331, but she found a more sophisticated approach. Responding to the climate which had seen the *lex Ogulnia* open the major priesthoods to plebeians a mere four years before, she found a feminine analogue; what the Ogulnian law had done to equalize the orders in the public religious sphere, Verginia did in the unofficial sphere.[21] She devised political action by women of a kind not dreamed of before, throwing down the gauntlet to traditional society without falling foul of the criminal law, and striking a telling blow against the unrealistic divisions between the two orders. In so doing she contributed more than the average male voter who merely cast his ballot. But Verginia was not competing with the average voter. Neither literally nor figuratively was she 'a woman of the people'. She was pressing the claims of the plebeian nobility, plebeian families who could point to at least one consul on their family tree. That is why Livy says that the admission of non-matrons (i.e., those belonging unequivocally to the lower orders) weakened the plebeian cult.[22] The reform was elitist, albeit on a somewhat broader basis than before.

TOWARDS MORE EQUITABLE DIVORCE

The Age of Verginia produced other relaxations of traditional rigidity. In 307 the censors expelled a certain L. Annius from the senate for divorcing his wife without summoning a *consilium amicorum*, a council of friends (VM 2.9.2). This was the first direct inroad into the *manus* marriage. In a marriage without *manus* divorce was a simple matter and was open to the wife as much as to the husband. But in the case of a *manus* marriage only the husband could untie the knot. Traditionally 'fault' divorce applied in such a case: Romulus, the founder of Rome, was said to have forbidden a wife to leave her husband, but to have allowed the husband to repudiate her for using poisons, drinking, substituting children, or committing adultery. None of those grounds was essential to the validity of the divorce, but the husband who divorced without relying on one of them forfeited his property (Plut. *Rom.* 22.3). In 307 Annius' case changed that, for once a referral to the council of friends was required, there had to be a debatable issue, namely specific grounds instead of the husband's will and pleasure. The rules imposed by 'Romulus' probably remained in place. The divorce was still valid without specific grounds, but in addition to the traditional property penalty a political punishment was now imposed.[23]

The ruling in Annius' case was one of the fruits of the events of 331. Patrician wives were beginning to reap the benefits of their predecessors' dedication. If one were to hazard a guess as to the names of the women who set the wheels in motion against Annius, Verginia would be the first choice. Her husband and Appius Claudius held the consulship in the year of Annius' misfortune, and Appius' extended censorship, which was noted for its innovative character, had ended only the year before, in 308.[24] Things favourable to the feminine cause had a habit of happening when Appius and Verginia's husband were in office: in their first consulship divorce was made more equitable, and in their second Verginia established her foundation. It is not too much to suggest that she was the driving force on both occasions.[25]

A PATRICIAN BACKLASH

In 287 BC a law of Q. Hortensius gave plebeian legislation parity with laws of the Roman people as a whole, and in the opinion of many that ended the conflict of the orders. The patricio-plebeian nobility was now firmly in place, though the time for social justice for the underprivileged was still in the future. But even amongst the upper classes there was still a residue of tension, for not all patricians welcomed the enhanced status of the plebs. A great patrician matron, Claudia, who was probably a daughter of Appius Claudius Caecus, was prominent amongst those who resented the change. In 249 her brother, P. Claudius Pulcher, lost 120 ships in the battle of Drepana. In 246 Claudia, when leaving the games in her carriage, was held up by the crowd and loudly regretted that her brother was no longer alive to reduce the rabble as he had done at Drepana. She was prosecuted by the plebeian aediles, and was fined 25,000 *asses*, a comparable penalty to the fine of 120,000 imposed on her brother for losing a fleet.[26]

The aediles in question, Fundanius Fundulus and Sempronius Gracchus, made both legal and political history in this case. They created a brand new charge especially for the trial, accusing Claudia of diminishing the *maiestas*, or 'greaterness', of the Roman people. That charge would later become the standard criterion for all acts of treason against the state. Claudia had spoken rashly at best; a reminder of the serious setback represented by Drepana could not have been more inopportune. But in fact her remark was more deliberate than rash; it was a political statement, a condemnation of the forces which had brought down her brother and would consign her family to the wilderness for the next forty years.[27] She had also reminded people that the conflict of the orders was still alive in some quarters. As the offence was unequivocally political, it was futile to charge her with sexual laxity, and a type of treason that a woman *could* commit was put on the statute book for the occasion. The plebeian aediles confirmed the conflict of the orders aspect by making her fine the nucleus of a fund with which they built a Temple of Liberty on that plebeian stronghold, the Aventine (L 24.16.19).

CONCLUSION

The theme of women's participation in the conflict of the orders stands up well. Both Verginia as a liberal patrician contributor and Claudia as an imperious conservative carry conviction. Livy's account of the cult of Plebeian Chastity is not an aetiological invention; the story lacks the aura of myth and legend that usually surrounds such inventions. Still less can Claudia's case be brushed aside; it goes back to an impeccable juristic source (Bauman 1967: 28). Nor is Claudia's denigration of the plebs rendered improbable by her relationship to Ap. Claudius Caecus. Despite his many liberal acts – including his postulated support for Verginia – that enigmatic figure was by no means an invariable protagonist of reform (Bauman 1983: 21–65).

The prosecution of patrician prostitutes by Gurges, and its interpretation as a corrective to the moral high ground claimed for the plebeian shrine by Verginia, are not open to any serious criticism. The one finding that is coloured by conjecture to some extent is the *manus*-eliminating motive of the patrician poisoners of 331. Livy himself had some difficulty with that case; he says that not all his sources attest it, but he must give it as it came to him (L 8.18.2). That there was such a case need not be seriously doubted; it was part of the official *acta* of a magistrate. But the matrons' motives can only be deduced by inference. And here there is not much on offer. Palmer's identification of the basis as 'a presumed aphrodisiac' (1974: 122–3, 134) tells us very little. Why did some two hundred matrons suddenly decide on such a move, and why did they all get it so horribly wrong? The concoctions must be taken as deliberate, and in that case our suggested reason is at least plausible.

3

WOMEN IN THE SECOND PUNIC WAR

INTRODUCTION

Prior to the Second Punic War, which played such a decisive part in creating the Roman empire, the third century exhibits very few significant developments in the area of women's participation in public affairs. Apart from Claudia's outburst in 246, there is only the passive evidence of the deaths, either by burial alive or suicide, of a number of Vestals, in pursuance of the barbaric policy of expiating prodigies and pestilences by killing members of that order.[1] But with Hannibal's irruption into Italy in 218 a new chapter opens in women's affairs, as in so much else in that momentous era. Women are significantly active in a number of areas, not all of which have been noticed before; nor has their cumulative effect been perceived. Broadly speaking, the period displays two distinct developments: on the one hand a continuation, and indeed an intensification, of discrimination and ill-treatment; on the other hand the encouragement, by the more liberal elements in male society, not only of co-operation by women, but also of a more active role in the management of their affairs. There is no clear-cut temporal division between the two developments until the last few years of the war. Until then the good and the bad alternate in seemingly haphazard fashion. Only from about 207 BC does an unequivocally favourable climate emerge.

THE EARLY YEARS: PROGRESS AND REGRESSION

The first development to attract our attention is a favourable one. In 217 an exceptionally large number of prodigies was reported, but instead of the traditional resort to the detection and burial alive of an unchaste Vestal, expiation was sought in a more civilized procedure. The senate decreed that there be animal sacrifices and a supplication (a solemn religious entreaty), and that offerings be made to the gods by both men and women. In the case of women the matrons were to offer a gift of money to Juno Regina on the Aventine, each contributing according to her means, and they were to celebrate a *lectisternium*, a feast to the gods. Even freedwomen, who usually laboured under the same disabilities as their male counterparts, were included: they were to make an offering to the Etruscan deity, Feronia (L. 22.1.8–18). This decree, far from discriminating against women as is sometimes supposed,[2] was quite progressive. Class differences were to some extent ironed out by locating the offerings in the plebeian quarter of the Aventine and including freedwomen. It is a safe guess that forward-looking matrons had a hand in promoting the idea. They will not have been far distant from M. Minucius Rufus, a determined opponent of the diehard patrician, Q. Fabius Maximus. Nor would another populist, the consul C. Flaminius, have refused them his support; his resistance to his own father's authority suggests a liberal position on family relations.[3]

Attitudes changed drastically in 216, after Cannae, though even then the first sequel to the disaster was a favourable one. A strong contingent of soldiers having escaped after the battle and made their way to Canusium in Apulia, a wealthy Apulian woman, Busa, received some ten thousand of them on their arrival in Canusium and gave them food, clothing and money. This made it possible for the young Publius Scipio, the future conqueror of Hannibal, to raise a levy in a private capacity and to transform the demoralized men into an effective force. The importance of Busa's contribution is shown by the fact that the town of Venusia equipped a whole force of cavalry and infantry at public expense, 'in order not to be outdone in good offices by a Canusian woman'. At the end of the war, when Scipio was at the peak of his popularity, Busa was voted honours by the senate.[4]

At Rome matters proceeded on a different course. Cannae produced a sharp reaction against women, both religious and secular. Two Vestals, Opimia and Floronia, were made the scapegoats for the disaster and were immolated in expiation. Having been convicted of unchastity, one was buried alive and the other would have suffered the same fate if she had not committed suicide.

Their unchastity was considered a prodigy, the *decemvirs* were told to consult the Greek Sibylline Books, and Fabius Pictor (the first annalist) was sent to consult the oracle at Delphi. The matter-of-fact tone of Livy's account reflects the attitude of Fabius Pictor, who witnessed the interment.[5]

The reaction against women in general was equally harsh. As accurate news of Roman losses at Cannae was not available, women mourned both the living and the dead. Fabius Maximus proposed that they be kept off the streets and cease their lamentations. When the full casualty list became known, the city was so filled with the sounds of grief that the annual rite of Ceres had to be deferred, because it might not be performed by mourners. The senate decreed that mourning be limited to thirty days to enable the rite to be celebrated. The women had no option but to comply, but made it clear that they were doing so under compulsion.[6]

The position of the cult of Ceres in the mourning crisis is important. The cult was the sacral focal point of the plebs. 'Romulus', mindful of the traditional morality of the rural plebs, had decreed the forfeiture to Ceres of half the property of a husband who divorced without cause (Plut. *Rom.* 22.3). The *lectisternium* of 217 had, for the first time, included Ceres amongst the divinities in whose honour the banquet was staged (Eisenhut 1964). Ceres was thus an essentially plebeian goddess, and the women who were forced to limit their mourning in order to carry out her rite were essentially plebeians. But we cannot go so far as to say that the senate's mourning decree was specifically anti-plebeian, for the goddess was so closely connected with the food supply that avoidance of any hitch in her rite was essential for the community at large. Nevertheless, we do note that this plebeian cult goddess was prominent in both the civilized expiation of 217 and the wartime stringency of 216. This provides some of the outlines of a politically significant perception amongst plebeian women. And it was, we recall, that patrician champion of the plebeian cause, Verginia, who had built on the divorce reform programme initiated by 'Romulus' and Ceres (see Chapter 2, p. 18).

There is one more piece to be added to the events of 216. Later in the year some of Hannibal's prisoners came to Rome to beg the senate to pay the ransom demanded by Hannibal. Women mingled with men in the crowd which gathered in (or near) the Comitium and pleaded with the senators to give them back their menfolk. After the senate had rejected the plea women joined in the throng which escorted the prisoners to the gates of the city. Livy notes that fear and destitution had driven the women to the unusual step of publicly mingling with men.[7] Although a tragic occasion, it illustrates how the pressures of war were beginning to break down the old barriers.

Another manifestation of the undermining of tradition occurred in 213. The year was marked by a rash of foreign superstitions. Roman rites were neglected, and new cults were freely practised. As Livy observes with some acidity, crowds of women congregated in the forum, on the Capitol and elsewhere, rejecting ancestral custom in their sacrifices and prayers; petty priests and prophets had taken hold of people's minds. The problem was aggravated by the masses of rural plebs who had taken refuge in the city. The minor magistrates being unable to disperse the crowds or dismantle their equipment, the urban praetor was directed to use his *imperium*, his military authority, against the cultists. He issued an edict requiring anyone in possession of prophetic books or ritual writings to bring them to him before the first of April. He also decreed that no new or foreign rites were to be celebrated in a public or consecrated place (L 25.1.6–12). Although Livy singles out the women for special criticism, it is clear that men were equally involved. The new cults, directing protests into new channels, are an early pointer to an important change in the co-ordinates of women's intervention in public affairs. Henceforth the tendency would be to orchestrate joint action by men and women, although exclusively feminine movements would by no means disappear.

SUMPTUARY LEGISLATION: DISCRIMINATION OR NECESSITY?

The year 215 brought a piece of legislation which imposed specific statutory restrictions on women, though whether anti-feminist thinking prompted it remains to be seen. The plebeian tribune C. Oppius carried a law laying down that no woman was to possess more than half an ounce of gold, or wear a purple garment, or ride in a two-wheeled carriage (*carpentum*) in, or within a mile of, the city, except in religious festivals.[8] On the face of it this law was discriminatory, but there are grounds for modifying this assessment, or at least for understanding it as something more than an arbitrary whim.

One of the consuls in 215 was Fabius Maximus, grandson of Fabius Gurges who had punished prostitutes in 295; the consul of 215 had already spoken harshly against mourning women in 216. In 215 he was responsible for the dedication of a statute of Venus Verticordia, Venus who turned women's thoughts away from lust (Palmer 1974: 135–6). The rite of Ceres also troubled the tender conscience on the subject of female impropriety that he had inherited. It was a mystery rite, requiring the celebrants to abstain from bread, wine and sex (Eisenhut 1964). Women's finery was also a sore point with anyone who felt as strongly about such matters as Fabius; it threatened the required standards of propriety even more than mourning had done.[9]

There were, however, more practical considerations in the minds of Fabius and the senate. Women were not the only section of the population saddled with the financial burdens of the war. In 210 senators agreed voluntarily to bring into the treasury all their gold, silver and coined bronze. Each man would retain only rings for himself, his wife and his children, amulets for his sons, and an ounce of gold each for his wife and daughters.[10] Although six years after Oppius' law, the war tax of 210 need not have been the first imposed on senators.

Fabius may have had a third, less excusable, motive. Later in the war he would stand forth as the bitter enemy of Publius Scipio, and even at this stage the sight of a woman of enormous wealth like Busa helping Scipio to take his first step on the road to greatness may have been most galling to Fabius. (When the senate honoured her at the end of the war Scipio was, of course, the hero who had no difficulty in putting through the decree.)

Fabius' instrument in getting the *lex Oppia* on to the statute book was the plebeian tribune, C. Oppius. But Oppius received no reward from the Establishment for his services, for he got no further than the tribunate. This contrasts sharply with Fundanius Fundulus, whose prosecution of Claudia while a mere plebeian aedile catapulted him into a consulship seven years later (*MRR* 1.217). Oppius' career may have been summarily terminated by the voters, who may not have liked his law. Sudden changes of heart by the Roman electorate were not unusual, and a measure that had slipped through in the darkest days of the war might have left smouldering resentment – as indeed proved to be the case when the law was repealed in 195 (see Chapter 4, p. 31).

EXPIATION AND THE WOMEN'S COMMITTEE

The last few years of the war saw a reaction against the excesses of the earlier years. As the Carthaginian danger receded, so did the severity of the Roman reaction. The year 207 provides a striking illustration of the change in attitudes. It was, on the face of it, a very bad year for prodigies. Special concern was felt at the birth of a hermaphrodite as big as a 4-year-old child. But instead of turning on the Vestals, the pontifical college decreed that the prodigy be drowned in the sea, and that twenty-seven girls sing a hymn composed by the poet, Livius Andronicus, by way of expiation. While they were practising the hymn, lightning struck the temple of Juno Regina on the Aventine. The soothsayers declared that the portent concerned matrons and the goddess must be placated by a gift. The government's response opened a new chapter in women's affairs. The curule aediles, again acting as a vehicle for innovation, issued an edict summoning matrons domiciled in the city or within 10 miles of it. The matrons chose twenty-five of their number as treasurers to whom they would bring contributions from their dowries, and with the money thus raised a golden basin was gifted to Juno Regina. A sacrificial procession was held, in which the twenty-seven maidens sang Andronicus' hymn. Livy criticizes the hymn as 'repellent and uncouth', but agrees that it might have appealed to the rough minds of the time.[11]

The minds might have been rough, but they were learning fast, for hymn-singing maidens were a distinct improvement on buried Vestals. It is no accident that the Pontifex Maximus at this time, and thus head of the college which decreed expiation by hymn-singing, was P. Licinius Crassus Dives. He was a close associate of Publius Scipio, and as such a member of a forward-looking group whose horizons went well beyond the confines of rural Italy (Bauman 1983: 92–110). The group's attitude to women may have owed something to Scipio's wife, Aemilia. She was noted for her magnificence in dress, ornaments and attendants (Pol. 31.26.3–5), which marks her out as an opponent of the *lex Oppia*. Her husband, owing a great deal to the wealthy Busa and at odds with Fabius Maximus, will have shared her sentiments. There is also a possible link between Aemilia and the tax on women's dowries, for one of the curule aediles involved in that operation was Ser. Cornelius Lentulus, a gentile connection of Scipio. It was not a time of austerity; the victory of Metaurus, later in the same year as the dotal tax, was followed by the restoration of a peace-time economy, with the matrons attending the thanksgiving in their richest garments (L 27.51.10). It was in this favourable climate that the dotal tax won the active co-operation of matrons. The idea of putting a rudimentary women's organization in place to collect it looks like the brainchild of the Scipionic group, and very possibly of Aemilia herself. The organization was, we recall, given some sort of official status by being formally created by the aediles. Aemilia could well have wanted matrons to start acquiring experience in administration, and to do so with official sanction. It was a far cry from the unofficial, and contentious, deputation arranged by Coriolanus' mother (see Chapter 1, p. 11).

Even errant Vestals were treated with more consideration at this time, and again Licinius Crassus was responsible for the improvement. When a Vestal negligently allowed the eternal flame to go out in 206, he did no more than scourge her. Expiation was made by an animal sacrifice and prayers at the temple of Vesta. The offence was a serious one, being taken to portend the fall of Rome; and the year was marked by an unusually large number of prodigies. A less enlightened Pontifex Maximus might have looked for evidence of unchastity against the Vestal in order to placate the goddess more adequately.[12]

THE SCIPIONIC GROUP AND CYBELE

The third century closed with a decisive political move by the Scipionic group in which women played an important role. The occasion was the importation, in 204, of the cult of Cybele, the Great Mother, from Phrygia in Asia Minor. By contrast with the cults of 213, this importation was officially sanctioned by the senate, after the Sibylline Books had revealed that it would precipitate the expulsion of Hannibal from Italy. Scipio Nasica, a connection of Publius Scipio, accompanied a great crowd of matrons of impeccable probity to Ostia to meet the goddess. They included Claudia Quinta, whose moral probity was in doubt, but who established her credentials by calling on the ship, which had run aground, to follow her if her chastity was beyond dispute. The ship obligingly moved and the matrons bore the goddess to Rome in triumph, nothing daunted by the fact that it had turned out to be a black stone.[13]

What was behind this episode? We know that the Scipionic group favoured the feminist cause; it also favoured exotic cults (Herrmann 1964, 58–9). But the matrons were assisting a more complex manoeuvre than the establishment of a new cult. In 205 Fabius Maximus had strenuously opposed a proposal to allow Publicus Scipio to cross over to Africa; Fabius maintained that the top priority was to get Hannibal out of Italy (L 28.40). The Scipionic answer was to import Cybele, which guaranteed Hannibal's expulsion. Someone wanted the matrons to be prominently associated with the move, and again Aemilia, in conjunction with Licinius Crassus, is a likely sponsor.

The cult of 204 succeeded because it had the right import permit; that of 213 failed because it did not. The message was that, for the most part, women's movements could not hope to succeed under their own steam. For better or for worse, they had to seek support from mainstream politicians, even if that meant abandoning a specifically feminist orientation. They had to become co-educational, so to speak.

CONCLUSION

The conflict between conservatives and progressives across the period, and its impact on women's affairs, does, it is felt, stand up well. That one and the same society should adopt the offerings of 217 and the Vestal victims of 216 bears eloquent testimony to the state of flux induced by the war. Busa is a minor epic that has hitherto gone unnoticed. But was she the only plebeian woman of means to help the war effort so unstintingly? There is no way of knowing; her saga became known to Livy only because of the senate's decree awarding her honours at the end of the war.

Whether the limit on mourning evoked criticism, as Valerius Maximus' *coactae* might seem to suggest, and whether that criticism was voiced by progressives who opposed Fabius in the senate, or by an unsuspected female critic, cannot be determined. But a progressive voice in the senate is more likely. We thus glimpse the tip of a veritable iceberg of controversy on women's affairs at this time. It is against a background of such controversy that conflicting ideas on such matters as the best way to expiate prodigies would make better sense. Progressive ideas had come under increasing scrutiny even in the decades preceding the war. One thinks in particular of the thinking involved in the divorce of Carvilius Ruga (Chapter 2, n. 25). All that the war did was to intensify the conflict.

Particular importance attaches to the formation, under the authority of an aedile's edict, of a women's committee to handle dotal contributions to the war effort in 207. The move was part of the radically improved method of expiation represented by the hymn-singing maidens. That women should then have gone on to play an important part in the complex political issue behind the importation of Cybele need occasion no surprise. It was a further manifestation of the much healthier climate prevailing at that time.

In a sense the sumptuary restrictions introduced by the *lex Oppia* do not fit too easily into the suggested confrontationist framework. We have provisionally thought of the Scipionic group and Aemilia as having opposed that law, but it must be conceded that there is no direct evidence to that effect. The question can, however, be reserved for further consideration in our next chapter, when we discuss the repeal of the *lex Oppia* (see Chapter 4, p. 31).

4

THE POLITICS OF PROTEST

INTRODUCTION

We turn now to the first half of the second century BC. The transition from the previous chapter to this one is not altogether abrupt. When we come to consider the repeal of the *lex Oppia*, the episode which generated the most striking manifestation of women's power in the whole of Roman history, we will recall the public appearances of women during the Second Punic War, and will see the events of 195 as an intensification, though in a much more goal-orientated fashion, of the earlier manifestations.

Similar considerations apply to our second topic in this chapter, the suppression of the Bacchanals. The cults of 213 and their suppression were prompted, albeit in embryonic form, by the same factors as the Bacchanalian movement, and women were as prominent in the one as in the other. Even the epidemic of poisoning cases in the second century (here presented as an adjunct to the Bacchanalian movement) can be said to some extent to have had roots in the past, in the shape of the events of 331.

But in spite of the qualitative similarities, the sheer magnitude and, in all cases except the *lex Oppia*, ongoing persistence of the phenomena oblige us to see the second-century developments as essentially part of the aftermath of the expansionist wars.[1]

THE REPEAL OF THE *LEX OPPIA*

Livy opens Book 34 of his history with the dramatic events attending the repeal of the *lex Oppia* which had imposed severe restrictions on women's finery in 215.[2] The incident was, says Livy,

31

trivial in itself, but because of the passions which it aroused it developed into a major issue.

M. Fundanius and L. Valerius, plebeian tribunes in 195, proposed that the Oppian law be repealed. Two other tribunes, M. and P. Iunius Brutus, opposed the repeal and threatened to use the tribunician veto to block it. The unusual division in the college of tribunes was reflected right across the board, for Livy says that many leading men spoke on the issue, and the Capitoline was crowded with supporters of both sides. Matrons were present in large numbers. Neither authority, modesty nor their husbands' orders could keep them at home. They blocked all the approaches to the forum, speaking to men and trying to convince them that in the current prosperity their former distinctions should be restored to them. The crowd of women grew larger every day as reinforcements flocked in from outlying areas. They even appealed to the consuls and other magistrates, but one consul, Cato, was adamant about his opposition to the repeal (L 34.1).

Livy then purports to give a verbatim account of Cato's speech opposing the repeal and the tribune Valerius' speech supporting it (34.2–4, 5–7). The speeches are probably not genuine, having been cobbled together from known speeches and writings of, especially, Cato,[3] but they are of some interest. Most of the material that Livy puts into Cato's mouth is simply designed to present the traditional Cato the Censor – the stern, uncompromising conscience of the rural plebs who believed as firmly as Fabius Maximus that a woman's place was in the home. But the tribune Valerius did not provide Livy with much documentation, and the annalist was obliged to improvise.[4] The general thrust of Valerius' remarks is that the women are simply asking for the restoration of their 'woman's world', the finery that constitutes their *insignia* and has been withheld from them too long, seeing that all wartime restrictions except the *lex Oppia* have been lifted.[5]

Valerius, then, is no more anxious than Cato to acknowledge the existence of a substantial political issue in this affair. There was such an issue, but first let us glance at the rest of Livy's account. He says that next day, after the speeches, an even greater crowd of women appeared. They formed a column which blockaded the houses of the Iunii Bruti, the tribunes who had threatened to veto the repeal. The women refused to raise the blockade until the threat of a veto was withdrawn. The tribunes withdrew their veto and the assembly unanimously approved of the repeal.[6]

What was behind the episode? The answer that I propose[7] is based on two passages in the speeches – a statement by Cato and a reply by Valerius. Cato warns his audience that once the law has ceased to set a limit to their wives' expenditure they will never set it themselves; let them not think that the situation which prevailed before the passage of the law will ever return. Valerius pours scorn on this, and assures them that their authority under *manus* or *patria potestas* will revive immediately if the law is repealed.[8] This can only mean that where restrictions of the sort included in the *lex Oppia* had been the private business of husbands and fathers prior to the *lex*, the statute had cut down the private power by imposing statutory maxima, it had suspended that aspect of family power. That is why Cato was so strongly opposed to the repeal: he was afraid that the abolition of the statutory restriction would not revive the common-law power of husbands and fathers to impose restrictions of their own choosing. But Valerius, acting on expert legal advice, was able to assure his audience that such fears were groundless.[9]

Who were the instigators of the move to repeal the law? Scullard identifies them as Publius Scipio, Flamininus and Scipio's wife Aemilia, because they were prime targets of Cato's attack on philhellenism and luxury imported from the East,[10] and the point is well taken. One of the items in Cato's speech that has an authentic ring is his tirade against Greek culture (L 34.4.3–4). Greece and things Greek were one of Cato's phobias. He fiercely attacked his great enemy, Publius Scipio, for his liking for Greek culture and a Greek lifestyle and, as we already know, Aemilia's lifestyle was of a magnificence that could easily have aroused Cato's ire. The only additions we need make to the names suggested by Scullard are other members of the Scipionic group like the Pontifex Maximus, Licinius Crassus, and the great jurist Sex. Aelius Paetus.[11]

If, as we may reasonably suppose, Aemilia was one of the instigators of the repeal – and there had to be some prominent matrons behind it[12] – she will have been associated in a political manoeuvre that went well beyond the immediate occasion. The reasons for saying this are twofold. First, the repeal proceedings forced Cato to postpone his departure for his consular province of Spain; this suited Scipio's book perfectly, for he had close links with Spain, and the later that Cato left for that province the better. Even more important, the strong response of women who flocked in from the rural sector was reflected in the way that their husbands subsequently voted, for when Cato stood for his most important office, the censorship, in 189 he was defeated, and had to wait until 184. The Scipionic group had temporarily alienated him from his constituency, the rural plebs.[13] It is a pity that we do not have more information about Aemilia. She may well have been a significant forerunner of the great political matrons of the late Republic. Her daughter certainly was (see Chapter 5, p. 42).

To a large extent the repeal of the *lex Oppia* is unique. It is the only occasion on which organized intervention by women on anything like such a scale was seen. This is most surprising in view of the sequel. In 169 Cato put up a tribune to propose the *lex Voconia*, a law which on the face of it was unequivocally anti-feminist. It forbade the institution of women as heirs to testators who were rated in the first census class, may have prohibited any woman from taking a legacy of more than half an estate, and probably cut down on women's rights of intestate succession (Bauman 1983: 176, n. 193). But there is no sign of any protest by women against this law. The fact that Livy makes no reference to the *lex* virtually guarantees that there was nothing of particular annalistic interest in it. The silence of women about a law of which Cicero says that 'this law, passed for men's advantage, is full of injustice to women' (*Rep*. 3.10.17) is matched by our uncertainty as to Cato's motives in sponsoring the law. In his speech in support of the law he spoke scathingly about the sort of woman who lent her husband money and demanded repayment whenever she felt like it, no matter how inconvenient it was to him (*ORF* fr. 158). But how did it help to eliminate women as heirs in the top census class while leaving their position undisturbed in all other classes? If the problem was simply arbitrary demands for repayment, the easiest way would have been to legislate for a period of grace. The most logical answer is that the law was not only a hindrance to women; it also stipulated that no one, male or female, could take by legacy or gift more than the heirs took (Bauman 1983: 176–7). It therefore seems that the reason why there was no protest against the *lex Voconia* is simply that it was not seen as exclusively anti-feminist, as the *lex Oppia* had been.[14]

THE SUPPRESSION OF THE BACCHANALS

The year 186 was dominated by the suppression of the Bacchanalian cult, an Italian version of the cult of Dionysus, and one
that is said to have given women a more enduring outlet for their
energies than that offered by *ad hoc* avenues like the repeal of the
lex Oppia. But whether the cult should be seen as specifically
feminist, and its suppression as specifically anti-feminist,[15] remains
to be seen. Equal importance attaches to the years of endemic
unrest that followed the Bacchanalian suppression; that will be
considered in the next section.

Livy, our major source for the suppression, treats us to what
is to some extent an exercise in historical fiction. But there is also
a hard core of fact.[16] Briefly stated,[17] the prostitute and former
slave, Hispala Faecenia, who had been a member of the cult,
revealed details of its operations to Sp. Postumius Albinus, one
of the consuls of 186. At first the cult had been practised only
by women and had been tolerated, but in the first decade of
the second century a Campanian priestess, Paculla Annia, started
initiating men as well. Paculla also introduced nocturnal rites,
held five initiations a month instead of three a year, restricted
membership to persons under 20, and encouraged promiscuity.
Initiates were bound by a *coniuratio*, 'a swearing together' which
obligated them both to fornication and to common-law crimes,
such as murder and forgery. There were more than 7,000 members,
including a number of men and women of rank, and the movement
almost formed a second state.

Postumius and his consular colleague, Q. Marcius Philippus,
were commissioned by the senate to conduct a special criminal
investigation (*quaestio*) into the Bacchanals and their nocturnal
rites. Livy's repeated allusions to the nocturnal aspect[18] point to
the possibly central position of women in the movement. In his
dialogue *On the Laws* Cicero advocates a ban on nocturnal sacrifices by women. The reputations of women must be protected by
the clear light of day. Initiations into the cult of Ceres must be
carried out by rites performed in the Roman manner; the senate's
decree concerning the Bacchanals demonstrated the traditional
strictness used in matters of this sort (Cic. *Leg.* 2.35–7). The
consul Postumius, in a speech written for him by Livy,[19] agrees
that women are at the root of the problem, but adds that young

men are also involved, since they are becoming effeminate and unfitted for military service (L 39.15.9, 13–14).

The consuls went ahead with their investigations and put large numbers of cultists of both sexes to death. Women who were condemned were handed over to relatives or to husbands in whose *manus* they were, for private execution; if no such authority figures were available, the public executioner obliged.[20] Postumius, who was allocated the greater part of the work, spent 186, and some of 185, on his investigation. In south Italy he found evidence of widespread depradations and destruction.[21] By using his full military authority he managed to sedate the situation – but only temporarily. On his return to Rome he arranged for a substantial reward to be voted to Hispala Faecenia. She received a cash payment of 100,000 *asses* which placed her in the first census class;[22] she was given the right to dispose of her property free of the patronal rights of her former mistress, to marry outside her clan, and to a freeborn citizen, and to choose her guardian.[23] Her lover, young Publius Aebutius who had put her in touch with Postumius, was also rewarded (L 39.19.3–7).

Hispala had rendered the ruling oligarchy an enormous service. But it was a service of an unprecedented kind. Instead of matrons who belonged to the Establishment, a woman from the lower orders had taken up the cudgels – but on behalf of the system, not on behalf of the underprivileged. The oligarchy manned the ramparts with rare unanimity. Cato delivered a speech of which only the title, *De Coniuratione (On the Conspiracy)* and one word from the speech have survived (*ORF* fr. 68), but the title tells us quite a lot. Cato was using the hard-working word *coniuratio* in a threefold sense. Primarily it meant the oath taken by initiates. But it also implied a plot against the state – hence Postumius' statement that the ultimate aim was control of the state (L 39.16.3). Thirdly, the women of Lemnos – whom Cato had cited in his speech against the Oppian repeal (L 34.2.3) – killed the men after swearing an oath under the impulse of Venus (*Veneris impulsu coniuratae*). Also, Terence refers to a swearing together of women – *coniuratio mulierum* (*Hec.* 198; Hyginus *Fab.* 15: 507). When Livy stresses both fornication and the potential danger to the state he is reflecting various uses of *coniuratio* in Cato's speech.

Where did the Scipionic group stand? The theory that their Hellenistic sympathies prompted them to support the cult has been refuted by Rousselle (1982: 71–195), and it need only be added that one of the three men who assisted in drawing up the senate's decree was Scipio's staunch supporter, Licinius Crassus (Bauman 1990: 345). If Scipio was not on the side of the Bacchanals, then neither was his wife Aemilia. Insofar as the movement was a feminist one, it was not Aemilia's kind of feminism. The bulk of the membership was drawn from the underprivileged – the lower levels of citizens, their counterparts in allied communities, and slaves, all loosely associated in a vast social protest (Gallini 1970: 11–45). There was nothing there to appeal to Aemilia. She was interested in advancing her husband's career and in relaxing restrictions on upper-class women, but this colonel's lady did not feel much subcutaneous sorority with Judy O'Grady.

Three other women are named in the episode, but the only one identified as a member of the cult is young Aebutius' mother, Duronia. Aebutius' paternal aunt, Aebutia, was opposed to the cult despite her residence on the Aventine, and so was the great patrician matron Sulpicia, mother-in-law of Postumius. As against the solitary example of Duronia, Livy names the four male leaders of the *coniuratio* without any hesitation.[24] In any event it is clear that Livy's statement about Paculla Annia's reforms means exactly what it says: an exclusively female cult was transformed into one open to both sexes. There can be no question of the *quaestio* of 186 having been anti-feminist.

THE INTENSIFICATION OF PROTEST

The suppression of 186 was by no means the end of the problem of the Bacchanals. The next few years disclose continued Bacchanalian activity, alternating with a rash of poisoning cases which were part of the cult programme rather than merely coincidental in point of time.

In 185 there was an uprising of slaves in Apulia. The praetor L. Postumius Tempsanus, a member of the same *gens* as the consul of 186, investigated a 'conspiracy' of shepherds (*pastorum coniuratio*) whose acts of brigandage had made the region unsafe; some seven thousand men were condemned to death (L 39.29.8–9). The following year Tempsanus broke up large conspiracies of shepherds and diligently prosecuted what was left of the Bacchanalian investigation – *reliquias Bacchanalium quaestionis* (L 39.41.6–7). Thus Tempsanus spread his *quaestio* over two years; the consul of 186 had done the same. Clearly the shepherds were both slaves and Bacchanalians. And as members of the cult had long been doing, they committed murder, forgery and brigandage not for the usual criminal purposes, but in order to generate funds for the cult.[25]

The year 184 witnessed a large-scale criminal enterprise, also on behalf of the cult, which, unlike that of the shepherds, encompassed women as well as men. The praetor Q. Naevius Matho held an investigation into poisonings. He was obliged to visit numerous rural communities (as the consul of 186 had done). The investigation caused him to delay his departure for his province of Sardinia for four months, and he is said to have condemned 2,000 persons. They included many women.[26]

Despite the exertions of the two praetors, the problem was not solved. In 182 the praetor L. Pupius was commissioned to reactivate the Bacchanalian *quaestio* in the same troublesome region of Apulia. He was to eradicate 'some seeds left over from the previous troubles', but the investigation achieved very little (L 40.19.9–10). In 181 the praetor L. Duronius (a relative of Aebutius' mother) was assigned to Apulia with a firm mandate. He was specifically to conduct a *quaestio de Bacchanalibus*; but we are not told the outcome of the investigation (L 40.19.9–11).

The poisoning cases of 184 were followed by an even more serious wave of similar cases in 180. The year was marked by the deaths of a consul, C. Calpurnius Piso, a praetor and other distinguished men. The deaths were seen as a prodigy, but again expiation was sought elsewhere than in Vestal interment. Two investigations were commissioned. One, under the praetor C. Claudius Pulcher, was to handle cases of poisoning in the city. The other, dealing with rural cases, was assigned to the praetor C. Maenius, to be completed before he left for his province of Sardinia. The death of the consul Piso was thought to involve his wife, Quarta Hostilia. When her son by a previous marriage, Q. Fulvius Flaccus, was defeated in the consular election which saw his stepfather victorious, Hostilia had upbraided him for his third failure but had advised him to try again, for she intended to secure his election within two months; and after Piso's death he was indeed elected, as suffect consul. Pulcher's *quaestio* found Hostilia guilty of the murder of her husband (L 40.37.1–7). The other *quaestio*, under Maenius, was making heavy going. He had such a congested trial list that after condemning 3,000 persons he advised the senate that evidence was continuing to accumulate and he would either have to give up the investigation or resign his province (L 40.43.2–3).

Is there a link between the Bacchanalian and poisoning trials of the 180s? Was poisoning part of the cult's fund-raising programme, in the sense that women poisoned their husbands in order, through forged wills, to swell the common fund,[27] as the shepherds were doing, after their fashion, in Apulia? Quarta Hostilia's case is against this, but there were at least 3,000 cases in the rural sector and an unspecified number in Rome itself, and they were not all prompted by the consular aspirations of stepsons. The poisoning trials of 154 may assist. Two women, Publilia (or Publicia) and Licinia, were charged with poisoning their husbands, respectively the consul L. Postumius Albinus and the consular Claudius Asellus. After a hearing by the praetor the women were handed over to their relatives for execution. There is reason to think that we have here yet another special investigation, prompted by yet another wave of mass poisonings.[28] One of the victims, Postumius Albinus, is also of special interest. He was a son of the consul of 186, and it may well be asked whether he had been following the cult-breaking family tradition. It was a time of great discontent, and another Postumius Albinus, consul in 151, pressed the levy for the war in Spain so ruthlessly that the tribunes imprisoned him (L *Per.* 48). We recall that one of the objections to the Bacchanalian cult was that it made young men effeminate and unfit for military service. It is not impossible that Publilia, the wife of the consul of 154, was a Bacchanalian sympathizer who killed for the cause.

CONCLUSION

Of the questions raised by the repeal of the *lex Oppia*, the proposal of a hitherto unsuspected reason for Cato's disquiet may be thought cogent; both speakers make much of the effect on *manus* and *patria potestas*. Aemilia's postulated role also carries conviction, given that some prominent matrons must have been involved. But on the *lex Voconia* we have been less successful and have been able to offer only a *faute de mieux* solution to that intractable law.

The most important finding about the Bacchanals is that the cult was far from being completely suppressed in 186. Over the ensuing five years, and possibly more, it engaged the energies of praetor after praetor despite their other commitments. Moreover, fund raising by means of common-law crimes, especially poisoning, was a prominent feature of the cult's operations, and women, including women of rank, showed their support for the cause of the underprivileged by joining in those operations.

5

WOMEN IN GRACCHAN POLITICS

INTRODUCTION

This chapter marks an important new development. It is concerned with three specialized women's groups, all of which are centred on the Gracchan period, though they all have a degree of continuity both in the past and down to the first century. Not surprisingly, these groups display a sharper degree of definition with respect to women's participation in public affairs than in any of the earlier periods. This is not entirely, or even mainly, due to good source material, for the absence of Livy is only partly compensated for by Plutarch, Appian, Dio and others. It is simply that some women in fact had a higher profile than their predecessors, and this has left its mark on the tradition.

The three groups assembled here have not been presented as groups before. Cornelia is well enough known in works dealing with the Gracchan period as a whole, but she has not been seen as the focal point of a politically meaningful group. Women lawyers who surface prior, and subsequent, to the Gracchan period have been discussed by some, though by no means all, writers on women and the law.[1] But the contribution by women to the great constitutional ferment of the Gracchan period itself has not previously been investigated. The third group, the Vestals, have been discussed in the context of the dramatic events of 114–13 often enough, but the political implications of those events from the feminist point of view have remained undetected.

CORNELIA, MOTHER OF THE GRACCHI

Cornelia, the younger daughter of Publius Scipio and Aemilia,[2] was born in the late 190s. She married Ti. Sempronius Gracchus (cos. 177), but after an illustrious career he died in c. 153. Cornelia refused an offer of marriage from Ptolemy VIII of Egypt and devoted herself to administering the family property and bringing up her children, personally supervising their education and imbuing them with the culture and erudition that she herself had absorbed in her parents' house. Of her twelve children, only three survived to maturity. They were Tiberius Gracchus, the reforming tribune of 133 whose assassination ushered in the long agony of the Roman Republic; Gaius Gracchus, who tried to exploit the plebeian tribunate even more systematically than his brother had done but eventually suffered a similar fate; and Sempronia, who married the ambiguous patrician, Scipio Aemilianus.[3]

Cornelia was a recognized writer; a collection of her letters was seen by Cicero.[4] The late Republican writer, Cornelius Nepos, quoted extracts from one of her letters, written to her son Gaius in 124. A slightly abridged version of the fragment runs as follows:

It is no doubt good to revenge oneself on one's enemies, but only if it can be done without harming our country. Since that is not possible, it is better for our enemies to remain in place indefinitely than for our country to be destroyed. I swear that except for the assassins of Tiberius Gracchus, you have recently caused me more trouble and annoyance than any enemy – you who should, as my only surviving child, have striven to cause me as little anxiety as possible in my old age; who should only have wanted to please me; who should consider it wicked to disregard my advice in any important matter, especially as so little of my life is left to me. Cannot even that brief time dissuade you from opposing me and ruining the Republic? Where will it end? When will our family abandon madness and turn to moderation? When will we stop causing trouble to others and inflicting it on ourselves? When will we be ashamed of throwing our country into disarray? But if you cannot be dissuaded, stand for the tribunate when I am dead; do what-ever you like when I am no longer aware of it. When I die and you invoke the family gods in my honour, will you not be ashamed to solicit the prayers of those whom you aban-

doned in their lifetime? May Jupiter not allow such madness
to enter your mind. But if you persist, I fear that through
your own fault you will bring such trouble on yourself that
you will never be at peace.

(Nepos fr. 1.1–2)

The letter is, if genuine, by far our most important document for
the political thinking, and indeed the entire *Weltanschauung*, of a
second-century Roman matron. Written on the eve of Gaius Gracchus' first tribunate of 123, the letter reveals a writer who is
passionately opposed to the radical programme of her younger
son. Cornelia is rallying to the defence of the traditional *res
publica*, she is castigating what she sees as a blot on the family's
escutcheon, besides being a deadly threat to the *res publica* itself.
Cornelia thus finds herself in harmony with members of her own
family – not the plebeian family into which she married, but the
patrician family into which she was born. Her sentiments would
have been endorsed, for the most part, by her cousin and son-in-
law, Scipio Aemilianus, despite the ambivalent relationship
between them. We might thus classify Cornelia as a moderate
conservative, and the first woman to articulate the thinking of
that sector, were it not for the controversy as to the genuineness
of the letter. However, it is reasonably safe to say that even if
Nepos has not given us the letter as Cornelia wrote it, he has
adapted his material without destroying its essential veracity.[5]

Cornelia's relations with her sons gave rise to a vast store of
anecdotes, not all of which need be treated with scepticism.[6] After
their deaths she said that the temples where they had been killed
were tombs worthy of such occupants, adding that having borne
the Gracchi she could never be accounted unfortunate. Her pride
in her son's achievements was such that she often complained that
she was known as Aemilianus' mother-in-law, not as the mother
of the Gracchi. She probably considered Tiberius her favourite
and identified with his programme; she chose Diophanes of Mytilene and Blossius of Cumae as his tutors, and was reported to
have engineered Aemilianus' death in order to prevent him from
nullifying Tiberius' agrarian law.[7] Cicero infers from her letters
that her sons were nourished more by her conversation than at
her breast (*Brut.* 104, 211). Despite Cicero's habitual bias against
the Gracchi, there may be some truth in his picture of a woman
of high intellect who would rather ensure that her sons served

43

the state than foster ordinary family ties. Her relations with Gaius, although more equivocal than those with Tiberius,[8] did inspire one most important statement by her younger son. When one of Gaius' enemies slandered her, he said, 'Do you dare to speak ill of Cornelia, who gave birth to Tiberius?' (Plutarch *Gaius Gracchus* 4.4). By using her name instead of 'my mother' Gaius almost elevated her to a concept. Caesar would one day refer to himself in conceptual terms,[9] thus following the precedent set by 'Cornelia who gave birth to Tiberius'. That status later received official recognition when a statue of her was erected in the Portico of Metellus, bearing the legend: 'Cornelia, Daughter of Africanus, Mother of the Gracchi'. Cato had denounced the erection of statues to women in the provinces, but in the elder Pliny's opinion that was more than offset by the erection of this statue in Rome itself.[10] Cornelia made a closer approach to official status than had ever been achieved by a woman before. The significance of her title would not be forgotten. Livia would remember it one day (see Chapter 10, p. 131).

After Tiberius' death Cornelia retired to Misenum on the Gulf of Naples. It is from Plutarch's account of her lifestyle there that we draw our evidence for a circle presided over by her. Plutarch says that at Misenum she continued her customary lifestyle. She had many friends, kept a good table at which she entertained Greeks and other literary personalities, and exchanged gifts with reigning kings. She regaled her guests with anecdotes about her father, but was most memorable when she spoke about her sons, giving no signs of grief and telling their stories as if she were speaking about men of early Rome. Some thought that grief or old age had impaired her mind, but Plutarch puts it down to her noble nature (*CG* 19.1–3). The passage points to contemporary criticism of Cornelia, but that is in itself an indication of her importance. As a moderate patrician whose mind was not closed to liberal ideas as long as they did not subvert the existing order, Cornelia shared her father's relatively progressive ideas about popular sovereignty, and found herself in sympathy with Tiberius' programme, insofar as he felt genuine concern for the peasants displaced in the aftermath of the great wars.[11] At her literary luncheons, which were already in place prior to her withdrawal to Misenum (*CG* 19.1), she will have entertained men like Diophanes of Mytilene, Tiberius' tutor and the ablest Greek speaker of the day; Blossius of Cumae, the Stoic ideologue who attacked the evils of private property; and Licinius Crassus Mucianus, noted as much for his interest in Greek culture as for his professional interest in the law.[12] Such men would have found Cornelia's house an ideal venue for their deliberations, especially as she was able to contribute significantly to the debate. We cannot even guess how much of the Gracchan ideology was worked out *chez Cornelia* – but only until Tiberius' death. Despite her affection for her younger son, Cornelia did not approve of his unabashed demagogy. Nor was she alone in that.[13]

An important conclusion can be drawn from Plutarch's seemingly obscure statement about Cornelia having spoken about her sons as if she were talking about men of early Rome (*CG* 19.2). On the face of it, it was simply a cruel attack on a great matron who kept her emotions under rigorous control, but there is more to it. Was she comparing them with legendary figures, with demigods? We recall her description of the temples where they had been killed as temples worthy of them, and we also learn from Plutarch that the people erected statues of the two brothers, consecrated the places where they had been killed, and sacrificed as if at the shrines of gods (*CG* 18.2). It is an intriguing thought that the daughter of Scipio Africanus, the man whose intimations of divinity had terrified Cato (Bauman 1983: 166–7), may have initiated the cult of the individual so favoured by populist leaders in the Republic and later on by the emperors. It is true that the outward sign was the popular manifestations attested by Plutarch, but someone, preferably someone educated in Hellenistic ideas, had to point the way.

WOMEN IN LAW

Was there at any time a feminine equivalent to the *iuris peritus*, the man learned in the law who placed his knowledge at the disposal of his fellow citizens?[14] And if there were feminine equivalents did they, like their male counterparts, use their expertise for political purposes? The answer is a qualified affirmative to both questions. There were, from about the turn of the third century, women lawyers, some of whom not only had a theoretical knowledge of the law but also gave opinions to consultants, though such opinions did not have the same capacity to make law as the *responsa* of male practitioners. And women did put their knowledge to good use in the political sphere, though unlike men they could not use it to attract votes in the chase for public office.

Our evidence prior to the Gracchan period is supplied by some of the titles and fragments of the comic poet Titinius, the first to compose *fabulae togatae*, or plays in Roman dress. He dates to the early part of the second century, to the age of Plautus rather than of Terence. Titinius is known to have written a play entitled *Iurisperita*, and it has been plausibly conjectured that the central character was a woman who was her own lawyer and lost no opportunity to parade her legal knowledge.[15] Our suggestion is, however, that she was very possibly more than her own lawyer in the light of one of the fragments: 'Someone wanted me to come to see him in order to discuss an important court case (*rem magnam*), but there he is, walking away!' The implication is that the *iurisperita* had arranged a legal consultation but the client let her down.[16] The poet was making fun of women's pretensions in a field reserved for men. An anti-feminist line has also been surmised, by Daviault, for other plays of Titinius. His *Barbatus* is thought to have attacked women's luxury and to have criticized the repeal of the *lex Oppia*; and his *Hortensius* may have satirized the feminists by having them demand membership of the assembly and the senate[17] – thus, we may add, taking the same line as that attributed to Cato in his *lex Oppia* speech. There is enough here to start the ball rolling, despite the doubts recently expressed by Marshall (1989).[18] The intellectual emancipation of women included an interest in the law, and women versed in both law and politics were arguably in the forefront of the attack on the *lex Oppia*.

Women as legal advisers in real-life situations do not surface until the early first century. But the second century does reveal women who are *iurisperitae* in the sense of having a legal grounding and putting it to political use. Our first example is an equivocal one, because although it involves some interesting legal issues, it is not certain that they were stirred up by a woman's legal expertise. In 151 a prostitute, Manilia, threw a stone at the curule aedile, Hostilius Mancinus, when he came to her premises intoxicated one night and tried to force his way in; he indicted her for trial by the people, but Manilia appealed to the tribunes, who vetoed the prosecution on the grounds that the aedile's conduct had been improper (AG 4.14). The question as to whether Manilia invoked *provocatio* or *appellatio* is important, but was the tribunes' ruling a response to an expert argument presented by Manilia, or was she merely a non-lawyer availing herself of an established right?[19]

A much clearer case of a woman's possession of legal expertise, and her employment of it to make new law, is that of the Vestal Claudia in 143. Her father, Ap. Claudius Pulcher (cos. 143), was a progressive patrician and one of the leaders of the Gracchan movement. As consul he made war on the Salassi and claimed a triumph, but the senate rejected his claim because he had suffered a reverse during the campaign. He decided to celebrate a triumph on his own authority. A tribune tried to veto the procession, but when he attempted to pull Claudius off his carriage, Claudia threw herself into her father's arms, thus interposing her Vestal sanctity between Claudius and the tribune. She maintained that position, and the triumph went ahead.[20]

The incident involved a number of challenges to tradition. Claudius bypassed the senate, as Tiberius Gracchus was to do ten years later. Claudia frustrated a tribunician veto; Tiberius would do the same when he deposed his fellow tribune, M. Octavius. In testing the limits of tribunician power, Claudia was in the mainstream of contemporary thinking. It was a time of doubting, of questioning conventions that had served a city-state perfectly well, but were less well suited to the needs of a Mediterranean empire. Since time immemorial the Vestals had been *sanctae*, sanctified, but sanctity was not the same thing as the sacrosanctity of a tribune. Vestal sanctity was a by-product of enforced chastity (L 1.20.3), sacrosanctity was the inviolability conferred on the tribunes by oath of the plebs during the conflict of the orders (Bauman 1981). Sanctity had never been defended in a positive way; it only surfaced when it was violated by unchastity. But now it was being given an extended meaning, it was being used as a constitutional, or would-be constitutional, weapon in the game of politics.[21]

There was a contemporary of Claudia's whose political thinking was also influenced by legal training. She is Laelia, daughter of the well-known politician and lawyer C. Laelius (cos. 140), and wife of Q. Mucius Scaevola (cos. 117), a member of the great legal family of the Mucii Scaevolae.[22] Cicero tells us that he often heard Laelia converse, and found that she was imbued with her father's *elegantia* – the precision of language appropriate to a lawyer. It is a safe guess that C. Laelius included legal instruction in his education of his daughter, as other jurists of the time were doing with their sons.[23] Cicero adds that Laelia's *elegantia* was passed on to her daughters, the two Muciae, and to her granddaughters, the two Liciniae. Cicero furnishes another important clue when he discloses that Laelia's father had nominated her husband as an augur though he was the younger of Laelius' sons-in-law, justifying his choice by saying that he had given the honour to Laelia, not to her husband (*Brut.* 101). The remark was not jocular. The meaning was that if she had been a man she would have made an ideal augur, combining her knowledge of augural law with political *nous* well suited to that most political priesthood.

Under what circumstances had Cicero 'heard' Laelia? There is no suggestion that she had spoken in public, nor was Cicero old enough to have attended any of Cornelia's literary luncheons. The conversations will have been held at the house of Laelia's husband, Q. Mucius Scaevola. Cicero studied law under Scaevola, and as was the custom lived in his mentor's house during his pupillage (Cic. *Amic.* 1). There were thus numerous opportunities for him to converse with Laelia. We know that Cicero heard criticisms of the Gracchi from Laelia's husband; Laelia herself had inherited a strong anti-Gracchan line from her father and may have contributed significantly to the shaping not only of her husband's thinking, but also of that of Cicero, whose opinion of the Gracchi was not favourable.[24] Cicero's dialogue *On Friendship*, in which Laelius heads the *dramatis personae*, may owe much to Laelia's reminiscences.

There is one more second-century figure who impinges on both the law and the politics of the period. She is Cornelia's daughter, Sempronia. Unloved and unloving in her marriage to Aemilianus because of her plain looks and childlessness (App. *BC* 1.83), she did not share her husband's anti-Gracchan sentiments any more than she shared his bed. In fact there were suspicions about her involvement in his death because of her known Gracchan sympathies (L *Per.* 59). There is no other trace of Sempronia in the Gracchan period, but at the turn of the century she was at the centre of a dramatic confrontation, when the populist forces put forward a certain L. Equitius as the illegitimate son of Tiberius Gracchus. The censor Metellus Numidicus having trumped that electoral ace by refusing to recognize Equitius as a citizen, the matter was brought before the people by a tribune. Sempronia appeared at a public hearing in the forum and flatly denied that

Equitius was her brother's son. Valerius Maximus comments on the incident as follows:

> What does a woman have to do with a public meeting (*contio*)? By ancestral custom, nothing. But in times of unrest custom goes by the board. It would be absurd to connect Sempronia with the weighty doings of men, but she deserves a mention because, when brought before the people by a tribune in unsettled times, she lived up to the grandeur of her family. Standing up in public, facing the stern looks of leading men, the browbeating of a tribune, and the demands of the crowd for her to kiss Equitius in recognition of his birth, she adamantly refused.
>
> (VM 3.8.6)

Sempronia was being interrogated as a witness at a criminal trial. The accused was the censor Metellus Numidicus, Saturninus' bitter enemy whom the latter was charging with dereliction of duty.[25] Sempronia's testimony saved Metellus. She had made a political statement, she had refused to forge the link that would have legitimized Saturninus' claim to be the political heir to the Gracchi. Her evidence may well have been true, Equitius may indeed have been an imposter. But it is also possible that his claim was genuine but that Sempronia, like her mother before her, had lost faith in the populists. For all we know, Cornelia's letter to Gaius may have owed its production for use against the populists to the good offices of Sempronia. As Cornelia's only surviving child, she will have had custody of the family papers.

Sempronia's presence in a court situation was a startling break with precedent. Even thirty years later Cicero was able to make a jury's flesh creep with a lurid picture of respectable women giving evidence before a gathering of men (Cic. *Verr.* 2.1.94). Attitudes had not changed. In 331 it had only been 'after the crowd had dispersed' that the matrons had agreed to drink their concoctions. Eyebrows had been raised at the invasion of the forum by women during the Second Punic War, and again during the *lex Oppia* demonstration. Even in the first century Dionysius of Halicarnassus was hardly able to contain his indignation at the thought of Veturia's mission to Coriolanus.[26] But the precedent established by Sempronia soon caught on, and a number of court appearances by women followed.

In 100, a year or two after Sempronia's innovation, Fannia of

Minturnae was divorced by her husband, C. Titinius, who tried to retain her dowry on the grounds of her adultery. But this namesake of the comic playwright met his match in the latest recruit to the ranks of the *iurisperitae*. Fannia brought an action for the return of the dowry. The case was tried by C. Marius, then in his sixth consulship. Fannia conducted the case herself, and showed that Titinius had known about her character before the marriage. Marius ruled that he had deliberately chosen an unchaste wife in order to get hold of her property; he awarded him a derisory single sesterce and ordered him to return the dowry to Fannia. She is our first nameable *iurisperita* in the sense of an active court participant.[27]

Valerius Maximus has left us a small dossier of cases conducted by women (VM 8.3). The three examples are gathered under the rubric, 'Women who conducted cases before magistrates on their own behalf or on behalf of others'. The first case is that of Maesia of Sentinum, who was arraigned before the praetor on a criminal charge. In the presence of a large crowd she dealt methodically and vigorously with the various points and was acquitted by an almost unanimous vote of the jury. Her achievement earned her the sobriquet of Androgyne, 'Man-Woman'. The senate, gravely concerned, asked an oracle what it might portend for the city (Plut. *Lyc. et Num.* 3.6). The oracle's reply has not been preserved, but as no Vestal interments are recorded it can be assumed that no expiation was considered necessary. The case is important, *inter alia* because Maesia's great proficiency in the early first century[28] was not acquired on the spur of the moment. It presupposes a line of women versed in at least the theory of the law, as we have already postulated, and possibly with some practical experience as well – if not in open court until Sempronia, then behind the closed doors of the family court and in private declamations.

The next case in the dossier is that of Afrania (or Carfania), wife of Licinius Bucco, who was a senator in the Sullan period (*MRR* 2.492). Afrania was much given to litigation and always appeared before the praetor in person, not because she lacked advocates but because she was so shameless (*inpudentia abundabat*). Her unprecedented barking in the forum constantly assailed magistrates' ears and she became a byword for chicanery (*muliebris calumnia*); her name was thrown up as a reproach against disreputable women. She survived until c. 48 BC.

Afrania/Carfania's excessive zeal was responsible for a change in the law. The Severan jurist, Ulpian, says that the praetor's edict prohibits women from postulating for others (*pro aliis postulare*). Ulpian defines *postulare* as 'expounding one's own or a friend's claim before a magistrate, or refuting the claim of another' (*D.* 3.1.2). Women were excluded from *pro aliis postulare*, adds Ulpian, so that they might not, contrary to the modesty (*pudicitia*) appropriate to their sex, perform a male function by involving themselves in the cases of others. This was put into the edict, he says, because of Carfania, a most mischievous woman who postulated shamelessly and caused much annoyance to magistrates.[29]

We may reserve the third case in Valerius Maximus' dossier for later consideration (see Chapter 7, p. 81), and turn now to another question. What really disturbed the legal establishment in the early first century? Was it the need to protect itself against competition, which three women had shown could assume alarming proportions, or was it just that conventional wisdom stressed that women were feeble-minded? Or, to put it another way, was the latter used in order to achieve the former? This cannot be specifically asserted, but there certainly was a gap between their perception of women and the reality. The lawyers never tired of the theme of *sexus infirmitas, inbecillitas,* women's weakness, their susceptibility to seduction and persuasion and, above all, their ignorance of the law. They needed to be protected against themselves, but sometimes even their ignorance of the law did not save them. Thus: 'Mistake of fact does not prejudice anyone; but ignorance of the law excuses no one, *not even women.*' The message was frequently repeated.[30] Roman society, conditioned as it was to accepting women's ignorance of the law as axiomatic, had to be specially alerted when that was not the case. In fact, of course, *iuris ignorantia* was a fiction. Women might no longer be able to postulate for others, but that in no way inhibited their interest in the law and the courts. In the late Republic women like Chelidon and Clodia knew all about the law and litigation, as did Livia and her friend Urgulania, and after them Messalina, in the early Principate (see Chapter 6, p. 65, Chapter 10, p. 133 and Chapter 12, p. 167). In Juvenal's Rome women had not forgotten the 'barking' of Afrania and the ban on postulating to which it had led, but they still managed to put their legal expertise to good use. There is an instructive picture in Juvenal:

51

There are hardly any cases that were not set in motion by a woman. If Manilia is not the defendant, she's the plaintiff. Women draw the briefs themselves, ready to dictate Celsus' opening and submissions. Do we as women ever conduct cases? Are we learned in the civil law? Do we disturb your courts with our shouting?

(Juv. 6.242–5, 2.51–2)

'Celsus' is the Trajanic-Hadrianic jurist, P. Iuventius Celsus, and Juvenal's dramatic date is the turn of the first century AD. Manilia is not in any way evading the ban on *pro aliis postulare*. She is simply a habitual litigant who knows some law and virtually runs her own cases by telling her counsel what to say. The phenomenon is not unknown today, in litigants of both sexes. Another character portrayed by Juvenal is the bluestocking who knows some law and releases a torrent of virtuosity at the dinner table, not allowing any lawyer, auctioneer, grammarian or rhetorician to get a word in edgeways (Juv. 6.434–40). Titinius' *Iurisperita* would have felt quite at home in Juvenal's Rome. Finally, in the very age when the classical jurists were most voluble in their assertion of women's ignorance of the law, women were busily engaged in seeking rulings on the law from the imperial chancellery.[31] The lawyers knew that this was happening (they sat on the emperor's *consilium* and drafted the replies to petitioners), but they still preserved the fiction of *iuris ignorantia*.

VESTALS IN REVOLT

One of the striking, but neglected, features of the Gracchan period is the surge of acts of defiance by Vestals. The phenomenon is not entirely new, for ever since Postumia (see Chapter 3, n. 9), there had been women who showed by dress and demeanour what they thought of the straitjacket imposed on the Vestal order. But Claudia's challenge in 143 signalled a new development, the Vestal who thought things out on an intellectual plane. The trend was intensified a generation later.

In 123 the Vestal Licinia dedicated an altar and sacred accoutrements at the temple of Bona Dea on the Aventine. The dedication immediately became a political issue. The urban praetor, Sex. Iulius Caesar, queried the Vestal's right to make a dedication without the authority of the people. The senate having referred the matter to the pontifical college, the Pontifex Maximus, P. Mucius Scaevola, ruled that 'What Licinia, daughter of Gaius, had dedicated in a public place was deemed not to be sacred'. The senate decreed that the altar be removed and that not a single letter of the dedication be allowed to stand (Cic. *Dom.* 136–7).

That at this time the Populares were challenging Optimate control of religion and striving to bring it under the people's control has recently been demonstrated (Rawson 1974). But what part did this incident have in the struggle? The crucial question is, Who was 'Licinia, daughter of Gaius'? If, as is often supposed, her father was C. Licinius Crassus who had tried as tribune in 145 to carry a law requiring vacancies in priestly colleges to be filled by popular vote,[32] then the difficulties are considerable. Licinia would be seen to have deliberately challenged her father's entire ideology. It is true that there was a precedent for Scaevola's ruling, for in 154 the censor, Gaius Cassius Longinus, had been told by the pontiffs that his proposed dedication of a statue to Concord required the authority of the people (Cic. *Dom.* 136). But Cassius had not violated any duty of piety. Licinia had, unless it be supposed that as a Vestal she had ceased to be a member of her family and was no longer under a filial duty; but that is not a certain inference from a change of family.[33] The alternative is to invent a conservative father, seeing that the orator Licinius Crassus, Licinia's cousin, who subsequently defended her on a charge of unchastity, was more of a conservative than a populist. But the invention would be an entirely gratuitous one. We must therefore accept the tribune of 145. Licinia, who certainly presents as someone flying in the face of expected standards, did refuse to be deterred by considerations of piety.

The second act of Vestal defiance is linked to the most sensational forensic event of the period, the trials of three Vestals in 114–13. Until then things had been quiet on the Vestal front for a long time; the last interments were a hundred years in the past, in the early years of the Second Punic War.[34] But the more civilized trend was abruptly reversed in December 114, when the pontifical college, headed by Metellus Delmaticus, tried the Vestals Aemilia, Licinia and Marcia for unchastity; Licinia can safely be identified as the independent dedicator of 123.[35] The pontiffs returned an uneven verdict, condemning Aemilia, who was tried first, but acquitting Licinia and Marcia. But they did not get away with it. There was a storm of protest, and in 113 the tribune Sex.

Peducaeus carried a law which censured the pontifical college and set up a special *quaestio*, to be presided over by L. Cassius Longinus, to investigate the two acquittals. Cassius convicted Licinia and Marcia, as well as a number of accomplices and men with whom the Vestals had consorted. Not even the forensic brilliance of Licinius Crassus was able to save Licinia.

This case raises three questions. First, what was the impact of Peducaeus' law on the traditional procedure for punishing errant Vestals? This question has not been raised before. Second, what exactly had the Vestals done? The answer to be offered here is new. And third, how does the case fit into the general political climate? This issue has been canvassed often enough, but our solution focuses more on the motivation of the Vestals themselves than on the mainstream political factions.

Peducaeus' law made drastic inroads into the control of religious affairs. The Cassii Longini, from whose ranks the president (*quaesitor*) of the Peducean court was drawn, had willingly accepted (and perhaps instigated) the ruling of 154 on dedication, and now they were driving deeper into the area of secular control. This had a most important result, in that the death sentences on Vestals condemned by the Quaestio Peducaeana could not be carried out by the traditional method of burying them alive. The ritual attending that punishment could only be performed by the Pontifex Maximus,[36] and he was *functus officio*. He had acquitted two of them, in accordance with the will of the gods, and the gods would not tolerate any further action by him. Nor would the secular law, for the Pontifex Maximus was nowhere recognized as part of the secular machinery for carrying out capital sentences. In effect, therefore, the law creating the special *quaestio* also created a new offence; it was analogous to Vestal *incestum* but was not entirely co-extensive with it. There is substance in the suggestion of Rawson (1974: 208) that Peducaeus' law created a *quaestio perpetua*, a permanent jury-court, for Vestal unchastity.[37] It was because the new offence was not fully co-extensive with the old one that Licinia and Marcia were not able to plead double jeopardy when arraigned before the *quaestio*.[38]

If the aforegoing proposition is sound, the secular procedure will have had yet another important consequence. It was no longer a means of expiation. The gods required religious ceremonies, not rhetoric and legal points. Hymn-singing maidens were an acceptable alternative to interment, but jury-trials were not. Thus by the very manner of their punishment the Vestals had placed their activities squarely in the realm of mainstream politics. There had been political motives in the past (see Chapter 2, p. 17), but merely as an adjunct to expiation. Now politics was a substantive objective. There was still, of course, a vital religious connotation, inasmuch as the protest threatened the very existence of the sacred flame. But that was a different consideration from expiation for a prodigy. And henceforth the way to save the sacred flame would be secular. (The politics of the protest will be discussed after we have analysed some other aspects of this matter.)

What had the Vestals done? Our only account of the factual basis of the charges is supplied by Dio (26.87):

> The punishment of the priestesses threw the whole city into confusion. The people punished not only the formally accused but all suspects. It all seemed to be due to a god's anger rather than to female immorality. Three women were involved. One, Marcia, had consorted with only a single knight, but Aemilia and Licinia had many lovers. They co-operated with each other, sometimes in private, sometimes in groups – Licinia with Aemilia's brother, Aemilia with Licinia's brother. They also extended their favours to those who could inform against them. It was kept secret for a long time, though many were in the know. But a slave, Manius, betrayed them because he had not been given what he had been promised. He was an expert at leading women into prostitution and teaching them to quarrel with each other.

This is as far as Dio takes us; the *Excerpta Valesiana*, on which we depend, breaks off at this point.

The picture of the Vestals running a brothel is a startling one. But it is not the sort of thing that Dio would have invented. Besides, it may have been confirmed by Livy. Book 63 of Livy is lost, but the epitome says that in that book Livy gave a full account of how the offence had been committed, how it had been detected, and how it had been punished. Clearly the wealth of detail had impressed the epitomator. Although the Livian derivatives do not reflect that comprehensive coverage, they do reveal that a prodigy started the chain of events and, more to the point, that soon after the prodigy a Roman knight, L. Veturius, seduced Aemilia, two other Vestals were drawn in, an information was laid by a slave and all were punished.[39] There is thus good confirmation of Dio's account, and he may well go back to Livy.[40]

For the actual trials our best source is Asconius (39–40 Stangl). He notes the original acquittals of the two Vestals and the creation of the *quaestio*, and has Cassius Longinus condemn the two and a number of other persons. Cassius acted with excessive severity – *nimia asperitate*. The exact force of this complaint has never been properly understood, although Asconius himself supplies the necessary clue. He says that whenever Cassius presided over a murder trial he charged the jury to consider who stood to benefit – *cui bono?* And it was because of this severity that the people appointed Cassius to head the Vestal commission (39 St.). In other words, Cassius attached great importance to inference and circumstantial evidence. That is why Dio says he condemned some on mere suspicion (CD 26.87.2). We conclude that Dio is basically a reliable reflection of Livy's account in the lost book 63.

The message of the sources is that moral decay in the Vestal order had assumed catastrophic proportions. Three defections out of the six priestesses making up the order (and possibly of all six[41]) meant that the Eternal Flame was in grave danger of going out. Even if that could be averted, one of the strengths of the order was its low turnover of members due to the minimum period of thirty years' service and the reluctance of many to leave even then (Plut. *Num.* 10.4; DH 2.67.2). Thus the replacement of a large part of the membership in one fell swoop was a daunting prospect.[42] It follows that faction fighting, that overworked panacea for the troubles of the Roman Republic, did not play a major part in the punishment of the Vestals. No doubt Metellus Delmaticus and Cassius Longinus were in different camps, but neither that nor any other shuffling of the cards suffices to explain this enormous dislocation of religious stability. Still less do any of the more esoteric solutions that have been proposed.[43]

The key to the whole affair is the Vestals themselves. There was clearly a great deal of misconduct going on, and it was being put on an organized basis. We have here the forerunner of a phenomenon that keeps cropping up in the early Principate, a coterie of rebellious spirits meeting together for some adultery and some sharpening of their wits on the foibles of the world (Bauman 1974a: 131–2). Nor was the coterie, the *coniuratio* if one likes, of 114 the first. The Bacchanalian movement had been condemned as a combination of organized sex and malpractice

threatening both religious and social stability. In such circumstances the nobility tended to present a united front. They had
done so with some minor exceptions in the Bacchanalian affair,
and to quite a large extent they did so now. Metellus Delmaticus
may have tried to cut down on the number of condemned, but
he dared not shut his eyes completely. The overwhelming support
for Cassius Longinus, the hanging judge, shows just how clearly
Roman society was alive to the magnitude of the threat.

Do we know anything about the membership of the coterie of
114? Not much can be made of the brothers of Aemilia and
Licinia, or of M. Antonius and Ser. Fulvius who were acquitted,[44]
but the Roman knight, L. Veturius, is instructive. It was he who
seduced Aemilia, who in turn drew Licinia and Marcia into what
proved to be quite a gathering; and it was Veturius' slave who
betrayed them (Oros. 5.15.20–2). Veturius has an interesting
family history. His links with women's organizations went back
to his remote ancestor Veturia, who led the deputation to Coriolanus. The patrician Veturii shared the Vestal Claudia's reservations
about the tribunate, for in ancient times Gaius Veturius had been
sentenced to death for refusing to make way for a tribune in the
forum (Plut. *CG.* 3.3). The Veturii had long-standing ties with
the families of both Aemilia and Licinia (Münzer 1920: 123–32).
If our Veturius was a direct descendant of L. Veturius, whom
Cato stripped of his equestrian status in 184 because of his neglect
of the family cult and his corpulence which rendered him unfit
for equestrian exercises (Fest. p. 344 Lindsay), indifference to
religion and the lifestyle of a *bon vivant* would have been a most
appropriate legacy for the man who seems to have played a leading
role in the coterie of 114.

Finally, what of the three Vestals themselves? What motivated
them? There have been suggestions that they simply supported
their families' populist moves against religion (Münzer 1920: 244),
but neither Licinia nor Claudia before her fits too well into that
category. It is better to suppose that these women were developing
an independent Vestal line, one not wedded to either of the ideol-
ogies current in mainstream politics. No doubt their family back-
grounds had inspired the independence of outlook that liberated
them from conventional thinking, but the problems that they
addressed were not the problems of their fathers. Their concern
was with matters specifically related to their situation as Vestals,
and it boils down to this: did Vestals like being Vestals? There is

no simple answer. On the one hand a Vestal enjoyed compensation through her special status in both the public and the private sectors; according to Plutarch very few left after thirty years' service, and were most unhappy when they did (*Num.* 10.2). But in the early Principate there would be strong resistance to attempts to recruit Vestals. Augustus found families using every possible means to keep their daughters' names off lists from which replacements would be drawn, even when he swore that if his granddaughters had been of the right age he would have put them on the list. He was forced to open the order to the daughters of freedmen, and to grant Vestals the *ius trium liberorum*, a privilege normally reserved for women with at least three children. In AD 24 two million sesterces were voted to Cornelia, which was a substantial increase in the 'bride-price'; and Livia was given the right to sit with the Vestals in the theatre, thus enhancing the order's prestige.[45]

In fact the problem of finding recruits was not peculiar to the Principate. Reluctance had been shown in the later Republic and had been highlighted by the orchestrated protest of 114. Many Vestals shared the feelings of the girl known to the elder Seneca, who wrote, 'Blessed nuptials! May I die if marriage is not sweet?' (Sen. Rhet. *Contr.* 6.8: 264 Mueller). She did not only mean marriage as such. She was expressing a deep longing for a normal life, for the life that women of her class could so easily enjoy in the capital of a world empire. It was time to discard the lopsided morality, to allow Vestals to live in the world.[46] But like so many of the progressive ideas thrown up by the Gracchan period, the impulse would dissipate most of its energy against the iron walls of tradition. But one improvement would survive, for the more civilized punishment flowing from Peducaeus' law would be perpetuated – at least for the period of this study.[47] Moreover, the trials of 114–13 would prove to be the last in the period in which convictions were obtained. And as a further bonus, the first century would display signs of a populist ideology amongst Vestals whom Aemilia, Licinia and Marcia had taught to think.

CONCLUSION

The discussion of Cornelia uncovers questions that have not been raised before. Her circle, her elevation to a concept, her promotion of a cult of her sons – all these are valid deductions from hard evidence. The same goes for women in law. Both as practitioners and as theoreticians they carry conviction. Their court appearances have been partly covered before, notably by Marshall (1989, 1990), but the significance of Sempronia's appearance in court is new. So are Claudia's constitutional challenge and Laelia's expertise and influence on Cicero. It can no doubt be said that these phenomena are sporadic and, in the case of postulating for others, terminating. But the cumulative effect of developments from Titinius to Juvenal cannot be ignored.

The one finding that may encounter opposition is the organized Vestal protest. But with Licinia's known attack in the matter of dedications, Veturius' credentials as a member of a coterie, Dio's credible description of the coterie's activities, and the lack of enthusiasm for recruitment into the order, the theory is by no means deficient in evidential underpinning. And one thing is certain. The expiation of prodigies by Vestal interment had been finally abandoned, at least for our period.

The most important topic in this chapter is Cornelia. She is our first unequivocal example of the matron who is fully immersed in public affairs. Verginia might have claimed primacy if the sources had been more generous on detail, and Aemilia has a strong claim, but as it is the distinction is Cornelia's. It was not only the magic of her sons' names that made her memory a standard of political behaviour for later generations; she was a major figure in her own right. Indeed, none of the great figures of the late Republic whom we are about to discuss ever became comparable criteria of excellence. If Cornelia ever had rivals, they did not surface until the triumvirate and the Principate.

6

THE POLITICAL STRATEGISTS OF THE LATE REPUBLIC

INTRODUCTION

The first century BC can properly be described as the Age of the Political Matron. Where previous ages had thrown up a few women whose status and abilities had enabled them to influence public affairs, the last century of the Republic saw the emergence of the influential woman almost as an institution. In the private law sector she was as emancipated as she ever would be, with *manus*-free marriage the general rule and guardianship little more than nominal.[1] In the public sector she foreshadowed the great imperial women, and in some respects outdid them, for the liberal climate of the time allowed her, like her male counterpart, to address a wider range of goals than would be possible later on. A Servilia was able to influence the proceedings of the senate without an elaborate comedy of curtains and concealment. A Fulvia did not need to wear an imitation of a military uniform; she commanded an army. Furthermore, there are signs of the extension to other matrons of the notion embodied in 'Cornelia, mother of the Gracchi' (see Chapter 5, p. 42). Even the Vestals are found intervening in public affairs, no longer as protestors but as active participants. There is also some interesting material on women who built up flourishing businesses as procurers of political and legal favours.

Organized feminine opinion, as distinct from powerful individuals, is on the whole less in evidence than before. This was partly due to the discouragement of women's presence in the forum, but it was also because women's horizons had expanded. The issues of mainstream politics took the place of demonstrations about finery. When an organized *démarche* did take place it was on a substantial question of fiscal policy.

VESTALS IN AN ENLIGHTENED AGE

That a new age had dawned is shown most clearly by the further history of the Vestals. In 73 a Vestal, Fabia, was accused of unchastity with Catiline (the later conspirator). Fabia was acquitted, though the sources are not sure whether this was due to the advocacy of M. Piso, the intervention of Cato of Utica, or the influence of Q. Lutatius Catulus. In the same year a charge was brought against both a Vestal, Licinia, and M. Licinius Crassus (cos. 70). They were acquitted when Crassus proved that his frequent visits to his Vestal relative had been made in order to persuade her to sell him a property.[2]

These trials were conducted by a secular court, the *quaestio*, modelled on that created by Peducaeus and now operating permanently.[3] That is why Cicero says that M. Piso, who defended Fabia, revived his fortunes as a court pleader by his success in the Vestal case (*Brut.* 236). One does not see a pontifical trial in the musty recesses of the Regia as an occasion for a display of forensic fireworks (assuming, which we do not know, that Vestals were allowed representation in the pontifical court at all).

It was not only in the forensic sphere that the Vestal order was taking on a popular coloration at this time. A *lex Papia*, possibly dating to 65 BC, laid down that twenty girls were to be chosen from the people by the Pontifex Maximus, lots were to be drawn in the *comitia calata*, and the successful candidate was to be made a Vestal. Whether this means that parental demand had exceeded pontifical supply, or that reluctance was being overcome, the effect of the law was to transfer partial control of the Vestals to the people. The Pontifex Maximus was no longer the sole arbiter of whom he was going to 'seize'.[4]

The most dramatic incident in this period occurred during Sulla's dictatorship. The young Caesar, who had been nominated as Flamen Dialis but not yet inducted, was told by Sulla to divorce his wife Cornelia, a daughter of the deceased populist leader, Cornelius Cinna. Caesar, having rejected Sulla's demand, was deprived of his priesthood and also lost his wife's dowry and his gentile right of succession. He was counted amongst Sulla's enemies, and was forced to go into hiding. In other words, he was proscribed. He was eventually forgiven through the good offices of the Vestals and of his kinsmen, Mamercus Aemilius and Aurelius Cotta (*SJ* 1.1–3).

Caesar never became Flamen Dialis.[5] Consequently, the practical result of intervention by the Vestals and the others was the removal of his name from the proscription lists and the restoration of his dotal and succession rights. That the Vestals played an important part in securing those concessions is clear. Suetonius says that for a long time Sulla had held out against members of his faction who interceded for Caesar, but they persisted and eventually got their way. The Sullan intercedents mentioned by Suetonius, namely Aurelius Cotta, a connection of Caesar's mother Aurelia, and Mam. Aemilius, are only noticed after the Vestals, which confirms that the latter were the last, and decisive, resort to whom they turned after all other means had failed. The idea of seeking Vestal support may have emanated from Caesar's mother, who was active in women's religious organizations. It is equally possible, however, that the initiative came from Cotta and Aemilius. Both were Pontifices,[6] and as such they had the ear of the Pontifex Maximus, Metellus Pius, and could have enlisted Vestal support through him.

One important question remains. Did the entire Vestal order join in the intercession, as Münzer thought (1937:221), or was it merely the work of individual Vestals? To this there is only one answer. We have the names of four Vestals who were in office at the time, but there is nothing to suggest individual initiatives.[7] When Suetonius speaks of *per virgines Vestales* (*SJ* 1.2) he means the entire order. If any confirmation is needed, it is supplied in full measure by what happened two decades later. In December 62 P. Clodius made his way by stealth into Caesar's house, where the festival of Bona Dea was being celebrated under the presidency of Caesar's mother.[8] The senate was prodded into taking action against this violation of an exclusively feminine cult,[9] and decreed that the matter be referred to the Vestals and the Pontifices. Those two orders, both acting in an official and collegiate capacity,[10] ruled that Clodius' act was *nefas*, a threat to the cosmic order desired by the gods. The result, as is well known, was that a special *quaestio* was established to try Clodius.[11] He was, as it happens, acquitted (much to Cicero's disgust[12]), but the consequences of the Vestal-Pontifical pronouncement were far-reaching, including, as they did, mortal enmity between Clodius and Cicero.

The *démarche* to Sulla and the Bona Dea affair are not the only matters in which the Vestals influenced mainstream politics in the late Republic. In December 63, in the evening of the day on which Cicero had had Lentulus and other Catilinarians convicted of conspiracy by the senate, the festival of Bona Dea was celebrated in Cicero's house. Cicero was plagued by doubts as to whether he should, as consul, put the conspirators to death. At that point the women in his house were sacrificing at an altar, and the fire which was thought to have gone out suddenly blazed up. The Vestals, who were present at the ceremony in their official capacity, declared that the goddess was giving Cicero a great light on his road to safety and glory, she was telling him to carry out the verdict which the senate had pronounced. The Vestals deputed Cicero's wife, Terentia, to carry the news to Cicero, who was greatly encouraged and had sentence of death voted by the senate next day.[13]

In the same passage (*Cic.* 20.2) Plutarch notes that Terentia was ambitious and more inclined to share Cicero's political interests than to trouble him with her domestic concerns. It would not be unkind to suggest that the sudden activation of the dead embers may have been planned in advance by Terentia and the Vestals. Indeed, Cicero himself seems to have had a special relationship with the Vestal order. Amongst the members at that time were Fabia and Licinia, who had been acquitted of unchastity in 73. Fabia was a half-sister of Terentia, and in 58, during Cicero's exile, she would give sanctuary to Terentia at the temple of Vesta. Licinia was prominent in 63, not long before the Catilinarian affair, when her relative, Licinius Murena, was a candidate for the consulship of 62. Licinia surrendered her Vestal seat at the games to Murena, thus lending the prestige of the order to his candidacy. As Cicero, the consul conducting the election, also favoured Murena, the latter was, not surprisingly, successful.[14]

It is clear that the Vestal impact on mainstream politics in the first century BC was quite a substantial one. The efforts of Claudia, the earlier Licinia, and the protestors of 114 had borne fruit.[15] Not the least of the achievements of the Ciceronian Age was its more enlightened attitude to the Vestals.

EULOGIES, PIETY AND POLITICS

In 102 Lutatius Catulus (cos. 78) pronounced a funeral oration over his mother, thus extending to women a custom long observed for male ancestors. This has been seen as a way used by men to gain status through their women; where Gaius Gracchus had used the technique during Cornelia's lifetime, Catulus extended it to eulogies (Pomeroy 1975: 182–3). If this were all it would still be an important proof of the impact of women's merits on the electoral consciousness. But there is even more to it, for Catulus should also be credited with an ideological motive. As already observed, he would defend Fabia on the charge of unchastity in 73. Even more important, he was a brother-in-law and ally of the orator Hortensius. He will have shared the orator's notable pride in his ancestors, and will have been acquainted with his daughter Hortensia. He may well have imbibed (or perhaps inspired) her feminist philosophy, which was more akin to Catulus' prosaic integrity than to her father's flamboyance. Catulus may have struck a telling blow for feminism.[16]

The political importance of the female eulogy became even clearer in 68, when Caesar pronounced a funeral oration over his aunt Julia, the widow of Marius, and also used the occasion to display images of Marius for the first time since Sulla had declared Marius a public enemy in 88. Caesar thus brought about a *de facto* annulment of that decree; the emperor Tiberius would be aware of the hidden pitfalls of the female eulogy.[17] In the same year Caesar pronounced an oration over his wife Cornelia; she was the first young woman to be honoured in that way (Plut. *Caes.* 5.2). Caesar was reminding the public of his rejection of Sulla's demand that he divorce Cornelia, thus striking a second blow at the dictator's memory by lauding a female connection.

The eulogy continued to have delicate political nuances later on. Porcia, sister of Cato of Utica, and widow of L. Domitius Ahenobarbus (cos. 54) who fell at Pharsalus, survived her husband for three years, dying at the end of July 45. Funeral orations were composed by Cicero, Varro and a certain Ollius. Cicero had some difficulty with the oration. He sent a draft to Atticus and asked him to pass it on to Porcia's son and her nephew Brutus, 'if it is to be sent at all' (*Att.* 13.37.3). Then, almost immediately, he sent Atticus a corrected version, to be sent to the son and Brutus in place of the first draft. He also asked Atticus to send him the orations of Varro and Ollius, especially the latter; Cicero had seen it already, but wanted to have another look at it, for it said things that Cicero could hardly believe (*Att.* 13.48.2). Porcia had evidently remained outspokenly loyal to the republican cause espoused by her brother and husband, and Cicero, intent on being seen to maintain an impartial stance, was worried about Caesar's reaction to the oration. We have no information as to what the otherwise unknown Ollius had said, but it was obviously not something that Caesar would want to hear.

THE FIRST 'FIXERS'

In a certain sense the eulogy was a negative accolade, a laudation of virtues which did not include political ambitions, though Porcia does not quite fit into that category. As a rule, when a woman did aspire to political influence she inspired the same outpourings of vituperation as that which greeted the forensic aspirations of Afrania/Carfania. The point is illustrated by the first female politician of the period, a certain Praecia who exerted considerable influence in the 70s. She was, says Plutarch, famed for her beauty and cheek (*lamyria*) throughout the city, though in other respects she was no better than a common prostitute. She headed a salon which promoted political ambitions, and established a reputation as a friend and a 'fixer' (*drastērios*). Cornelius Cethegus, a populist turned Sullan who virtually controlled the city, became her lover, and political power passed into her hands; no public business could be transacted without Cethegus' approval, and he did nothing without Praecia. In 74 Lucullus (cos. 74) won her over by gifts and flattery; it was a great thing for such a 'pushy' woman (*sobara kai panēgyrike*) to be seen as a connection of the great Lucullus. Praecia enlisted Cethegus' support and Lucullus duly obtained the province of Cilicia, his stepping-stone to the much sought after command against Mithridates (Plut. *Luc.* 6.2–4). In the same year Cethegus had a hand in securing the command against the pirates for M. Antonius (Ps.-Ascon. 259 St.). Praecia will have had something to do with it; Plutarch does not note that item in her career because he is writing about Lucullus.

Plutarch's insinuations of immorality have damned Praecia for all time.[18] But for a woman whose family displays no senators or magistrates, and at the most one obscure jurist,[19] she must have

had exceptional ability to put Lucullus in the way of a command
that had been contested by Sulla and Marius to the point of
bloodshed, and would be wrested from Lucullus by that most
powerful dynast, Cn. Pompeius Magnus.

The other great 'fixer' of the time is Chelidon, though we know
of her only through some references in Cicero's speeches against
Verres. We begin with a summary of Cicero's characterization of
Chelidon:

> She was Verres' mistress, and while he was praetor she
> controlled the civil law and private disputes, and was also
> dominant in maintenance contracts. She only had to whisper
> in Verres' ear and he would change a decision already given,
> or disregard his own precedents. People flocked to her house
> in search of new laws, new decisions, new procedures, while
> the houses of the jurisconsults were deserted. Some of her
> customers paid her in cash, others signed notes of hand. It
> was more like the praetor's tribunal than a prostitute's house.
>
> (*Verr.* 2.1.136–40, 120)

The attack is long on generalization, short on detail. Chelidon is
linked with only two concrete cases. In the one, in which she has
only a supporting role, a testator had made his daughter his heir,
on the basis that as he was not on the census roll the *lex Voconia*
did not apply. Verres used his edict to give possession of the
property to the substitute heir, a man. In other words, he ruled
that the *lex Voconia* did apply and the daughter was disqualified.
Cicero claims that Verres presented himself as an adversary of
women only in order to conceal the fact that his entire edict had
been composed to suit Chelidon (*Verr.* 2.1.104–6). The criticism
is not an impressive one. Apart from the fact that Verres may
well have acted quite properly,[20] the vague generalization about
'Chelidon's edict' is not accompanied by any specific indication
of how she stood to benefit. We have to take Cicero's word for
it that her control of the civil law and private disputes flowed
from what she had got Verres to include in his edict.

Cicero does somewhat better with his other concrete example,
though in the end he fails to substantiate his contention that
Chelidon dominated maintenance contracts. A contract for the
upkeep of the temple of Castor had long awaited an official cer-
tificate of proper completion (*probatio*). The original contractor
having died, Verres conspired with the new contractor to defeat

the rights of the minor heir by withholding certification on the most trivial grounds, namely that the columns were not plumb. The minor's guardians went to see Chelidon. Cicero paints a lurid picture of their shame and disgust at having to enter a harlot's house. In return for a promise of money Chelidon undertook to do her best. But next day she told them that Verres could not be moved. The guardians were forced to come to terms with the new contractor (*Verr.* 2.1.130–40).

So much for Chelidon's domination of maintenance contracts. But with that forensic brilliance so peculiarly his own, Cicero does manage to extract some profit from the incident. He cites as his source L. Domitius (cos. 54?), who had had the story from one of the minor's guardians. But when cross-examined by Cicero, Domitius had refused to mention Chelidon's name, and had only done so when pressed (*Verr.* 2.1.139–40). Cicero attributes his reluctance to a sense of shame, and asks Verres if he does not feel ashamed of being dominated by a woman whose very name Domitius hesitates to mention. There is a subtle purpose behind this observation. People are, it is implied, generally reluctant to name Chelidon, and for that reason – but only for that reason – Cicero is unable to cite chapter and verse. Cicero thus invites us either to take his word for it or to reject his picture of Chelidon completely. On balance the first alternative is to be preferred. Chelidon probably did have a reputation as an intermediary, and she may well have been running a flourishing business in that commodity. Amongst her qualifications is one of special interest to us, for she must have had a good understanding of the law. It is no accident that she was active in the same period as Praecia. Although the edict against Afrania/Carfania was probably already in place,[21] the repercussions of what she had started were strong and clear. Instead of postulating for others, women with a legal background were now interceding for them.

WOMEN AND THE CONSPIRACY OF CATILINE

Two women, Sempronia and Fulvia, played roles of some importance in the conspiracy of Catiline in 63. They were on opposing sides, but the sources, with the unanimity that they seem to reserve for this sort of thing, tar both women with the same brush of immorality. Sallust has left us a detailed report on Sempronia. He says that Catiline won the support of women who had financed their expensive lifestyles by prostitution, but had fallen into debt when age restricted their activities. Catiline calculated that through them he could win the support of their slaves, set fire to the city, and win over or kill their husbands. These women included Sempronia – the only one whom Sallust names. Well born, well favoured, well read, well versed in the courtesan's craft, she knew nothing of modesty or chastity. Under the pressure of extravagance she had committed wrongful acts of masculine audacity (*virilis audaciae*); she had broken her word, repudiated her debts, been a party to murder. Yet she did not lack talent: she wrote poetry, told jokes, used language which was modest, tender or wanton, and displayed much wit and charm (Sall. *Cat.* 24.3–25.5, 40.5–6).

In connection with the conspiracy, envoys of the Allobroges were taken to the house of Sempronia's husband, Decimus Brutus, a confirmed enemy of the populists.[22] Brutus was away, but Sempronia's presence made it a suitable venue, for she was indispensable to the meeting with the envoys.[23] Gabinius, one of the ringleaders, was also present. This is all that we know about Sempronia's part in the affair. She was not prosecuted for it, no doubt because women could not be charged with aspiring to supreme power, which is what the conspiracy was about (see Chapter 1, p. 12). For similar reasons Catiline's wife, Aurelia Orestilla, was allowed to go scot free, despite a record which, if the sources are to be believed, included a demand for the murder of Catiline's son.[24]

Sempronia's family background is of interest. She did not belong to the Sempronii Gracchi branch of the Sempronii. She was a daughter of Sempronius Tuditanus (cos. 129), the well-known Optimate, historian and constitutional lawyer; and she was a sister of the orator Hortensius' wife.[25] An anecdote about her brother is unexpectedly apt. He is described by Cicero as an eccentric who used to ascend the rostra wearing a tragic robe and actor's boots, scattering coins to the people as he went (*Phil.* 3.16). Cicero regrets that he did not bequeath his contempt for money to his family. As he was the last male member of the family, Cicero appears to be criticizing Sempronia (and her sister) for their extravagance. Hence, perhaps, the financial stringency that drove Sempronia into Catiline's camp. Cicero was only too ready to aim a barb at Catiline's associate.

The other Catilinarian woman is Fulvia who gave Cicero information about the conspiracy. The mistress of Q. Curius, her ardour had been dampened by his straitened circumstances, following his expulsion from the senate for immorality. In an attempt to improve his image Curius boasted to her of his part in the conspiracy, saying that he would soon 'give her the earth'. Fulvia, aghast, told some people about it, though without naming names. When Cicero entered on his consulship in 63 Fulvia got in touch with him, and acted as an intermediary to carry Cicero's inducements to Curius and the latter's disclosures of the plot to Cicero. We depend for this information on sources other than Cicero himself,[26] for he does not once refer to Fulvia in his four orations against Catiline. But Fulvia achieved immortality in spite of Cicero, for the Severan jurist, Papinian, notes that she uncovered the conspiracy and informed Cicero, from which Papinian derives a general rule that in cases of treason even women are heard (*D* 48.4.8.). Cicero had, through Fulvia, promised Curius great rewards, but there is no trace of Curius or Fulvia having received them. Hispala Faecenia, the Bacchanalian informant who preceded Fulvia as the first woman to lay an information, was more fortunate.[27] But it was not only in the matter of rewards that Fulvia was badly done by. Some of the sources (though not all) tried to damn her as a prostitute.[28]

CLODIA

With Clodia we meet our first sustained political strategist. As true a scion of the arrogant and eccentric Claudii Pulchri as her brother,[29] she was a daughter of Ap. Claudius Pulcher (cos. 79), a niece of the Vestal Claudia who defied a tribunician veto in 143, and a remote descendant of Claudia who vilified the Roman plebs in 246. Born in c. 94, she married Metellus Celer (cos. 60) in c. 63 – a surprisingly late date if it was her first marriage – but was widowed in 59. She was almost certainly the 'Lesbia' who drove Catullus to distraction, and after giving the poet his congé moved on to the well-born orator, M. Caelius Rufus. Rumours swirled around her throughout her life. She was said to have been responsible for Metellus' death. She was known as 'the bargain-basement Clytemnestra' (*Quadrantaria Clytemnestra*) whose large, brilliant eyes said 'yes' at the dinner-table but 'no' in the bedroom. There was talk of incest with her brother. It was also said that she had tried to break up Cicero's marriage in order to marry him herself.

Most important of all, she was the driving force behind the prosecution of Caelius Rufus which she instigated in 56, in order to punish him for breaking off with her.[30]

Cicero defended Caelius in 56, and his speech is our prime source for Clodia.[31] The prosecution was launched by L. Sempronius Atratinus, then only 17 years old, as chief accuser. His natural father, Calpurnius Bestia, had been charged with electoral corruption earlier in the year and had been successfully defended by Cicero. Caelius proposed bringing a second charge of corruption against Bestia. As that would prejudice Bestia's candidacy for the praetorship, Atratinus is thought to have prosecuted Caelius in order to block the attack on Bestia (Gardner 1958: 400–1). Two subscribers supported Atratinus. One of them, Herennius Balbus, is criticized by Cicero for his involvement in the social whirl, including visits to Clodia's favourite resort, Baiae (*Cael.* 25–7). The other was a certain P. Clodius, but he was not Clodia's brother.[32] The speakers for the defence were Caelius himself, Licinius Crassus Dives, and Cicero. Caelius was charged with public violence under the *lex Plautia de vi* of 70 BC.

Cicero has a great deal to say about Clodia's part in the case (*Cael.* 30, 35, 50, 53, 55–69), but there is no consensus as to the implications of what he says. Some see Clodia as the driving force behind the prosecution; others assign her a subordinate role; and still others almost write her out of the case.[33] Our preference is for the first alternative, and an attempt will now be made to add to what others have said in support of that solution.

The indictment covered five counts, but Clodia is mentioned in only two of them. It was alleged that she had lent Caelius some gold which he had used to procure the murder of Dio of Alexandria; and Caelius was said to have obtained a supply of poison to be given to her (23, 30, 51). The other three charges were dealt with by Crassus, who spoke before Cicero (23). The significance of this division of labour has never been fully appreciated. It is simply that Cicero had deliberately arranged for Clodia to be left to him. She was, in effect, the complainant in the poisoning charge, and the key witness in the Dio of Alexandria charge. Thus her evidence was crucial. She had to be handled roughly, a technique for which Cicero was better qualified than Crassus. Cicero makes straight for the jugular in his opening: his client is being attacked by the resources of a prostitute – *opibus meretriciis* (1.1). This was not mere abuse, for under the *lex de vi* a prostitute was not a competent witness.[34] Cicero does not raise it as a formal objection to Clodia's evidence, but his forbearance is simply due to the fact that he cannot formally stigmatize her as a prostitute in view of the wording of the ban on prostitutes' evidence: 'who publicly earns a living with his/her body' (D 22.5.3.5). Whatever Clodia's morals, she did not ply her trade in public. But Cicero was a past master at insinuation. Crassus could not have done it; as a member of the so-called First Triumvirate with Pompey and Caesar, he could not speak ill of the sister of P. Clodius. When Crassus spoke for Caelius, the conference of Luca, at which the three dynasts would patch up their differences, was only two weeks away. The third speaker, Caelius himself, was under no constraint; the barbs about the bargain-basement Clytemnestra and the tantalizer were fired off by Caelius at the trial (QIO 8.6.53).

There is no need to analyse all Cicero's thrusts at Clodia,[35] and we turn to our next question. Was there any reason for the attack on Clodia apart from the need to discredit her evidence? In other words, was she the mastermind behind the prosecution? If it is found that she was able to stir up prosecutions at will, she will have been a most formidable performer in the political arena. For that we need some proof of her involvement in cases other than that of Caelius, and it so happens that such proof is to hand, in a neglected passage in Cicero's speech:

> The accusers have cited the condemnation of M. Camurtius and C. Caesernius. How dare they, coming from 'that woman', mention these names? How dare they revive the memory of that great wrong which, though not entirely forgotten, has been dulled by time? On what charges were they condemned? No doubt because they avenged the resentment felt by the same woman for a wrong done to her, revenge which they took on her behalf by committing a sexual assault on Vettius. Has their condemnation been brought up, then, so that Vettius' name may be heard in this case, so that the old story about the copper may be quoted? They were not liable under the law concerning violence, but they had contravened some law.
>
> (71, adapted)

It should be noted that here, as consistently throughout the speech, Cicero does not identify Clodia by name. She is 'that woman', 'the same woman'. The reason is that Cicero could be held liable for defamation only if he identified his victim by name.[36] This has a bearing on the strength of Cicero's insinuations against Clodia; he was not sure enough of his ground to come right out with it. As for the case of Camurtius and Caesernius, it seems that a certain Vettius had done Clodia an injury; according to Plutarch she was called *Quadrantia*[37] because one of her lovers had put copper coins into a purse and sent them to her as silver. Instead of suing Vettius she put up two henchmen to assault him sexually.[38] If the perpetrator was the notorious L. Vettius who was a tower of strength to Cicero in the Catilinarian affair, Clodia will have struck a powerful blow at an enemy of her brother and Caesar, while also avenging a private wrong. Violence rather than litigation was almost forced on her by her lifestyle; an action might have earned her a contemptuous award of nominal damages.

Clodia is at the very heart and centre of the case. Of the three accusers, one was a trained advocate attached to the Clodii, one was a social connection of Clodia, and one was a figurehead in the person of Bestia's son.[39] But Clodia's motives were not unilateral. On the one hand she was motivated by personal considerations, in order to be revenged on Caelius. That in itself establishes her political importance; not everyone could make free use of the public criminal courts in pursuit of a private vendetta. Men had been doing that sort of thing for hundreds of years, but Clodia was the first woman. But over and above that she gave effect to a link which she had, I suggest, forged with Calpurnius Bestia, a link that was analogous to the all-male *amicitia*, or political friendship. Clodia and Bestia had a mutual interest in co-operating with each other. Bestia was a candidate for the praetorship in 56 and needed to silence Caelius. He therefore made common cause with Clodia. But it would be a mistake to think that he merely used her as a pawn. The pawn, if any, was on a different square. Clodia supplied the charges and the bulk of the prosecuting team, and all that Bestia contributed was the nominal chief accuser. As in any *amicitia*, the 'friends' aimed at more than one goal. In Clodia's case the desire for revenge was conjoined with an interest in promoting Bestia's career, perhaps for the purpose of a liaison with yet another man younger than herself.[40]

Clodia is known to have been beautiful, and she is generally assumed to have been intelligent, educated and witty.[41] There is no need to quarrel with that assessment, but the point is that those qualities are only peripheral to her consequence. Determination, at times bordering on ruthlessness, a profound understanding of politics and politicians and consummate skill in manipulating them, and indifference to, and even contempt for, the traditional curbs on women's political mobility – in a word, *muliebris audacia* in the true sense – these are the marks of the great feminine political strategist. Whether we base our assessment solely on the evidence adduced above, or supplement it by additional possibilities,[42] Clodia's claim to the title is not open to question.

SERVILIA

Servilia, half-sister of the irredentist Republican and Stoic, Cato of Utica, mistress of Caesar and mother of Brutus who killed Caesar, is something of an enigma. She ought to be the greatest political strategist of the late Republic, but does not quite present as such. This is partly due to the sources, which divide into two distinct halves. The one half consists of the letters of Cicero, with whom Servilia was politically involved both during Caesar's lifetime and after his death, but it is only very late in the piece that any substantial information about Servilia surfaces in the letters. Prior to June 45 there are only two references; dating respectively to May 51 and February 50, both relate to Servilia's role in finding a husband for Cicero's daughter (*Att.* 5.4, 6.1). If we had only Cicero we would have no idea that during this most critical period in Caesar's career his liaison with Servilia was at its height, or that the woman who would later show such mastery of political strategy had been (as she must have been) in close touch with him on such burning issues as the terminal date of his Gallic governorship.[43] In June 45, when things are starting to move towards the climax of 15 March 44, Cicero asks Atticus whether Servilia has come, and whether Brutus has done anything about arranging a meeting between Cicero and Caesar (*Att.* 13.11, 16). Cicero was hoping for a meeting after Caesar's return from Spain. This is the tip of the iceberg. It points tantalizingly to a mass of negotiations in which Servilia acted as an intermediary and, we may well suppose, as the confidante of both Caesar and leading personalities like Cicero. But we cannot even guess which of the innumerable issues of the time were handled by Servilia.

After Caesar's death Servilia is given more exposure. In May 44 Cicero tells Atticus that according to Caesar's old lieutenant, Balbus, Servilia has returned and says that Brutus and Cassius will not leave Italy (*Att.* 15.6). But even this information, so crucial to Cicero's own plans, has come to him only at second hand. Why did he not have any direct correspondence with Servilia? The question is not answered in *Att.* 15.24, where Cicero's messenger to Brutus is told by Servilia that Brutus had left for the east that morning.

Cicero at last comes into direct contact with Servilia in June 44, when a meeting in Antium is attended by Cicero, Servilia, Brutus, Brutus' sister and wife, Cassius, and others. The senate having offered Brutus and Cassius supervision of grain supplies as their propraetorian provinces, the meeting was called to decide on a response to the offer. Cicero embarked on a rambling exposition of what senate, people and republicans ought to have done, but he was cut short by Servilia: 'Well, I must say, I've never heard anything like this!' Cicero kept his temper at this brusque interruption. Servilia announced that she would see to it that the derisory appointments were removed from the senate's decree (*Att.* 15.11, 12.1). Cicero's editors do not take this as evidence of Servilia's ability to exercise any special influence.[44] Perhaps rightly; Praecia had done much the same for Lucullus with less fuss. But in her other major appearance Servilia gave a very clear demonstration of her importance. On 25 July 43 Cicero was asked by Servilia, whom he describes in a letter to Brutus as 'a woman of great ability and energy', to meet her in order to discuss Cicero's plan for Brutus to bring his army to Italy. The meeting was attended by Labeo (a jurist), P. Servilius Casca (tyrannicide and kinsman of Servilia), and Scaptius (Brutus' agent). Servilia took charge of the meeting. She put the question as to whether they should tell Brutus to come, and asked Cicero for his opinion. It was almost as if she was a consul presiding at a meeting of the senate.[45] Cicero then gives Brutus a full account of what he had said at the meeting, and does not mention Servilia again until the end, when he tells Brutus how he had drawn the senate's attention to the children of Lepidus, the husband of one of Servilia's three daughters who was showing signs of deserting the republican cause. Brutus has, adds Cicero, no doubt heard of the matter 'from your mother's letters'. Which confirms that Servilia did write letters, even if not to Cicero. But as Lepidus did defect to the Caesarians, the question is, what stance did 'your mother's letters' take up? Only one answer is possible. Servilia was opposed to the Caesarians, the party of her former lover. The memory of the man who had, according to Suetonius, loved her above all others, who had bought her a pearl worth six million sesterces and had knocked a valuable property down to her at a nominal price (*SJ* 50.2), did not survive his death.

The liaison had encountered opposition even during Caesar's lifetime. Cicero said of the property knocked down to her that 'It's a better bargain than you think, for he bedded Tertia at a discount' (*SJ* 50.2). The insinuation was that Servilia had prostituted her youngest daughter to Caesar in return for the property. Plutarch tells us that in 63, during the Catilinarian debate, Caesar was handed a note, which caused Cato to exclaim that Caesar was being briefed by the conspirators; Caesar gave the note to Cato, who found it was a love letter from Servilia and threw it back with the words, 'Take it, since you're besotted with her' (*Brut.* 5.2–3). Cato's rigid morality could not tolerate the liaison, but he was also opposed to it on political grounds. Caesar was already a threat to everything that Cato believed in.

Did Servilia, who had an almost maternal influence over Cato (Ascon. 23 St.), allow political considerations or romantic considerations to deny the very principles that she had helped to inculcate in him? If there is any truth in Cicero's witticism about the property, political considerations were her main motivation. Caesar's decision to spare Brutus after Pharsalus, out of regard for Servilia (Plut. *Brut.* 5.1–2), has been condemned as a blatant attempt by Servilia to exploit the liaison (Hallett 1984: 51–2). But that could be said of any *amicitia*. The only difference here is that a romantic interest may have been combined with a political motive – assuming that the former survived Caesar's abrupt decision to marry Calpurnia in 59 despite the fact that Servilia was available.[46] Political considerations may have prompted Servilia to oppose Brutus' marriage to Cato's daughter, Porcia, in 45, a year after Cato's death; but her opposition was lukewarm, for the marriage did take place.[47] (Porcia, the feminine counterpart of the Stoic saint who was her father, is prominent in Plutarch's *Life of Brutus*. She persuaded Brutus to confide in her by cutting her thigh and bearing the pain with fortitude. She was privy to the plot to kill Caesar. While the assassins were at work in the senate-house she was in a state of such acute anxiety that she fell into a trance. And when she learnt of Brutus' death she swallowed live coals.[48])

There is not much more to be said about Servilia's politics

during Caesar's lifetime,[49] and only one or two points to be added to what Cicero has told us about the period after his death. Plutarch says that Servilia traced her lineage back to Servilius Ahala who had killed the tyrant Sp. Maelius in 439 (*Brut.* 1.3). Although Plutarch insists that the story is true, it must be dismissed as propaganda. But the republicans clearly felt that the canard was sufficiently consistent with Servilia's reaction to Caesar's death to warrant its dissemination. It is also disturbing to find Servilia buying the house of Pontius Aquila who had helped to kill Caesar (Cic. *Att.* 14.21.3). And if Atticus, a close friend of Servilia, had to give her asylum in 42, at a time when her son-in-law and other members of the triumvirate were hard at work proscribing anti-Caesarians, our uneasiness is intensified.[50]

Servilia's apparent changes of front are best explained by an adaptation of Münzer's suggestion that if Servilia had an ideology, it was a family oriented one which aimed at reviving the fortunes of the Servilii Caepiones, the family into which she had been born (1920: 427). Hence, for example, her decision, after the death of her first husband, to have her son Iunius Brutus adopted by her full brother, Q. Servilius Caepio. Her preoccupation with the advancement of her son is perhaps the major strand in her entire involvement in politics after that, though much of her time was spent extricating that accident-prone young man from predicaments rather than positively promoting his career. We have already noticed one example, after Pharsalus, and another occurred earlier, in 59, when the informer L. Vettius tried to implicate Brutus in a charge of plotting to kill Pompey; the case was adjourned overnight, and Servilia is believed to have persuaded Caesar, then consul, to get Vettius to remove Brutus' name from the list of suspects.[51] Foreshadowing the aspirations of imperial women, most of Servilia's hopes were centred on her son. We do not know whether he confided in her as he did in Porcia, and cannot say whether she was privy to the plans for the Ides of March. The more charitable supposition is that she was not.[52] But she was still Brutus' mother, and so, putting her best face on it, she took charge of the situation in masterly fashion. The cause which she then espoused was probably much closer to her own basic thinking than any ideas that she might have exchanged with Caesar.[53]

CONCLUSION

The collegiate role of the Vestals throws new light on the order. Moreover, both that role and the improved methods of dealing with transgressors contribute usefully to our understanding of that *humanitas* for which the Ciceronian age is noted.[54] Our analysis of Chelidon, taken with the reappraisal of Praecia, adds a new dimension to women's affairs. Politics is no longer confined to the salon. Nor is it always fuelled by that dedication to sons' careers that loomed so large in Cornelia's thinking. Many others followed her example, but there were exceptions. Clodia, for one, displays few signs of maternal motivation. Nor, if Sallust is to be believed, does Sempronia in the Catilinarian affair. Even Cato's wife, Porcia, gives her loyalty to her husband rather than to her son, though hers is a special case. Both she and her aunt (on whose death Cicero uneasily composed an oration) owed their true allegiance to an idea, the traditional *res publica*. The triumviral period would produce a woman who also thought deeply about the higher imperatives of politics, but Fulvia's thinking would be unequivocally Caesarian. In the Principate the two Agrippinas would be cast in a similarly thoughtful mould, though their ideas would not coincide with those of either the Porcias or Fulvia.

Servilia does not quite fit into any of the above categories. That she was dedicated to the advancement of her son is beyond doubt, but she also had a wider horizon in the shape of the revival of her family's fortunes. Moreover, she was far from indifferent to self-interest and material gains. She also gives no sign of philosophical speculation; *ad hoc* solutions, the approach of the politician rather than of the statesman, were her *forte*. She was a master craftsman, but not an architect.

7

THE TRIUMVIRAL PERIOD: DIPLOMACY, ORATORY AND LEADERSHIP

INTRODUCTION

In keeping with its transitional character, the triumviral period (43–30 BC)[1] sees women in new roles which involve them in public affairs in ways that had not – as far as our information goes – been attempted before. There may have been diplomats before Mucia and Octavia, but there is no sign of them.[2] There almost certainly were no public orations before Hortensia's single, but significant, contribution. Above all, neither before nor after was there a woman with Fulvia's unique combination of qualities, a combination that almost allows her to pre-empt the title of the first empress that Augustus awarded (after his death) to Livia.

As already foreshadowed (see Chapter 1, p. 5), two separate chapters are being devoted to the women of the period. Octavian's sister, Octavia, and his wife Livia are so much a part of the Augustan Principate that they cannot simply be treated as contemporaries of Mucia, Hortensia and Fulvia. But their role in this period needs to be kept separate from their later careers if it is not to lose much of its special significance.

MUCIA

Mucia Tertia, daughter of the great Republican lawyer, Q. Mucius Scaevola (cos. 95), begins her career with an intriguing question mark. As governor of Asia over 95–4 her father received semi-divine honours from the provincials, and it has been suggested that when a statue was erected to him at Olympia as 'saviour and benefactor', a statue was also erected to his wife or daughter.[3] If so, Mucia may have been the first woman to receive a distinction that later became standard practice for members of the emperor's house. But too much should not be made of this.

As a half-sister (or first cousin) of Q. Metellus Celer (Clodia's husband) and Q. Metellus Nepos (cos. 57), Mucia belonged to a powerful family.[4] It was as a result of their influence that she became Pompey's third wife in c. 80 and had three children by him – the only known children from his five marriages. Pompey was absent from Rome over 67–2, but on his return he divorced Mucia. There was talk of Caesar having seduced her, but Pompey was criticized for promptly marrying Caesar's daughter Julia.[5] After the divorce Mucia married Aemilius Scaurus. When Scaurus was tried for extortion in 54 Pompey refused to stand by him; he still bore Scaurus a grudge for having made light of his verdict against Mucia by marrying her (Ascon. 23 St.). Pompey's treatment of Mucia alienated Metellus Celer, who refused to support the ratification of the arrangements made by Pompey in the east over 67–2, despite the fact that Pompey had secured his election as consul for 60 for that very purpose (CD 37.49.1–5, 50.1–6). Pompey's urgent need for ratification drove him into the so-called First Triumvirate with Caesar and Crassus; one of the conditions was Pompey's marriage to Caesar's daughter.

Mucia made her political debut in January 62, some eleven months before the divorce, in a matter concerning her relative, Metellus Nepos. Nepos had, as tribune, vetoed Cicero's valedictory oration as retiring consul at the end of 63, on the grounds that Cicero had put citizens (the Catilinarians) to death without trial. In January 62 Nepos continued the attack, proposing that Pompey be summoned from the east to suppress the remaining Catilinarians. Caesar was a party to these manoeuvres, which supports Suetonius' statement that a coalition with Caesar was in the pipeline before Pompey divorced Mucia.[6] Cicero appealed to both Mucia and Clodia to intercede with Nepos. As Cicero puts it in a letter to Metellus Celer (*Fam.* 5.2.6), 'When I learned that he planned to use his tribunate to destroy me, I appealed to your wife Clodia and your sister Mucia, to dissuade Nepos from his injurious plan; Mucia's goodwill towards me, as a friend of her husband, had been made plain to me many times'. Cicero here attaches more importance to Mucia than to Clodia, only mentioning the latter first because he is writing to her husband. Mucia was already known for her diplomacy. She was, however, unable to persuade Nepos, who joined Pompey in the east. But a few months later, after the divorce, Nepos broke with Pompey; the *iniuria* to Mucia influenced his decision, possibly as a result of direct prompting by her.[7]

Mucia is said to have been a frequent target for attacks on her character. In a left-handed sort of way this would be a tribute to her political importance, but in fact the evidence is very weak and can be ignored.[8] We therefore turn to her most important diplomatic role, in the negotiations between her son, Sextus Pompeius, and the triumvirs Antony and Octavian. Sex. Pompeius was a thorn in Octavian's side and forced a deeply troubled *res publica* on to rocks that nearly wrecked it altogether. From his base in Sicily, Sextus had mounted a blockade which cut off corn shipments to Italy. In an attempt to get negotiations going, Mucia was sent to her son in Sicily, while Sextus' father-in-law, L. Scribonius Libo (cos. 34) went to Rome from Sicily. There is talk of the people having exerted pressure on Mucia, by threatening to burn her house down (App. *BC* 5.69.291). A possible explanation of this obscure statement is that Mucia was known as a devoted supporter of her son's cause, and was as active in promoting his interests as Servilia had been with Brutus. Mucia's importance will have been known to the starving populace, and a violent demonstration outside her house – an everyday occurrence at this time (App. *BC* 5.67–8) – will have sent her flying post-haste to Sicily. There was a definite link between Octavian and Mucia. They were related by affinity, for at about this time Octavian married Scribonia, sister of Scribonius Libo who was Sextus' father-in-law. Dio correctly makes Octavian the instigator of Mucia's mission to Sicily (CD 48.16.3).

The combined efforts of Mucia and Scribonius Libo produced a meeting between the three dynasts, but their demands were a long way apart and the negotiations were broken off.[9] The people, urged on by famine, pressed the triumvirs to continue the discussions, and a further meeting was arranged by Mucia and Sextus' wife, Scribonia.[10] This time Mucia's efforts were successful, for the outcome, in 39, was the treaty of Misenum which made Sextus a fourth partner in the triumvirate. Mucia does not surface in the four stormy years that followed, culminating in Sextus' execution, probably on Antony's orders, at Miletus in 35. But she is seen again in 31, after Actium. Her son by her second marriage, M. Aemilius Scaurus, had betrayed his half-brother, Sextus, to Antony's lieutenants in 35, and had fought on Antony's side at

Actium. The victorious Octavian condemned him to death, but spared his life in response to a plea by Mucia (CD 51.2.4–5).

HORTENSIA AND THE *ORDO MATRONARUM*

Hortensia, daughter of the great orator who rivalled Cicero in the courts, is known for only a single episode, but it is one that raises even more questions than has hitherto been realized. In 42 the triumvirs, Antony, Octavian and Lepidus, were badly in need of funds for the prosecution of punitive action against Caesar's assassins. They published an edict requiring 1,400 of the richest women to make valuations of their properties and to contribute to the war chest such amounts as the triumvirs might determine. Fraud would be punished by fines, and rewards would be paid to informers, whether free persons or slaves.[11] The women affected by the decree appealed to the triumvirs' womenfolk. They were well received by Octavian's sister, Octavia, and by Antony's mother, Julia, but were brusquely rebuffed by Antony's wife, Fulvia. Thereupon they staged a demonstration, forcing their way to the triumvirs' tribunal in the forum. Hortensia, whom they had chosen as their spokeswoman, addressed the triumvirs. Her speech, as we have it from Appian,[12] runs as follows (my emphases):

> As was proper for *women of our rank* petitioning you for something, we addressed your womenfolk. But Fulvia's rudeness has driven us here. As relatives of those whom you proscribed, we have already lost our menfolk. If you also strip us of our property you will diminish *our status*. If we have wronged you, proscribe us. But if we have not voted you public enemies, nor destroyed your houses, nor led an enemy against you, nor prevented you from gaining offices or honours, why should we share the penalty when we do not share the guilt? *Why should we pay taxes when we have no part in the honours, the commands, the policy-making?* 'Because there's a war on', you say. But when have there not been wars, and when have women ever been taxed? Our mothers contributed when you faced the loss of the empire in the Second Punic War, but they funded their contributions from their jewellery and on a voluntary basis, not from their property or dowries under duress. We will gladly contribute

to war with the Gauls or the Parthians, but not to civil war. We did not contribute to either Caesar or Pompey, nor did Marius or Cinna tax us, or even Sulla.

The triumvirs were angry that women should dare to hold a public meeting when men were silent, should demand from magistrates the reasons for their acts, and should refuse to give money when the men were serving in the army. They ordered their lictors to drive the women away, but the shouts of the crowd forced them to desist. Next day they announced that the number of women was being reduced from 1,400 to 400; the shortfall would be made up by a tax on men who possessed more than 100,000 drachmas, including foreigners. Thus *peregrini*, who were as voteless as the women, were being heavily taxed.

Two questions arise. The first, which has not been raised before, is whether the matrons for whom Hortensia spoke had a specific group identity. Second, were they demanding the franchise? On the first question, Valerius Maximus' little dossier of women who spoke for others (VM 8.3) refers to the tax being imposed on *ordo matronarum*. Is he being facetious – a quality not prominent in his gossip column – or were the wealthiest matrons recognized as an 'order' analogous to the senatorial and equestrian orders and delimited by the censors in similar fashion to those groups? Traditionally the senate had granted the *ordo matronarum* purple garments, golden patches and other insignia in recognition of the success of Veturia's mission to Coriolanus (VM 5.2.1), but there is no suggestion of the conferment of any corporate status on the *ordo*. As stated by L. Valerius in the Oppian debate (see Chapter 1), adornment and finery were a woman's insignia. But in spite of that, is there any basis for the idea that there may have been some sort of corporate identity? There is some support for this in the speech. First, the rules required 'women of our rank' (*gynaixi toiaisde*) to observe protocol by applying to the triumvirs' women-folk. Also, if they lost their property they would be reduced to a status unbecoming to their birth, way of life and sex. We recall the official recognition of some sort of feminine corporate identity when a committee of treasurers was set up in the Second Punic War (see Chapter 3, p. 27). The trouble is, though, that the triumvirs' edict required the 1,400 women to submit valuations of their property, which would not have been necessary if the censors had done that already. On the other hand, how did the triumvirs (or anyone else) know who the 1,400 wealthiest women were, if no records were already in existence? One might postulate the maintenance of some sort of record of properties in connection with the Matronalia, or on a more secular level the formation of action groups belonging to the obscure category of *conventus matronarum*.[13] But neither of these conjectures is secure. A technical meaning for *ordo matronarum* cannot be driven home.

As to the scope of Hortensia's demands, a specific demand for the franchise is not authorized by anything in the speech.[14] But Valerius Maximus says that she displayed something of her father's eloquence; he lived again in his daughter. One wonders if the resemblance extended to her knowledge of history, given that Q. Hortensius' *Annales* contained the best account of the Social War and the Italian demands for the franchise (VP 2.16.3–4). That she shared the ideology of the proscribed is clear, and would explain the hostility of Antony's wife, Fulvia. But that she was the wife of Brutus' adoptive father, Q. Servilius Caepio,[15] is not provable. But what does seem certain is that she took the question of women's rights much further than anyone had done before. Building on recent Vestal thinking, and drawing logical conclusions from the politicizing of women like Praecia, Clodia, Servilia and Mucia, Hortensia was not content to underpin the status quo by limiting her demands to the restoration of finery.[16] 'No taxation without representation.' Better still, 'No taxation because of no representation'. The message was not lost on the crowd of male bystanders who would not allow the lictors to disperse the demonstrators.

FULVIA: *L'IMPÉRATRICE MANQUÉE*

Fulvia has the highest profile of any woman prior to the great figures of the Principate, despite her modest ancestry. Her father, M. Fulvius Bambalio, was a nonentity, and her maternal grandfather, C. Sempronius Tuditanus, was an eccentric who used to mount the rostra in tragic costume and scatter coins to the people (Cic. *Phil.* 3.16). Her mother was a Sempronia, a sister of the Sempronia who helped Catiline. But her great-grandfather, C. Sempronius Tuditanus (cos. 129) was important. His *Libri Magistratuum* was one of the earliest works on Roman public law. If Fulvia had a talent for constitutional experimentation it was genetically predictable.

Fulvia was married in succession to P. Clodius (*ob.* 52), C. Scribonius Curio (*ob.* 49), and Mark Antony (*ob.* 30). Her most dramatic involvement in public affairs was a brief one, from 44, after Caesar's murder, to 40 when she herself died. But she made her debut before that. In 52 she and her mother gave evidence against Milo when he was charged with the murder of P. Clodius, who had died in a 'shoot-out' on the Appian Way. Their evidence was taken last, which was the decisive position, and made a deep impression on the jury (Ascon. 36 St.). Cicero's defence of Milo failed, for which he never forgave Fulvia. He attacked her evidence by the same indirect technique that he had used against Clodia (see Chapter 6, p. 70); he says that she accompanied Clodius everywhere, and then casually adds that Clodius usually travelled with an entourage of prostitutes and eunuchs (*Mil.* 28, 55). Valerius Maximus has Clodius tied to Fulvia's apron strings, wearing a dagger as a sign of his subjection to a woman's *imperium* (VM 3.5.3.). It has been plausibly suggested (Marshall 1985: 167) that she worked actively in Clodius' interests, and that the ability to organize recruiting which she displayed on Antony's behalf in 40 was foreshadowed by her organization of *collegia* on behalf of Clodius.

Cicero launched a scathing attack on Fulvia in 44. The Galatian tetrarch, Deiotarus, had been tried by Caesar and defended by Cicero, but Caesar had not handed down his verdict at the time of his death. In April 44 Antony produced a decree purporting to come from Caesar's papers, restoring Deiotarus' kingdom (Bauman 1985: 54–6). Cicero says that when Deiotarus' envoys posted a bond to cover the restoration, the arrangements were made in the women's quarters, where most things were bought and sold; there was a roaring trade in public assets in Antony's house, where his wife, luckier for herself than for her husbands, was putting provinces and kingdoms up for auction; Deiotarus was worthy of any kingdom, but not of one bought through Fulvia.[17]

Cicero had time to deliver one more tirade against Fulvia before events caught up with him. In *Philippics* he has her with Antony at Brundisium in 44, watching the execution of some disaffected centurions. Referring to her throughout as 'his wife' because the attacks were being delivered in public speeches, Cicero has 'that most avaricious and cruel woman' look on, while the blood of 'the bravest of men and the best of citizens' spatters over her face

(*Phil.* 3.4, 5.22, 13.18). Fulvia got her revenge on 7 December 43, when Cicero perished in the proscriptions. When his head was brought to Antony, she is said to have spat on it, pulled out the tongue and pierced it with hairpins, with many cruel jokes.[18] Appian also incriminates Fulvia, though not specifically in Cicero's death. He says that Caesetius Rufus had refused to sell her a handsome house that he owned, but when the proscriptions started he offered it to her as a gift. He was, however, proscribed and his head was brought to Antony. But Antony said it had nothing to do with him and sent it to Fulvia. She had it impaled in front of Rufus' house instead of on the rostra (App. *BC* 4.29.124). Valerius Maximus has part of the story; he records Antony's receipt of the head and his failure to recognize it (VM 9.5.4).

Whatever the truth about the heads of Cicero and Rufus,[19] it is clear that Fulvia had acquired an unenviable reputation for her part in the proscriptions. Nor do the sources adduce any extenuating circumstances. Appian's little compendium of women's roles in the proscriptions includes some cases of outstanding heroism.[20] Even Antony is credited with 'the only decent thing that he ever did' when he was persuaded by his mother to remove the name of his uncle, L. Iulius Caesar, from the lists. But no one has anything good to say about Fulvia. Octavian waged a savage propaganda campaign against her later on, but it cannot all be dismissed as propaganda, for Fulvia is not the only woman to have made improper use of the proscriptions.[21]

Yet the picture of Fulvia is not all dark. Her one great redeeming feature was her unswerving loyalty to Antony, a quality not exactly in plentiful supply amongst either men or women in the circles in which she moved. She looked after Antony's interests with unshakeable courage and determination, and it is by her actions in that regard that she should finally be judged. She first showed her mettle in 43, after Antony's defeat at Mutina. Attempts were being made to declare Antony a public enemy, but Fulvia was able to block them. Accompanied by Antony's mother and others, she spent a whole night visiting senators' houses. Next day, wearing mourning clothes and uttering loud lamentations, they waylaid senators on their way to the senate-house. Their efforts bore fruit, for despite a *Philippic* by Cicero the motion to declare Antony a public enemy was defeated (App. *BC* 3.51, 61). The strategy was brilliant. Displays of mourning were normally paraded by the relatives of someone facing a criminal charge, in order to arouse sympathy for the accused. But here there was a more subtle purpose. Senators were being reminded that a *hostis* declaration violated all law and custom, for the victim was outlawed in summary fashion, without being heard in his defence. Fulvia was canvassing a burning constitutional question that had been in contention, in one form or another, ever since the Gracchan period – which was, incidentally, the period in which her great-grandfather had written on public law.[22]

Fulvia showed great strength of character at this time. Antony's enemies were trying to strip her of all her possessions. When Fulvia was struggling to cope with a torrent of lawsuits she found a strong supporter in Cicero's friend Atticus, who appeared in court with her and gave her an interest-free loan to pay for a property that she had bought some time before (Nepos *Att.* 9.1–7). Atticus showed his complete lack of ideological bias by standing by Fulvia as he would also do for her political antithesis, Servilia, when she was threatened by the proscriptions (see Chapter 6, p. 76). It is pleasing to be able to report that when Antony returned he remembered Atticus, removed his name from the proscription lists, and sent him an escort (Nepos *Att.* 9.7,10).

We next encounter Fulvia in 42, when she stood out against the fiscal relief sought by Hortensia. There is an important angle to this that we have not had occasion to notice before, and that is that Fulvia's opposition overrode the views of Antony's mother. Fulvia, not Julia, was authorized to speak for Antony, then in the east. Her attitude speaks well for her perception of the higher imperatives, for she was a very wealthy woman[23] and may well have been amongst the 1,400 hit by the new tax. This was how an empress could have been expected to act.

The year 41 ushered in the last, and greatest, period in Fulvia's life. It was then that she displayed qualities of leadership, courage and dedication matched by very few people in our entire period, whether men or women. Dio says that nominally the consuls of 41 were Servilius Isauricus and Mark Antony's brother, Lucius Antonius; but in reality, adds Dio, it was Lucius Antonius and Fulvia. At that time Fulvia was Octavian's mother-in-law, having betrothed her daughter Clodia to him. Antony being in Bithynia and Octavian in Macedonia, she ignored the third triumvir, Aemilius Lepidus, and managed affairs herself. Neither senate nor people transacted any business without her approval (CD 48.4.1). Even Lucius Antonius was her subordinate. He wished to celebrate a triumph for a victory over some Alpine tribes, but with Fulvia opposing it on the ground that he had not killed the requisite 5,000 of the enemy or otherwise waged 'a just war', he was not able to get it through the senate. Eventually he managed to persuade her, whereupon it was voted unanimously. Nominally, adds Dio, the triumph was his, but in reality it was Fulvia's (CD 48.4.2–6). One wonders whether the incident was deliberately engineered by Fulvia in order to test her control of the senate, in view of Octavian's imminent return to Rome (CD 48.5.1). Servilia had enjoyed a measure of control over the senate (see Chapter 6, p. 74), but nothing like this.

When Octavian returned from the east, still in 41, he immediately put in hand the implementation of the triumvirs' plan to confiscate lands from eighteen Italian cities for the purpose of founding colonies of military veterans.[24] This was going to be a key factor in what was already shaping up as a conflict between the two major members of the triumvirate, Antony and Octavian, and Fulvia wanted to delay matters until Antony returned. She therefore appeared before the soldiers with her children, exhorting them to stand by Antony (App. *BC* 5.14). It was a far cry from the days when a woman's public appearance, even in the civilian ambience of the forum, had evoked raised eyebrows. Fulvia was setting a precedent which only one or two members of the Domus would come anywhere near following in the early Principate.[25]

A tortuous series of moves and countermoves on the subject of the veteran settlements ensued.[26] The question was whether Octavian would carry out the entire resettlement, or whether Fulvia and Antonius would take charge of the allocations to Antony's veterans. Octavian made Fulvia his main target; according to Dio he could not stand her difficult temper and chose to be at odds with her rather than with Antonius (CD 48.5.3). Octavian repudiated Fulvia's daughter Clodia, sending her back with a sworn statement to the effect that she was still a virgin – a gratuitous insult, since no grounds for the divorce were needed. Octavian then launched a propaganda war against Fulvia, subjecting her to scurrilous attacks that may have inspired some of the canards against her.[27] At some point Fulvia and Antonius changed their tack, switching from support for the veterans to support for the proprietors who were being stripped of their properties in order to provide land for the veterans.[28] This change of direction reveals great foresight on Fulvia's part. She was cultivating 'the flower of

Italy', the *villae* proprietors clustered around those great urban centres, the *municipia*. Ten years later (with Fulvia long dead) they would carry Octavian to victory over Antony.

Eventually Fulvia decided to resist Octavian by force. Appian says that this was when she was told by Antony's procurator, Manius, that Antony's liaison with Cleopatra would continue as long as Italy was at peace, but if war broke out he would return immediately. Thus, says, Appian, a woman's jealousy incited L. Antonius to war (*BC* 5.19). This latest use of the *muliebris* syndrome can be ignored, for Fulvia, not L. Antonius, took decisive charge of the arrangements for the coming campaign. She stirred up Octavian's soldiers against him by bribes; and she sent L. Antonius and her children to follow Octavian on the last of his colonizing missions. Then followed a new phase in this extraordinary woman's story. She girded on a man's sword and led an assault on Praeneste, giving the soldiers the watchword, haranguing them, holding councils of war with senators and knights, and sending orders to key points under her own hand.[29] Octavian's reply was to convene a meeting of veterans which was conducted in the form of a trial, at which Fulvia and Antonius were held to be the wrongdoers (CD 48.12.3–4).

Both sides now prepared for war. In 40 Antonius was besieged by Octavian in the Etruscan city of Perusia. Fulvia, who was not in Perusia, summoned sympathetic generals from Gaul and collected reinforcements which she placed under the command of L. Munatius Plancus and sent to Perusia (App. *BC* 5.23). But shortage of food forced L. Antonius to surrender at Perusia. He was spared by Octavian, though there is a nasty story about 300 senators and knights being sacrificed at the altar of the deified Julius Caesar. Fulvia fled with her children to Brundisium, from where she found her way to Antony and his mother at Athens.[30]

Fulvia had come to the end of the road. Blamed by Antony for the Italian disaster, she took ill at Sicyon on the Gulf of Corinth, where Antony left her, while he set sail for Italy. Fulvia died at Sicyon in mid–40 BC, heartbroken at Antony's infidelity and reproaches. He had not visited her sickbed before leaving for Italy, and after that she had not wanted to live. Her death precipitated a reconciliation between the warring factions.[31] Appian tries to suggest that this became possible because the *casus belli*, Fulvia's jealousy of Cleopatra, was no longer in operation (*BC* 5.59). But

Appian knew better than that. The organizing genius behind the attempt to outmanoeuvre Octavian had gone.

In the final analysis Fulvia's heroism in the Perusine War had an even deeper root than loyalty to Antony. Appian says that Fulvia favoured 'monarchy' (*BC* 5.54), by which he means that she, unlike L. Antonius, saw no point in trying to resuscitate the senatorial republic. She was a true Caesarian. The great dynasts had come to stay, and she did not have any objections to Octavian in principle. All that she held against him was his attempts to exclude her husband from a full share in the new order. The 'first empress of Rome', as Münzer had no hesitation in calling her,[32] also lived up to her role by foreshadowing the honours that eastern communities would one day shower on the women of the emperor's Domus. The Phrygian city of Eumeneia was called Fulvia in her honour, and her face appeared on Antony's coins.[33]

The one respect in which Fulvia was unique was in her ability to organize military campaigns. That was what really upset the sources. Hence Velleius' statement that she had nothing feminine about her except her sex.[34] The last word belongs to Plutarch (*Ant.* 10.3):

> She was a woman who gave no thought to spinning or housekeeping, nor did she consider it worthwhile to dominate a man not in public life. She wished to rule a ruler and command a commander.

CONCLUSION

The chapter is dominated by one woman to an extent not seen anywhere else in our discussions up to this point, and indeed not often to be seen in what lies ahead. Fulvia was the first empress in all but name, and not only for her good qualities. If her acquisitive instincts led to abusive use of the proscriptions, she was simply anticipating what some empresses, notably Messalina, would do later on. But it is rather for her positive attributes that she should be remembered. To repeat a point that we have already made, she is matched in courage and determination only by the elder Agrippina and her daughter, while in political *nous* and organizing skill she has no peer. And despite the routine bias of the sources, her treatment by Antony arouses more sympathy than the fate of any imperial woman, again with the exception of the elder Agrippina, and possibly of Augustus' sister, Octavia.

The other two women in the chapter are quite comfortable in their supporting roles. Mucia's diplomatic skills are not usually presented *in extenso*, and our attempt to do so casts new light both on Mucia and on the period. Hortensia's speech, though worked on by scholars often enough, has not previously prompted an enquiry into the significance of *ordo matronarum*.

8

THE FOOTHILLS OF THE PRINCIPATE

INTRODUCTION

The 30s BC witnessed an intensification of the struggle between Octavian and Antony, to which Fulvia had made such a notable contribution until her death. The third man, Lepidus, left the triumvirate in 36, but meanwhile Sex. Pompeius had forced his way in, assisted by the diplomatic efforts of his mother, Mucia. But by 35 it had resolved itself into a straight fight between Octavian and Antony. Until the final military confrontation which settled the issue in 31–30, the struggle was waged with non-warlike weapons. Diplomatic activity was prominent, as we have already gathered from Mucia's history. An even more extensive participation in that aspect of the struggle is attested for Octavian's sister, Octavia. She and Octavian's wife, Livia, also played a prominent, albeit passive, part in another 'peaceful' aspect, namely the intensive propaganda war of the 30s. That war indirectly prompted the weaving of the first strand in the creation of the Domus Caesarum, and the Domus in turn was the crucial factor in defining the status of the imperial women.

THE DIPLOMATIC SKILLS OF OCTAVIA

It is no accident that our discussion of imperial women in the prelude to the Principate begins with Octavia. Although by no means ignored by the sources, she has, in general, a much lower profile than Livia, but as far as the 30s are concerned Octavia is the more important figure of the two.

Octavia Minor, full sister of, and some six years older than, Octavian,[1] married C. Claudius Marcellus (cos. 50) before 54; a son and two daughters were born of the marriage. Marcellus died in 40, in the same year as Fulvia, and later that year Octavia married Antony. Thus the dynastic marriage, already an established practice among noble families, was being put to one of its most important uses. As brothers-in-law the two dynasts might be better placed to reach an accommodation. Or so it was hoped, although the history of such alliances in recent decades ought to have counselled caution.[2]

The marriage was harmonious at first. Antony struck a coin to commemorate the union, with Octavia's portrait head on it. This probably made her the first Roman woman to be so honoured, unless Fulvia's appearance on Antony's coins was as herself and not as a personification.[3] Octavia spent the winter of 39–8 in Athens with Antony, in what the sources describe as the most idyllic happiness, and it was probably then that she was given divine status (in the eyes of the Greek east, though not of the Roman west) as Athena Polias.[4] In 37 the triumvirs experienced one of their endemic crises, and it was then that Octavia showed her paces as a diplomat. Accompanying Antony to Italy at her express request, she used some highly skilled diplomacy. She won the support of Octavian's friends, Maecenas and Agrippa, respectively his advisers on domestic affairs and war, and with their help she prevailed on Octavian not to let her, the wife of one dynast and the sister of the other, witness the defeat of either. The result of her intervention was the Treaty of Tarentum extending the triumvirate for five years. She persuaded Antony to increase the number of ships that he was lending Octavian for use against Sex. Pompeius, and she got Octavian to add a bodyguard of 1,000 for her to the soldiers that he was lending Antony for the Parthian campaign. For good measure she arranged the betrothal of Octavian's infant daughter, Julia, to M. Antonius Antyllus, the elder son of Antony and Fulvia. Antyllus would not be allowed to live long enough to celebrate the formal marriage, but Octavia deserves full marks for trying.[5]

OCTAVIA BECOMES A *CASUS BELLI*

The immediate results of Octavia's intervention in triumviral politics were encouraging. Antony's coins began displaying Octavia's portrait head and his own together, and also Octavia with both Antony and Octavian.[6] But in reality Tarentum had been the pinnacle of her achievement, and from now on it would be downhill all the way. Antony returned to the east with her, but when they reached Corcyra he sent her back to Italy. The pretext was that he did not want to expose her to the dangers of his forth-coming Parthian campaign, but it was widely believed that he wanted to be free to continue his liaison with Cleopatra (CD 48.54.5). On her return to Rome Octavia devoted herself to look-ing after the children of Fulvia and Antony as well as her own. This was not the only indication of Antony's uncanny ability to inspire Octavia with the same loyalty that he had evoked in Fulvia. Despite learning, in 36, that Antony had acknowledged his paternity of three of Cleopatra's children, when his Parthian campaign ran into trouble in 35 Octavia sought and obtained her brother's permission to take reinforcements to Antony in the east. But when she reached Athens the story was the same as before: she found letters from Antony telling her to go home. She was greatly distressed, but simply wrote to ask him where she was to deliver the troops and equipment that she had brought with her.

Octavian felt that his sister had been grossly insulted, and told her to live in her own house – that is, to divorce Antony. But she steadfastly refused to leave Antony's house, and begged Octav-ian not to plunge Rome into civil war because of a woman. She continued looking after Antony's children, and even received his friends and interceded for them with Octavian. This simply brought Antony greater odium, but there can be no doubt about Octavia's sincerity. It was not until 32 that Antony formally divorced her, and until then she continued to appear before the world as his wife.[7]

Antony's injurious treatment of Octavia furnished Octavian with his one clear-cut constitutional pretext for the war which had been waiting to happen for some time but had needed a proper *casus belli*. It had to be a cause that involved something more than a private wrong to an individual, it had to be able to be seen as an injury to the state. We turn now to consideration of how wrongs done to Octavia were fitted into that category.

OCTAVIA, LIVIA AND TRIBUNICIAN SACROSANCTITY

In 36 BC, nine years before he founded the Principate, Octavian created the first of the institutions that would determine the consti-tutional and political shape of the new order. He secured a law of the people granting him the same sacrosanctity as that enjoyed by the tribunes of the plebs. As Dio puts it, 'They voted him protection against insult whether by word or by deed, and decreed that whoever violated his protection would be liable to the same penalties as those that had been laid down for the tribunes'. Thus Octavian, although a patrician and not eligible for the plebeian office of tribune, was able to acquire one of the attributes of that office.[8]

The grant to Octavian was, although a break with tradition, not entirely without precedent.[9] But a year later, in 35, he did something that had never been done before. Another law of the people 'granted Octavia and Livia security and protection against insult on a similar basis to the tribunes'. At the same time they were given statues and were exempted from the perpetual guardianship of women.[10] Statues and release from tutelage were not particularly startling; both had sufficient precedent.[11] But the grant of tribunician sacrosanctity[12] meant that women had been given one of the attributes of a public office – and an office that was at the very core and centre of the concept of popular sovereignty. If Cato the Censor had been alive he might well have seen this as the thin end of a wedge leading to the very evils that he had foreseen in his *lex Oppia* speech (see Chapter 4, p. 32). Indeed, there was a backlash amongst traditionalists at this time. It was felt that if for any reason the imperial women needed protection, they could have been granted the sanctity of Vestals, the possession of which by non-Vestals would have been no more of a fiction than the possession of tribunician sacrosanctity by persons who were not, and could never be, tribunes.[13] But Octavian thought otherwise, and, as we will now attempt to show, for good reason.

Why was official protection of this sort introduced, and why was it done precisely at this time? There are two answers, one general and the other more specific. In general terms, the protection was a response to the propaganda war between Octavian and Antony during the uneasy years of the triumvirate. Insults and abuse were freely exchanged by the dynasts, and although it was simply an amplification of the invective that had been part and parcel of republican politics, a new dimension had been added by the attacks on Fulvia (see Chapter 7 n. 21). Octavian knew better than anyone how injurious such attacks on a woman could be, for he had initiated them. And it was precisely through the female members of his family that he was most vulnerable. Amongst the many attacks on his relations with women levelled at him by

Antony (*SA* 69), the most embarrassing focused on his hasty marriage to Livia in January 38. At that time Livia was already six months into the pregnancy which resulted in the birth of her second son, Drusus; the latter's ostensible father was Livia's first husband, Tiberius Claudius Nero. Further evidence of haste was seen in the fact that in 39 Octavian had divorced his previous wife, Scribonia, immediately after the birth of their daughter Julia, and had then asked the Pontifical College if he could marry Livia while she was pregnant. The pontiffs replied that if it was certain that conception had already taken place the marriage could go ahead, but Dio doubts if they found any precedent and thinks they would have said this anyway.[14] The bizarre nature of the whole affair was further emphasized when Livia's previous husband gave her away at the wedding as if she were his daughter. When Drusus was born Octavian sent him to his father; but there was much talk about 'Children being born to the fortunate in three months'.[15]

Octavian would have liked to take immediate action against the propaganda barrage surrounding his marriage, but that would only have added fuel to the flames. In any case, the third triumvir, Aemilius Lepidus, was still something of a force to be reckoned with in 38, and would not have minded a breach between the other two. But in 36 Octavian managed to depose him, although allowing him to retain his office as Pontifex Maximus – in consideration, we might well think, of the pontiffs' helpful ruling on the marriage to Livia.[16] In 36, with Lepidus out of the way, and Antony absorbed in affairs in the east, Octavian was the unchallenged ruler of the west. But as so often, absolute power corrupted absolutely. It was in 36, at a time when a serious famine was raging, that Octavian and Livia chose to stage 'The Banquet of the Twelve Gods'. The guests appeared in the guise of gods and goddesses, with Augustus playing the part of Apollo. We are not told which goddess Livia represented, but she was undoubtedly present and took part in 'the novel adulteries of the gods' which an anonymous lampoon quoted by Suetonius noted as a feature of the banquet. Next day there was an outcry; people said that the gods had eaten all the grain, and that Octavian was Apollo the Tormentor. Suetonius also notes that Antony wrote letters disclosing the names of all the guests.[17]

Suetonius does not furnish the date of the banquet, but it can be deduced from other evidence. Dio notes, under 36, that the honours voted to Octavian for his victory over Lepidus included the right to hold an annual banquet in the temple of Capitoline Jupiter. Also, the lampoon quoted by Suetonius ends with the words, 'Jupiter himself fled from his golden throne'. It seems clear that the banquet had been held in the temple of Capitoline Jupiter, as voted that year. Moreover, it was precisely in 36 that Augustus adopted Apollo as his special deity;[18] Apollo was the guest of honour at the banquet.

So far so good. But Octavian had not yet extended tribunician sacrosanctity to the women, and would not do so for another year. In other words, despite recent attacks he did not yet consider an extension necessary. Two conclusions are possible: either his hand was forced by some new, even more scurrilous, attacks; or a factor other than local propaganda attacks was responsible for his decision to bring the women under the protective umbrella. The first alternative can be ruled out right away. There is no sign of any attacks on Livia after 36. As for Octavia, at no time does she appear as a victim of scurrilous local attacks. The most that we are told is that when she married Antony she was pregnant by her first husband; and the marriage took place within the *annus luctus*, the mandatory period before a widow remarried, but the senate granted Octavia dispensation from that rule. Later on, Augustus condemned a man to the galleys for claiming to be the son of the emperor's 'noble and sanctified sister Octavia'.[19] And that is all.

We conclude, then, that there was a special reason, independent of run-of-the-mill insults, for the extension to the women in 35. That reason is not far to seek. It was, clearly and unequivocally, Antony's persistent humiliation of Octavia. Both the reason and the date can be identified quite easily, for both were known in antiquity. Plutarch says that when Octavia sought permission to sail to Antony in 35, Octavian allowed it not as a favour to her, but in order to have plausible grounds for war if she were insulted (*Ant.* 53.1). In other words, her sacrosanctity was official and any violation would be a hostile act against the Republic. Octavian remembered January 49, when the tribunes Antony (*sic*) and Cassius were roughly handled in the senate and fled to Caesar, who was able to claim that he was crossing the Rubicon in order to vindicate the dignity of the tribunes (Caes. *BC* 1.22.5). Octavian did not have any violated tribunes, but he could cast Octavia in an equivalent role, delivering polemics on Antony's treatment of her before both senate and people (Plut. *Ant.* 55.1). Plutarch does not link those events with the grant of sacrosanctity, but it was, I suggest, precisely when Octavia asked to be allowed to go to Antony that Octavian, well aware of how Antony had already treated her, saw the advantages to be gained from the conferment of sacrosanctity on her. That is why he chose sacrosanctity rather than Vestal sanctity. The latter would have sufficed if it had simply been a matter of protecting her from scurrilous local attacks, but there was no basis on which Vestal sanctity could furnish a constitutional pretext for war. Not even Claudia's successful confrontation with the tribune (see Chapter 5, p. 47) could support that.[20]

Octavia was, then, the primary reason for the first step in the creation of the imperial Domus. Livia was included almost incidentally. Some nine years younger than Octavia, and still in the first flush of what seems to have been a most successful marriage, Livia was not a factor in Octavian's *casus belli* against Antony. She had survived the attacks on her marriage and on the banquet without undue discomfort, and if it had not been for Octavia's special problem the law of 35 would not have been introduced. But the formula on which the law was based was (necessarily) in general terms, covering the concept of *iniuria* in both its verbal and its physical aspects.[21] Livia could not possibly be left out of that, though from the practical point of view she may have been more interested in the release from guardianship which accompanied the grant, for she possessed substantial property.[22] But once the grant was in place it was perfectly able to be used for less esoteric purposes than declarations of war. And in Livia's case it was so used on at least one occasion. Dio reports that once some naked men who met Livia were only saved from death when she said that to a chaste woman such men were no different from statues (CD 58.2.4).

The grant did not, however, outlive the two original beneficiaries; it was not repeated for any later members of the Domus. Octavian's own tribunician sacrosanctity continued to be conferred on his successors,[23] but alternatives were found for the women. They began being included in the oath of allegiance sworn to the emperor, and they were also, as 'eminent persons', protected by the treason laws when insults were subsumed under that crime in AD 8.[24] It is quite conceivable that criticism of a dangerously close approach to the admission of women to public office caused the idea to be abandoned. Similar resistance to other close approaches would be encountered in the Principate.

CONCLUSION

This chapter is perhaps the most homogeneous so far, for it is focused on a single theme. Octavia, the sister of the future emperor Augustus, was both an active and a passive agent in the creation of a bridge between the great political strategists of the late Republic and the women of the imperial court. She was not alone in her employment of diplomatic skills, for the contemporary Mucia was working in the same field, and under conditions which were just as difficult as those confronting Octavia. But Mucia's son never occupied the box-seat, he was never in a position to give his mother the enormous, and official, enhancement in status that Octavian was able to give his sister. It is true that the grant of sacrosanctity was made by Octavian primarily for his own ends, and for immediate ends rather than with any thought of creating the first institution of a new order, but that *ad hoc* process is how all the institutions of the Augustan Principate were created. But Octavia was much more than a mere occasion for an act of creation. She was a not unworthy successor to Fulvia as a forerunner of (and later as a participant in) the new style of feminine politics that would emerge in the Principate.

9

WOMEN IN THE AUGUSTAN PRINCIPATE

INTRODUCTION

When Octavian[1] 'restored the Republic', that is, founded the Principate in 27 BC,[2] he initiated the most far-reaching change in Roman history. It was one that had a profound effect on every aspect of life, including women's role in public affairs. That role was still dominated by the upper echelons of society, but with a difference, for there was now an elite within the elite. The women of the Domus Caesarum, the House of the Caesars, stood apart from the general run of women from senatorial and equestrian families. Socially an Octavia, a Livia, or a Julia might have been content to describe herself as *prima inter pares*, but in reality there was the same subtle distinction between her peers and herself as between the emperor and his peers. It is not for nothing that Tacitus says of Livia, offended by someone's disregard of her wishes, that she felt 'violated and diminished' (*TA* 2.34.4). This is the language normally reserved for attacks on the *maiestas*, or majesty, of the emperor himself.[3] There had been nothing like it in the Republic, even in the days of the great first-century dynasts.[4] Tribunician sacrosanctity had initiated the change, and a number of later developments fuelled it.[5]

With ultimate power now concentrated, at least in theory, in the hands of one man, the spotlight was on women who stood closest to the throne. A new kind of political activity replaced the cut, thrust and parry of senatorial politics, and it was within the new framework that the political role of women acquired a new definition. The present chapter explores that role in the Augustan Principate. Our approach is necessarily a selective one, for women have a high profile in so many sectors of the Augustan

99

kaleidoscope that an all-embracing presentation is hardly possible. Three topics have been chosen; all of them have a bearing on one or other of the areas of public life that were of special concern to women.

The first topic focuses on the succession to the throne, an endemic issue not only in Augustus' reign but throughout the Julio-Claudian period. The women of the Domus devoted a vast amount of energy to that issue. Each contender strove to secure the prize for one of her sons, and a labyrinthine network of dynastic marriages and adoptions, which sometimes tax the ingenuity of modern genealogical cartographers to the full, was the result. Battle was joined on a broad front – palace intrigue, factionalism, popular support, political trials, and sometimes judicial murder. The topic covers the second and third sections of the chapter.

The second topic deals with the policy of family rejuvenation which was one of the showpieces of the reign. Women were to be encouraged to marry and have children, and the stability of the family was to be secured by punishing sexual laxity. First mooted in the triumviral period, and put in place by a series of laws on morals and marriage extending over most of the reign, the policy probably aroused more opposition than any other Augustan reform. Aspects of that opposition will occupy our attention, with special reference to the politics of protest spearheaded by Augustus' daughter, Julia, and the sensational trials to which her politics led. Opposition to matrimonial reform was also responsible, in a way not previously identified, for the disgrace of the poet Ovid. (See further pp.105–24).

This chapter is rounded off by the third topic, which attempts an overview of Livia, concentrating on matters not covered in the first two topics, and culminating in an evaluation of her position in the state. The discussion focuses on the Augustan Livia, for Tiberius' reign marks a new phase in her career, a phase so clearly distinguishable from what went before that the two cannot be merged without a serious loss of clarity.

THE SUCCESSION: OCTAVIA AND LIVIA

The first phase of the succession question is dominated by Octavia. Indeed, one of the puzzles of the period is the apparent inability of Livia to promote the claims of her sons, as long as

Octavia was alive. The rivalry between two powerful women foreshadows the later Julio-Claudian rivalries that are so prominent in Tacitus' pages.

The first step in the search for a successor was taken by Augustus in 25 BC, when he married his daughter Julia to M. Claudius Marcellus, Octavia's son by her first marriage. The match gave expression to Augustus' cardinal belief that the successor should be a member by blood of the Julian *gens* to which both Augustus and Octavia belonged. That hope could not always be realized, but it remained a counsel of perfection.[6] Marcellus had been marked out for preferment for some time. In September 31 he and Livia's son, Tiberius, had ridden in Augustus' triumph after Actium, but it was Marcellus who rode the right-hand trace-horse (*ST* 6.4). The hand of Octavia, her brother's senior by some six years, and familiar with the Hellenistic dynastic marriage since her stay in the east,[7] is discernible in these arrangements. The two years following the marriage saw another phenomenon new to Rome, when Marcellus' public career was given rapid acceleration. It is true that when Augustus fell seriously ill in 23 he gave the accounts of the empire to the consul Piso, and his ring to his great general, Marcus Vipsanius Agrippa, thus apparently bypassing Marcellus. But it is likely that this was because Marcellus was himself ill at the time; he died shortly after Augustus' recovery.[8]

Marcellus' death left Octavia inconsolable. She hated all mothers, says Seneca, and most of all Livia, because the happiness earmarked for her had passed to Livia's son (*Ad Marc.* 2.3–4). But Octavia's fears were unfounded, for Livia was no closer to getting Tiberius on to the right-hand trace-horse now than she had been before. And again it was Octavia who dictated the course of events. In 21 Julia was married to Agrippa, despite the fact that he was old enough to be her father. Octavia's manipulations recalled the great diplomat of 37 (see Chapter 8, p.91). At this time Agrippa was the husband of her daughter, the elder Marcella. Octavia had arranged the marriage in 28, when Agrippa's star was in the ascendant, and there were children. But now Octavia prevailed on Agrippa to divorce Marcella and marry Julia. She compensated Marcella by marrying her to Iullus Antonius, the son of Antony and Fulvia.[9]

Octavia's dispositions resulted in the first constitutional regulation of the succession in 18, when Agrippa was given a share in the proconsular *imperium* and the *tribunicia potestas*, the two powers that would henceforth mark a man out as the destined successor. The following year Augustus reintroduced the cognatic principle, but fortified this time by an agnatic link, by formally adopting Gaius and Lucius, the sons of Agrippa and Julia. There was now a two-tier system of succession: Augustus would be succeeded by Agrippa, and the latter would be succeeded by either Gaius or Lucius, who were now Augustus' sons in virtue of their adoption.[10]

Where was Livia while all this was going on? After so many years of marriage, was she able to challenge Octavia's influence, or did the latter alone have Augustus' ear? Syme would have said that Livia fully supported the arrangements, for in his view she had taken the initiative as far back as 32, when Tiberius was betrothed to Vipsania Agrippina, Agrippa's daughter by a previous (pre-Marcella) marriage; this masterstroke by Livia will have 'bound the great general to herself and to Augustus' (1939: 345). But this view is not persuasive. When Tiberius, aged 10, and Vipsania, barely a year old, were betrothed in 32 the 'great general' still had a year to go before qualifying for that accolade at Actium. The driving force behind the Tiberius-Vipsania betrothal was in fact Cicero's old friend, Atticus.[11] If anyone in the Domus cultivated Agrippa it was Octavia. When she married her daughter to him in 28 she was clearing the ground for Marcellus' marriage to Julia three years later. She knew that Agrippa would not take too kindly to that match,[12] but by making him her daughter's husband she tied his hands.

Agrippa's marriage to Julia ought to have evoked an energetic protest from Livia. She might not have been able to object to Marcellus in view of his cognatic credential, but what was her reaction in 21, when Tiberius, very possibly not yet married to Vipsania,[13] was passed over in favour of a stranger? Unfortunately little more than speculation is available. If we take Seneca literally, Octavia broke up her own daughter's marriage and married Agrippa to Julia in order to revenge herself on Livia for having sons still living. This inference has been drawn, but it is not altogether convincing; Augustus needed Agrippa in the family rather than outside it. Another solution that has been proposed is that Livia in fact tried to forestall the choice of Agrippa by suggesting to Augustus that Julia marry a Roman knight; C. Proculeius was mentioned as someone who led a quiet life and kept out of politics.[14] The theory has one rather macabre point in its favour. We are told that Proculeius ended his life by swallowing gypsum in a vain attempt to relieve the pain of a stomach complaint (*PNH* 36.183). Livia could thus have calculated that a brief union between Proculeius and Julia would check Agrippa, and would leave Tiberius with the chance of another bite at the cherry within a short space of time. But this must remain conjectural. We can only conclude that on the evidence Octavia had things very much her own way.

THE SUCCESSION: LIVIA

In 11 BC, by a strange quirk of fate in the year of Octavia's death,[15] Tiberius married Julia, who had been a widow since Agrippa's death the year before. Tiberius was forced to divorce Vipsania, to whom he was deeply attached (*ST* 7.2–3). Livia is not mentioned, but when Suetonius says that it was a hurried marriage we immediately ask why. It was not Augustus who was in a hurry, for he settled on Tiberius only reluctantly (CD 54.31.1). Nor was there any urgency of the sort that had accelerated the marriage of Livia and Augustus in 38. Julia was carrying Agrippa's last child, Agrippa Postumus, at the time of Agrippa's death, but the *annus luctus* was duly observed by Julia; the only reference to pregnancy in connection with the Tiberius-Julia marriage is that Vipsania was carrying Tiberius' second child at the time of her divorce (*ST* 7.3.2). That is the indecent haste of which Suetonius speaks. With Octavia probably out of the way already, Livia was determined that this time no one – not even her son – was going to snatch the prize from her. The imperious mother had started to emerge at last.

The decade following Tiberius' marriage to Julia saw Livia's efforts crowned with complete and final success, though only after she had overcome obstacles of a much more formidable character than anything with which Octavia had had to contend. Livia's younger son, Drusus, having died in 9 BC, Tiberius seemed to be on target for comparable preferment to that shown to Agrippa. In 7 BC he held a second consulship, Livia's contribution to which he publicly acknowledged: he and Livia dedicated the Precinct of Livia, he gave a banquet for the senate on the Capitol, and Livia gave one for the women 'somewhere or other' (CD 55.8.2). In 6 BC Tiberius received the tribunician power for five years and a special *imperium* in the east (VP 2.99.1). With Gaius and Lucius still there to furnish the ultimate successor, the two-tier system was once more in place. And then suddenly, in the same year 6 BC, Tiberius left Rome and retired to the island of Rhodes, where he was to remain until AD 2 (*ST* 10.2–11.1). The withdrawal is closely bound up with our third great Augustan figure, Julia, but first let us complete the story of the succession.

In 1 BC Tiberius appealed to Augustus to allow him to return to Rome. The request was refused, and the only concession that Livia managed to extract from Augustus was that Tiberius be given the title of Augustus' envoy (*legatus*), to conceal the fact that with the lapsing of his tribunician power he was a mere private citizen (*ST* 11.5, 12.1). Livia's strenuous efforts to secure something more concrete were frustrated by the faction supporting Augustus' son/grandson, Gaius Caesar, and it is from about this time that we can date an intensification of the succession struggle. Ultimately, Livia would triumph, but whether she could have done so without a series of fortuitous deaths is doubtful.

Tiberius was finally allowed to return in AD 2. Livia's urgent prayers played a part in Augustus' decision, but he would not have consented without the agreement of Gaius Caesar, who stipulated that Tiberius was to take no part in public affairs (*ST* 13.2, 15.1). The two-tier system had degenerated into a struggle for the first tier. But in the same year the wheel turned in Livia's favour, when the younger Caesar, Lucius, died. Livia was blamed for his death, as she had been for that of Marcellus and would be for others. There was no truth in the allegations – if the sources had been more selective they would have been more credible – but they testify to the decisive character of Livia's ultimate triumph.

The fates again came to Livia's assistance in AD 4, when Gaius died of wounds received in Armenia. Augustus now had to rebuild the succession system from the ground up, and he decided (or agreed) to make Tiberius the focal point. In June he adopted both Tiberius and Agrippa Postumus, the surviving son of Julia and Agrippa, after having first arranged for Tiberius to adopt Germanicus, the elder son of Livia's other (deceased) son, Drusus. This made Germanicus Augustus' grandson by adoption, as he was Livia's grandson by birth. The adoption of Tiberius included a significant innovation. Augustus declared that 'I do this for reasons of state – *rei publicae causa*' (VP 2.104.1). This was much more than an expression of reluctance on Augustus' part. Livia had in fact scored an impressive double. She had had an official rider added to her son's adoption, thus giving dynastic arrangements a constitutional force that they had not had before; and she had got her grandson into the two-tier system.

In AD 6 Augustus severed Agrippa Postumus' ties with the Julian family by pronouncing an *abdicatio* ('get out of my sight!'). Soon afterwards Postumus was banished (*SA* 65.1), and he was effectively out of the race. Propaganda and politicizing would try hard to reinstate him, but would achieve little more than an obfuscation of Augustus' last years that still persists today.[16] The final seal was placed on Livia's efforts in AD 13, when Tiberius' tribunician power was renewed, and he was given in all provinces and armies a power equal to Augustus' own (VP 2.121.1).

THE AUGUSTAN PROGRAMME OF MORAL REFORM

In 2 BC Roman society was rocked by a scandal involving Augustus' daughter, Julia, and half *la jeunesse dorée* of Rome. The scandal sparked off the most dramatic series of trials of the entire reign, including as they did the unique impeachment of an emperor's daughter. But the affair has so many ramifications that it cannot be properly understood if presented in one continuous narrative. It is therefore proposed to develop the story from a number of separate vantage points, starting with the programme of matrimonial and moral reform that was one of the showpieces of the Augustan legislative achievement.

In 18–17 BC Augustus enacted the main body of the great *leges Juliae*, the laws which enjoyed the special distinction of bearing his name. Two of those laws put the moral reform programme in place. One, the *lex Julia de maritandis ordinibus*, regulated marriage, encouraged procreation by privileges and rewards, and penalized the unmarried and the childless, in particular by restricting their rights of inheritance. A later law, the *lex Papia Poppaea* of AD 9, amended the marriage ordinance in a number of respects. The other law of 18–17, the *lex Julia de adulteriis coercendis*, made sexual laxity, hitherto mainly confined to the privacy of the family court, a public crime to be adjudicated on by a permanent jury-court specially created for the purpose. The law applied both to *adulterium*, illicit intercourse by and with a respectable married woman, and to *stuprum*, fornication with a widow or unmarried free woman who was not a prostitute. The *adulterium* part could be committed only by wives and their lovers; a husband's extra-marital affairs did not create problems of legitimacy. The punishment was banishment to an island and partial forfeiture of property.[17]

What was the precise purpose of the legislation? The issue has been keenly debated, but without the emergence of a clear consensus. However, in terms of the most viable theory the aim was to strengthen the traditional family unit, to stimulate the Italian birthrate, and to reinforce *pudicitia*, the strict moral standard expected of women. In short, to rejuvenate the Italian stock. The long years of anarchy and civil war had taken their toll. The decline in the birth-rate had created an acute shortage of manpower, not only in the military sphere but also in the civil. People were reluctant to marry, and when they did they were reluctant to have children. Easy divorce was also a destabilizing factor, and although Augustus did nothing to restrict freedom of divorce, he laid down that no divorce be valid unless witnessed by seven citizens (*D* 24.2.9). The hope was, *inter alia*, that women would no longer be able 'to date the years by their husbands instead of by the consuls'.[18]

The programme encountered intense opposition in some quarters, but it won such acceptance from the community as a whole that it ultimately earned Augustus the highest honour within his country's gift. That honour, the status of *pater patriae*, or father of his country, was destined to be the principal target of the politics of protest that would be spearheaded by Augustus' daughter and would give rise to the trials of 2 BC.

The legislation of 18–17 BC had a long history, both in terms of awareness of the problems and in terms of actual earlier laws. As far back as 131 BC one of the censors had spoken forcefully about the need to produce more children. In the late Republic Cicero had given thought to it. And in the critical years of the triumvirate a practical step had been taken, when tribunician sacrosanctity was granted to Octavia and Livia. In the early 20s the Augustan propaganda machine was hard at work, coaxing laudations from the poets and not hesitating to use the well-worn technique of falsifying history. Horace condemns moral laxity, calls on Augustus to curb licence, and bestows fulsome praise on the emperor for protecting Italy with arms, gracing it with morals, and reforming it with laws. A generation later Ovid has Maiestas, the goddess who personified the 'greaterness' of Rome, born of Honour and Reverence in lawful wedlock, and attended by Chastity. The falsifiers came up with a law of 'Romulus' making marriage compulsory and prohibiting the exposure of children. Augustus' claim to have restored many ancestral traditions also belongs here, as does Suetonius' selection of the laws on adultery, chastity and marriage as prime examples of Augustus' restatement of old laws and enactment of new ones. In 28–7 an important practical step was taken ahead of the legislation, when Augustus revived the cult of Pudicitia, which had gone into a decline since the epoch-making efforts of Verginia.[19]

We have spoken of opposition to the programme, but when did that opposition first make itself felt? A pointer is supplied by the elegiac poet Propertius. Writing in c. 26 BC, the poet rejoices with his mistress, Cynthia, at the elimination of a law which had made the lovers fear that it would separate them.[20] The passage is usually taken to mean that in 28–7 Augustus had made an unsuccessful attempt to legislate on marriage and morals; he had either passed a law which he had then been forced to repeal, or he had proposed a law but had withdrawn the proposal when the strength of the opposition became clear.[21] Despite a recent claim that there was neither a law nor an abandoned proposal prior to 18–17 BC,[22] one or other of those alternatives is undoubtedly correct. In fact there was legislation long before Augustus. Plutarch learnt from Sallust that Sulla had legislated on marriage, which Sallust had found strange for someone living in lechery and adultery himself (Plut. *Comp. Lys. et Sull.* 3.2). There is no need to ask how Sallust obtained the information; Sulla's criminal laws survived him and went down to posterity.[23] Even earlier, in 204 BC, there is a trace of a *lex lenonia* which penalized *lenocinium*, or procuring for immoral purposes[24] – oddly enough, at a time when the Scipionic group was making a feature of moral probity (see Chapter 3, p. 28). It is because of laws like these that Suetonius says that Augustus revised some existing laws – *leges retractavit* (*SA* 34.1). It is for the same reason that the Severan jurist, Paul, says that the first chapter of the *lex Julia de adulteriis* obrogated (that is, tacitly repealed) *a number of earlier laws* (*Coll.* 4.2.2).

The question as to whether a law was actually passed, or merely proposed but abandoned, in 28–7 can be answered in the light of information supplied by Dio. He notes, under 27 BC, that Augustus brought some laws before the people before formally submitting them, in order to find out what was unpopular and to rectify it (CD 53.21.1–3). In other words, at public meetings (*contiones*), Augustus tested the climate and, finding it unfavourable, abandoned the proposed law. Dio is, as so often, generalizing from a single incident, and that incident can only be the abortive attempt to legislate on marriage and morals. No other proposal is on record as having struck trouble in 27 BC. Opposition in the late 20s is also implied by Livy in his *Preface* (written c. 27–5 BC): 'Morals declined to the present low level, when we can endure neither our faults nor their remedies' (*Praef.* 9). Confirmation is supplied by Tacitus, who notes *two* Julian rogations prior to the *lex Papia Poppaea* (*TA* 3.25.1, 28.3); one of them is the proposal of c. 27 BC.

We conclude, then, that in 27 BC Augustus, who was consul at the time, proposed an ordinance on marriage and morals. He chose as the legislative body the centuriate assembly, effective control of which was in the hands of the people most affected, namely the well-to-do.[25] The proposal failed to get acceptance and was dropped. But the need for family rejuvenation remained acute. In 23, as compensation for giving up the consulship, Augustus received the full tribunician power. But that power had never been used to initiate legislation by anyone who was not a tribune, and before working out how to use it he cast around for some other solution to the difficulties that he had encountered in c. 27. He was offered a *cura legum et morum* in 19, and again in 18, but this overriding power to legislate without reference to the people smacked too much of the discredited institution of the dictatorship. It was then that the legislative potential of the tribunician power was probed, and the *leges Juliae* were put on the statute book. This was not the end of the opposition, but for a long time there was peace.[26]

THE TRIALS OF 2 BC

We now have the necessary background, and can address the trials of 2 BC as well as the politics of protest which led up to them. The bare facts are soon told. In 2 BC Augustus sent Julia a bill of divorcement in Tiberius' name and mounted a series of trials against Julia and a number of men with whom she had consorted.[27] Julia was banished to Pandateria, a small, inhospitable island north of Naples; her mother, Scribonia, who had not remarried since being repudiated by Augustus, voluntarily shared her exile. Julia was later transferred to Rhegium on the mainland, but was never allowed to return to Rome. She was denied wine and luxuries, and was not allowed to see any man without Augustus' permission. He even thought of putting her to death. She was treated as no longer belonging to his family. He had given her a modest allowance during her internment, but it was not confirmed by his will and Tiberius discontinued it. When she died in AD 14 she was denied burial in Augustus' mausoleum.[28] Tiberius is said to have allowed her to waste away by slow starvation, thinking that she had been in exile so long that her death would pass unnoticed (*TA* 1.53.3), but the accuracy of this is doubtful.

Of the men involved, one, Iullus Antonius, was a son of Antony and Fulvia who had been brought up by Octavia and had married her daughter after the latter's divorce from Agrippa. Despite his antecedents Augustus had – no doubt through Octavia's influence – given Iullus a consulship and a governorship. He was sentenced to death, but was allowed to commit suicide (VP 2.100.4). He might have got off more lightly if Octavia had been alive; she was noted for her ability to influence Augustus towards clemency.[29] Julia's other lovers were treated more leniently, being sentenced to banishment under the adultery law. They included Q. Crispinus, Ap. Claudius, Sempronius Gracchus, Scipio, and Demosthenes, as well as a number of unidentified senators and knights.[30] The mildness of their punishment was greeted with surprise. They were no worse off, it was said, than if they had consorted with the wife of an ordinary citizen; instead of putting them to death Augustus had given them travel documents and sent them away for their own safety.[31] But one of them, Sempronius Gracchus, ultimately fared less well. This 'persistent adulterer' had first seduced Julia when she was still Agrippa's wife and had continued the liaison after she married Tiberius. He was tried about a year after Julia and the rest, being protected until then by the tribunate which he held in 2 BC. He was banished to Cercina off the African coast. But at some earlier point he had helped Julia to write a letter to Augustus attacking Tiberius; the latter remembered it when he became emperor, and soldiers were sent to Cercina to kill Gracchus (*TA* 1.53.4–9).

JULIA'S RELATIONS WITH HER FAMILY

What was behind the trials? The question is a complex one. Julia's conduct was of long standing. Her liaison with Gracchus was more than ten years old; Agrippa had known about it, and had suffered torments because of his wife's adulteries (*PNH* 7.45). It was even said that she had tried to seduce Tiberius while Agrippa was alive (*ST* 7.2). Why, then, did a state of affairs that had been tolerated for so long suddenly blow up in 2 BC? What exactly had Julia and her friends been doing – was it simply immorality, or was there more to it? A consensus on such questions has not yet emerged, and perhaps never will. The very nature of the events veils them in secrecy. The most that can be done is to offer a plausible solution.[32]

Our first task is to attempt to put Julia's relations with other members of the Domus in proper perspective. How did she stand *vis-à-vis* her father, her stepmother Livia and her husband Tiberius? And what light do those relationships shed on her political thinking?

We are able to see Julia as a three-dimensional figure, rather than as a pawn on a matrimonial chessboard, thanks to the collection of anecdotes about her compiled in c. 400 by Macrobius (*Sat.* 2.5.1–9). As she is here speaking for herself,[33] the collection is one of our few sources of direct evidence in the whole affair. Julia presents herself as well-educated, with a taste for literature, and a pungent, if bawdy, wit. When people expressed surprise that her children looked like Agrippa, she replied that 'I only take a passenger on board when I have a full cargo' (2.5.9). A number of her sayings testify to her easy relationship with her father. When he spoke to her about her unconventional lifestyle, she drew attention to the children's resemblance to Agrippa (2.5.3). She once offended Augustus by appearing provocatively dressed. Next day her attire was more modest. He asked whether that was not more suitable for Augustus' daughter, but she replied that 'Today I dressed for my father's eyes, yesterday for a man's' (2.5.5). Coming upon her one day while her women were plucking out grey hairs, he asked, 'In a few years' time wouldn't you rather be grey than bald?' 'Yes, indeed.' 'Then why are they in such a hurry to make you bald?' (2.5.7). This is of special interest; the incident took place within a year or two of the catastrophe,[34] thus pointing to continued good relations and supporting Augustus' claim to have known nothing concrete about her activities until the scandal broke (see this chapter, p. 113).

The anecdotes also furnish evidence of ill-feeling between Julia and Livia. On one occasion, at the games, eyebrows were raised at the difference between Livia's entourage of solemn men and the rowdy troop (*grex*) of young men around Julia. Augustus wrote to her to complain about her unseemly familiarity with young men. She wrote in reply, 'Don't worry, I'll soon make old men of them' (2.5.6). On another occasion Augustus declared that Julia was brash but innocent, as Claudia had been in days gone by (2.5.4). The reference was to Claudia Quinta, who had proved her chastity by moving a ship (see Chapter 3, p. 28). Augustus was in all probability replying to a complaint by Livia on something or other that Julia had done. Augustus replied by reminding Livia that the Claudian family to which she belonged had its own problems. Yet another difference between the two women can be inferred from Julia's reply to a family friend who had urged her to abandon her extravagance and to imitate her father's frugality; she replied that 'He forgets that he is Caesar, but I remember that I am Caesar's daughter' (2.5.8). The parsimonious Livia will not have been impressed. But Augustus never lost his affection for Julia. There is even a note of tolerance in his remark that 'He had two spoilt brats, the state and his daughter' (2.5.4).

The most difficult relationship to unravel is that between Julia and Tiberius. The marriage was, we are told, happy at first, but the death of the son who was born in 10 BC changed that, and from about 7 BC Tiberius stopped living with her.[35] This was followed by his sudden withdrawal to Rhodes in 6 BC (see this chapter, p. 104). What prompted that drastic move? For the most part the sources have no idea. Suetonius offers four guesses: Tiberius was disgusted with Julia but dared not accuse or divorce her; he wanted to show the regime how indispensable he was; he wanted, as he is said to have stated subsequently, to leave the field clear for Julia's sons, Gaius and Lucius; he needed a rest from his labours, as he said at the time, and in the face of Livia's entreaties and Augustus' complaints to the senate he went on a hunger strike and finally got his way. Velleius, who was there, confirms Suetonius' first reason when he says that Julia did not neglect any act of extravagance or lust, claiming the right to do whatever pleased her; Velleius also confirms Suetonius' third and fourth reasons – what he said afterwards, and what he said at the time. Dio, groping in the dark, thinks that Tiberius did not so much seek leave to go as receive orders to do so because of his attitude to Gaius and Lucius.[36]

Only the insight of Tacitus enables us to get close to the truth. He says that Julia looked down on Tiberius as an inferior, and this was the real reason for his withdrawal – *spreverat ut inparem; nec alia tam intima Tiberio causa cur Rhodum abscederet* (*TA* 1.53.2). Tacitus was well aware of the speculations and, in the case of the fourth reason, the official explanation known to Suetonius, but he wanted to probe below the surface. What does he mean by *inparem*, 'inferior'? One recent answer is that Julia extolled the Claudii Pulchri, the family of her lover Ap. Claudius, and denigrated the Claudii Nerones to whom Tiberius belonged. But Suetonius stresses Tiberius' descent from both the Claudii Nerones and (through Livia) the Claudii Pulchri.[37] An esoteric suggestion which we notice only as a curiosity is that Julia was determined to be an empress, even at her sons' expense; but Tiberius refuses to supersede Gaius and Lucius, thus proving 'unequal' to the task, whereupon she blackens his name with Augustus.[38]

There is a question that needs to be asked. Does Tacitus mean an ordinary, almost routine claim of superior ancestry by Julia, or is he describing something entirely new, a special attribute of the Julian *gens* into whose care the *res publica* had been entrusted? To ask the question is to suggest the answer. Julia was the first to claim superiority because of the divine blood of Augustus that flowed in her veins. Her daughter Agrippina would taunt Tiberius with precisely that notion in AD 26: 'How can you sacrifice to Divus Augustus while persecuting his descendants? His divine spirit does not reside in mute statues; I am his true image, born of his heavenly blood' (*TA* 4.52.4). Agrippina was repeating her mother's sentiments: *spreverat ut inparem*. Already a political slogan, the divine blood would supply an entire ideology to Agrippina's son, Caligula (see Chapter 11, p. 159). If c. 7 BC seems a bit early for the birth of the Julian myth, it should be remembered that the family had, since Caesar, claimed descent from Venus Genetrix. Also, the man who was already the *de facto* father of his country had enough intimations of divinity for his daughter to be encouraged to propagate the new message.[39] She was referring to more than her penchant for extravagance when she 'remembered that she was Caesar's daughter'. She was using a weapon not available to her Claudian adversary, Livia, to devise a pattern that would dominate the politics of the next reign. We cannot go so far as to say that it was Julia, rather than Augustus himself, who first detected the potential of the divine blood, but it is clear from the Macrobius passage that she was contrasting the splendid lifestyle of Caesar's daughter with the (Livia-imposed) frugality of Augustus himself. As Velleius says, she made licence to sin her only measuring rod, claiming that whatever it pleased her to do was lawful – *quidquid liberet pro licito vindicans* (VP 2.100.3). Augustus and Livia had claimed a somewhat similar right in 36 (see Chapter 8, p. 95), except that they had had to disguise themselves as gods. Julia found a more subtle disguise in the divine blood.

THE AVANT GARDE AND THE *PATER PATRIAE*

We must now attempt to draw the threads together. As already observed, we require answers to three questions. What exactly had the defendants of 2 BC done? Why was it only penalized in 2 BC? And what part did the animosity between Livia and Julia play in the *dénouement*?

The most circumstantial account of the case is supplied by Seneca:

> The emperor Augustus banished his daughter and made public the scandals of his House. She had received lovers in droves (*admissos gregatim adulteros*). She had roamed the city in nocturnal revels, choosing for her pleasures the Forum, and the very Rostrum from which her father had proposed his adultery law. Turning from adultery to prostitution, she had stationed herself at the statue of Marsyas, seeking gratification of every kind in the arms of casual lovers. Enraged beyond measure, Augustus revealed what he should have punished in private. Later he regretted not having drawn a veil of silence over matters of which he had been unaware until it was too late.
>
> (*Ben.* 6.1–2)

Augustus disclosed the scandal in a letter to the senate which was read by his quaestor because he was too ashamed to read it in person (*SA* 65.2). The letter was also published in an edict for general information. That is how the elder Pliny, not a senator, got to know of it. He says that in her nocturnal frolics Julia placed a chaplet on the statue of Marsyas; Pliny compares P. Munatius who had taken a chaplet from Marsyas' statue and placed it on his own head, for which he was imprisoned when the tribunes refused to intervene. Dio also knows of nocturnal revels and drinking bouts in the forum and on the rostra; Augustus had previously suspected something, but now he was very angry and notified the senate. Dio's evidence is important because he makes it clear that the revels in the forum were the last straw. Tacitus calls the offence *inpudicitia* and says that by giving the solemn name of 'an injury to religion and a violation of majesty' to a common peccadillo of men and women Augustus exceeded the scope of his own laws.[40]

Up to this point the picture is consistent and credible. The basis of the complaints against Julia and her friends was adultery and intoxicated revelry. The industrious Seneca adds an important detail: 'His failing years were alarmed by his daughter and the noble youths who were bound to her by adultery as if by a military oath (*velut sacramento*); again he had to fear a woman in league with an Antony' (*Brev. Vit.* 4.5). The same Seneca, we recall, attests lovers as being admitted in droves – *gregatim*. Julia's entourage at the games, to which Livia took such strong exception, was a *grex*. She headed a coterie which included adultery amongst its pursuits.

There are, however, two passages which need careful scrutiny, for they appear at first sight to point to something more sinister than frolics. Dio says that Iullus Antonius was punished capitally because by taking part in the revels (*touto praxas*) he was considered to have designs on the monarchy (*hōs epi tēi monarchiai*). And in his catalogue of the misfortunes that befell Augustus, Pliny includes Julia's adultery and the disclosure of plots by her against his life – *consilia parricidae palam facta* (*PNH* 7.149).[41] Augustus was thrown off balance by the scandal, and so are some modern investigators, for on the strength of these throw-away lines it is asserted that Julia and the rest conspired to kill Augustus, to marry Julia to Iullus Antonius, and to place him on the throne as caretaker for Gaius and Lucius.[42] But there is no possible foundation for this view. Even if there were no contradictory evidence it would hardly be possible to see Julia as her father's murderer. In any case, there is overwhelming evidence to the contrary. Firstly, there is Seneca's careful summary of Augustus' letter. Moreover, Tacitus, like Pliny, sets his account of the case in the context of Augustus' misfortunes, but far from describing it as a plot to kill anyone, he makes it quite clear that it was a case of adultery, although one that had been elevated to treason in breach of Augustus' own laws. Tacitus' criticism was misunderstood by Pliny, and perhaps by Dio, although he is not nearly as specific as Pliny, to mean treason in the sense of a murderous plot, instead of in the sense that it actually bears in Tacitus' context.[43] Pliny was also confused by Seneca's 'youths bound to Julia by adultery as if by a military oath', for this made him think of a *coniuratio*[44] – though, oddly enough, Pliny does not use the word in his account. One final point – would Augustus have agreed to furnish 'travel documents' (see this chapter, p. 109) to men who had sworn to kill him? There is no need to labour the point. Julia did not mount a conspiracy against Augustus.

The aims of the *grex Iuliae* were not lethal. The group was one of those coteries of rebellious spirits that made their appearance from time to time. They had something in common with the Bacchanals, whose *coniuratio* expressed by oaths what Seneca attributes only notionally to the *grex Iuliae*. The two movements also shared nocturnal activities and the consumption of wine, those 'infallible' proofs that women were up to no good. The Vestals of 114–13 also had a certain group cohesion, and shared the various interests of that *bon vivant*, L. Veturius (see Chapter 5, p. 57).

Adultery, though prominent on Julia's agenda, was not the only item thereon. Her literary bent, her mordant wit, and her generally avant garde lifestyle were shared by members of her circle. Gracchus may have been a tragic poet and was also an orator of some note; Iullus Antonius had literary pretensions; Q. Crispinus (cos. 9 BC) was related to the Crispinus who, as praetor in the crucial year 2 BC, gave the first entertainment at which knights and matrons appeared on the stage; Scipio was a friend of that bitter enemy of the adultery law, Propertius; Demosthenes could have been both a musician and a notorious adulterer; and if Ap. Claudius was P. Clodius' grandson he will not have been a stranger to nocturnal revels.[45]

Were there any women in the circle besides Julia? According to Dio the scandal saw accusations against many other women; but Augustus, though showing no mercy to Julia, was disposed to be lenient with the others, and decreed that they were not to be punished for anything done more than five years before (CD 55.10.16). This five years' prescription (limitation of actions) was introduced in order to prevent a witch-hunt. But we only have one name. Julia's freedwoman, Phoebe, who was one of her accomplices, hanged herself, whereupon Augustus said that he would rather have been Phoebe's father than Julia's (*SA* 65.2–3). Why did Phoebe take this drastic step? A possible answer is that she followed the example of Hispala, who was initiated as a Bacchanal by her mistress and then betrayed her (L 39.10.5–13.14). If Phoebe had betrayed her *patrona* to Augustus, it is arguable that, facing a penalty of reversion to servitude, she decided to end her life.[46]

The coterie was protesting, but what about? Was it merely a non-specific protest against convention, or was there something specific? Protests with no discernible objective are not unknown. In AD 37 a coterie very similar in format to Julia's was presided over by a certain Albucilla and amused itself with adultery interspersed with witticisms at Tiberius' expense. There was no succession struggle at the time, nor was there a plot to kill the moribund Tiberius, but that did not save them from the criminal law (Bauman 1974a: 130–4). This is the extreme case. Julia's circle did have a somewhat more specific objective. It was an intensification, precisely in 2 BC, of the attacks on tradition that the group had been mounting for some time. There was a reason why that intensification occurred precisely in 2 BC. There was also a reason why Augustus reacted precisely at that time to a state of affairs that had been going on for ten years or more.

It was in 2 BC that the status of *pater patriae*, father of his country, was conferred on Augustus. The status was his last constitutional acquisition and set the final seal on his reign. It was seen as a transfer of the state into the power of Augustus, as if into the power of the head of a family. Suetonius has preserved the words with which Valerius Messalla saluted Augustus: 'May good and auspicious fortune attend you and your Domus, Caesar Augustus, for in praying for that we are praying for lasting good fortune for the state; the senate and people of Rome hail you as Father of your Country.' With tears in his eyes Augustus replied that 'I have attained my highest hopes, Conscript Fathers, and have no more to ask of the immortal gods than that I may retain your approval to the end of my life'. The literary chorus which greeted the new title leaves us in no doubt as to the profound importance of what had happened. Augustus ends the official record of his achievements with the conferment of the title, although he survived for another sixteen years.[47]

The idea of making Augustus *pater patriae* had been in the pipeline for a long time. As early as 29–7 BC Horace had reminded him that 'If he seeks to have *Father of Cities* inscribed on his statues, let him dare to curb licence and be famous through the ages; fault must be discouraged by punishment, for without morals laws must fail' (*Carm.* 3.24.27–36). This adds another dimension to the moral regeneration propaganda of the 20s. The persistence with which Augustus strove to enshrine his programme in legislation, despite one major setback and strenuous opposition thereafter, is now seen to have been moved by personal considerations as well as by social needs. But Julia and her friends were not impressed, and they showed their contempt by perpetrating the most outrageous acts in the forum and on the rostra.[48] Prior to 2 BC displays of contempt for the Establishment might have been tolerated. But as *pater patriae* Augustus almost took on a new identity, one compounded of a religious aura (*numen*) and personal majesty. The new charisma could brook no continuation of the old patterns of filial behaviour, for the head of a family which now embraced the whole community had to uphold the highest standards of morality – not only for the sake of the community but also for the sake of the *pater patriae* himself.

Did Augustus bring matters to a head before or after the conferment of the new title? Had he been advised that conferment could not take place until the scandal had been sedated, or was it only after conferment that the need for action became apparent to him? Interesting as the first alternative is, the second is the correct one. Dio locates *pater patriae* before the trials (CD 55.10.10, 14), and rightly so; the title was conferred on 5 February, which hardly gives time for the trials before that. There is an even stronger reason for preferring Dio's sequence. The revels in the forum had, as Dio himself implies, been anything but a regular feature over the years. In fact they were of very recent occurrence indeed. However unaware of the group's activities in general Augustus may have been, this particular act of defiance could not have failed to become notorious literally overnight. In other words, the desecration of the forum and the rostra happened only once. The focal point is Marsyas' statue. If Julia plied the prostitute's trade there, it was more than an isolated incident, but the crucial event, which happened only once, was the placing of a chaplet on the statue. The statue stood in the forum, where *Marsyas caussidicus*, Marsyas the court pleader (Mart. 2.64.8), was in competition with Apollo, the god who had inspired the *ius respondendi* by which Augustus had given formal efficacy to the opinions of jurists.

Apollo was, to Augustus, the supreme jurisconsult, and he was also the ultimate inspiration of Augustus' legislation. In effect, therefore, Julia and her friends crowned Marsyas as a better lawyer than Apollo. The crowning was thus one of the acts that denigrated the moral reform programme; whatever it was that took place on the rostra from which Augustus had proposed his adultery law was another.[49]

The *grex Iuliae* had given a devastating reply to the honour which had just been conferred; they had made a mockery of Augustus' lifelong dedication to morals and the family.[50] Julia, hostile to the reform programme which sought to restrain her 'right' to do whatever she liked, long resentful of her role as a matrimonial pawn, responding both to public (especially equestrian) opinion (see this chapter, p. 123) and, in the vinous ambience of the moment, to pressures from the group that under normal circumstances she might have resisted, allowed herself to stage this monumental insult to the newly created *pater patriae*. Augustus, horrified, had no alternative but to react vigorously and at once. There was not even time to regain his composure sufficiently to appear in person to tell the senate what had happened.

There remains Livia's possible role in the *dénouement*. But this can more conveniently be dealt with in our overview of Livia (see this chapter, p. 125), and we therefore end this section with a postscript. There is some evidence of popular agitation for Julia's recall from exile. Dio notes under AD 3 that the people pressed Augustus to bring his daughter back, but he replied that fire and water would mix before that happened. Thereupon the people threw blazing torches into the Tiber (as the Bacchanals had done – L 39.13.12). Later that year Julia was transferred from Pandateria to Rhegium on the mainland (CD 55.13.1). How reliable is this information, coming not from Dio himself but from a Xiphilinus excerpt? Things get out of hand in the Zonaras excerpt which follows the Xiphilinus fragment in the editions, for we are told that Julia was brought back to Rome and persuaded Augustus to adopt Tiberius (CD 55.13.1a). We cannot even guess what Dio himself had actually said. But there is something in Suetonius. He says that in response to vigorous popular demands, Augustus summoned a public meeting, but called on the gods to curse the people with similar daughters and wives (*SA* 65.3). Elsewhere (*SA* 19.1–2) Suetonius includes in his catalogue of the conspiracies of the reign (which does *not* include Iullus Antonius) the plan of the lowly Epicadus and the aged Audasius to take Julia by force from Pandateria to the armies. If this is not a doublet of what was suggested for Julia's daughter in Tiberius' reign (see Chapter 10, p. 152), it reveals a further aspect of the succession struggle. By AD 3, the year when these popular demonstrations were taking place, Tiberius was back in Rome. Although temporarily barred from politics, he was a threat to Julia's surviving son, Gaius, and the latter's friends looked around for a counterweight and thought they might find it in Julia. But this was an entirely new phenomenon, having very little to do with the events of 2 BC. Neither the half-Parthian Epicadus nor Audasius who had been charged with forgery (in connection with the proposed recall?) can be considered as heirs to the elegant dilettantes of 2 BC.

OVID, THE YOUNGER JULIA AND THE OPPOSITION

In AD 8 Ovid, the last of the great Augustan poets, was banished by Augustus. Ovid, then in his fifty-first year, was sent to Tomis on the Black Sea, and despite endless appeals, both to Augustus and to Tiberius, he was never allowed to return to Rome and died in exile in AD 18.

While in exile Ovid wrote two poetical works, *Tristia (Miseries)* and *Epistulae ex Ponto (Letters from the Black Sea)*. The constant theme is Augustus' displeasure and his hopes of forgiveness. But despite his incessant allusions to his misfortunes, Ovid has succeeded in compiling the most opaque account of anything in the last decade of Augustus, a period not noted for its lucidity at the best of times. The only certain facts are that he was sentenced to the milder form of banishment, *relegatio*, but was sent to a remote outpost instead of to a nearby island; that he was left in possession of his property; and that he retained his equestrian status.[51]

According to Ovid he was ruined by two things, a poem and a mistake – *carmen et error* (*T* 2.207). The poem is identified by Ovid himself as the *Ars Amatoria, The Art of Love* (*T* 2.211–12 and *passim*). The work is usually taken to have been written in about AD 1,[52] thus leaving an interval of some seven years before Augustus reacted to it. But details of the mistake are extremely hard to come by. Ovid says a great deal about what he did not do, emphasizing that he did nothing forbidden by the criminal law. He says that he saw something that he should not have seen, and raises a tantalizing corner of the veil when he observes that Actaeon unwittingly saw the naked Diana but was set upon by dogs all the same.[53]

The naked Diana opened the floodgates of conjecture. Ovid has been seen committing adultery with Julia, Livia, or anyone else whose name could be dredged from the archives. He has been seen unwittingly witnessing Augustus in bed with Livia, or Julia, or a youth. The naked Diana has been identified as Julia or Livia in the bath; but Julia's reaction would hardly have been a hostile one.[54]

The problem moved out of fairyland when scholars began searching for a link between Ovid and the disgrace of Julia's daughter, Vipsania Julia. In AD 8 the younger Julia was charged with adultery and was relegated to the island of Trimerus in the Adriatic, where she died twenty years later. But she is a mere pasteboard by comparison with her mother; apart from her disgrace, the only facts known about her are that she owned the biggest house and the smallest dwarf in Rome (*PNH* 7.75). Her punishment was harsh: her house was razed to the ground; Augustus refused to acknowledge, or to allow to be reared, the child born after her condemnation; in exile she depended for her sustenance on the generosity of Livia, no doubt acting for Augustus who had surreptitiously sustained the elder Julia in a similar way; she was forbidden burial in his mausoleum; and her daughter, Aemilia Lepida, was not allowed to marry Claudius 'because her parents had offended Augustus'.[55]

The younger Julia's case raises a number of questions. D. Iunius Silanus, her only lover to be named as such, was not formally prosecuted at all; he was simply excluded from Augustus' friendship (Bauman 1974a: 112). Ovid was not so lucky; where Silanus, having left Rome voluntarily, was able to return of his own volition, Ovid could not go back without permission. It seems that a more serious view was taken of whatever Ovid had done; it was more offensive than adultery with the emperor's granddaughter.

A note by the Juvenal scholiast started scholars down a trail leading nowhere. The scholiast says that Julia committed incest with her brother, Agrippa Postumus (ad Juv. 6.158). On the strength of this evidence it was argued that Julia allied herself to Agrippa in order to challenge the extant two-tier system under which Germanicus, the husband of their sister Agrippina, was installed as the ultimate successor to Tiberius. Julia, resenting

Agrippina's boasts about Germanicus, will have committed incest with Agrippa in order to cement an alliance with him. Ovid will have been her accomplice (Norwood 1963). The trouble is that the scholiast completely misunderstood the Juvenal passage. The poet says of a diamond worn by Berenice that 'It was given as a present by the barbarian Agrippa to his incestuous sister, in the country where kings celebrate the sabbath and clemency allows pigs to reach old age' (6.156–60). 'Agrippa' is the Jewish king Agrippa II (Meise 1969: 41). There is no other tradition for Julia's incest.

The Juvenal scholiast is also responsible for another crux. He says that the sister who was given the diamond was the wife of L. Aemilius Paullus, who was executed for treason. She was relegated, was later recalled, gave herself over to vice, and was permanently exiled. This does not make sense. Temporary relegation for treason, permanent banishment for adultery: it should have been the other way around. The conspiracy of Paullus is genuine enough (*SA* 19.1), but its date is a movable feast. Whether one opts for AD 1 or AD 6, there is a technical problem: Augustus' disavowal of the child born after Julia's condemnation requires Paullus still to have been alive when she was condemned (for adultery).[56] Her double banishment is also worrying, and it has been suggested that there was a single episode, a conspiracy in AD 8 which saw Paullus executed and Julia exiled; Augustus will have disavowed the child in order not to endanger the succession. The theory links Ovid to the conspiracy as someone who knew of it but failed to pass on the information.[57]

This is as far as we can take the *error*; the problem is insoluble and may well remain so. We therefore turn to the *carmen*, whose prospects are somewhat brighter. The *Epitome de Caesaribus* of c. AD 400 states the reason for Ovid's relegation as follows: 'He exiled the poet Ovidius Naso for writing the three books of the *Ars Amatoria*' (1.24). This official version[58] provides the key that we need. When *Ars Amatoria* was published in c. AD 1 it consisted of only two books, both of which gave instruction to men. At a later date the third book was added, giving instruction to women.[59] The work applied the principles of didactic poetry; what Vergil had done for farming, Ovid set out to do for love-making. Most of the material would scarcely raise an eyebrow today, but Ovid comes close to the borderline at the end of book 3, when he announces that it is time to deal with 'naked matters, which I blush to tell', and proceeds to give completely uninhibited practical advice to women (*AA* 3.747–808). He takes the precaution of pointing out that the book is intended only for courtesans (*AA* 3.57–8); registered prostitutes were, of course, exempted from the adultery law. But this did not satisfy the regime, for by praising extra-marital relationships the work discouraged matrimony. The authorities were not impressed by aphorisms like 'Childbirth shortens youth, A field constantly harvested grows old' (*AA* 3.81–2). Marriage, procreation, chastity – all the values of the programme were put at risk by the third book. Teaching courtesans how to attract men was not likely to turn men towards respectable matrons. Ovid knows that this is one of the complaints, but vigorously denies the charge:

> [My Art] does not contravene the laws, it does not teach the young married women of Rome. Four times have I declared that 'I shall sing only of what accords with the laws, of permissible secret loves'. But, you say, the matron can use arts intended for others. Let the matron give up reading then, for every poem can teach her something wrong.
>
> (*T* 2.243–56)

Book 3 was the last straw. Ovid was well aware of the adverse reaction. Three years later he published *Remedia Amoris (The Remedies for Love)*, in which he observes that his advice on falling out of love must leave some things to the reader's imagination, because 'Some people have recently criticized my works as shameless' (*Rem. Am.* 357–62).

When was book 3 published? There are no chronological indications in the work. If books 1 and 2 were published in AD 1 and subsequently reissued in a second edition to which book 3 was added, the interval between the two editions must have been appreciable.[60] When Ovid completed the first two books he thought the work was finished (*AA* 2.733–44). But this is followed by an addendum: 'Lo, the girls are asking for counsel. You will be my next concern' (*AA* 2.745–6). What happened after publication of the first two books to cause Ovid to decide on a third? Conjecture supplies an answer.

Let us return to the opposition to Augustus' programme. The five years' proscription for adultery was introduced in 2 BC (CD 55.10.16). We recall Dio's words: 'Many women were accused but Augustus set a definite date as a limit.' Now, who but the women concerned would have pressed for relief? It is very likely that they mounted a concerted campaign, the first women's demonstration for many years. Ovid gave the female lobby support, by precept if not by active assistance. It is even possible that his legal knowledge, acquired in a progressive law school,[61] pointed the way to the by no means traditional idea of a limitation of actions in criminal cases.[62]

The opposition kept up the pressure after 2 BC. In AD 9 there was a disturbing demonstration against the marriage ordinance by the Equites, who took advantage of a public spectacle to voice their demands. Augustus tried to fob them off by displaying Germanicus' children as proof of the advantages of a family (*SA* 34.2). But he was forced to yield, albeit with a bad grace. The *lex Papia Poppaea* which substantially amended, and ameliorated, the marriage ordinance, was proposed by the consuls – both of whom were bachelors.[63] This time there was no question of Augustus being the proposer himself under his tribunician power; he did not want his great laws of 18–17 BC to be seen to have been less than adequate, which would have happened if the new law had borne his name.[64]

The presence of Equites in the forefront of the pressure groups of AD 9 brings Ovid into the picture. As one of the intellectual leaders of the equestrian order, he was writing furiously throughout the ten years up to AD 9, and was concentrating on the one basic theme. The second edition of *Amores* belongs to this period; it was followed by books 1 and 2 of the *Art*, and after that by book 3 and *Remedia Amoris*.[65] Thus the entire corpus of works critical of the puritanical-demographic policy so dear to Augustus belongs to the one decade. But there needs to have been a crucial point at which what had been tolerated suddenly became unacceptable. That point was book 3 of the *Art*, that ill-concealed invitation to the matrons of Rome to tread the primrose path with 'the girls'.

Book 3 should be located in close proximity to AD 8. This is because AD 6–8 witnessed a sustained literary assault on the regime. Prompted by unrest and famine, anonymous epigrams defaming eminent persons began to be posted up, and the regime was forced, in AD 8, to make such attacks treason (Bauman 1974a: 25–51). There is nothing to prove that Ovid was one of the anonymous pamphleteers, but if he chose precisely at this time to take up the cudgels in the equestrian cause with even greater vigour than before, by blatantly teaching matrons how to break the law, a regime already oversensitive to criticism may well have reacted harshly. Hence Ovid's banishment in, precisely, AD 8, the year when literary attacks reached their peak.

LIVIA, CONSORT AND CONFIDANTE

What sort of woman was Livia? She has figured in our discussions often enough, but only now, when we are in possession of the essential pieces, is it possible to attempt an overview of the most important woman of the reign. More precisely, we are here undertaking the first of two overviews, for there are two Livias. One, the mother of the emperor Tiberius, emerges as a fully three-dimensional figure from the pages of Tacitus. The other, the wife of the emperor Augustus, has to be cobbled together from scattered pieces of evidence in various sources.

Livia Drusilla, to give her the full names bestowed on her by her father, M. Livius Drusus Claudianus, at her birth in 58 BC, presents as the quintessential Roman matron. Chaste in herself, she demanded the same standard of others. Helpmate and confidante of her husband, she controlled his household with quiet, albeit frugal, efficiency, and acted as his ever-present adviser in both private and public affairs. Strong minded and not easily swayed, she was pleasant enough in personal contacts, but lacked the erudition and panache of a Julia. Hardly any memorable sayings of hers have come down to us; Dio lists only two (CD 58.2.4). This idealized portrait papers over some cracks, but its main outlines are accurate enough. The only sustained attack that a hostile tradition was able to mount against her concerned her alleged responsibility for the convenient disappearance of those who stood between Tiberius and the throne – Marcellus, Lucius, Gaius, Agrippa Postumus, Augustus himself, and her grandson Germanicus.[66] The very length of the list defeats it.

Until 35 BC there were some more credible insinuations. The precipitate haste of her marriage is one. Even assuming a political motive for the marriage (Sirago 1983: 59–60), why could they not wait three months until Drusus was born? We also recall with some uneasiness 'the novel adulteries of the gods' enacted at the Banquet of the Twelve Gods (see Chapter 8, p. 95). Suetonius takes special precautions to establish the credentials of the story (SA 70.1–2). But Livia's brief flirtation with the avant garde ended in 35, when she was given tribunician sacrosanctity. After that she concentrated on living up to the standard expected of an accredited member of the Domus. There was no better way of doing that than by promoting strict morality. Livia acquired a legendary reputation for integrity: 'Chastity stood beside her marriage-bed'; 'she guarded her good name jealously'; 'her private life was of traditional purity'.[67] When Augustus died she was probably given a lictor,[68] a privilege previously allowed only to Vestals among women, and ten years later, in AD 24, she was granted the right to sit with the Vestals in the theatre (*TA* 4.16.6). Tacitus says that this was done in order to induce women to become Vestals, but the fact remains that Livia was the criterion of Vestal virtues.[69]

The tradition which has Livia not only tolerate Augustus' infidelities, but pander to them by providing him with virgins to deflower is probably a canard,[70] but it has hidden depths. Livia's enemies were accusing her of *lenocinium*, or pandering, which was penalized by Augustus' adultery law. The attack on Livia is on all fours with the criticism of Augustus in 16 BC, when his departure from Rome with Terentia, Maecenas' wife and his mistress, evoked the comment that under his own laws he punished some, spared others, and broke the laws himself (CD 54.19.2–3). This raises a larger issue. Can the *lenocinium* allegation against Livia be seen as a reproach to someone whose connection with the adultery law was almost that of a co-author? This would have appealed to Ferrero, who floated the idea of Augustus having made Livia the criterion of excellence when he addressed the senate on the adultery law in 18–17 BC (1911: 69–70). The idea wins support from Livia's careful handling of the household economy[71] which gave practical expression to a sumptuary law enacted by Augustus contemporaneously with the adultery and marriage laws of 18–17 BC (*SA* 34.1, 40.5). The extravagance of the Banquet of the Twelve Gods had contrasted sharply with the famine raging at the time, and the subsequent switch to frugality could well have been Livia's idea, as part of her conversion to rectitude. There is one tantalizing direct hint of Livia's involvement in the legislative programme: in Egypt she was honoured as the patron of marriage.[72]

We now address the most important question of all. Did Livia play any part in the downfall of Julia in 2 BC? The idea has been canvassed before, mainly by inventing scenes in which Livia discloses the awful truth to Augustus,[73] but is such a scenario in fact possible on *a priori* grounds? Some of the evidence militates against such a possibility. Julia's disgrace did not enhance the absent Tiberius' prospects; Livia's attempt, in 1 BC, to secure permission for Tiberius to return achieved no more than a cosmetic appointment as Augustus' emissary on Rhodes. But there is one factor that has not previously been brought into the equation. Livia, we are told, showed great generosity in rearing friends' children and paying their daughters' dowries; and people began calling her *mater patriae*, mother of her country (CD 58.2.3). The appellation was not official, but after Augustus' death it was proposed in the senate that it be officially conferred; however, Tiberius vetoed it on the grounds that honours for women should be kept within bounds (*TA* 1.14.1–2). The point is, though, that the senators who supported the idea knew that it would be welcome to Livia; Tacitus has them propose this and other honours in a rush to flatter her.

There is accordingly reason to believe that in 2 BC the potential *mater patriae* saw it as her duty, as well as the duty of the *pater patriae*, to restrain immorality and licence. Co-sponsor of the family rejuvenation programme from the start, she had suffered the frustration of seeing Julia flaunt her indiscretions and earn no more than a mild rebuke from Augustus long enough. We cannot assert positively that when word of the desecration of the forum and the rostra reached the palace, it was Livia who aroused a reluctant emperor to action, but it is likely enough. She disliked Julia as an affront to the moral standards that she was pledged to uphold, and on personal grounds as well. She was certainly able to exert enormous influence over Augustus. He made a practice of discussing important matters with her, compiling a list of topics to be dealt with at their next meeting, and noting her replies for future reference.[74] This custom came close to giving Livia a status equivalent to that of an *amicus principis*, a friend of the emperor whom he would summon to his council. The classic case is the conspiracy of Cornelius Cinna which was mounted in, probably, AD 4.[75] Augustus summoned a council of his friends, but before it met he consulted Livia, being uncertain what to do with this grandson of Pompey. Livia advised him to pardon him, arguing that a physician achieved more by curative medicine than by surgery.[76] Augustus accepted her advice, cancelled the projected meeting of the *consilium*, and later made Cinna consul. According to Seneca there were no further plots against Augustus. Even if this is not true, it confirms the high opinion that later ages had of Livia's knowledge of affairs.[77] In Dio's version Livia delivers one of those boring rhetorical exercises with which Dio hoped to entertain his readers, but the point is that he considers Livia a suitable vehicle for the sort of homily that he usually puts into the mouth of a politician like Maecenas, so that he, too, is paying tribute to her political knowledge.

Tacitus pays Livia a rare compliment when he says that she was a match for Augustus in the subtleties of intrigue (*TA* 5.1.5). The extent to which he relied on her advice is confirmed by the fact that she often accompanied him on his travels, despite his own ruling against such practices.[78] One of the occasions was the eastern tour of 22–1 BC, when Sparta was visited and honoured because it had sheltered Livia and her family in the triumviral period, during their flight (CD 54.7.2). It was probably during this tour that Athens, which was in disfavour for having supported Antony, attempted to restore itself to favour by showering divine honours on Livia and Julia. While in the east Livia was also instrumental in collecting privileges for both communities and individuals; cities were named after her in Pontus and Judaea. A feature of her acquisition of divine honours was that, unlike previous recipients – Fulvia and Octavia – she was not restricted to honours in the Hellenistic world. In AD 3 a cult inscription in Africa was dedicated to Juno Livia, and another in the west to the goddess Livia.[79]

One of the most dramatic episodes in Livia's career, and one that graphically illustrates her resolution and strength of character, took place at the time of Augustus' death. In August 14, when Augustus lay dying at Nola, Livia despatched an urgent letter recalling Tiberius from Illyricum. She then proceeded to cordon off the house and the adjoining streets, and to issue favourable bulletins about Augustus. She continued these measures while the steps demanded by the situation were being taken. That done, one and the same edict announced that Augustus was dead and that Tiberius was in control (*TA* 1.5.5–6). Tacitus is corroborated by Dio (56.31.1), who states categorically that Livia took these steps in order to forestall a coup. Suetonius makes the concealment the work of Tiberius, who wanted to dispose of Agrippa Postumus first; but Suetonius adds that the letter in which Augustus allegedly ordered Agrippa's death might have been written by Livia in Augustus' name (*ST* 22). Velleius makes no mention of either Livia or concealment; instead this devoted Tiberian invents a touching scene in which Augustus dies peacefully in the arms of 'his beloved Tiberius' (*VP* 2.123). There have been sporadic attempts to reject Livia's role, but Tacitus and Dio are demonstrably accurate.[80] Livia had at last[81] assumed the dominant role to which she was so well suited by both birth and character. She would come close to institutionalizing that role in her son's reign.

CONCLUSION: LIVIA AND THE *RES PUBLICA*

The conclusion to this chapter is devoted to the elaboration of a point touched on earlier, namely Livia's use of language appropriate to the emperor's personal majesty when a 'subject' displeased her (see this chapter, p. 99). That incident dates to Tiberius' reign, but the question is whether it was simply the end result of a process that had begun under Augustus.

The question – or its equivalent – has been considered in two recent works, namely Sirago (1983: 59–61) and Purcell (1986). Sirago's thesis is that Livia modelled herself on Fulvia, and shared the latter's perception of feminine autonomy in confrontation with the decisions of men. This proposition leads Sirago to assign to Livia 'a juridico-political position which aimed at putting her on the same level as Augustus, it aimed at the legal and open recognition of prerogatives of absolute parity with him, at real power not as the emperor's wife but *per se*, at the assignment of a specific share in power by the emperor'. But this sweeping statement is not supported by any documentation. It also goes further than anything that could be postulated for Fulvia. Sirago has transposed the Tiberian Livia to Augustus' reign and has added a dash of Agrippina Minor for good measure.

Purcell bases himself on the *Consolatio ad Liviam*, a consolation to Livia on the death of her son Drusus which is thought to have been written by a Roman Eques after attending Drusus' funeral in 9 BC. The poem's reference to Livia as Romana Princeps[82] is said to elevate Livia to a position comparable to that of Augustus. The focal point of her 'principate' is the *ordo matronarum* of which she is the Patrona. She is also said to have possessed *auctoritas*. The idea is an interesting one, but the nature of the *ordo matronarum* is not clarified any more than we were able to do in our discussion of Hortensia (see Chapter 7, p. 81). Nor is it made clear why Livia's patronage of the *ordo* should have placed her on the same plane as the emperor. Hortensia's leadership of the same shadowy organization did not threaten the triumvirs, any more than Verginia's leadership of plebeian matrons had challenged the consuls (see Chapter 2, p. 15). As for *auctoritas*, it is no more than a word unless the suggestion is that it is here analogous to *auctoritas principis*. But if that is the suggestion it cannot be endorsed.

What Purcell has succeeded in doing is to cover, although not in so many words, a phenomenon to which we have already drawn attention, namely Livia's *de facto* status as *mater patriae*. Romana Princeps is simply another manifestation of the same thing. Other manifestations can be cited. For example, Ovid's desperate attempts to have his case put up to Livia are as fulsome a recognition of her influence as anything in the *Consolatio*.[83] But in essence all this is simply an intensification – admittedly by several degrees of magnification – of the influence of a Servilia or a Mucia. Even Praecia and Chelidon must have been thanked in extravagant terms by grateful clients. It might be thought that the one manifestation rising above the level of flattering language was Livia's elevation to the status of a cult figure, especially in the west. To the examples already noted we might add *Livia Augusti dea*; and the unfortunate Ovid wrote from exile predicting her eventual deification. But again this was more of an intensification than an innovation. It had happened to Fulvia and Octavia, and perhaps to Mucia before that (see Chapter 7, p. 78). The point need not be pressed; other honours and privileges showered on Livia lead to the same conclusion.[84]

At what point does a quantitative difference become a qualitative one? There is no easy answer, but that point was not reached in Augustus' reign. It was only after his death that Livia received any official title; and even then *mater patriae* was refused (see Chapter 10, p. 131). So was her consecration as an official god when she died; it was only authorized thirteen years later, when her grandson gave her what was no longer a very novel honour (see Chapter 12, p. 166). Even her decisive control of the situation at Nola took place after Augustus' death; she had not ventured during his lifetime to emulate the military or organizational skills of Fulvia.[85]

10

TIBERIUS, LIVIA AND
AGRIPPINA

INTRODUCTION

Tiberius' reign marks the start of a new phase. The change is
exemplified by two women, Livia and Agrippina. Livia, greatly
enhanced in status after Augustus' death, claimed from a reluctant
son, and to a large extent succeeded in obtaining, a share in the
business of government. She did so only in a *de facto* capacity,
though if she had had her way it would have been more than
that. Agrippina, a daughter of Julia and Agrippa, and wife of
Livia's grandson, Germanicus, headed a faction, the *Partes Agrippinae* (Agrippina's Party), whose purpose was presumably to
secure the throne for one of her sons, though it sometimes seems
that destabilizing the regime was the principal aim. Agrippina set
a new standard for women in public life. Left a widow early in the
piece, she stood up to Tiberius and his *Eminence Grise*, Sejanus, in
an unflinching confrontation, relying more on her own birth and
determination than on the support of any man – except one. She
was the antithesis of the ideal member of the Domus in nearly
every way, sharing the loyalty, courage and lack of domestic
serenity of Fulvia rather than the more deliberate virtues of Livia.
The only quality that she and her step-grandmother[1] had in
common was the rejection of sex as a political weapon; Agrippina
was as noted for her *pudicitia* as Livia was. But that did not
alleviate the state of hostility that dominated relations between
the two women, with some remissions, for a large part of the
reign.

130

JULIA AUGUSTA

Livia's status changed dramatically after Augustus' death. His will adopted her into the Julian family with the title of Augusta; her name thus became Julia Augusta. Henceforth she was Augustus' adopted daughter, and technically she was Tiberius' sister. Cumbersome, but there was no other way of bringing her into the *gens Julia*. The will also appointed her as heir to one-third of Augustus' estate, with the other two-thirds going to Tiberius. As the bequest exceeded what a woman could inherit under the *lex Voconia* (see Chapter 4, p. 34), the senate exempted her from the restriction. When Augustus was deified she became priestess of his cult, and was (probably) given a lictor (see Chapter 10, n. 6). To a senator who swore that he had seen Augustus going up to heaven Livia paid the going rate of a million sesterces.

It has been suggested that Livia was adopted in order to create a co-regency, but this deduction from what happened at the start of the new reign is not sound.[2] The adoption was an attempt to bridge the gap between the Julians and the Claudians – both Livia and Tiberius were now honorary Julians – and to make it possible for Livia to style herself *divi Augusti filia*, 'Daughter of the god Augustus'. But there was something anomalous in Julia's position. Like so many of Augustus' innovations, 'Augusta' was ambiguous. As 'Augustus' was a more specific designation of the ruling emperor than 'Caesar',[3] so it could be (and was) argued that 'Augusta' meant something more than a mere dowager; it designated an empress. Tiberius was well aware of the anomaly. He could not avoid an honour that had been decreed by Augustus, but wherever he could intervene he did. As already observed, he vetoed a proposal to make Livia *mater patriae*.[4] He also blocked a move to add *Iuliae filius*, 'Son of Julia', to his own nomenclature, thus rejecting a matronymic that had matriarchal implications.[5] Holding that only moderate honours should be paid to women, he forbade the erection of an altar to commemorate her adoption; and according to some sources he vetoed her entitlement to a lictor. He would also not allow her name to be given to the month of October.[6] Somebody was pressing very hard for the formal recognition of Livia as a constitutional entity. She may not have actually been Romana Princeps before, but there were those who felt she ought to be it now.[7]

The sources ascribe Tiberius' opposition to jealousy and

resentment. He considered, says Tacitus, that to elevate a woman would diminish his own status; Suetonius defines the diminution as a claim to an equal share of power.[8] But at the very start of his reign Tiberius had made it clear that he had been called to office by the *res publica*, not by Livia's intrigues or an old man's adoption, and in vetoing honours for Livia he was simply upholding the traditional republican ideology which he applied to himself as well.[9] Tiberius, lacking Julian panache (some would say Julian instability), did not want to set either his mother or himself too far above the state. But he did not take it upon himself to make all the decisions regarding Livia's honours. When Gytheion in the Peloponnese wanted to establish a cult of the deified Augustus, Tiberius and Livia, he rejected it on behalf of Augustus and himself, but left it to Livia to communicate her decision to them. He did the same when authorizing the cities of Asia to erect a temple to Tiberius, Livia and the senate, and again when refusing to allow Further Spain to build a temple to Livia and himself. And when Octavia's granddaughter, Appuleia Varilla, was charged with making insulting remarks about Augustus, Tiberius and Livia, Tiberius ruled on Augustus and himself, but consulted Livia on her position.[10]

Livia assiduously collected divine honours, and equally assiduously promoted the cult of Augustus in her capacity as its priestess.[11] She was the major contributor to developing the imperial cult which played such a key role in the propaganda, and in the satisfaction of the public's emotional needs, in the early Principate. To Tiberius, the man who told the senate that the only temple he wanted was in their hearts (*TA* 4.38.2), all this was anathema, and it remained so after her death. When Livia died in AD 29 the senate voted her deification, but Tiberius vetoed it, declaring that she had not wanted it.[12] There were seemingly no limits to Tiberius' determination not to allow Livia to become an institution. After her death priests introduced the practice of celebrating her birthday. When the celebration was held in AD 32, M. Cotta Messalinus got into trouble by describing the celebration as 'a funeral feast' (*novendialis cena*), by which he meant that as she had not been deified her birthday was no more important than the feast on the ninth day after a funeral. Cotta was charged with *maiestas*, or treason, by someone who realized that a successful prosecution would institutionalize Livia after all. But Tiberius ruled that 'words loosely spoken on a festive occasion should not be treated as criminal'.[13]

LIVIA AND THE SHARING OF POWER

Tiberius' ban on constitutional encroachment was merely the most visible sign of a deep-seated malaise in the relations between mother and son. The root cause was Livia's incessant demands for a share in power. The veto might have blocked the constitutional road, but if Livia could not become a co-ruler in law she was at least going to do so in fact. Her ambitions antedated Tiberius' reign. Discord surfaces as early as AD 6–8, when a rash of anonymous pamphlets attacking eminent persons reached such proportions that Augustus was obliged to punish such attacks as treason. The lampoons were, in Tacitus' opinion, aimed at Tiberius' cruelty, arrogance and poor relations with his mother. Suetonius has preserved a number of examples, in one of which both Tiberius and Livia are involved: 'You cruel monster! I'll be damned, I will, if even your own mother loves you still.' The cause of the bad feeling is not far to seek. Livia was constantly reminding Tiberius of how she had persuaded Augustus to make him the first successor instead of nominating Germanicus outright. For this, say the sources, she constantly demanded payment.[14] As Augustus gradually handed over the reigns of government to Tiberius, so Livia began claiming payment. But the man who had set his face against political power for women did not respond.

For Tiberius' reign the picture of discord is not an unequivocal one, largely because of conflicting presentations by Tacitus. But he does not directly address the problem until AD 22. There is, however, earlier evidence (in Tacitus) from which important conclusions can be drawn. The evidence relates to the processes of both the criminal and the civil courts, and goes back to the very start of the new reign. In AD 15 an attempt was made to determine the constitutional status of the deified Augustus. A certain Falanius was charged with enrolling a male prostitute as a celebrant in the cult of Augustus. But Tiberius vetoed the charge, pointing out that the suspect cultist was a mimist who had taken part in the festival staged by Livia in memory of Augustus (Bauman 1974a, 71–2). Livia was clearly implicated. She had, as priestess of the cult, put up an accuser (name unknown), to lodge charges in the hope of securing a juristic definition of the new god. But because of an unfortunate oversight a vulnerable example was chosen. Livia's attempt to augment her influence by augmenting the cult over which she presided, had failed.[15]

In AD 21 Livia was the instigator of a case that is well enough known, though her part in it has not been suspected before. A certain Clutorius Priscus, whose elegy on Germanicus (*ob.* AD 19) had won him a prize from Tiberius, composed a poem about Tiberius' son Drusus, during the latter's illness, hoping to win a prize with it when Drusus died. But Drusus recovered. Priscus was, however, unable to resist reading the poem at a gathering of matrons presided over by Vitellia. A professional informer got wind of it and decided to investigate. Vitellia denied having heard anything but the others were frightened into testifying. Priscus was charged with black magic; the poem was seen to have cast a spell or curse on Drusus. He was sentenced to death by the senate and was hurried off to execution; the senate wanted to get rid of the evil eye as soon as possible. Tiberius, who was away from Rome at the time, was most distressed when he heard of it. He had already marked Priscus out as a man of promise, but someone had taken advantage of his absence. He signalled his displeasure by introducing a rule which required an interval of ten days between verdicts of the senate and their implementation, to give the emperor time to veto a verdict if he so desired.[16]

Livia's connection with the case is to be inferred from the identity of the man who proposed the death penalty against Priscus, namely the consul designate, D. Haterius Agrippa. He was a friend of Livia's grandsons, Germanicus and Drusus (*TA* 2.51). Even more important, he was a son of Q. Haterius Agrippa, who owed his life to Livia. In AD 14, when Tiberius seemed reluctant to become emperor, Q. Haterius offended him by asking how long he proposed leaving the state without a head. Afterwards Haterius went to the palace to apologise. He grovelled at Tiberius' feet, causing him to stumble and fall to the ground. The guards nearly killed Haterius, and only Livia's urgent intervention saved him (*TA* 1.13.4–7). Two years later he partly repaid the debt by promoting one of Livia's favourite projects, restraints on extravagance, in the senate, much to Tiberius' annoyance (*TA* 2.33.1, 6). Q. Haterius' son repaid the rest of the debt in 21, when he responded to Livia's request for help against the man whose black magic had threatened her grandson. Livia's interest in the case was obviously known; the matrons who agreed to testify because they were terrified (*TA* 2.49.3) knew exactly what pressure was being applied to them. Livia had won this round; she had forced Tiberius to amend the law relating to the death sentence.

In the sphere of civil suits Livia was quite open about her participation. In 16 L. Piso brought suit against her friend Urgulania.[17] Urgulania, 'whose friendship with the Augusta had placed her above the law', refused to respond to the summons and drove to the palace. Piso tried to drag her from her refuge by force, as he was legally entitled to do, but Livia complained that she felt 'violated and diminished'. In other words, this was the occasion on which she used the language of imperial *maiestas* (see Chapter 9, p. 99). The early date of the occurrence is significant; she was challenging Tiberius' refusal to accord her constitutional recognition. The outcome of the case was that Tiberius was forced to support his mother to the extent of ageeing to appear at the praetor's tribunal as Urgulania's counsel. But Livia, having made her point, gave instructions for the disputed sum to be paid. Urgulania was Livia's special vehicle for the transmission of messages of this sort. On another occasion she was summoned to appear before the senate as a witness, but refused to attend. A praetor was sent to take her evidence at her house, a facility not available even to Vestals (*TA* 2.34.3–8). On still another occasion, in 24, when Plautius Silvanus was awaiting trial on a charge of throwing his wife out of a bedroom window, Urgulania, who was his grandmother, sent him a dagger; this was taken as an imperial hint (*TA* 4.22).

So much for the forensic side of Livia's drive for constitutional recognition. We turn now to Tacitus' specific notices of the antagonism. Under AD 22 he notes that Livia dedicated a statue to Augustus near the theatre of Marcellus, and placed her name before that of Tiberius on the inscription. According to Tacitus, Tiberius was gravely offended but did not say anything. But Dio, in a somewhat garbled version, says that Tiberius insisted on the dedication being authorized by the senate.[18] It might be argued that in making a dedication without authority Livia was simply following the (unsuccessful) precedent set by the Vestal Licinia in 123 BC (see Chapter 5, p. 52), but this is a case where a qualitative difference must be predicated. Livia was once more claiming a special relationship with Divus Augustus, and was publicly proclaiming her superiority to the reigning emperor in that regard.

The unauthorized dedication is, however, something of a

problem, for it was followed, in the same year, by an incident that testifies to good relations between mother and son at that time. Livia took suddenly ill, whereupon Tiberius returned urgently from Campania. The senate decreed that games were to be organized by the four major priesthoods and the Augustan Brotherhood. Tiberius did not interfere, except to veto the inclusion of the Fetiales amongst the organizers, quoting ample precedent for the inferior status of the Fetiales in the past; he would, he said, have not agreed to the Augustan Brotherhood if they had not had a special link with the Domus. Tacitus concludes that relations were either still cordial or were being presented as such behind a facade (*TA* 3.64.1, 3–5). But Tacitus might have gone a step further. Tiberius had acted with due filial piety, but there was a slight sting in the tail. Supplications for Livia's recovery were not to go beyond the regulation pattern. There was nothing special about her position.

There are also cases of co-operation without any hidden reservations. Thus in 17 Tiberius asked Livia to write to Archelaus of Cappadocia, a client who owed Tiberius a debt of gratitude for having once successfully defended him before Augustus. Archelaus had not remembered the debt when Tiberius was at Rhodes. Livia's letter held out hopes of indulgence to Archelaus if he came to Rome to beg for it. The letter brought Archelaus to Rome post-haste, but he was then put on trial before the senate and either died of aggravation or committed suicide (*TA* 2.42). Co-operation is also likely in the case of Vistilia who in 19 registered with the aediles as a prostitute. She was charged with adultery and banished. The senate then passed a decree banning prostitution by the daughters, wives and granddaughters of Roman knights (*TA* 2.85, *ST* 35.2). These measures will have enjoyed Livia's wholehearted support.

Despite one or two promising signs, however, the general trend was not favourable. Tacitus notes Livia's imperiousness as a possible reason for Tiberius' withdrawal to Campania in 26 (*en route* to Capri). Tiberius was, he says, in a dilemma: to share power with her was intolerable, but to dislodge her was impossible, for he owed his position to her (*TA* 4.57.4). Suetonius, in a useful overview, makes one of his favourite divisions into two stages. At first her claim to a share of power caused Tiberius to avoid frequent meetings, in order not to be seen to be guided by her advice, though from time to time he sought it. When she attended the scene of a fire near the temple of Vesta and urged the rescuers to greater efforts, he warned her not to meddle in affairs unbecoming to a woman. The second stage, of open enmity, was ushered in when she pressed Tiberius to make a new citizen a juror, to which he agreed on condition that the entry be marked, 'Forced on the emperor by his mother'. Livia lost her temper and produced some old letters of Augustus criticizing Tiberius' abrasive and stubborn character. Some of Suetonius' sources considered this the prime reason for the withdrawal. Suetonius goes on to note that after the withdrawal Tiberius saw her only once, for a few hours. When she fell ill shortly after that, he did not even visit her.[19] Dio also supplies an overview. Her station was so exalted that she held audiences to which senators and others were admitted, and had the details entered in the public records. For a time Tiberius' letters bore her name as well, and communications to them were addressed to both. Although never visiting the senate, the assembly or the camps, she endeavoured to manage affairs as if she were not merely co-ruler, but sole ruler. Eventually Tiberius removed her entirely from public affairs, but allowed her to direct domestic affairs (*ta oikoi*). But she gave so much trouble even in that capacity that he tended to avoid her, and it was mainly because of her that he withdrew to Capri.[20]

Tiberius' hostility after her death did not manifest itself only in the ban on deification. When she died the funeral was held over, pending word from Capri as to whether Tiberius proposed attending, but a letter from him advised that important business made it impossible for him to be present. At the modest funeral (in Augustus' mausoleum) the eulogy was delivered by her great-grandson, Caligula. Tiberius failed to carry out the provisions of her will; that, too, was discharged by Caligula, eight years later. And in his letter to the senate disallowing honours that it had voted, Tiberius attacked 'womanish friendships' (*amicitias muliebres*), which Tacitus understands as a veiled reference to C. Fufius Geminus, consul at the time of Livia's death and said to owe his advancement to the influence of Livia, to whom he had access through his wife, Mutilia Prisca. But Tiberius also disliked the witticisms that Geminus had uttered at his expense. The following year Geminus was charged with treason and committed suicide; his wife stabbed herself in the senate-house.[21]

Livia became something of a political football after her death. Apart from the attack on her friendships, there were the forces that tried to secure her indirect deification by celebrating her birthday (see this chapter, p. 132). The deification issue outlived Tiberius. On his accession her grandson, Claudius, had it officially proclaimed that she was a goddess of the state, although still not in a completely independent capacity; she shared a temple with Divus Augustus in the Palatium (CD 60.5.2; EJ 125). She had had to wait a long time even for that limited recognition. She should have been the first woman to receive the honour of deification, but Caligula, otherwise so dutiful to 'Ulysses in petticoats',[22] reserved that honour for his sister. Despite her honorary membership of the Julian family, Livia was a Claudian.

We shall meet Livia again, but the obituary written by Tacitus is a fitting conclusion to this section:

> (In AD 29) the aged Julia Augusta[23] died. Of the highest nobility through her own Claudian family and Livian and Julian adoptions, her first marriage was to Tiberius Claudius Nero. But Caesar (Octavian), captivated by her beauty, took her from her husband (with or without her consent) in a great hurry, and married her without even waiting for the birth of the child that she was expecting. She had no more children, but the marriage of Agrippina and Germanicus created a blood-tie with Augustus and gave them great-grandchildren in common. A traditionalist in domestic virtues, in courtesy she went beyond the approved standards of the women of old. A dominating mother and an accommodating wife, she was a match for both her devious husband and her insincere son.
>
> (*TA* 5.1.1–5)

DISCORD IN THE DOMUS: AGRIPPINA IN GERMANY AND THE EAST

In AD 5 Vipsania Agrippina, daughter of Julia and Agrippa, married Germanicus. He was the elder son of Livia's son Drusus, and of Antonia, a daughter of Octavia and Mark Antony. Germanicus' adoption by Tiberius in AD 4 had brought him into the two-tier succession system. Agrippina was Augustus' granddaughter by direct descent, as Germanicus was Livia's grandson. With two of Agrippina's brothers dead, her third brother on the verge of destruction, and her sister, the younger Julia, an exile (see Chapter

9, p. 120), Agrippina was effectively the only child of Julia and Agrippa to survive into Tiberius' reign.

When Germanicus' father died in 9 BC his mother, Antonia, went to live with Livia, taking with her Germanicus, his brother Claudius and their sister Livilla. Antonia was the ideal matron – chaste, strong minded, influential, devoted to her children and to the Domus. After Livia's death her house became a centre of social and political influence. She did posterity one disservice, however, for in collaboration with Livia she dissuaded Claudius from writing a history of the civil wars, as had been suggested to him by the historian Livy (SC 41.1–2). Augustus' wife and Antony's daughter were determined to keep that sensitive period under wraps.

During the fourteen years of their marriage Agrippina and Germanicus had nine children. We know of Nero Caesar, Drusus Caesar, Gaius (Caligula), Julia Agrippina, Julia Drusilla and Julia Livilla. Nero and Drusus perished in the internecine struggle that rocked the Domus for the greater part of Tiberius' reign. Caligula survived to become emperor. The younger Agrippina would dominate much of the reigns of Claudius and of her son Nero. Drusilla was deified after an ambiguous relationship with Caligula.

In a brief pen-portrait of Germanicus, Tacitus says that he was hated by Livia and Tiberius because his father had been suspected of wanting to restore the Republic (TA 1.33.1–4). Whether this is true, or is merely used by Tacitus to foreshadow Agrippina's populist ideology, is a moot point.[24] At all events, he is on stronger ground when he says that ill-feeling between Livia and Agrippina made things worse. Livia, he tells us, had a stepmother's (in reality a step-grandmother's) dislike of Agrippina, who was self-willed and excitable, though her chastity and love for her husband made those qualities a virtue (TA 1.33.5). Tacitus has set the scene for the coming drama, the first act of which was played out in Germany.

Agrippina was with Germanicus on the Rhine over 14–16, on that desultory mission so oddly reminiscent of the Duke of York and his ten thousand men. In 14, at a critical stage of the Rhine legions' mutiny, there were fears for the safety of Agrippina, then pregnant, and of the infant Caligula. Germanicus prevailed on her to seek safety among the Treveri. But the mutineers tried to prevent her departure, ashamed at the thought of her ancestry and feeling great affection for Caligula, who had got his nickname from his habit of toddling around the camp wearing the *caliga*, or common soldier's boot. The choice of footwear will, we may well think, have owed more to the populist sentiments of Agrippina than to the patrician severity of the Claudian Germanicus. At the men's insistence Germanicus agreed to bring Caligula back, but excused his wife because of her condition (*TA* 1.39–44; *SG* 9).

The following year saw Agrippina give the first demonstration of her indomitable spirit. A rumour having spread that Germanicus' army was cut off, there was panic, with some proposing the demolition of the Rhine bridge to stop the Germans. Agrippina stopped the rot. Assuming the role of a commander after the fashion of Fulvia, this 'big-hearted woman' (*femina ingens animi*) dispensed clothes and dressings to the needy and the wounded. Later she stood at the head of the bridge to thank the returning legions. Tiberius was, says Tacitus, highly suspicious of this cultivation of the army: what was left for generals to do, Tacitus has him asking, when a woman reviewed the troops, stood by the standards, offered largesse? She had more authority than the officers, she had suppressed a mutiny which letters from the emperor had been unable to do (*TA* 1.69). Tacitus' speculations about Tiberius' reaction need not be taken literally.[25] He is epitomizing the general reaction to what was, except for Fulvia,[26] an astonishing innovation. To apply populist doctrines to the army, in a way that not even Marius or Caesar had dreamed of, was bad enough. But when it was spearheaded by a woman it was more of a shock than if she had stood for the consulship.

Agrippina's example was to be followed by another matron during Germanicus' next mission. Unrest in the east prompted the despatch of Germanicus, late in 17, on a special mission which gave him authority over all governors in the region. Agrippina accompanied him, giving birth to her last child, Livilla, at Lesbos on the way (*TA* 2.54.1). Tiberius knew that her presence put the Syrian legions as much at risk as those of the Rhine had been, and in order to keep an eye on the pair he appointed Cn. Calpurnius Piso as governor of Syria. Piso's wife, Munatia Plancina, was a close friend of Livia; her father had proposed the name 'Augustus' for Octavian in 27 BC. Before leaving for the east, Plancina received advice from Livia. The Augusta was, says Tacitus, 'bent on persecuting Agrippina through feminine jealousy (*aemulatio muliebris*)', which was inspired by the fact that Germanicus had a more aristocratic lineage than Livia's grandson, Drusus (Tiberius' son); what made it even worse was the fact that Agrippina out-shone Drusus' wife, Livilla, both in lineage and in fecundity (*TA* 2.43.5–7). Again Tacitus is making a point with scissors-and-paste, but the point is well taken. He is crediting Agrippina, not for the last time, with superiority derived from the divine blood of Augustus. *Vis-à-vis* the Claudian Livia, it was once more a case of *spreverat ut inparem* (see Chapter 9, p. 112).

In Syria, Plancina and her husband began cultivating the legions. Plancina, 'unable to stay within the limits of feminine decorum',[27] attended cavalry parades and uttered insults against Agrippina and Germanicus. The troops believed that the sentiments had Tiberius' approval, and when to this was added financial inducements and relaxations of discipline, they began calling Piso 'Father of the Legions' (*TA* 2.55.4–5). The title was uncomfortably close to *pater patriae*, and was anathema to Tiberius (see Chapter 10, n. 9).

The situation between the two families grew steadily worse, but matters did not take a really ominous turn until 19, when Agrippina and Germanicus toured Egypt, disregarding Augustus' ban on visits by senators to that special imperial preserve (*TA* 2.59.33–4). A visit by Mark Antony's grandson was particularly disturbing, nor was the regime impressed by Germanicus' edict admonishing the Alexandrians for their godlike shouts about Agrippina and himself, shouts which he declared were 'only appropriate for Tiberius and Livia' (EJ 320b). Who had sown the idea of the shouts in the crowd's mind? Agrippina, ever conscious of the divine blood of Augustus, had welcomed divine honours for herself at Mitylene to mark Livilla's birth,[28] and she took the same line at Alexandria. But she had slightly miscalculated. The visit earned Germanicus his first open rebuke from Tiberius (*TA* 2.59.3; *ST* 52.2).

When Germanicus returned to duty he found that his orders regarding the army and cities of Syria had been countermanded. There was a violent quarrel, after which Germanicus fell ill. Convinced that Piso had had him poisoned, he wrote to Piso terminating his command. The dying prince begged Agrippina to put away her pride and not to provoke those stronger than herself (*TA* 2.72.1–2). Tacitus thinks he gave her secret instructions, but there was only one mastermind in that family. The funeral was unassuming. The new governor of Syria arrested Martina, a notorious poisoner and a friend of Plancina. Agrippina, impatient for revenge, took ship with Germanicus' ashes.

Agrippina was received by large crowds all the way from Brundisium to Rome. Drusus and Claudius met the cortege at Tarracina, but Livia, Antonia and Tiberius were not present. This, however, was not a deliberate slight; Tiberius provided two cohorts of praetorians to escort the cortège from Brundisium to Rome.[29] But Tiberius was worried. The rising tide of popular enthusiasm for Agrippina was disturbing. The people, resenting the absence of a state funeral, were calling her the glory of her country, the true descendant of Augustus, the acme of traditional morality; they prayed that her children might outlive their enemies (*TA* 3.4.3, 5.1). This was no 'rent-a-crowd' demonstration, and Tiberius knew it. He published an edict enjoining a return to normal life; 'rulers were mortal, the *res publica* was eternal' (*TA* 3.6). It was not the memory of Germanicus that caused disquiet. That was a convenient prop, but the real danger was Agrippina and her sons. They would rock the boat for the next ten years.

In AD 20 the senate tried Piso and Plancina for the death of Germanicus. After the second day's hearing Piso, finding that Plancina had distanced herself from him, withdrew his defence and killed himself. Assured by Livia that she would be pardoned, Plancina had abandoned her loudly proclaimed determination to share her husband's fate. Piso left a note begging Tiberius to spare his sons, but saying nothing about Plancina (*TA* 3.15.1–3, 16.5–7). Two days were then devoted to a sham trial of Plancina. Tiberius, greatly embarrassed, spoke for her,[30] but only to the extent of putting forward Livia's entreaties. No one in the senate supported him, but the consul Cotta Messalinus proposed that in deference to the Augusta's wishes Plancina be absolved. There was much private criticism of Livia's intervention on behalf of 'her grandson's murderer'. Thirteen years later, with Livia no longer there to protect her, Plancina paid the penalty. Charged with unidentified crimes, she died by her own hand.[31]

The case had a sequel in 21, when Aulus Caecina proposed in the senate that no provincial governor be allowed to take his wife with him. In an unmistakeable reference to Plancina, he launched a tirade against 'the female entourage that makes a Roman column look like a barbarian procession', accused governors' wives of practising extortion to the point where they virtually set up an alternative seat of provincial government, and ended with the gloomy observation that with salutary laws like the *lex Oppia* no longer holding them in check, women now ruled at home, in the courts, and even in the army. Caecina's tirade did not attract support, and the motion lapsed. But three years later a decree of the senate was carried, on the motion of Cotta Messalinus, laying down that governors were to be liable for their wives' crimes even if they themselves were innocent and quite unaware of what had been done.[32] So extreme an application of the principle of vicarious liability bears eloquent testimony to the bad impression that Plancina (and Livia) had created.

DISCORD IN THE STATE: AGRIPPINA, TIBERIUS AND SEJANUS

After Piso's trial matters improved in the Domus for a while. Agrippina's eldest son, Nero, was given accelerated entry into a magisterial career and married Julia, the daughter of Tiberius' son Drusus. The grant of tribunician power to Drusus in 22 filled the vacancy resulting from Germanicus' death and marked him out as the destined successor, but there was no immediate reaction from Agrippina; Tacitus does not mention her after the Germanicus affair until 23. Tiberius followed up the elevation of his son Drusus by giving her son Drusus the same career acceleration as had been given to Nero three years before. Moreover, it was during the three years' lull that Livia fell seriously ill; at least for the present 'feminine jealousy' ceased to dominate Domus politics. But in September 23 two things happened to change all this. Tiberius' son Drusus died; and Sejanus began the ascent that almost took him to the top.[33] These events were the great watershed, in Agrippina's political life as in Tiberius' reign as a whole. Agrippina's sons became the heirs apparent – at least in the eyes of the Julian members of the Domus. The pressures building up around that issue gave rise to the first specific political movement to be headed by a woman, and the Julian identity began crystallizing as something separate and distinct from the Claudian part of the Domus.[34] What had hitherto been largely kept within the domestic circle was now poised to erupt into the public sphere. The reaction of the regime would be to enlist the assistance of the public criminal law; disputes within the Domus would now begin to be submitted to the arbitration of the criminal courts.[35]

Tacitus was well aware of the significance of what had happened in 23. After noting Tiberius' eulogy for Drusus, he sums up the position as follows:

> Senate and people were secretly pleased at the revival of Germanicus' family, though its new popularity and Agrippina's inability to conceal her ambitions would ultimately prove fatal. For now that her sons were marked out for the succession, Sejanus decided to eliminate them. As poison was ruled out by their attendants' loyalty and Agrippina's unassailable chastity, he decided to rely on her stubborn refusal to conform (*contumacia*). Playing on Livia's animosity and Livilla's complicity in his recent crime,[36] he would get them to persuade Tiberius that pride of family and popular support were driving Agrippina to a bid for power (*dominatio*). Through Livia's friend, Mutilia Prisca, and her lover he would play on the Augusta's own thirst for power (*potentia*); and he would fan Agrippina's restlessness through her closest friends.
>
> (*TA* 4.12)

Tacitus introduces the next year, 24, with the news that the pontifical college had decided to include Nero and Drusus in the prayers for the emperor's safety. It was a special occasion, the completion of the first ten years of the reign, but Tiberius was annoyed at this coupling of Agrippina's sons with himself. He asked the Pontifices whether they had yielded to entreaties or threats by Agrippina. We note with some surprise that Tiberius, Pontifex Maximus since 15, learnt of the college's ruling only at second hand. However, the pontiffs accepted full responsibility, but received only a mild rebuke. According to Tacitus this was because many of them were Tiberius' relatives or eminent persons, but in fact the Julian connection was well represented; Agrippina's son Drusus and her close friend C. Asinius Gallus were Pontifices.[37] Tiberius complained to the senate about the unwisdom of heaping honours on young men too soon. Tacitus discloses what was behind the complaint:

> The complaint was prompted by Sejanus, who kept on claiming that the state was split in two, as if by civil war. There were those, he said, who called themselves members of 'Agrippina's Party' (*Partes Agrippinae*), and unless checked

their numbers would increase. The only cure for the deepen-
ing discord was to remove some of the leaders.

(*TA* 4.17.4)

Partes Agrippinae is the most explicitly political label attached to
any woman so far; it is matched only by what Tacitus will say
about her daughter, the younger Agrippina (see Chapter 13,
p. 195). The label has persuaded some writers that there was a
conspiracy headed by Agrippina which aimed at forcibly replacing
Tiberius by her son Nero. The conspiracy theory depends, apart
from a supposed prelude,[38] on the trials that followed Sejanus'
urgent call. Those trials began in 24 and continued until 29, when
Agrippina and Nero were themselves brought down. Our investigation will determine our attitude to the conspiracy theory. It will
also help us to explain what Tacitus means by *Partes Agrippinae*.

THE TRIALS OF AD 24–9

Tacitus cites the attacks on C. Silius and Titius Sabinus as the
main instances of Sejanus' policy of eliminating the leaders of
Partes Agrippinae. Both owed their downfall to their friendship
with Germanicus, but Silius was the more important. He had been
legate of Upper Germany[39] during AD 14–21 and had suppressed
Sacrovir's rebellion in 21, for which he had been awarded triumphal emblems. Therefore Sejanus decided to begin with him,
leaving Sabinus for later. Silius' wife, Sosia Galla, was charged as
his accomplice; Tiberius disliked her because she was Agrippina's
friend (*TA* 4.18.1, 19.1). We may safely suppose that the friendship
went back to their time together on the Rhine, when Agrippina
had been sent for safety to Colonia Augusta Treverorum, which
was the main centre in Silius' province (*TA* 1.41.2).

The consul Visellius Varro was allowed to be an accuser at
Silius' trial, in spite of the rule forbidding a magistrate in office
from filling such a role. Varro's father had been legate of Lower
Germany in 21 and had fallen out with Silius over the conduct
of the campaign against the Gallic insurgent, Sacrovir.[40] Varro had
undoubtedly been briefed by his father in regard to Silius' dealings
with Sacrovir. Information about that tenebrous episode was of
paramount importance to the case, because despite Tacitus'
attempt to conceal the fact, the gravamen of the charges was that
Silius had connived with Sacrovir and had delayed taking steps to

suppress the revolt.[41] The outcome of the case was that Silius died by his own hand before the verdict. Sosia's trial proceeded, and the senate sentenced her to exile. But a concession was made in regard to her property. Instead of the usual total confiscation, Agrippina's friend, Asinius Gallus, proposed that half be allowed to her children. M. Lepidus improved on this by proposing the release of three-quarters to the children.[42]

There is an obvious question: was Agrippina implicated in what Silius and Sosia had done? The answer is conjectural but persuasive. Both Julius Sacrovir, leader of the Aeduan section of the revolt, and Julius Florus, leader of the Treveran section, owed their Roman citizenship and their family name to Julius Caesar.[43] As the revolt started only after Germanicus' death (*TA* 3.40.5), was Agrippina able to claim the allegiance of Caesar's Gallic *clientela*, the vast network of dependants that he had built up during his years in Gaul? The idea is possible both in principle and in detail. The example of Junia Silana, who put up two of her clients to accuse the younger Agrippina (*TA* 13.19.3), disposes of any difficulty in designating a woman as *patrona* of a *clientela*. And Agrippina, the true heir to the Julian name, in fact had a patron-client relationship with the other leader of *Partes Agrippinae* whom Sejanus wanted to destroy, Titius Sabinus.[44] There is thus room for the suggestion that Agrippina communicated with her friends Silius and Sosia, still on the Rhine, with a view to instigating a revolt which would destabilize Tiberius' regime but, thanks to *clientela*, would not threaten the basic link with Rome. The whole situation in the region favoured such an enterprise. Agrippina had not forgotten the legions' offer to put Germanicus on the throne. She also remembered her own special relationship with the soldiers because of her name and lineage, of which the Rhine bridge and her selection of the infant Caligula's footwear were merely two manifestations.[45] There is a curious statement in Tacitus: as no official statement about the revolt was released in Rome, rumour ran riot, and although all good citizens deplored the country's difficulties, many disliked the regime so much that they welcomed the prospect of change even if it meant danger to themselves (*TA* 3.44.1–2). The meaning is that Tiberius knew perfectly well that a member of the Domus was implicated, but that fact had to be kept under wraps. Hence Tacitus' statement that Tiberius released no information until the revolt was over, informing the senate simultaneously of the outbreak of the war and its conclusion (*TA* 3.47.1–2).

Tacitus reports eight cases under AD 24, but only that of Silius and Sosia is specifically linked to the attack on *Partes Agrippinae*. There are, however, two other cases that may have formed part of the attack. In 24 Vibius Serenus was accused by his son of having, while governing Baetica in Spain the year before, sent subversive agents to the Gallic rebellion. He was found guilty. Caecilius Cornutus, who had funded Serenus' Gallic venture, committed suicide before he could be brought to trial. Also in 24, P. Suillius Rufus was convicted of judicial corruption and exiled, after Tiberius had opposed a lighter sentence. He had been Germanicus' quaestor in Germany.[46]

In 25 Sejanus wrote to Tiberius for permission to marry Livilla, the sister of Germanicus and widow of Tiberius' son Drusus. Sejanus declared that his sole aim was to protect the Domus against Agrippina's malice. But Tiberius replied that the marriage would split the Domus in two, destabilized by feminine rivalry as it already was.[47] In this regard Tacitus notes that Livilla was pressing Sejanus to honour his promise of marriage. This is a reference to a widespread tradition, according to which Sejanus had decided to get rid of Drusus. He chose as his ally Livilla, whom he seduced, beguiled with promises of marriage and power, and drew into a plot against Drusus. To lend credence to his promises Sejanus divorced his wife, Apicata. Eight years later, after the fall of Sejanus, Apicata revealed the truth in a letter to Tiberius.[48] The story has come under intensive scrutiny, but when all the improbabilities have been sifted out a substratum of truth remains.[49] From our point of view one of the significant features of the episode is that Sejanus, no friend of the Julians whatever he was to Tiberius, allied himself to a Claudian woman.

In 26 Sejanus, baulked of a dynastic solution to the problem of Agrippina, returned to the courts. His first target was Claudia Pulchra, a granddaughter of Octavia, second cousin to Agrippina, and widow of P. Quinctilius Varus who had lost an army in Germany in AD 9. That she was a descendant of Ap. Claudius, one of the elder Julia's lovers, is possible but cannot be proved. Her case was seen as the first in a series of events destined to lead to Agrippina's downfall (*TA* 4.52.1; *ST* 53.1). Claudia's accuser was Cn. Domitius Afer, soon to become the greatest orator of the age, and the charges were *stuprum* with a certain

Furnius, dabbling in magic, and attempting to poison Tiberius. Before the case was tried there was a confrontation between Agrippina and Tiberius. Agrippina, 'forthright as ever', was incensed at the impeachment of her relative and went straight to Tiberius, bursting in on him while he was sacrificing to the deified Augustus. Agrippina addressed a strongly worded reproach to Tiberius (*TA* 4.52.3–5), forcibly making the point about the superiority of the divine blood of Augustus to which we have already referred (see Chapter 9, p. 112), and claiming that Claudia was only a pretext; like Sosia, Claudia had been singled out because she was Agrippina's friend. Stung by her words, Tiberius caught hold of her and quoted a Greek line: 'My girl, do you think you are badly done by if you do not rule?' (*ST* 53.1; *TA* 4.52.6).

Pulchra's sentence is not recorded, but it was probably banishment. Some devious undertaking was afoot in the counsels of *Partes Agrippinae*. This is suggested by what happened in 27, when Pulchra's son, Quintilius Varus, was prosecuted by the same Domitius Afer. The charge is not known, but the co-accuser was P. Cornelius Dolabella, who was related to the defendant. The latter in turn was betrothed to one of Agrippina's daughters. But where *Partes Agrippinae* had been taken unawares in 26, this time they were ready. With Tiberius absent, the senate blocked the charge by resolving that nothing be done until the emperor returned (*TA* 4.66). As Tiberius had by this time left Rome for good, nothing more was heard of the case. That in itself is significant, for it guarantees that no 'conspiracy' was involved. But just what it was that *Partes Agrippinae* was doing it is not possible to say.

In 26, shortly after Pulchra's trial, Agrippina fell ill. When Tiberius visited her she wept quietly for some time, and begged him to help her in her loneliness by giving her a husband. She was, she said, still young enough (about 40), marriage was the only proper consolation for the virtuous, and there were men who would welcome Germanicus' wife and children. Tiberius caught her drift, but did not want to show either anger or fear, and did not commit himself. Tacitus here specifically names his source, the memoirs of the younger Agrippina, daughter of this Agrippina; Tacitus notes that the incident is not recorded by any other historian (*TA* 4.53). We might have guessed the source even without the acknowledgement, for the incident is handled quite differently from Tacitus' usual portrayal of Agrippina. Although generally sympathetic to her cause, he does not hesitate to emphasize her *atrocitas*, her 'toughness', as well as her excitability, and only here does he introduce a more personal note.[50] It is likely, however, that the memoirs did not hide the stronger side of her character; the outburst in regard to Claudia Pulchra comes immediately before the marriage request in Tacitus, and may well go back to the same source.[51]

It has been surmised that the specific husband whom Agrippina had in mind was C. Asinius Gallus,[52] and his qualifications for the post are certainly impressive. He had been mentioned by Augustus as a possible, though unsuitable, candidate for the throne; he had married Tiberius' divorced wife (and Agrippina's half-sister), Vipsania, and had added fuel to the flames by behaving provocatively towards Tiberius. Since Vipsania's death in 20 he had been available for remarriage. In 30, a few months after Agrippina's own trial, he was condemned by the senate and held under house arrest until he starved himself to death in 33. In the latter year, after Agrippina's death, Tiberius burst into a tirade, accusing her of adultery with Gallus and saying that after the latter's death she had lost the will to live.[53] We also recall that Gallus proposed a lighter sentence for Sosia Galla.[54] All in all, this mischievous destabilizer had enough links with Agrippina for us to see him not only as a possible husband, but also as the possible architect of some of the ideas of *Partes Agrippinae*.

The abortive marriage request was followed by the incident of the apple. Agrippina, having been warned by Sejanus about a plot to poison her, when invited to dine with the emperor sat silent, leaving her food untouched, and even refusing an apple selected for her by Tiberius. He remarked to Livia that it would not be surprising if he reacted harshly against someone who thought he was trying to poison her (*TA* 4.54; *ST* 53.1). Soon afterwards Tiberius withdrew to Capri,[55] leaving Sejanus a free hand. Sejanus began undermining Nero Caesar, playing on Drusus' jealousy of the elder brother, who was Agrippina's favourite. There is also talk of Nero's wife, Julia, acting as a 'mole' on behalf of Livilla and Sejanus (*TA* 4.59–60). But none of this is much more than background noise. The next major development was the case of Titius Sabinus, one of Tacitus' focal points for the attack on *Partes Agrippinae*. The case came to a head on 1 January 28, after a period of lengthy preparation. Tacitus presents the case as pure black comedy. Sejanus commissions L. Latiaris and three other ex-praetors to build up a case against Sabinus. Latiaris wins Sabinus' confidence, casts aspersions on Tiberius and Sejanus, while praising Germanicus and Agrippina, and persuades Sabinus to do the same. The next step involves what can only be described as the ancient precursor of 'bugging'. The other three agents conceal themselves in the roof of Latiaris' house, while Latiaris engages Sabinus in further treasonable conversation. The listeners in the roof write down everything that is said. The record was handed over to Tiberius, who wrote to the senate accusing Sabinus of tampering with his freedmen and plotting against him. On 1 January 28 Sabinus was condemned by the senate and led away to summary execution, crying out that 'This is a fine way to welcome the New Year!'[56]

What do we know of Titius Sabinus apart from the trial? Tacitus describes him as a distinguished Roman knight (*inlustris eques Romanus*) who looked after Germanicus' wife and children, visiting them at home and escorting them in public, the sole survivor of a great crowd of dependants (*clientes*). He was respected by decent people (*boni*) but resented by the small minded (*TA* 4.68.1). Originally, then, Sabinus was a client of Germanicus; Tacitus says that friendship with Germanicus was responsible for his being dragged off to prison. After Germanicus' death the *clientela* passed to Agrippina; as we have shown, there was nothing to prevent her as a woman from being a *patrona*. But when Sejanus launched his attack on the movement in 24, he clearly did not have an indictable case against Sabinus. Whether this means that Sabinus had no part in the Sacrovir scandal, which essentially concerned provincial governors, it is not possible to say. Perhaps he worked behind the scenes but could not be incriminated, though Serenus' financier, Cornutus, suggests otherwise. At all events, it was only by arranging a trap that a case was able to be made against him. It was time for Sejanus to come to grips with his real objective, Agrippina and her sons; Sabinus was simply eliminated in order to deprive her of her surest prop.

Our material for the trials of Agrippina and Nero poses something of a problem. The greater part of book 5 of *Annales*, in which Tacitus described the climax of the long struggle, is lost. Some material on preliminary matters has survived, together with information in other sources, but great care has to be taken with the chronology. One is always reluctant to claim better knowledge of the minutes of the Roman senate than Tacitus, but he has displaced some key items, and in order to obtain a coherent picture some relocation is necessary.[57] The most likely scenario opens in AD 27. In that year there were criminal proceedings against Agrippina and Nero, though the main trial would not be held until 29. In 27, then, Tiberius wrote to the senate accusing Nero of homosexuality and Agrippina of disobedience and insubordination. There was, Tacitus specially notes, no mention of rebellion. But Cotta Messalinus, that indefatigable friend of the regime, proposed a capital penalty. Others felt, however, that Tiberius' intentions were not clear, and Iunius Rusticus, chosen by Tiberius to keep the minutes of the senate, warned against precipitate action. It was therefore decided to treat Tiberius' accusations as sub-capital, thus supporting a penalty of relegation, of banishment to some area in Italy rather than the full-blown deportation to a remote island that was imposed for capital crimes.[58] Agrippina was sentenced to confinement in a villa at Herculaneum; Nero's place of internment is not known.[59] Sejanus then proceeded to mount a campaign of destabilization against them. Soldiers were posted to shadow them, and to report 'with the precision of an annalist' on their correspondence and visitors. *Agents provocateurs* were sent to urge them to escape and to make their way to the German armies (still loyally disloyal a decade after the Rhine bridge), or to embrace the statue of Divus Augustus in the forum while calling on the people and senate for aid.[60] They did not respond to these suggestions, but the evidence was used at the main trial in 29 as if they had.[61] The same technique of self-incrimination as was used against Sabinus was being applied.

It was while Agrippina was interned at Herculaneum that the destruction of Sabinus was brought to fruition.[62] Tiberius wrote to thank the senate for punishing that enemy of the state at a time when other enemies were threatening his life; the letter did not name names, but everyone knew that Agrippina and Nero were meant (*TA* 4.70.7). The stage was being set for the final act; instead of sub-capital charges there were now hints of capital crimes. But nothing could be done until Livia's death; while she was alive neither Tiberius nor Sejanus dared challenge her authority.[63] But when she died in 29 a letter came from Tiberius, denouncing Agrippina and Nero, this time by name. It was so soon after Livia's death that it was suspected that it had been delivered to the consuls earlier but had been held back on the instructions of Livia; one of the consuls was Fufius Geminus, whom we recall as a protégé of Livia's.[64] The senate met to consider the letter in an atmosphere of extreme tension, indeed of near anarchy. A violent demonstration was being staged outside the senate-house. The demonstrators carried images of Agrippina and Nero and, while expressing their loyalty to Tiberius, shouted that the letter purporting to have come from Tiberius was a forgery, for the emperor could not possibly favour the destruction of his Domus. The senate adjourned without taking a decision. Thereupon forged pamphlets, purportedly written by ex-consuls and attacking Sejanus, began circulating. Sejanus was enraged and used this to frame fresh charges on the basis of the amendment of the treason laws introduced by Augustus in AD 8.[65] Sejanus declared that the senate had spurned the emperor's anger; the people had defected; seditious speeches and fictitious decrees of the senate were being circulated; and all that remained was for the people to take up arms under the leadership of those whose images they had brandished like banners. Tiberius issued an edict reprimanding the populace. He also reproached the senate for not acting on his letter, pointing out that the delay had increased the unrest and had exposed imperial majesty to ridicule. He directed that the whole case be reserved for his decision (*TA* 5.4.5, 5.5.1).

This is as far as the sources take us. The actual trial is not described anywhere. We know that a certain Avillius Flaccus was Agrippina's accuser; his completion of a difficult task earned him the prefecture of Egypt in 32.[66] We also know that Nero was tried, declared a public enemy, and exiled to the island of Pontia, where he was driven to suicide in 31.[67] It can be safely supposed that his trial, and that of Agrippina, were held before the senate in Rome; though Tiberius did conduct some trials on Capri, these particular defendants were far too dangerous to risk transporting.[68]

One question remains. Have we at last got the full-scale conspiracy to kill the emperor and seize the throne that we have been resisting ever since 2 BC? Tacitus did not think so. He has the demonstrators raise a cheer for Tiberius while parading the images of Agrippina and Nero (*TA* 5.4.3). But the punishment inflicted on Agrippina makes it clear that the regime took an extremely serious view of the whole affair. She was exiled to Pandateria, where her continuous vilifications of Tiberius earned her a beating from a centurion in which she reportedly lost an eye. There is also talk of her being force-fed and ultimately starving herself to death. Her ashes were left on Pandateria. She died on 18 October

33, two years to the day after the fall of Sejanus. The death of her persecutor had kindled hopes of a relaxation, but when this proved illusory she lost all hope. It was then that Tiberius accused her of adultery with the recently deceased Asinius Gallus, claiming that after his death she had not wanted to live. But Tacitus denies that she was capable of such feminine frailty, and says that she was preoccupied with masculine pursuits – the androgyne syndrome again. Tiberius claimed credit for not having had her strangled or cast out on the Gemonian Steps, as had happened to Sejanus. The senate voted thanks for this act of clemency, added Agrippina's birthday to the days of ill-omen, and voted an annual sacrifice to Jupiter on the anniversary of her death.[69] She was not declared a *hostis*, or enemy of the state, as Nero had been, but that does not prove any less serious perception of her role. It was simply that such a declaration was not competent against a woman. As Tacitus says, a woman could not be charged with aiming at supreme power – *occupandae rei rublicae* (*TA* 6.10.1). So they did the next best thing.[70]

Our conclusion must be that *Partes Agrippinae* was in a state of sedition in the concluding stages of the drama. But that still leaves a question. Against whom was the sedition directed? The whole tenor of Tacitus' account supplies the answer. The purpose was not to get rid of Tiberius, but of Sejanus. In AD 8 Augustus had made anonymous pamphlets a form of treason not only if directed against the emperor himself, but also if aimed at eminent persons (*inlustres*).[71] That is precisely what spurred Sejanus on in the final stages; he, not Tiberius, was the object of the attacks. It was still sedition, because Augustus had so decreed, but the purpose was not usurpation.[72]

The banishment of Agrippina and Nero signalled the virtual end of *Partes Agrippinae*. Her younger son, Drusus, was imprisoned and was eventually charged and declared a *hostis*, finally dying of starvation in 33, shortly before Agrippina.[73] There were reports that when Tiberius was planning the destruction of Sejanus in 31 he ordered Macro, in the event of Sejanus trying to resist by force of arms, to release Drusus from custody and to present him to the people as their leader.[74] Whether Tiberius would have contemplated a coalition with *Partes Agrippinae* after expending so much energy on destroying it is a very moot point.[75] It looks more like Julian propaganda.

CONCLUSION: THE NATURE OF *PARTES AGRIPPINAE*

What exactly does Tacitus mean by *Partes Agrippinae*? Does it imply, if not a political party in the modern sense, at least a *factio* with a degree of cohesion and continuity, ascertainable objectives and a recognized leader? The only scholar to have given this matter much thought is Marsh (1926, 1931). He traces three groups in Tiberius' reign – the party of Germanicus and Agrippina, the party of Drusus, and the party of Sejanus. Allen (1941) has disproved the party of Sejanus, and has also refuted Marsh's belief that the Germanicus and Drusus groups were the successors of the republican Populares and Optimates. But Allen is less successful with his contention that there were no parties at all in Tiberius' time, that 'the best that Tacitus can discover are court intrigues' (1941: 4–5). If the groups did not go back to republican precedents, then divisions in the Principate had to be of a different order, they essentially had to be 'court intrigues', because that is where the new centre of gravity was.

What needs to be emphasized is that it is only with specific reference to Agrippina that Tacitus uses a collective noun, *partes*. For Germanicus he says only that the court (*aula*) was split by unspoken partisanships (*tacita studia*) for Drusus and Germanicus; Tiberius favoured Drusus, but Germanicus benefited by Tiberius' hostility, as well as by his own lineage and that of Agrippina, who outshone Drusus' wife Livilla both in lineage and in the number of her children (*TA* 2.43.5–7). But, adds Tacitus, Germanicus and Drusus were good friends, undisturbed by the rivalries of their partisans. *Tacita studia* is not of the same order as *Partes Agrippinae*. In the case of the latter Tacitus' full reference is to 'those who call themselves members of the Party of Agrippina' (*TA* 4.17.4). The sponsors of *tacita studia* did not call themselves anything.

Marsh sets great store by a statistical analysis of consuls from AD 4 to 37. He finds that Tiberius and Drusus favoured the older families, while the Germanicus-Agrippina group drew its support from lesser nobles and new men. But in fact Marsh's figures tell quite a different story. The only period in which lesser men do significantly better than the old nobility is from 16 to 19, when Germanicus-Agrippina consuls outnumber those of Tiberius-Drusus by ten to seven. During 20 to 27, the very heyday of

Agrippina's faction, there are sixteen old nobility and only four lesser men. These are the crucial periods, for after 27 the Agrippina faction was virtually defunct. The correct conclusion therefore is that lesser men only predominated when Germanicus himself was in the saddle and had consular nominations in his gift. When he was no longer there the ratio of lesser men to old nobles suffered a drastic decline. In other words, consulships were not in Agrippina's gift and her party was *not* a mere continuation of the Germanicus faction. That faction ceased to exist when Germanicus died, and for the next four years there was a recess while efforts were made to reconcile the warring sections of the Domus. But in 24 hostilities were resumed; the initiative came from the Agrippina side, when Tiberius was somehow bypassed as Pontifex Maximus and Nero and Drusus were included in the prayers. It was then that the old Germanicus faction was revived, but in a more specific form: it was given a definitive identity and was called *Partes Agrippinae*.

Why did Agrippina authorize the act of defiance of 24? Speculation yields little profit. If, as Tacitus says, Drusus' death had placed her sons in the direct line of succession (*TA* 4.12.3), why did she rock the boat? Meise thinks she was afraid that Tiberius was not genuine about making her sons his successors and wanted to supplant them by his grandson, Tiberius Gemellus (1969: 72–3). But this leads nowhere. What happened to Gemellus after the destruction of *Partes Agrippinae*? A better solution is that Drusus' death indeed removed the last defence against outright hostility. Drusus had continued the policy of preserving outward harmony that he had maintained with his cousin Germanicus. He had toned down the rivalry between Livilla and Agrippina, and had perhaps even persuaded his grandmother to moderate her dislike of Agrippina. But with his death the moderating influence disappeared and *tacita studia* erupted into open warfare. Sejanus did not create the new situation; he simply capitalized on the opening that rivalries within the Domus gave him. And it was in the new atmosphere of unrestrained ambition and hostility that various interest groups coalesced under the Julian banner, and *Partes Agrippinae* was born.

Do the occurrences of *partes* elsewhere in Tacitus shed any light on our problem? *Partes* in the sense of a political faction occurs mainly in *Historiae*, but there are fifteen occurrences in *Annales* (*Lex. Tac.* s.v.). Seven of these are not linked to the name of any leader. Of the other eight, two have the leader's name in adjectival form, both referring to the Republic: *Partes Pompeianae, Iulianae* (*TA* 1.10, 2). Six have the leader's name in the genitive. Two of these are republican or triumviral (Caesar and Antony), and one refers to the Germans (*TA* 4.44, 3.62, 1.60). This leaves a mere three references for the early Principate, and here an extraordinary fact appears: one of the three is *Partes Agrippinae*, and the other two refer to that Agrippina's daughter, the younger Agrippina. The key passage is *TA* 13.18.3–5: After the murder of Britannicus, Agrippina had secret talks with his sister, Octavia, and raised funds from all quarters; she was affable to tribunes and centurions, and honoured such nobles as were still left, as if she were seeking a leader and a party – *quasi quaereret ducem et partis*. The previous year she had had Pallas on her side (*in partibus*) against Burrus and Seneca (13.2.3).

Tacitus' concentration on the two Agrippinae is no accident. He uses the word for the mother because it denotes something special, an organized movement against the emperor; and he uses it for the daughter for exactly the same reason. The techniques of the two women were very similar. Both cultivated the military, both had links with the nobility, and both made a special point of fund raising.[76] But there may be one difference. The daughter was looking for a leader for her group; she did not plan to be its titular head herself. Does the same apply to the mother? On the one hand we might say that when she sought permission to marry in 26, she was looking for a *dux* and hoped to find him in Asinius Gallus. But her *Partes* was already in place. Then what about her son Nero? Born in AD 6, presented to the senate in 23, included in the prayers the following year, by 26 he was the object of Sejanus' special venom; Tacitus has his freedmen and clients exhort him to show decisiveness, to give the people and armies what they wanted (*TA* 4.59.5). The exhortation suggests that Nero was not up to the task. We are therefore inclined to think that Agrippina's name was given to the group not only for its propaganda value, but also because she was the driving force. Tacitus is saying something important when he stresses her *atrocitas*, her greed for power, her unfeminine preoccupation with masculine concerns (6.25.3). The elder Agrippina's mother had headed a *grex*. She did not adopt her mother's methods, but she did inherit the idea of a woman heading a political group. If any Roman woman was a politician in her own right, it was the elder Agrippina.

11

CALIGULA'S SISTERS

INTRODUCTION: THE LATER JULIO-CLAUDIANS

Women members of the Domus are as prominent now as they were before, but there is a difference. The Principate is an established fact, destined to outlast the strenuous attempts of two Julian rulers to destroy it. Because it is established, there is no longer the same sense of urgency about consolidating it. The empire will survive without the consummate duplicity of Augustus or the solid competence of Tiberius; it will survive without the sanity and balance of Livia and Octavia. Palace circles can now afford the luxury of offbeat experimentation. Each of the three reigns exhibits innovations. Caligula will put his ideas about his sisters into practice – in a distinctly un-Roman fashion – but the phenomenon will die with him. Claudius will be remembered as a mere tool in the hands of his womenfolk and his freedmen. And while Nero's domination by his mother has a precedent, killing her is new.

CALIGULA AND HIS FAMILY

When Caligula became emperor early in 37 he made the affairs of his family his prime concern. It was partly familial piety, but he was also building up the image of his Domus, not only as propaganda but also for constitutional purposes. His grandmother Antonia, with whom he had lived after Livia's death before being taken into protective custody on Capri, was granted all the honours once enjoyed by Livia – the privileges of a Vestal, priestess of Augustus, and the title Augusta. She may have declined this last, but in any case she did not enjoy her honours for long, for

157

she died on 1 May 37, less than seven weeks after the death of Tiberius. Caligula gave special attention to the memory of his mother. He journeyed to Pandateria and Pontia to retrieve her ashes and those of his brother Nero, and installed them with all the pomp of a triumph in the mausoleum of Augustus. As the remains of his other brother, Drusus, were irrecoverable he erected a cenotaph. The declaration of Agrippina's birthday as a day of ill omen was annulled, and sacrifices were offered on her birthday. Games were instituted in her honour, and a carriage bore her image in procession. The villa at Herculaneum where she had been incarcerated was destroyed. The month of September was renamed Germanicus, thus including it in a dynastic trio with July and August, named after Caesar and Augustus. Caligula's uncle, Claudius, was made consul; and Tiberius' grandson, Gemellus, was adopted by Caligula and made Prince of the Youth, though this was only a prelude to the unfortunate youth's death. The legacies under the will of Livia (his 'Ulysses in petticoats'), which Tiberius had left unpaid, were now paid. The memory of Agrippina continued to be his special concern. On his accession he declared that he had burnt the records of the court cases against his mother and brothers, but later on he revived the treason law and took his revenge on the enemies of his House.[1]

Some of the familial acts attributed to Caligula are clearly the work of a biased tradition.[2] For example, we are told that when Antonia sought a private interview he refused to allow it unless the praetorian prefect, Macro, was present (*SG* 23.2). The truth of the matter is that Antonia had been responsible for alerting Tiberius to Sejanus' plot, and she had a common interest with Macro, who engineered Sejanus' fall and opened Caligula's path to the throne. Antonia saw Caligula on Capri at least once, when in the presence of Macro she persuaded Tiberius to interrogate Herod Agrippa's accuser, Eutychus. Then, in 37, when Caligula arrived in Rome with Tiberius' body, he wanted to release his friend Herod Agrippa immediately, but Antonia restrained him, arguing that a speedy release would give the impression that he welcomed Tiberius' death. This is the interview that Suetonius has distorted. Macro was indeed present, as he had every right to be as the magistrate in charge of Herod's case, and there is no difficulty about fitting the interview into the remaining weeks of Antonia's life; Herod's fate was one of Caligula's top priorities.[3]

The example of Antonia and Macro cautions us to treat Caligula's statements on their merits.[4] When we read of his boast that his mother had been born of incest between Augustus and Julia (*SG* 23.1), we must ask whether there may have been some method in his madness, in the sense that he was building up the image of the Domus, of the divine blood of Augustus. Similarly with his letter to the senate claiming that Livia's maternal grandfather had been a mere decurion, which Suetonius indignantly refutes by citing the public records which showed that he had held Roman magistracies (*SG* 23.2). The truth could be that he occupied the two statuses in succession, but Caligula chose only to emphasize the first. Livia was, after all, only a notional Julian. So was Germanicus. Hence perhaps the lesser prominence accorded to him than to Agrippina in Caligula's arrangements. But in the last resort the touchstone of Caligula's perception of 'the Divine Domus' is his relations with his sisters.

THE THREE SISTERS

It became clear at the start of the reign that Caligula's sisters, Julia Agrippina, Julia Drusilla and Julia Livilla, were to occupy a special position in the Domus, they were to be privileged amongst the privileged. All three received Vestal privileges (*PIR* 319) and seats in the imperial enclosure at the games, but that was only the icing on the cake. The most important part was their acquisition of constitutional status. First, they were included in the annual vows for the emperor's safety.[5] This was the issue on which *Partes Agrippinae* had declared war on Tiberius in 24. The history of that issue over the rest of Tiberius' reign is of interest. In 29 Sejanus, who had made the inclusion of Nero and Drusus in the vows for Tiberius a *casus belli*, was himself included in such vows (Hennig 1975: 124–33). In 31, after his fall, the senate forbade the taking of oaths in the name of anyone except the emperor (CD 58.12.6). When Caligula included his sisters he was in fact repealing the senate's decree, thus reasserting what had been attempted in 24. The Domus was simply reclaiming its own.

Two other honours took the constitutional status of the sisters even further. Firstly, they were included in the annual vows of allegiance to the emperor (not to be confused with the vows for his safety). The pattern formula is quoted by Suetonius: 'I will not hold myself and my children dearer than I hold Gaius and his sisters.' The honour has been described as unprecedented.[6] But in fact there were precedents, though only in the Greek east. Thus, the oath of Gangra of 3 BC included Augustus' children and grandchildren (EJ 315). But with the accession of Caligula we have a western, Latin oath from Aritium in Lusitania (*ILS* 1.190). It has been surmised that this oath, though sworn as late as 11 May 37, was a response to instructions sent by Macro immediately after Tiberius' death (Barrett 1989: 54). If so, there is a question: did Macro have a sudden inspiration when Tiberius died, or had Caligula's friends been working on the idea of elevating the sisters for some time? There can only be one answer. The remnants of *Partes Agrippinae* had been thinking hard ever since their party's demise, and they had lent Caligula an attentive ear when he proposed special provision for the sisters in the familial package that was being put together.

The other innovation saw the sisters included in the preamble to proposals submitted to the senate by the consuls. Again Suetonius supplies an example: 'May this be good and propitious for Gaius Caesar and his sisters' (*SG* 15.3). Here, too, it has been asked whether there was any precedent,[7] but again Caligula was able to cite examples. In the Republic the formula had been: 'May this be good, propitious and fortunate for the Quiritiary Roman People.'[8] But when Valerius Messala proposed the status of *pater patriae* for Augustus, he prefaced his motion with, 'May this be good and auspicious for you and your Domus, Caesar Augustus' (*SA* 58.2). One therefore suspects that the Caligulan practice was not entirely new.[9] But what was original was the cumulative effect of the various measures. Caligula was reminding the world that he was not the only assurance of the continuity of the regime.[10] The message was also propagated numismatically. In 37 Caligula issued a sestertius portraying his image on the obverse and the three sisters on the reverse; Agrippina represents Securitas, Drusilla Concordia, and Livilla Fortuna.[11]

DRUSILLA

If the sources are to be believed, his sister Drusilla was the most important person in Caligula's life. With the possible exception of his fourth wife, Milonia Caesonia, she was the only woman that this unhappy psychopath[12] ever loved. The sources make vague, almost routine allegations of incest by Caligula with all three sisters,[13] but the only part that even they believe is that relating to Drusilla. Suetonius offers a suitable basis for discussion.[14] According to him Drusilla was rumoured to have lost her virginity to Caligula while they were both under age and living in Antonia's house; Antonia is said to have caught them in the act. Later on Caligula took her from her husband, L. Cassius Longinus,[15] and openly treated her as his lawfully wedded wife.[16] When Caligula fell seriously ill, late in 37, he made Drusilla his heir both to his property and to the throne – *heredem quoque bonorum atque imperii aeger instituit*. Then, when she died in June 38 he proclaimed a period of public mourning (*iustitium*), during which it was a capital crime to laugh, bathe or dine with parents. Drusilla was deified, and was to be known as Panthea (Universal Goddess). A temple was planned, and elaborate games were to commemorate her birthday. From this time Caligula never took oath about anything, whether at public meetings or on military occasions, except by the godhead (*numen*) of Drusilla. He also required all women to swear by her *numen*. Some time later, when Caligula's fourth wife bore him a daughter, he named the child Drusilla. Suetonius concludes that he did not love his other sisters as much, or accord them the same honours.[17]

The public honours were matched by an avalanche of private grief. Caligula rushed off to his Alban villa before the funeral, spent some time there gambling furiously, then wanderd aimlessly down to Campania, and thence to Syracuse, returning after some time with his hair and beard still uncut in token of mourning.[18]

That there was an intense emotional relationship is clear, but was there a political aspect as well? What are the implications of the quasi-marriage and the institution as heir to the throne? The answer often given is that Caligula wanted to introduce Ptolemaic brother-sister marriage, so as to preserve the sacred Julian bloodline and give coherence and stability to a regime based unequivocally on the Domus.[19] It is thus a Ptolemaic question and the roots are Hellenistic.[20] That Caligula had a Hellenistic orientation is sufficiently attested. He reacted harshly against the consuls of 39 for commemorating the anniversary of Actium, thus honouring both his great-grandfather, Mark Antony, and the latter's Ptolemaic connection.[21] His boast that his mother had been born of incest between Augustus and Julia (*SG* 23.1) was in complete harmony with a Ptolemaic stance. So were the repeated taunts of his mother and grandmother to Tiberius, about the superiority of the divine Julian blood. Yet another strand was Caligula's denigration of Livia's ancestry (*SG* 23.2). She might have been a notional Julian, but basically she was still a Claudian.[22]

So much for the general shape of Caligula's ideology. But the crucial question is his designation of Drusilla as his successor.[23] This was, if true, the most destructive of all his assaults on tradition. It contemplated the unthinkable, the elevation of a woman to the purple.[24] It might be argued that as Caligula and Drusilla were, in our view, not lawfully married (see n. 16), the case for her designation must be rejected, since in the Ptolemaic model marriage and succession were interdependent. But the Roman version was in an experimental stage, and in principle it would have made no difference if emperor and sister had been only good friends. Continuity of the divine blood was the essential aim. But there is a question. Could a successor be designated by will? The answer is that this question had been in issue at the start of the reign, when it was claimed by some that Tiberius' will instituting both Caligula and his grandson, Gemellus, as heirs was tantamount to designating them as successors. Hence Caligula's immediate steps to have the will set aside.[25] But the issue dragged on. Dio says that Caligula granted Drusilla's second husband, Aemilius Lepidus, five years acceleration of office, and repeatedly declared (verbally) that he would leave him as his successor (CD 59.22.6–7, 11). The acceleration may be true, but Caligula's 'repeated assertions' are always suspect,[26] and it is quite possible that Dio's version originated in circles which objected to the idea of a female ruler, and invented the proposed designation of a man. There was, after all, nothing to commend Lepidus to Caligula as a successor. His only Julian credential was that the disgraced younger Julia was his grandmother. Even less likely to have impressed Caligula was the fact that Lepidus' other grandmother, Cornelia, was a daughter of Scribonia by an earlier marriage than that to Augustus.[27] Nor will Caligula have forgotten that Lepidus' sister had betrayed her husband (Caligula's brother, Drusus) to Sejanus.[28]

If it is simply a matter of choosing between Suetonius and Dio, the former is to be preferred. He attests an actual designation of Drusilla, whereas the best that Dio can do for Lepidus is a promise. But does either source have to be rejected? If Drusilla married Lepidus early in 38,[29] that is, after Caligula's illness of October 37, her designation might be seen as a temporary expedient pending her marriage to Lepidus. But this will not work either. The reason is Caligula's second marriage, to Livia Orestilla, in late 37 or early 38.[30] That marriage gave Caligula an expectation of children of his own, and takes Lepidus out of contention, leaving Drusilla once more as the only candidate. Unless and until the sources compose their differences, that must be our conclusion.

TWO SISTERS

With the death of Drusilla, the spotlight shifts to Agrippina. She and her sister Livilla were involved in an obscure association with their brother-in-law, Lepidus, in 39. As coherent an account as it is possible to extract from the garbled tradition informs us that when Lepidus was put on trial, Caligula also condemned the two sisters, on charges of adultery and of having been accomplices in a plot against him. He made public letters in their handwriting which he had obtained by fraud and seduction.[31] He dedicated to Mars the Avenger three swords that had been intended to kill him. Lepidus was executed and the sisters were banished to the Pontian Islands, though Caligula warned them that he had swords as well as islands. The urn containing Lepidus' bones was given to Agrippina, who was ordered to carry it back to Rome, clutching it to her bosom all the way. (This seems to be connected with a proposal by the future emperor Vespasian, then praetor, that special games be held to celebrate Caligula's victory in Gaul, and that the conspirators' bones be cast out unburied.) In Gaul, Caligula sold his sisters' jewels, furniture, slaves and even freedmen. He told the senate that no more honours were to be conferred on members of his family. The friends of Lepidus and the sisters who were punished included Nero's future praetorian prefect, Tigellinus, who was exiled for adultery with Agrippina (see n. 32).

What exactly was the crime of Agrippina and Livilla? The sources are at their most opaque here. It has recently been suggested that Lepidus himself was guilty of no more than adultery with the sisters. This is no doubt a possible inference from Dio's reference to their *synousia* with Lepidus – 'intercourse' not necessarily sexual but frequently so. We also have the statement of Tacitus that as a girl Agrippina had allowed Lepidus to seduce her in the hope of winning power; and in the fifth century Rutilius Namatianus recalled that Lepidus had wanted the throne and had paid the penalty for his incestuous adultery.[32] But Dio amplifies his *synousia* by observing that in a letter to the senate Caligula accused the sisters of many impious and immoral acts – *polla asebē kai aselgē*. We recall that *asebeia* is Dio's regular word for *maiestas*, or treason (Bauman 1974a: 4–7). There is also Suetonius' reference to adulteresses and accomplices in plots – *adulteras et insidiarum adversus se conscias* (*SG* 24.3).

The search for a conspiracy throws up Cn. Lentulus Gaetulicus, governor of Upper Germany since 29, who rebelled and was put to death in the autumn of 39, after Caligula had (it is said) moved rapidly north, taking with him his sisters and Lepidus. The link with that incurably obscure episode is a tenuous one,[33] and leads to some absurdities. Whatever Gaetulicus' aims, how did they square with the aims of Agrippina and Lepidus, who presumably[34] wanted to kill Caligula, marry, and install Lepidus as caretaker for Agrippina's son Nero, then two years old? And if those were their aims, what did Livilla hope to get out of it? Childless herself, did she risk her neck for her young nephew? Perhaps, but it has been pointed out that her husband, M. Vinicius, patron of the historian Velleius Paterculus, was not involved in whatever she was doing and emerged unscathed from the affair.[35]

There is no sure way through the maze, but one question is worth asking. Do we have here yet another of those coteries of free spirits that we have met before? Gaetulicus was something of a poet and a liberal thinker; Livilla, after being recalled by Claudius, was banished for adultery with the philosopher Seneca; Agrippina may also have had a liaison with Seneca. Let us again recall Albucilla and her coterie.[36] She and her friends had come under fire as recently as 37. Her group included literary figures, but also an exponent of more direct action, in the person of Agrippina's husband, Cn. Domitius Ahenobarbus. Charged with both adultery and treason like the others, where some committed suicide, he was saved by Tiberius' death. The prosecution was supervised by Caligula's mentor, Macro. The point is that Albucilla's *coniuratio* was not a plot to kill the moribund Tiberius; like the *grex Iuliae*, its objectives were adultery and denigration of the emperor.[37] If Lepidus headed a coterie of this sort, which somehow became entangled in Gaetulicus' enterprise,[38] it might explain why Suetonius speaks of *Lepidi et Gaetulici coniuratio* (*SG* 9.1) – naming Lepidus before the military leader because his group was behind the whole affair. If the group was as wild as its predecessors, Caligula himself, with his bizarre sense of humour, his brazen impudence, and his free-spirited attitude to his sisters,[39] would not have been out of place in their company. But eventually, driven either by paranoia or by hard evidence, he turned on his boon companions and destroyed them.

CONCLUSION

Three matters call for a final comment. First, was Drusilla a willing collaborator with Caligula or his victim? This is best answered by Tacitus' comment on Livia's desertion of her husband for Octavian: *incertum an invitam* (*TA* 5.1.3). The Julian women were as much in favour of the divine blood concept as the men. Second, we know that Caligula eventually had a child by his fourth wife, a daughter whom he named Julia Drusilla and commended to all the goddesses (*SG* 25.4). One wonders – but can put it no higher than that – whether he entertained the same thought of making this Drusilla his successor as he had in the case of her namesake. Third, the one solution that may meet opposition is the link between Lepidus' coterie and Gaetulicus. Why, it will be asked, did the coterie get involved if its aims were so different from those of Gaetulicus? But this is something that the sources leave entirely up in the air, and only conjecture is available. Whether the particular conjecture offered here is plausible is something that readers will decide for themselves.

12

MESSALINA, AGRIPPINA AND CLAUDIUS

INTRODUCTON: THE CLAUDIAN DOMUS

'Almost the whole conduct of his reign was dictated not so much by his own judgment as by that of his wives and freedmen.'[1] What the sources are trying to say is that the Claudian Domus was not simply a continuation of what had gone before. Claudius was not a Julian. He had not even received the specious imprimatur of adoption into the *gens*, and he paid little more than lip service to Julian traditions. Even that modest acknowledgement was concentrated at the start of his reign. A decree of the senate recalled Agrippina and Livilla from exile and restored their property; the official reason was that they had been unlawfully banished by Caligula.[2] Games were instituted to mark the birthdays of his mother Antonia and his father Drusus; Antonia's image was displayed at the games; and the name Augusta, which she had probably declined when it was offered by Caligula, was again conferred. But the recognition accorded to Claudius' maternal grandfather, Mark Antony, could not have been more perfunctory. Claudius simply recommended in an edict that Drusus' birthday be celebrated with special solemnity because it was also Antony's birthday.[3]

His attitude to the founding couple, Augustus and Livia, is instructive. So little did he belong to the Julian family that he had to appropriate the *cognomen* of 'Caesar', to which he was entitled neither by birth nor by adopton. But the acid test is supplied by his paternal grandmother, Livia. In 42 she was deified, thus giving her the recognition that neither the previous Claudian ruler, Tiberius, nor Caligula had seen fit to accord her. She was also given a statue in Augustus' temple (again the shared honour signifying the co-founder), the sacrifices were entrusted to the Vestals, women were ordered to use her name in oaths, and she received games and the parading of her image.[4] These honours, impressive at first glance, were much more modest than those that had been decreed for Diva Drusilla.[5] Moreover, the motive was more immediate political need than piety. Claudius did not have access to the title of 'Son of a god' that would have given a certain Julian continuity to his assumption of the throne. It is unlikely that he declared himself Augustus' grandson;[6] auto-adoption would have to wait for Septimius Severus. But *Divae Nepos*, 'Grandson of a goddess' who happened to be a co-founder, would do almost as well, if given wide enough exposure. Hence her appearance on his coins, the first Diva to be so honoured.[7] But after that Diva Augusta receded into the background. There is no trace of the protection of her divinity by the criminal law, as there had been for Divus Augustus and Diva Drusilla.[8] At long last Livia had ceased to matter politically.

Claudius took some steps, then, to tone down the gulf between the Julian House and himself, but his Domus was a new creation. As the last hope of the Claudians,[9] he gave the Domus a new direction and new techniques. But whether the architect of the new format was Claudius himself or his third and fourth wives, Messalina and Agrippina, remains to be seen.

MESSALINA AND THE NEW POLITICS

Valeria Messalina was very well connected, being a great-granddaughter of Augustus' sister, Octavia, through both her mother, Domitia Lepida, and her father, M. Valerius Messala. She was Claudius' third wife, having been preceded by Plautia Urgulanilla, a granddaughter of Livia's friend Urgulania, and by Aelia Paetina.[10] The date of Messalina's marriage to Claudius is not known. Estimates range between 37 and 41, with c. 39 as the best guess. Her date of birth is also unknown, and here conjecture is in free fall; guesses range from AD 3 to 26.[11] The uncertainty is most unfortunate. If she married while still a teenager her spectacular sexual exploits might simply be the experimentation of a girl who had married a man three times her age; but if she was already a mature woman it might mean something else. Even more important, the new style of politics associated with her presupposes some knowledge of the world. Would an adolescent have possessed such knowledge? We should be wary of a late date of birth. None of the great female politicians – Livia, Octavia, the elder Agrippina – were in the first flush of youth when they began making their mark. Even the younger Agrippina was 24, and Julia already had a problem with grey hair. It might of course be argued that if Messalina was largely motivated by the succession rights of her children, maternal instinct might have compensated for inexperience; therefore the birth of her daughter Octavia in 40, and of her son Britannicus in 41, could have given even an adolescent Messalina a powerful incentive. Alternatively, if there were any evidence to support the theory that Claudius was not her first husband[12] it would underpin an early date of birth. But even without that a fairly mature Messalina is the better guess, and a date of birth before 20 is probable.

The Messalina of the sources is one of the great nymphomaniacs of history. The literary barrage attesting to this cannot be brushed aside.[13] Juvenal's circumstantial account of her regular attendances at brothels under her trade-name of Lycisca is supported by the elder Pliny's attestation of a twenty-four hour marathon, Tacitus' list of twelve of her lovers, and Dio's description of group sex sessions in the palace at which the matrons' husbands were present.[14] Dio gives us our first indication of the new politics centred on the criminal courts that was Messalina's one contribution to the science of government. Dio says that husbands who agreed to be present were rewarded with honours and offices, but those who withheld their wives from the orgies were destroyed (CD 60.18.2). Messalina thus acquired a most ingenious hold on compliant husbands, for if they ever chafed at the bit they could be prosecuted for *lenocinium*, that is, as panders under Augustus' adultery law. In this way Messalina not only protected herself against the disclosure of her own activities to Claudius (CD 60.18.2–3), she also built up a following by manipulating the criminal law. That, coupled with the judicious use of sex, was to be her principal weapon in the game of politics. The combination evolved by '*Partes Messalinae*' was unique.

Messalina opened her account in 41 or 42, when Caligula's sister Livilla, recently recalled, was again banished, this time to Pandateria, which was rapidly becoming a summer cottage for the Julian family. The charge was adultery with Seneca. He was banished to Corsica and was not allowed to return until after Messalina's death. Much is made of the fact that Livilla was condemned without being charged, but there was nothing unusual about that; her guilt was manifest. Subsequently she was put to death, probably by soldiers despatched to Pandateria. She was interred in Augustus' mausoleum.[15]

The motives for this early forensic foray by Messalina are important. Dio says she was enraged because Livilla did not honour and flatter her, and also because Livilla was very beautiful and was often alone with Claudius (CD 60.8.5). A perfectly viable motive is disclosed by Dio. By insisting on proper respect Messalina was trying to compensate for the reverse that she had suffered after the birth of Britannicus in 41, when Claudius vetoed the titles of 'Augusta' for her and 'Augustus' for her son that the senate had voted; Claudius confined himself to issuing coins portraying the infant as *Spes Augusta* and publicly presenting him as his successor.[16] Messalina's influence must have been very great if she could get the senate to entertain 'Augusta' that had hitherto been conferred so sparingly,[17] let alone 'Augustus' which, unlike 'Caesar', had never been granted to a son. Messalina's reaction to the rebuff was a carefully calculated move against Livilla. Even if there was no formal trial, there was an edict of Claudius sentencing his niece to exile, and by including a complaint of insufficient respect in the verdict Messalina hoped to secure some sort of quasi-judicial confirmation of her status as empress.[18] She had thus let it be known that even if she was not an Augusta, it was wise to treat her with respect. The message was not fully received, for she never became Augusta,[19] but she did achieve some results, for in 42 some praetors publicly celebrated her birthday on their own initiative, without any official decree (CD 60.12.4). A somewhat similar technique had been used in an attempt to confer quasi-deification on Livia (see Chapter 10, p. 132). There were also some official honours. In 43 Messalina was allowed to ride in a *carpentum* at Claudius' British triumph, and received the same privilege of occupying the front seats at the games as Livia had enjoyed. She also held audiences as Livia had done.[20]

Dio's second motive for the attack on Livilla, namely jealousy, is not necessarily fanciful. Livilla, born in 18, might well have been seen as a threat by an older woman. But even then it was not a simple case of jealousy.[21] The real danger, as Messalina saw it, was that Livilla might divorce her husband, M. Vinicius, and become Claudius' fourth wife. Livilla's sister, Agrippina, had shown what tactics the sisters were capable of in 40, when she tried to break up Galba's marriage. It had earned her a slap in the face from Galba's mother-in-law (Suet. *Galb*. 5.1), but the message was not lost on Messalina.

It has been argued that Seneca was included in the attack on Livilla because of his history as a supporter of Caligula's sisters.[22] It is true that a charge of adultery was often simply a procedural trigger to uncover evidence of something more serious,[23] and although we do not know what was uncovered against Seneca, it was grave enough to warrant the death penalty. Seneca himself tells us that Claudius spoke against that penalty at his trial in the senate, and saved his life (*Ad Polyb*. 13.2). Livilla, however, was not tried by the senate. She was dealt with by Claudius himself, holding court in the palace and, literally, in his bedroom (*intra cubiculum*). Messalina might very well have been present.[24]

The year 42 also saw the downfall of Appius Iunius Silanus. Governor of Eastern Spain, he was recalled by Claudius in order to marry Messalina's mother, Domitia Lepida. But Lepida was not fated to enjoy her third venture into matrimonial bliss for long, for in the same year Silanus was executed. His destruction was engineered by his stepdaughter, Messalina, in collaboration with the freedman Narcissus. We are told that Silanus had offended Messalina by refusing to make love to her, and this had alienated Narcissus (CD 60.14.3). The sources inherited this tired substitute for genuine information from Octavian's lampoon against Fulvia (see Chapter 7, n. 21). It has been suggested that Silanus was involved in the conspiracy of Scribonianus,[25] and that is as good a guess as any. Having got wind of that, but not being able to pin anything concrete on Silanus,[26] Messalina and Narcissus concocted an ingenious scheme in order to avert a serious danger to the throne. They invented a dream in which Silanus killed Claudius. Narcissus disclosed the dream to Claudius, and Messalina gilded the lily by claiming to have had the same dream for several nights. Orders were sent to Silanus to come to the palace to attend Claudius' audience, but when he arrived they reported that he was trying to force his way in. Claudius, who was notoriously terrified by such omens, took this 'corroboration' of the dream as proof of Silanus' manifest guilt, and ordered that he be immediately summoned and executed. Next day he commended Narcissus in the senate for his devotion to the emperor's safety even in his sleep.[27]

Messalina's use of the criminal law now begins to become clear.

In a certain sense she was Claudius' Sejanus, searching out his enemies and destroying them. Her motives were no doubt personal as well as protectionist. Silanus was no threat to her son's prospects, but threats to her own position and influence weighed heavily with her, and Silanus looked dangerous in that regard. In the course of time more mundane interests, like the appropriation of other people's property, would be added to her agenda, but even then the element of a threat to Claudius would be present.

The conspiracy of L. Arruntius Camillus Scribonianus erupted shortly after Silanus' death,[28] and Messalina was prominent in the aftermath, when a series of trials was held (CD 60.15.1–16.8). Messalina and Narcissus worked as a team (SC 37.2), with Narcissus attending the trials (in the senate) and reporting to her. Dio paints a lurid picture of the trials. They got slaves and freedmen to inform against their masters and patrons; torture was employed against free men in violation of Claudius' oath; and women were executed in droves. The last is a gross exaggeration, but parts of it are true. Arria, wife of A. Caecina Paetus, encouraged him to suicide by stabbing herself in the breast and exclaiming, 'Look, Paetus, it doesn't hurt'. She was a friend of Messalina but refused to appeal to her. At an earlier point of the proceedings Arria had soundly rebuked Scribonianus' widow, Vibia, for having turned informer.[29] Another woman known to have been involved in the trials is Cloatilla, wife of a conspirator who was executed. She was pardoned by Claudius for burying her husband in breach of the law, which denied burial to those convicted of treason (QIO 8.5.16).

A decisive stage in Messalina's forensic history was reached in 43. She got rid of one of the praetorian prefects, Catonius Justus, allegedly because he had threatened to reveal her infidelities to Claudius. No further details are available, but there was some link between Catonius and Julia, the daughter of Tiberius' son Drusus and widow of Germanicus' son Nero, and as Messalina instigated the prosecution of Julia, so she can safely be assumed to have done the same for Catonius.[30] It has been plausibly suggested that there was an understanding between Catonius and Julia to undermine Messalina; she would be replaced as Claudius' wife by Julia, whose son Rubellius Plautus would then be able to challenge for the succession. Catonius' death was followed by the downfall of his colleague, Rufrius Pollio, and Messalina was able to staff the praetorian prefecture with two men who were devoted to her,

Lusius Geta and Rufrius Crispinus.[31] We cannot but be impressed by Messalina's political skill; her ability to make a pre-emptive strike against Catonius before he betrayed her to Claudius points to her possession of a most efficient intelligence service. The further consolidation of her political machine was helped by Claudius' absence in Britain for six months of 43. While he was away the consul L. Vitellius was virtually in charge of the empire (Suet. *Vit.* 2.4); he was so devoted to Messalina that he begged to be allowed to take off her shoes, one of which he carried with him constantly and frequently kissed (2.5).

In 46 or early in 47 Messalina turned her attention to the marriages of Claudius' daughters. The elder daughter, Antonia, born of Claudius' marriage with Aelia Paetina, had become the wife, in 41, of Cn. Pompeius Magnus, scion of a powerful family. The other daughter, Octavia, who was Messalina's own child, was betrothed to L. Iunius Silanus, a member of a family which was a constant thorn in the side of the early emperors; Domitia Lepida's unfortunate third husband was a Iunius Silanus.[32] But Messalina was not aiming an attack at Octavia's betrothed.[33] Her target was Pompeius Magnus. Dio says that Messalina brought false charges against him; he lost his life because of his family and his relationship to the emperor, but the formal charges related to things not known to Dio.[34] Suetonius, also drawing a bow at a venture, says he was caught in bed with a young boy and was stabbed on the spot (*SC* 29.1–2). His father, and his mother Scribonia (a great-niece of the elder Julia's mother) perished at the same time, and their two younger sons were exiled.[35] Why Messalina wanted this genocide defies comprehension.[36] The only thing that makes any sort of sense is the fact that after Magnus' death Antonia was married to Messalina's half-brother, Faustus Sulla (*SC* 27.2). The replacement of a dangerously independent contender by her brother was a great comfort to Messalina.[37]

In 47 Messalina launched a *cause célèbre*, one which in its dramatic impact was second only to her own catastrophe a year later. It was the trial of Asiaticus, a case which marks Tacitus' return from the long exile to which the vagaries of textual survival had condemned him ever since the end of Tiberius' reign: by a queer quirk of fate, the first words of the extant book XI are *nam Valerium Asiaticum*. D. Valerius Asiaticus of Vienna in Narbonese Gaul had helped to kill Caligula and had prospered under Claudius, reaching the consulship and accompanying the emperor

172

to Britain. Tacitus starts by telling us that Messalina believed that Asiaticus had been Poppaea Sabina's lover; she also coveted the Gardens of Lucullus which he owned. Messalina got her regular prosecutor, P. Suillius Rufus, assisted by Britannicus' tutor, Sosibius, to charge Asiaticus and Poppaea. Sosibius warned Claudius about Asiaticus' connections at Vienna and about his proposed visit to the Rhine armies; the emperor, alarmed, sent troops to arrest Asiaticus. Refusing to remit the case to the senate, Claudius tried Asiaticus in a bedroom of the palace (*intra cubiculum*) with Messalina present. Suillius charged corruption of the army, adultery with Poppaea, and effeminacy. Asiaticus replied (or so Tacitus would have us believe) that Suillius' sons could vouch for his masculinity. When Asiaticus spoke, Claudius was deeply moved; and, again according to Tacitus, Messalina left the room to dry her tears, after warning L. Vitellius (the custodian of her shoes) not to let Asiaticus get away.[38]

Vitellius, then holding his third consulship with Claudius as his colleague, carried out Messalina's instructions faithfully. Pretending to be defence counsel, he asked that Asiaticus be allowed to choose the manner of his death. This was a concession sometimes made, but Asiaticus had not yet been found guilty. Messalina and Vitellius, well aware of Claudius' tendency to take the shadow for the substance, counted on his taking the statement by 'defence counsel' as an admission of guilt, and so it turned out; Claudius granted the concession. Asiaticus, complaining that he had been brought down by a woman's guile (*fraus muliebris*) and Vitellius' shameless mouth, opened his veins. Messalina also organized Poppaea's destruction, employing agents to threaten her with imprisonment and driving her to suicide. A few days later, when Claudius asked her husband why she had not come to dinner, he was told that she was dead.[39]

There is a question about Messalina's motives. In a sequel to Asiaticus' case, her resident prosecutor, Suillius, brought charges in the senate against two knights by the name of Petra. It was alleged that one of them had had a dream in which Claudius was wearing either a wheaten wreath with inverted ears or a wreath of withered vine leaves, which portended either a shortage of grain or Claudius' death in the autumn. Again, a dream was taken as reality, this time by the senate, and they were put to death. But, adds Tacitus, their real offence was that they had lent their house as a rendezvous for Poppaea and a mimist, Mnester (*TA* 11.4.1–5).

This Mnester was, it seems, one of Messalina's lovers. He had refused a liaison, but she had persuaded Claudius to order him to carry out all commands that she gave him. She took him away from the theatre and kept him with her in the palace.[40] Tacitus' allusion to the real cause of the two knights' offence thus implies that Poppaea's usurpation of Mnester was at the base of the entire Asiaticus affair. But this does not make much sense. In an attempt to reconcile the anomalies, Koestermann suggests that Asiaticus was merely a scapegoat. To charge Poppaea with adultery with Mnester would have meant charging him as well, and therefore charges of adultery between Poppaea and Asiaticus were trumped up; hence Asiaticus' complaint about 'a woman's guile' (Koestermann 3.25). But this leaves the other charges against Asiaticus up in the air, besides giving undue prominence to a routine charge of adultery between two persons not belonging to the Domus.

One fixed point can be relied on in our search for a solution. Messalina orchestrated the entire drama of Asiaticus' destruction. She was responsible for the decision to locate the trial in the palace, which enabled her to be present and also made it possible to concoct the fraudulent confession. There was no need to bypass the senate in the case of the two Petrae. Their names were *added* to the list of accused (*TA* 11.4.1), but they could be left to the senate, for the dream sequence did not require the connivance of Messalina and Vitellius.[41] But what event was of such magnitude as to demand not only the elaborate drama staged by Messalina in the palace, but also proceedings in the senate against accomplices who almost certainly included others besides the two Petrae?[42] The answer is that Tacitus has in fact told us what it was all about, but his penchant for the ridiculous has again coloured his narrative. He has Sosibius warn Claudius that Asiaticus had organized Caligula's murder and could, judging by his proposed visit to the Rhine armies, be planning something sinister now. But he then devalues the warning by having Claudius immediately despatch the praetorian prefect, Rufrius Crispinus (Messalina's friend), with a military force, 'as if they were going to crush a rebellion', only to find Asiaticus at the holiday resort of Baiae; but none the less they brought him to Rome in chains (*TA* 11.2–3). Then follows Asiaticus' equivocal reply to the charge of effeminacy, Messalina's tears, and Vitellius' equally tearful appearance as defence counsel.[43] We cannot assert as a fact that Asiaticus was planning a coup,[44] but Claudius' advisers certainly thought so. Thus once again Messalina consulted the interests of Claudius (and of Britannicus) as well as her own. She probably gratified her resentment of Poppaea, and she certainly did acquire the Gardens of Lucullus,[45] but she also rendered an important service to the regime.

P. Suillius, Messalina's resident prosecutor, proceeded immediately after the case to launch a relentless series of prosecutions (*TA* 11.5.1). A Roman knight, Samius, paid Suillius 40,000 sesterces to take his case, only to commit suicide when he discovered that Suillius was collaborating with the other side (*TA* 11.5.2). Messalina is not mentioned here, but her overall link with Suillius is not in doubt. That worthy's court cases yielded him a total of three hundred million sesterces (*TA* 13.42.6), and when he was charged with fraudulent prosecutions in 58 he first claimed that he had acted on the orders of Claudius, and then that he had been ordered by Messalina. It was asked why only Suillius had been chosen as the mouthpiece of 'that vicious whore', but the senate ruled that the acid test was Suillius' enormous earnings: 'one who was paid for crimes must pay for them' (*TA* 13.43.4–5). The victims named at his trial included Livilla, Poppaea and Asiaticus (*TA* 13.43.3).

Some disquiet may be caused by C. Silius' proposal in 47 that the ancient *lex Cincia* prohibiting the acceptance of payment by pleaders be rigorously enforced. In Tacitus' opinion the proposal was aimed specifically at Suillius, whom Silius hated. Silius was the man with whom Messalina would soon contract a bigamous marriage. But this does not in any way require the rejection of her link with Suillius. Silius may have had his own reasons for hating the delator; Suillius had, after all, restored Mnester to Messalina by getting rid of Poppaea. Silius' hatred is no more than an incidental frill to draw attention to the looming catastrophe of Messalina and Silius.[46]

Messalina's last forensic venture took place in 47 or 48, when she fell out with one of the imperial freedmen, Polybius. Dio says that she accused him falsely, even while maintaining a liaison with him, and caused his death; and after this the freedmen as a whole distrusted her (CD 60.31.2). Polybius was at one time Claudius' literary secretary, but later handled petitions to the emperor as *a libellis*. Seneca addressed his *To Polybius on Consolation* to him during his exile, in the hope that he would use his influence with Claudius to secure his recall, though in the end he had to wait for Messalina's death.[47] It has been argued that Polybius fell because he tried to prevent Messalina from marrying Silius.[48] Another possibility, it is suggested, is that Polybius wanted to respond to Seneca's appeal, but was put down in order to prevent it.[49]

THE MARRIAGE OF THE EMPEROR'S WIFE

Messalina's marriage to C. Silius in the autumn of 48, while still married to Claudius, is one of Tacitus' great set-pieces (*TA* 11.12, 26–38). But even with generous support from other sources this extraordinary episode remains shrouded in darkness. The voluminous modern literature has not evolved a consensus, and possibly never will.[50]

Messalina formed an association, probably in 47, with C. Silius, son of the elder Agrippina's ally who had perished in 24; through Messalina's instrumentality Silius was designated as consul for 48, though he does not seem to have taken up the office. Messalina was captivated by Silius and pressed him to divorce his wife, Junia Silana. Silius wanted a formal marriage, and offered to adopt Britannicus and to leave Messalina's power intact. After some hesitation she agreed, and when Claudius left for Ostia they were married.[51] At Ostia the imperial freedom broke the news to Claudius. Narcissus, once Messalina's ally but hostile since Polybius' death, advised Claudius to take prompt action, for Silius threatened to make himself master of Rome.

Meanwhile Messalina and her company were at her residence in Rome, celebrating a simulated vintage festival with strong Bacchic connotations. But when it became known that Claudius was on his way seeking vengeance, the group split up. Messalina went to the Gardens of Lucullus, Silius to the forum. Others, less lucky, were arrested by centurions who hunted them down. Knowing how susceptible to her presence Claudius was, Messalina decided to meet him face to face. She asked the senior Vestal, Vibidia, to appeal to Claudius to give her a hearing. She then set out for Ostia, possibly travelling in a refuse cart, as Tacitus says, in order to arouse sympathy.[52]

The scene shifts back to Claudius. The loyalty of Lusius Geta, Messalina's appointee as praetorian prefect, being in doubt, Narcissus took over from him for just the one day. Messalina's friends, Vitellius and Caecina, travelled with Claudius on the journey to Rome; Narcissus joined the party in order to forestall any pleas for leniency. On the way they met Messalina. Narcissus immediately handed Claudius a detailed dossier of her adulteries. When the Vestal Vibidia demanded that she be given a hearing, Narcissus assured her that this would be done. In Rome, he took Claudius to Silius' house, showed him the image of Silius' father, on display in breach of the senate's decree of 24, pointed out the imperial possessions given to Silius by Messalina, and elicited from Claudius his first positive expression of indignation.

They then went to the praetorians' camp, where Claudius proceeded to conduct a series of summary trials. Silius refused to defend himself. Others tried to do so, but without much success. The condemned included Titius Proculus, appointed by Silius as Messalina's 'guardian'; Mnester, whose plea that he had only obeyed orders impressed Claudius but was rejected on the advice of the freedmen; Sulpicius Rufus, procurator of gladiators, who may have assisted Messalina in 46 when she intervened on behalf of the gladiator Sabinus who had been her lover; Decrius Calpurnianus, prefect of the Vigiles; Iuncus Vergilianus, the only senator named by Tacitus; and Traulus Montanus, whose plea that Messalina had dismissed him after only one night did not save him. A number of knights whom Tacitus does not name also perished. He attests only two acquittals – one because he had played a woman's part, the other because of his connections.[53]

After his exertions at the camp Claudius went home, had dinner, and ordered word to be sent to 'the poor woman' to appear next day to plead her case. Narcissus, remembering her power over Claudius, told the tribune on duty that her execution was to proceed, 'as the emperor has ordered'.[54] Messalina was at the Gardens of Lucullus, where her mother, Domitia Lepida, standing by her in spite of her betrayal of Ap. Silanus, tried to persuade her to take her own life. But Messalina could only weep and lament. When the tribune and the freedman Evodus burst in on her she tried to kill herself, but failed, and the tribune ran her through. Her body was given to her mother for burial. When Claudius was told of her death he did not ask for details; he remained impassive even when he saw her children mourning her. The senate helped him to forget by decreeing the removal of her name and statues from all public and private places. Narcissus received quaestorian honours, which made him eligible for the senate.[55]

What lies behind this extraordinary affair? The numerous

theories include a considerable measure of scepticism. Some would deny that there was a marriage at all; a Bacchic orgy was distorted by the freedmen to blacken Messalina's name. But the sources make it clear that it was *iustae nuptiae*, a lawful marriage.[56]

A theory propounded by Meise calls for comment. He argues that Silius hoped to be accepted as a serious contender for the throne by presenting Messalina and Britannicus to the praetorians, commanded by two of her supporters as they were. She also had the support of L. Vitellius and Caecina Largus, and the military side was in the hands of Decrius Calpurnianus, prefect of the Vigiles, and Sulpicius Rufus of the gladiatorial school. Thus all the essentials of a plot were in place. The reason for the whole enterprise was Messalina's fear of Agrippina's ambitions for Nero. Agrippina was a greater threat than any that Messalina had faced so far, because of her marriage to Passienus Crispus, her great wealth, and Nero's popularity with the people.[57]

This conspiracy makes somewhat better sense than that attributed to the elder Julia, but there are difficulties. The comparison with previous threats is unfortunate; Messalina had averted those threats by judicial action, not by marrying anyone.[58] Even more to the point, why did she favour the conspiracy? In what way would Britannicus be better off with a stepfather who might have sons of his own, than with his own father?[59] As for Silius' promise to preserve Messalina's power intact, even Tacitus says that she was lukewarm about marrying him because she was afraid that once in power he would abandon her (*TA* 11.26.5). Moreover, L. Vitellius' loyalty at this stage is doubtful; he exchanged his custody of Messalina's shoes for cultivation of Narcissus' image, which he placed amongst his household gods, and later he sponsored the decree allowing Claudius to marry Agrippina.[60] Finally, what sort of conspiracy was it that did nothing except stage a Bacchic festival when Claudius' back was turned? That was surely when the presentation to the praetorians should have taken place.

Tacitus believes that it was purely a love affair which aroused great apprehension in the minds of the freedmen. The observation with which he opens his account strikes the keynote for the entire episode: 'Bored with the facility of her adulteries, she was rushing into new thrills.'[61] The vintage festival has no point except in that context; it typifies the new excitements to which boredom had propelled Messalina. Tacitus has told us, then, what he considers the key to the whole affair. There is not sufficient reason to disagree with him.

AGRIPPINA: MARRIAGE AND THE SUCCESSION

The death of Messalina opened a new chapter in Agrippina's career. There is no suggestion that she had anything to do with her rival's destruction, but the beneficial effect on her fortunes is clear. Not yet in quite the top rank as a politician, the eldest daughter of Agrippina and Germanicus would now come into her own, dominating the politics of her time as no member of the Domus, not even Livia, had ever done. In some respects she would be a worthy successor to Messalina, eliminating those who stood in her way with the same ruthless efficiency. She also shared Messalina's indifference to conventional morality, except that she kept a tight rein on her passions. As Tacitus puts it, 'She held honour, modesty, her body, everything, cheaper than sovereignty'. A strong tradition, which Tacitus finds it difficult to reject, has her offer herself to her son in order to retain her grip on power. She had one supreme ambition, to place her son Nero on the throne: 'Let him kill me, but let him rule.' But not far behind that was her determination to secure a position of unprecedented eminence for herself. She proposed coming as close as it was possible for a woman to come to a partnership in power; she would be, in fact though not in law, a *socia imperii*. The story of Agrippina in Claudius' reign is the story of her successful realization of both her objectives.[62]

The first step was to marry Claudius. His freedmen wanted him to marry again, but could not agree on a successor. Tacitus, still in pursuit of the absurd, stages a process of selection which is a parody of the emperor's *consilium*.[63] Claudius summons the freedmen to a meeting. Narcissus favours Claudius' former wife, Aelia Paetina, whom he had divorced after the birth of their daughter Antonia. Callistus nominates Caligula's former wife, Lollia Paulina, who had disgusted the elder Pliny by appearing at a dinner party smothered in emeralds and pearls to the tune of forty million sesterces. Pallas supports Agrippina. She was opportunely available, having killed her second husband, the wealthy Passienus Crispus, in, probably, 48. She had married him in 44, taking him away from Domitia, the elder sister of Messalina's mother.[64] Pallas stresses Agrippina's descent from Gemanicus (*not* from Agrippina and the divine blood), and urges Claudius to ally himself to a noble line, to unite two branches of the Claudian family,[65] so that a woman of proven fertility should not transfer the grandeur of the Caesars to another house. Agrippina promoted her cause by paying frequent visits to Claudius, to whom as her father's brother she had an access denied to her rivals. She was chosen. But before the wedding could proceed an obstacle had to be overcome. The marriage of an uncle and a niece violated the spirit, and in all probability the letter, of Roman law, and steps were taken to obtain special dispensation from both senate and people. The necessary legislation was piloted by that master strategist, L. Vitellius. The dispensation was a limited one, applying only to an uncle marrying his brother's daughter; marriage with a sister's daughter remained forbidden.[66]

The marriage was celebrated at the beginning of 49. But even before that Agrippina had begun planning her strategy for the succession. She wanted to marry her son Nero to Claudius' daughter, Octavia, but Octavia was betrothed to L. Iunius Silanus. A solution was found by the ingenious L. Vitellius. In his capacity as censor he removed Silanus from the senate on the grounds of incest with his sister, Junia Calvina. The fact that Junia had recently married Vitellius' son did not deter him; it may even have furnished him with ammunition. Claudius cancelled the betrothal; Silanus resigned his praetorship and killed himself; Junia Calvina was exiled.[67] Nero was then betrothed to Octavia; the marriage would take place in 53 (*TA* 12.58.1). Here, too, there was a problem, because in 50 Agrippina had persuaded Claudius to adopt Nero. The intermediary in urging Claudius to do this was Pallas, who had become Agrippina's lover; he cited the Augustan precedent of having two potential successors in the interests of stability (*TA* 12.25.1–4, 26.1). Claudius not only adopted Nero, he gave him precedence over Britannicus because he was three years older. The lawyers noted that this was the first adoption in the patrician branch of the Claudian family.[68] As Nero was now a Claudian,[69] the agnatic link between his bride and himself had to be broken, and Octavia was given in adoption to another family (CD 60.33.2[2]), thus enabling the marriage to be duly celebrated in 53.

Nero's adoption in 50 was followed, a year later, by his election to the consulship on 4 March 51, the office to be held when he turned 19 in six years' time. He was given the title of Prince of the Youth, together with proconsular *imperium* outside Rome, co-option into the four major priesthoods, and the right to wear the triumphal toga at the games given in his honour.[70] Within two or three years of her marriage Agrippina had virtually ousted Britannicus from the succession. She had forced an emperor whom she dominated completely to bypass his own son in favour of an outsider. Little remained for her to do on the succession front except to be on the alert for any sign of opposition. In 51, a year after the adoption, Britannicus greeted Nero one day as 'Domitius', thus pretending to ignore the fact that 'L. Domitius Ahenobarbus' was now 'Ti. Claudius Nero Caesar' (*TA* 12.41.6–8). This sent Agrippina flying to Claudius to complain that a legislative act of the people[71] had been flouted by Britannicus. Claudius responded obediently by exiling or executing the best of Britannicus' tutors and replacing them by men nominated by Agrippina.[72] One of the victims was Sosibius who had helped to destroy Asiaticus on Messalina's behalf (CD 60.32.5).

AGRIPPINA AND THE SHARING OF POWER

Agrippina used her influence over Claudius not only to consolidate Nero's claims, but also to enhance her own position. Immediately after the marriage she secured Seneca's recall from eight years' exile, and also obtained a praetorship for him. She felt, says Tacitus, that his literary renown would make his recall popular with the public, and he would be a distinguished tutor for Nero (*TA* 12.8.3). Tacitus is well aware of the importance of Agrippina's interest in Seneca's literary accomplishments; she was a literary figure herself, and one of Tacitus' sources (see Chapter 10, p. 148), and that is why he adds that she had Seneca recalled in order not to be known only for her crimes.[73]

Agrippina had won the contest for Claudius' hand, but one of the contestants, the bejewelled Lollia Paulina, had left her with a feeling of uneasiness. She therefore arranged, in 49, for Lollia to be charged with having consulted astrologers about Claudius' marriage. Claudius gave one of his ambiguous performances during the trial in the senate. He spoke about her distinguished family connections, carefully avoiding all mention of her having once been married to Caligula; but then he suddenly went on the attack, describing her plans as destructive to the state and proposing that she be sentenced to confiscation and exile. The senate allowed her five million sesterces and confiscated the rest of her vast fortune. But Lollia was not fated to enjoy a relatively comfortable exile, for Agrippina had a tribune despatched to force her to suicide (*TA* 12.22). According to one account her head was brought to Agrippina, who identified it by certain dental peculiarities (*CD* 60.32.4). But Agrippina herself had a dental peculiarity in the shape of two canine teeth on the right side (*PNH* 7.71), and this may have confused Dio. In any case the story is not convincing, for immediately after Agrippina's death in 59 Lollia's ashes were brought back to Rome for burial (*TA* 14.12.6).

Was Agrippina just being vindictive to a former rival, or did she still have reason to fear Lollia? The latter had been Agrippina's main rival in the contest (*TA* 12.1.3), but why was she a threat after Agrippina had won? The answer must be that Lollia consulted astrologers *after* Agrippina's victory, in the hope of reversing Claudius' decision. Consultations with astrologers were always viewed with suspicion, especially by Claudius. And despite her victory Agrippina still had to be cautious; the decisive stage represented by Nero's adoption was still in the future. Nor was Lollia the only danger to be warded off at this time. It was at this same delicate stage that Agrippina ruined the illustrious Calpurnia, whose beauty had been praised by Claudius in a casual remark. As he had not shown any serious interest in her, Agrippina contented herself with having her banished; she was recalled after Agrippina's death.[74]

Nero's adoption in 50 ushered in a string of successes. Agrippina received the title of Augusta, the first living consort of a living emperor to be so honoured. She was given the right to use the *carpentum* at festivals. She attended a mock battle on the Fucine Lake wearing a military cloak, but one made of cloth of gold, in contrast to Claudius and Nero who wore regular military uniforms.[75] In order to display her power to the provincials, she arranged for the foundation of a veteran colony at the principal town of the Ubii, where she was born; the colony was named after her, Colonia Claudia Augusta Agrippinensium – the modern Cologne.[76] She often accompanied Claudius when he received foreign dignitaries. She sat on a separate tribunal, and was so seated in 50 when the British leader Caratacus and his family rendered the same homage to her as to Claudius. The innovation was not well received. Tacitus is highly critical of a woman being seated before the Roman standards, preoccupied with her own dignity and flaunting herself as a partner in the empire (*imperii socia*) which her ancestors had created. Dio observes that she was not satisfied to have all the privileges of Livia and more, and to exercise the same power as Claudius; she wanted the same formal title as his.[77] Later on, after her death, she was accused of having sought a partnership in the empire (*consortium imperii*), of having tried to get the praetorians to swear allegiance to her, and of having wanted to subject senate and people to similar ignominy (*TA* 14.11.1). The reference to the praetorians relates to an occurrence in 51 when Agrippina got rid of the praetorian prefects Geta and Crispinus, who were pledged to the cause of Messalina's children. She persuaded Claudius that two prefects led only to discord, and got Afranius Burrus appointed as a single incumbent. Unlike Seneca, Burrus would not forget his debt to Agrippina.[78]

Some of her distinctions at this time were more or less routine, such as divine honours in the east, or were no greater than those possessed by Livia, such as the entry of her audiences in the official records.[79] But one item is more significant. In the Acts of the Arval Brethren, dating to between 50 and 54, Nero is twice described as 'the progeny (*subolem*) of Agrippina Augusta and the son (*filium*) of Claudius' (SMW 14). She thus came close to the *Iuliae filius* that had eluded Livia (see Chapter 10, p. 131). But she did not quite get there. As with the golden cloak at the Fucine Lake, a near miss was the best that she could do. The *de iure* heartland of power, *tribunicia potestas* and *imperium*, was beyond her reach. The cloak was no doubt an attempt to graze the fringes of *imperium*, but it fell far short of the *de facto* exercise of military authority by her mother at the Rhine Bridge, or by Fulvia at Praeneste. She was no less at a disadvantage in the sphere of civil power. Tribunician sacrosanctity might have put Livia's feet on the first rung of the constitutional ladder proper if she (or Augustus) had so chosen, but Agrippina only had Vestal sanctity – effective enough against insults, but not on the main line.

In 51 charges of *maiestas* and aspirations to empire were lodged against that sterling character, L. Vitellius. Claudius would have accepted the charges, but the entreaties, or rather (says Tacitus) the threats of Agrippina, caused him to change his mind. The accuser, Iunius Lupus, was forced into exile (*TA* 12.42.4–5). What does Tacitus mean by saying that Agrippina resorted to threats? The answer testifies to her excellent grasp of public law. On his accession Claudius had suspended charges of *maiestas*; the suspension remained in force throughout his reign, and was a distinct plus in his final balance sheet. But the suspension did not mean that a would-be accuser was prevented from lodging such a charge; he might get it accepted, in which case the *maiestas* law would be revived. But there was a penalty for failure; he would be taken to have prosecuted for a non-existent crime and would be liable to be punished for malicious prosecution, or *calumnia*.[80] This explains Agrippina's threats. She simply reminded Claudius of his undertaking on his accession, and added for good measure that Britannicus' incorrect salutation of Nero, which immediately preceded the attack on Vitellius,[81] could found a charge of *maiestas* if the law were revived. Forces hostile to Agrippina had put up Iunius Lupus in an attempt to punish her minion for his part in legalizing her marriage,[82] but they had nearly stirred up a hornets' nest.

AGRIPPINA AND THE FREEDMEN

Where did Agrippina stand *vis-à-vis* the imperial freedmen? The great crux is her relationshp with Narcissus. Although he had created the vacancy that she was chosen to fill, Tacitus has him support Aelia Paetina in the three-cornered contest to select Claudius' fourth wife (*TA* 12.1.3). But Dio says that the freedmen as a whole supported Agrippina, in order to protect themselves against Britannicus, who might seek revenge for his mother's death (CD 60.31.8). Elsewhere Dio says that Agrippina was all-powerful because she had won over Narcissus and Pallas. But since that refers to a later stage than the matrimonial contest,[83] is Dio telling us that after the marriage Agrippina and Narcissus composed their differences? Unfortunately this will not work. In 52, three years after the marriage, there was a most unfriendly confrontation at the mock battle on the Fucine Lake. A defective tunnel having released an alarming flood of water, Agrippina accused Narcissus, who was in charge of the project, of having pocketed the money allocated to it and arranged the collapse in order to conceal his crime; Narcissus replied with an attack on her feminine imperiousness (*impotentia muliebris*) and overweening ambition.[84] There was not yet any sign of harmony between the two antagonists, nor would further developments yield anything to support the picture painted by Dio. In the final stage of the reign (see the following two sections), when Agrippina's fortunes declined sharply but were resuscitated by firm action on her part followed by the timely death of Claudius, Narcissus was quite specifically not on Agrippina's side (see the following section).

AGRIPPINA: THREATS AND COUNTER THREATS

There was an early warning of a change in Agrippina's position in 53, when she put up Tarquitius Priscus to bring charges of occult practices and extortion against Statilius Taurus, whose gardens she coveted.[85] (The charges were brought up in the senate; unlike Messalina, Agrippina did not use the chamber court.)[86] Statilius killed himself before the verdict, but the senate punished Tarquitius, formerly Statilius' legate in Africa, by expelling him from its ranks. The senate was marking its disapproval of Agrippina's intrigues as much as of the accuser's disloyalty, and the ruling is seen as the start of a reaction against her.[87] Narcissus is not mentioned, but if the solid freedmen support postulated by Dio had been in place the adverse reaction would probably have been forestalled.

The year 54 brought an intensification of Agrippina's worries. The sources say that a series of prodigies portended a change for the worse,[88] but what really alarmed Agrippina was a remark made by Claudius in his cups, to the effect that he was fated to endure, and eventually to punish, the misconduct of his wives. He made the comment to the freedmen when they expressed their approval of a trial the day before, at which Claudius had condemned a woman for adultery. The remark came at a time when he was showing signs of regretting his marriage and his adoption of Nero; it was at this time that Claudius showed great affection for Britannicus and declared his intention of giving him the *toga virilis*, immature as he was, 'so that the Roman people might at last have a genuine Caesar'.[89] These ominous developments, says Tacitus, determined Agrippina to act immediately.[90]

The first step was to destroy Messalina's mother, Domitia Lepida, in what Tacitus describes as 'a womanish case' – *muliebris causa*. He says that in ancestry, beauty, age, wealth and determination Agrippina and Domitia were evenly matched, as they also were in unchastity and other vices. The issue was who would control Nero. Domitia used liberality, but Agrippina, 'who gave her son empire but could not tolerate his rule', was grim and threatening (*TA* 12.64.4–6).

Agrippina's fears were fully justified. Domitia had not only enjoyed Nero's confidence ever since she had taken him in while Agrippina was in exile, she was also Britannicus' grandmother. The case against her was much more than 'womanish'. It was part of the last phase of the succession struggles that had plagued the Domus for seventy-five years. The case was also aimed at Narcissus, whose loyalty to Claudius and his natural children was beyond question.[91]

The charges against Domitia were that she had used black magic against Agrippina, and was disturbing the peace of Italy by failing to control her regiments of slaves in Calabria.[92] Nero, forgetful of his debt to Domitia, gave evidence against her (SN 7.1). She was sentenced to death, in spite of the protestations of Narcissus. Tacitus speculates on the considerations that prompted Narcissus to give such dedicated support to the Claudian cause: he felt that if Nero became the successor there would be a witch hunt against the Claudians, but with Britannicus in the saddle Claudius would be safe; he condemned Agrippina's treachery which was tearing the Domus apart, attacked her improper liaison with Pallas, and accused her of subordinating all modesty and integrity to her drive for sovereignty (TA 12.65.2–5). In an odd conclusion to these 'thoughts of Narcissus', the latter calls on Britannicus to take revenge on his mother's murderers. Little sense can be made of this portrait of an architect who condemns his own work, and the only useful fact to emerge from the 'thoughts' is that there was now open hostility between Narcissus and Agrippina and her henchman, Pallas. The schism on the matrimonial issue had reached its inevitable climax.

Having got rid of Domitia, the next logical step for Agrippina was to get rid of Claudius. But first something happened to Narcissus. His health broke down and he went on holiday to the coastal spa of Sinuessa in Campania. At some point during his stay there Agrippina had him imprisoned, ill treated and driven to suicide.[93] Dio adds a curious postscript. He says that before he died Narcissus burnt all the letters in his possession incriminating Agrippina. Such altruism does not ring true. If there was any destruction of documents it will have been carried out by Agrippina's agents. Dio may reflect (with a slight change of emphasis) a story put out by Agrippina (in her memoirs?) to the effect that Narcissus had destroyed his records in order to cover up his guilt. She had said something similar about the Fucine Lake tunnel.

Alternatively, we may have here a scrap of information about the obscure attempt to prosecute Agrippina shortly before Claudius' death.[94]

THE DEATH OF CLAUDIUS

The way was now clear for Agrippina to eliminate Claudius, and the sources almost unanimously agree that that is what she did.[95] But though they agree that poison was administered and Agrippina was responsible, they differ on details. A serviceable working model has Agrippina employ Locusta, a professional poisoner, who infuses poison into a dish of mushrooms. But the poison works too slowly, and Claudius' physician, Xenophon, is called in. He introduces a feather smeared with a speedier poison into Claudius' throat, and Claudius dies. The date is 13 October 54. Claudius is deified, which prompts Nero to call mushrooms 'the food of the gods'.

Modern investigators divide about equally into believers and unbelievers.[96] There is little point in attempting to arbitrate. It has been said that much depends on whether one believes that Claudius planned to reinstate Britannicus.[97] That is true, and it raises a large issue. What do we think was contained in the will that Suetonius says Claudius made? It was sealed with the seals of all the magistrates, but before Claudius could take it any further he was cut off by Agrippina, who was herself facing charges at the time.[98] Tacitus thinks that the will was not read in case the preference shown to the adopted son left the people with a sense of injustice. This is noted by Tacitus after Nero has become emperor, but Dio has Nero first destroy the will and then become emperor.[99] At a guess one would say that Dio is right; the will instituted Britannicus as joint heir, thus raising the same issue as that which had confronted Caligula on Tiberius' death (see Chapter 11, p. 162). For the second time in seventeen years a Claudian will had been frustrated by Julian manipulation. But Agrippina's tactics were even less commendable than Caligula's. He had at least produced Tiberius' will and adduced legal argument for setting it aside. Agrippina dared not let Claudius' will see the light of day, any more than she had allowed Narcissus to live and publish his correspondence.

CONCLUSION

The elaborate political apparatus, geared to the criminal law, that we have postulated for Messalina does, it is felt, carry conviction. Her motives were a mixture of self-interest and attention (devotion is too strong a word) to the interests of Claudius and the state. She may have been more generous, and less discriminating, in her private life than seemed appropriate to the real success stories, Livia and Octavia, or to the tragic elder Agrippina. But she had a keen appreciation of the realities of power. She realized very early in the piece that the Claudian Domus was something more than a mere continuation of what had gone before. Not all the factors in the equation had changed; the need to pick one's way through a minefield in order to secure the succession for one's own son was as acute as ever. But the instability of Claudius' seat on the throne was something new. Whether by birth or by adoption, membership of the Julian family had ensured a relatively secure tenure of power to all his predecessors. Despite oath taking, treason and plot, neither Augustus nor Tiberius had really come within hailing distance of deposition. Caligula had been less lucky, but his problem was pathological. Claudius the non-Julian needed new techniques if he was to survive, and Messalina played a not inconsiderable part in providing them. In the end her personal peculiarities proved to be her undoing, but Claudius' survival over the critical first decade of his reign owed more than we will ever know to the shrewd political intelligence of Valeria Messalina.

Agrippina inherited more than a husband from Messalina. Endowed with a particularly keen intellect and a literary bent that enabled her to impress Claudius more than the *Hausfrau* Aelia Paetina or the bejewelled Lollia Paulina, she learned from her predecessor what to do in order to exploit the full potential of the new politics, and also what not to do if she wanted to enjoy the fruits of her labours. When Pallas stressed her descent from the Claudian Germanicus but said nothing about her mother and the divine blood, he simply reflected her realization that the ideology of *Partes Agrippinae* belonged to the past. She would attempt to form her own *Partes* in her son's reign, but it would have a Claudian, almost an anti-Julian, slant. But she really believed in only two things, her son's claim to the throne and her claim (modelled on that of Livia but pursued with much greater insistence) to a share in his power. She concentrated on those aims with such iron determination that she was able to impose rigorous controls on a disposition which, given her previous history, could easily have led her on to the same slippery path as her predecessor.

13

AGRIPPINA, NERO AND THE DOMUS

INTRODUCTION

The first five years of Nero's reign were dominated by his relations with his mother. There were two areas of contention. On the one hand Agrippina pressed even harder than she had done under Claudius for a full share of power, for a partnership in empire. On the other hand she guarded her position jealously against anyone, whether wife or mistress, who threatened her influnce over Nero. She even fought fire with fire, forming some sort of alliance with Nero's first wife, Octavia, in a desperate attempt to bring Nero to heel. But on the whole Agrippina's few years as an emperor's mother were not felicitous. She was constantly striving to come from behind, to equalize a minus, but history had passed her by. Nero's advisers saw no future for the regime in continuing to treat the Principate as a branch of the Domus. Agrippina's tragedy was that she was unable to accept the change.

After Agrippina's death in 59 two of Nero's wives, Octavia and Poppaea, managed something of a continuation of the political life of the Domus. Octavia as the focal point of a Claudian revival is completely convincing. And though Poppaea is less well cast as the champion of the Julian cause, her struggle with Octavia was one of the closest approaches to an entirely feminine political operation in the history of our period. But Statilia Messalina, Nero's third wife, who survived him, had no scope for political action; there was nothing left of the Julio-Claudian dynasty for her to work on.

'THE BEST OF MOTHERS'

On the day of his accession (13 October 54) the 17-year-old Nero, asked by the tribune of the guard for a password, replied 'Optima Mater – The Best of Mothers'. Thus was struck the initial keynote of the reign, and for a while the honours showered on Agrippina seemed to bear out the promise of the password. When Claudius was deified she was appointed priestess of his cult and given two lictors. Coins were an early mark of distinction; Agrippina appeared in tandem with Nero, sometimes in the senior position, and sometimes as a goddess complementing Nero's depiction as a god.[1]

The priesthood of Divus Claudius would prove to be the barometer of Agrippina's declining fortunes (see this chapter, pp. 192–3), but one of the distinctions has a more immediate impact. It is the legend, 'Procurator of Caesar and Agrippina Augusta' (SMW 264). This shared authority over imperial procurators has a bearing on what Tacitus calls 'the first death of the new reign', namely the murder of M. Iunius Silanus, governor of Asia, who was poisoned through Agrippina's machinations but, according to Tacitus, without Nero's knowledge. The crime was carried out by Nero's procurator in Asia, P. Celer, in conjunction with the freedman Helius; the poison was, it is said, supplied by Agrippina from the residue of what she had used against Claudius. The victim was a brother of the Silanus whom Agrippina had destroyed in order to end his bethrothal to Octavia (see Chapter 12, p. 180). Tacitus rather illogically says that Agrippina was afraid that M. Silanus would seek revenge for the death of his brother (after four years?), but he also notes another reason: 'popular talk' considered an adolescent who owed his throne to a crime a less suitable ruler than a mature aristocrat, innocent of crime and of equally distinguished ancestry.[2] We conclude that if Agrippina acted without Nero's knowledge,[3] it was because the procurator of Asia fell into the category of 'Procurator of Caesar and Agrippina Augusta'. Strictly speaking she would still not have discharged a state function, since procurators were servants of the Domus, not of the *res publica*, but the dividing line was fading.[4]

THE SEPARATION OF DOMUS AND *RES PUBLICA*

The sources make some sweeping generalizations about Agrippina's authority in the early months of the reign. Tacitus says that there would have been other murders had it not been for Burrus and Seneca. They guided Nero into more acceptable outlets for his perverted desires, displaying rare unity in their opposition to the violent and domineering Agrippina, supported as she was by Pallas.[5] Locating the opposition at the very start of the reign is simply intelligent anticipation by Tacitus.[6] What actually happened was that Agrippina's ambitions alienated one of her staunchest supporters, Burrus, and drove him into an alliance with the more flexible Seneca. Burrus had been Agrippina's most vital instrument on the day of Claudius' death, when he presented Nero to the praetorians, reassured them about the absence of Britannicus, and conducted Nero to their camp, where he was saluted as imperator, leaving the senate's confirmation as little more than a formality. Burrus had not forgotten that he owed his praetorian prefecture to Agrippina. Seneca's recollection of past favours was less of an embarrassment to him. But even Burrus, it seems, could not allow personal loyalty to outweigh the public interest indefinitely.[7]

The accession speech that Nero delivered in the senate was written by Seneca.[8] The philosopher took the opportunity to launch an immediate, if indirect, attack on Agrippina. Outlining the proposed shape of his principate, Nero renounced everything that Claudius was being criticized for. He would not judge every case himself; he would not assist a few powerful individuals by holding court behind closed doors; corruption would be suppressed; his Domus and the *res publica* would be kept separate and distinct (*TA* 13.4.2). Renunciation of the chamber court did not worry Agrippina very much; she had not made use of that speciality of Messalina's, preferring to entrust her judicial operations to the senate. Nevertheless, trials *intra cubiculum* were part of the apparatus of the Domus, and the proposed downgrading of the Domus was aimed squarely at her. By blocking her ambition to become a partner in empire, Seneca had nailed his colours to the mast. The burning question of the day was how Agrippina would respond to the challenge.

The answer was not long in coming. At the end of 54, a mere month or two after Nero's accession, Agrippina made a dramatic attempt to use her position as priestess of Divus Claudius as a means of participating directly in politics instead of leaving it to a male intermediary. Two measures were proposed in the senate, both amending laws that had been passed in Claudius' reign. The one concerned the *lex Cincia* of 204 BC. Originally prohibitive of the acceptance of any court fees by pleaders, it had been amended in 47 so as to allow a maximum fee of 10,000 sesterces per case. It was now proposed that the full rigour of the *lex* be revived.[9] The proposal was in line with the new policy of discouraging the corruption which was endemic amongst court pleaders like P. Suillius (see Chapter 12, p. 175). But Agrippina was hostile to the proposal, claiming that it subverted Claudius' legislation; as he had been deified his *acta* were protected from interference, and as the priestess of his cult she had a right and a duty to interfere. Agrippina was raising an important issue. If they insisted on deifying their rulers, they must accept the constitutional consequences of their decision. And those consequences included the possibility that a woman would have the right to defend the Divus' acts. When Livia became priestess of Divus Augustus she had tried to punish insults to him under the criminal law, but that remedy was not open to Agrippina; there was no such thing in Roman law as punishment for unlawful legislative proposals.[10] The other proposal to which Agrippina objected was that quaestors be exempted from the obligation to stage gladiatorial games. We do not have details of the Claudian legislation, but there clearly was some, and she opposed this proposal as well.[11]

Agrippina's opposition was taken seriously – as it had to be once she forced them to look at the consequences of deification – and the senate specially arranged to meet on the Palatine, probably in the Palatine library. A door was built at the back of the chamber, through which Agrippina was admitted; she then stood concealed behind a curtain and listened to the debate.[12] The amending laws were passed, but Agrippina had achieved the unthinkable: she had attended a meeting of the senate. In doing so she had not only set up a counterweight to Seneca's policy, she had also responded to an attack on herself as the priestess of Divus Claudius; and although she may not have won security of tenure for Divus Claudius, she had at least delayed his deconsecration.[13]

It was also late in 54 that Agrippina fired a second shot in her constitutional campaign. A delegation from one of the warring factions in Armenia was given a hearing by Nero. Agrippina approached the tribunal with the evident intention of mounting it and seating herself at Nero's side. This advance on the separate dais that she had occupied in Claudius' reign (see Chapter 12, p. 182) would have given practical expression to the jugation of mother and son on Nero's early coins (see Chapter 13, p. 191). It could have been the introduction to a new definition of the *res publica*. But Seneca was equal to the occasion. While everyone stood stupefied, he advised Nero to step down to meet his mother. Thus a show of filial piety averted a scandal (*TA* 13.5.3). Dio joins Burrus in the impromptu solution, and adds that after this Seneca and Burrus strove to ensure that no more public business was entrusted to Agrippina; they took the entire administration into their own hands (CD 61.3.3–5.6). They gave proof of that, still in 54, when a commander had to be appointed for Armenia. 'Public talk' was divided between those who saw little hope in a youth ruled by a woman, and those who hoped that Burrus and Seneca would persuade Nero to appoint a competent commander; the hopes of the Seneca-Burrus lobby were realized, for Corbulo was appointed (*TA* 13.6.1–6, 8.1).

DECLINE AND DESPERATION

Agrippina might have achieved an honourable draw in late 54, but 55 saw a distinct weakening in her position. Nero fell in love with an imperial freedwoman, Claudia Acte, held clandestine meetings with her, at first without Agrippina's knowledge and later in defiance of her wishes, and very nearly married her.[14] The liaison, which was favoured by Seneca and Burrus, was destined to last for the rest of Nero's life.[15] Agrippina reacted to this development with extreme uneasiness. She railed against 'her freedwoman rival', 'her daughter-in-law the skivvy', but her attacks only intensified Nero's passion. Yet his mother's influence was still so strong that he was obliged to resort to subterfuge; Seneca's close friend, Annaeus Serenus, pretended to be the donor of the gifts that Nero gave Acte. Agrippina decided to change her tactics. She admitted that she had been too hasty, and offered Nero the use of her bedroom for his assignations, as well as financial support. But Nero's friends urged him to be on his guard against a ruthless and insincere woman.[16]

Nero, wishing to conciliate his mother, sent her a splendid jewelled robe selected from the wardrobes of former empresses, but Agrippina declared that he was only returning a fraction of what belonged to her (*TA* 13.13.5–6). Ungracious, but she was again asserting a claim as a partner in empire. That is why Tacitus says that some put a sinister construction on her words (*TA* 13.14.1). Their forebodings were soon confirmed. When Nero decided to check the mainstay of this female arrogance (*superbia muliebris*) by getting rid of Pallas, Agrippina became thoroughly alarmed. She declared in Nero's hearing that 'Britannicus was now of age and a worthy heir to his father's throne, at present occupied by an adopted intruder who used it to ill-treat his mother'. She threatened to expose all the wickedness of the Domus, including her marriage and her poisoning [of Claudius].[17] It was only thanks to the gods and her efforts that Britannicus was still alive. She would take him to the praetorians' camp and would let them see Germanicus' daughter[18] standing up to men who would rule the world – Burrus with his crippled hand and the exile Seneca with his pedantic tongue. Hurling abuse, she invoked the deified Claudius, the shades of the Silani, and all her other crimes, now rendered vain (*TA* 13.14.4–6). Nero's worries were increased by an incident at the Saturnalia, when Britannicus was loudly applauded for a song about his exclusion from the throne. But Nero was unable to frame a viable charge against him, and therefore arranged, in February 55, for him to be poisoned, while dining with other children in the presence of Agrippina, Octavia and others. Nero claimed that he had died of epilepsy and gave him an unpretentious funeral.[19]

It now came close to open hostilities. Agrippina's fear and rage at the death of 'the last of the Claudians' (*TA* 13.17.3) knew no bounds. She allied herself to Octavia, Britannicus' sister and Nero's (neglected) wife. She held secret meetings to raise funds, cultivated military tribunes and centurions, honoured those of the nobility who still survived, and gave the impression that she was searching for a leader and a party- *quasi quaereret ducem et partis*. Pallas had been her party leader, but now Nero removed him from office as financial secretary.[20] As for the successor to Pallas for whom Agrippina was looking, names, especially of senators, are not particularly thick on the ground. P. Celer, the procuratorial poisoner, was not without influence, but there is nothing to suggest that he was at the centre of a sub-senatorial lobby; still less can it be supposed that it was he who put Agrippina in touch with the great Stoic opposition to Nero.[21] Her friends certainly included C. Ummidius Quadratus, legate of Syria, who was noted for his long tenure of the office (51–60), but precisely for that reason he distanced himself from the politics of the capital; nor does Pallas' brother, Antonius Felix, procurator of Judaea, present as a likely leader, despite his marriage to a Drusilla.[22] The answer is, of course, that Agrippina did not have a suitable leader available; she was in fact only starting to put an organization in place in 55, in the hope of halting the sudden decline in her fortunes. But Nero was too quick for her. Acting no doubt on the advice of Seneca and Burrus, he withdrew the military escort which she had been given as Claudius' wife, together with some German troops that had been added as an additional honour. This effectively put an end to her negotiations with tribunes and centurions (Koestermann 3.269). She was also moved from the palace to the house previously owned by Antonia, in order to cut off the morning salutations at which crowds of friends and dependants attended her. When Nero visited her at her new establishment he was accompanied by an armed guard and did not stay long.[23]

Agrippina was effectively isolated (CD 61.8.6), and her isolation exposed her to dangers. Junia Silana, the wife of C. Silius whom he had abandoned for Messalina, precipitated the greatest crisis in Nero's Domus up to this time. She had been on good terms with Agrippina, but the latter had spoilt Silana's chances of marrying Sextius Africanus by telling him that Silana was getting older and her morals had deteriorated. Agrippina's motive was, it is said, to keep Silana childless and unmarried in order to inherit her property herself (*TA* 13.19.2). Whatever the motive, Silana now took what could have been a terrible revenge. She put up her clients, Iturius and Calvisius, to charge Agrippina with plotting to incite Rubellius Plautus to revolt and to marry him. As a son of the Julia who was Tiberius' granddaughter, he was a dynastic threat. Even more important, his Stoic connections and great wealth made him an ideological enemy of Nero, for which he would later pay with his property and his life (Bauman 1989: 111–12). Adversity makes strange bedfellows. Under different circumstances Agrippina would cheerfully have sent him to join the Silani, but now she wanted to marry him.

Tacitus notes that there were 'old and often repeated charges' that could have been raised against Agrippina, such as mourning Britannicus and publicizing Octavia's wrongs (*TA* 13.19.3) – in other words, accusing Nero of Britannicus' murder and of humiliating Octavia by his liaison with Acte. But the accusers concen-

trated on the Rubellius Plautus affair. Understandably: he was
potentially the leader that Agrippina wanted. An elaborate attack
was mounted against her. Junia Silana's clients disclosed their
evidence to Atimetus and the actor Paris, who were clients of
Nero's aunt Domitia. The latter was no friend of Agrippina, who
had taken Passienus Crispus from her; presumably she was also
not impressed by Agrippina's destruction of her sister, Domitia
Lepida. Domitia told her clients to divulge the plot to Nero in
the most sensational terms. The meaning of this is that as charges
of *maiestas* were still in abeyance, something drastic was needed
in order to persuade Nero to revive the treason law.[24] Paris, who
was one of Nero's boon companions, found Nero in his cups and
so terrified him that he resolved not only to kill his mother and
Plautus, but also to remove Burrus from the praetorian prefecture
because his obligation to Agrippina made him suspect (*TA*
13.19.4–20.1). This partial contradiction of what he had said about
Burrus at the start of the reign (13.2.1–3) worried Tacitus and
prompted him to do some research. His investigations having
convinced him that there was no truth in the story about Nero's
hostility towards Burrus,[25] he has Nero eager to proceed with his
mother's destruction. But he is restrained by Burrus, who points
out that everyone is entitled to be heard in their defence, especially
a parent. Next day Burrus visited Agrippina, accompanied by
Seneca and some freedmen. Burrus informed her of the charges
and the names of the accusers, and confronted her with the threatening stance of an accuser. She gave a spirited reply:

> The childless Silana knows nothing of a mother's feelings;
> it is easy for a loose woman to change lovers, but not
> for a mother to change sons. The impoverished Iturius and
> Calvisius can repay an old hag, but I am not going to incur
> the infamy of causing my son's death, nor is he going to
> cause mine. As for Domitia putting up Paris and her lover
> Atimetus to concoct a drama for the stage, while I was
> securing the succession for Nero she was worrying about
> her fish-ponds at Baiae. How can they claim that I tampered
> with the praetorians, undermined the loyalty of the prov-
> inces, or bribed slaves and freedmen? If Britannicus had
> become emperor would I have survived? If Plautus had won
> the throne and had sat in judgment on me, I would have
> been charged not with a few indiscreet remarks prompted

by a mother's love, but with the crimes that I committed on my son's behalf.[26]

Agrippina demanded an interview with Nero. Displaying considerable understanding of the legal issues involved, she neither spoke in her defence nor reminded him of what she had done for him.[27] She demanded punishment for the accusers and benefits for her friends.[28] Junia Silana was exiled, Iturius and Calvisius were expelled from Rome, and Atimetus was executed. Paris, the boon companion, was left alone. So too, was Plautus – for the present.[29] The benefits to her friends augment our list of her supporters. Faenius Rufus was put in charge of the corn supply; he would later become praetorian prefect, but would be brought down by Tigellinus on the grounds of friendship with Agrippina. Arruntius Stella was appointed to supervise the games planned by Nero, and Ti. Claudius Balbillus (Nero's former tutor) was made prefect of Egypt. The governorship of Syria was earmarked for P. Anteius, but his departure was delayed by various pretexts and he was finally kept in Rome.[30]

PEACE AND TRANQUILLITY

Agrippina's repulse of the attempted prosecution had won her an important round. It had also enabled her to retain, or to regain, some of Burrus' loyalty. The opposition was well aware of that, and the immediate sequel was the prosecution of Burrus and Pallas (still prominent despite his demotion). They were charged with conspiring to give the throne to Faustus Cornelius Sulla, Messalina's half-brother and husband of Claudius' daughter, Antonia. The story told by the accuser Paetus, a notorious delator, was manifestly untrue, and he was exiled. At the trial Burrus, who was a member of Nero's *consilium*, took his seat and voted although he was an accused; but this was on a preliminary point.[31] Clearly there was still a significant link between Agrippina and Burrus. He would not be able to save her when the supreme crisis came, but he would refuse to kill her.[32]

Burrus' return to his allegiance appears to have had a calming effect, for the next two or three years are devoid of stirring events on the domestic front, as Tacitus notes with some disappointment.[33] It has been suggested that by 57–8 Agrippina was capitalizing on the rebuff of Nero's attempt to abolish indirect taxes; she is thought to have allied herself with dissatisfied elements in the senate. But despite Agrippina's wealth and Pallas' financial expertise, there is nothing save conjecture to link her with the episode.[34] There is, however, one matter that seems to have a bearing on her position at this time, although Tacitus does not forge a link. In 57 the distinguished Pomponia Graecina, wife of A. Plautius, was charged with foreign superstition. She was tried by her husband, sitting with a *consilium* of relatives, but was acquitted. Tacitus observes that her long life was always unhappy, because after the murder of her relative, Julia Livilla, through Messalina's instrumentality, Pomponia wore mourning and grieved for forty years.[35] This protracted demonstration of hostility to Messalina would have been far from unwelcome to Agrippina, and one wonders if Pomponia was a friend of Agrippina who was charged as a reminder that the struggle for control of Nero was not over. But this does not mean that there was any tension between mother and son at this time. It has been argued, on the strength of Arval records of sacrifices to Concordia on Agrippina's birthday in 57 and 58, and on Nero's birthday in 58, that there was anxiety because of a rift,[36] but her total exclusion from *Annales* over 56–8 suggests that Tacitus found nothing important to report about her.[37]

It seems, then, that the three years' hibernation marked something of a revival in Agrippina's fortunes. She was no longer the domineering figure of the first three months, but the setbacks of 55 had not been followed by any further inroads into her position. On the contrary, it must be assumed that she retained a degree of control over Nero and still cherished hopes of a partnership in power. Her reaction to the advent of Nero's second wife, Poppaea Sabina, is the guarantee of that.

POPPAEA SABINA

Poppaea Sabina was destined to achieve what the professional politicians of two reigns had not been able to do, namely the complete and final destruction of Agrippina. Someone as powerful as that deserves a brief biographical notice. Tacitus, in one of the most striking contrasts between his treatment of a topic and that of Suetonius,[38] introduces Poppaea Sabina with the observation that hers was the kind of immorality that proved to be a national disaster; she had every virtue except Virtue. A daughter of the

199

Poppaea Sabina who had been driven to her death by Messalina, she had the same names as her mother because her father, T. Ollius, had been implicated with Sejanus, as a result of which she had taken the name of her illustrious maternal grandfather, C. Poppaeus Sabinus (cos. AD 9). From her mother, the most beautiful woman of her day, she had inherited a lineage and beauty; her wealth measured up to her birth; and she was a charming and witty conversationalist. She professed respectability, wearing a veil on her rare public appearances, though Tacitus is not sure whether this was to arouse interest or because it suited her. She bestowed her favours on husbands and lovers alike, but always in a calculating fashion. While married to Rufrius Crispinus (one of Messalina's appointees as praetorian prefect, by whom she had a son), she was seduced by the young, urbane M. Salvius Otho (the future emperor) and married him (TA 13.45). Her amber-coloured hair inspired a poem by Nero and a new fashion amongst Roman women. She also set a fashion by bathing in asses' milk, which she believed smoothed out wrinkles, and by devising a heavy cosmetic which came to be known as 'Poppaea's cream'. Noticing some wrinkles in her mirror one day, she prayed that she might die before she lost her looks.[39]

Tacitus dates the start of Nero's liaison with Poppaea to 58. Otho sang his wife's praises to Nero, hoping that possession of the same woman would strengthen his hold over Nero.[40] Poppaea soon established her ascendancy over Nero, but allowed him to spend only a limited amount of time with her; she did not want to jeopardize her marriage to Otho, whom she described as a real man compared with Nero and his subservience to Acte.[41] Nero sent Otho off as governor of Lusitania, where he remained until the civil war.[42]

Tacitus ushers in the year 59 with one of his keynote statements: 'In the consulship of C. Vipstanus and C. Fonteius, Nero no longer delayed his long-premeditated crime' (TA 14.1.1). Poppaea saw no prospect of his divorcing Octavia and marrying her while Agrippina was alive. She taunted him with being a pupil under guardianship rather than a Princeps, claiming that Agrippina was afraid that as Nero's wife she would disclose her mother-in-law's oppression of the senate and her arrogance and greed (14.1.1–3). By alternating tears and seduction Poppaea won him over. There was no opposition, adds Tacitus; everyone wanted Agrippina's power broken, though no one thought Nero's hatred would drive him to murder (14.1.5).

In a last desperate attempt to reassert her domination, Agrippina reportedly tried to lure Nero into incest, though the sources are far from clear as to what happened. Tacitus notes two versions. In the one Agrippina began visiting Nero at midday, his regular time for feasting; all dressed up and ready for incest, she drew her inebriated son into sensual caresses. The attendants reported to Seneca, who enlisted the support of Acte; she warned Nero that the army would never tolerate such sacrilege. But according to another account the initiative had not come from Agrippina but from Nero himself. Tacitus considers the first version more likely (*TA* 14.2). An Agrippina who outdoes Jocasta, and a Nero who cannot plead Oedipus' ignorance, are a lot to swallow. Dio realizes that; he thinks that Nero had a mistress who looked very much like Agrippina, and Nero used to say that when he was with her he thought of his mother (*CD* 61.11.4). But Dio also learned that after Poppaea's death Nero first attached himself to a woman who looked like her, and then to the boy Sporus who also looked like her (*CD* 63.13.1). Suetonius thinks that when Nero rode with Agrippina in her litter he used to commit incest with her; but he also has Nero and Sporus in a litter (*SN* 28). It has been observed that the one part of the story that Suetonius believes is the intervention of Seneca with the help of Acte.[43]

Whatever the truth of the incest story, there is evidence of a more conventional nature regarding the worsening relations between mother and son over 58–9. We are obliged to Suetonius for the information, because Tacitus is deeply immersed in one of his Grand Guignol modes and moves straight from the incest set-piece to the collapsible ship set-piece, pausing only to note in passing that Nero avoided being alone with her because of the attempted incest, and expressed his wholehearted agreement whenever she left for her properties at Tusculum and Antium (*TA* 14.3.1). In Suetonius, after cancelling her guard of honour and driving her from the palace (which we know happened in 55), Nero begins a campaign of systematic harassment. He bribes people to annoy her with lawsuits while she remains in the city, and when she withdraws to the country he passes by her house both by land and by sea and destabilizes her with shouted abuse and mockery (*SN* 34.1). As Suetonius then turns immediately to Nero's experiments with ways of killing her, the campaign of lawsuits and abuse must be much closer to 58–9 than to 55. The harassing lawsuits recall the torrent of suits that Atticus helped Fulvia to cope with in the triumviral period (see Chapter 7, p. 86), and one wonders if persuading creditors to foreclose was habitually used as a political weapon. Livia, we recollect, felt herself diminished by a litigious attack on her friend Urgulania (see Chapter 10, p. 135). At all events, the stage was now set for the *dénouement* in the long saga of Agrippina.

'LET HIM KILL ME, BUT LET HIM RULE'

Agrippina's resistance to Nero's plans to marry Poppaea was said to be the major factor in Nero's decision, in 59, to end his mother's domination once and for all. He had some difficulty in devising a suitable way to kill her, since she had reputedly built up resistance to poison by swallowing antidotes. He experimented with a mechanical device for dropping ceiling panels on her while she slept, but this leaked out. A solution was proposed by Anicetus, commander of the fleet at Misenum, Nero's former tutor and an old enemy of Agrippina. His plan was to construct a ship with a detachable section which would hurl Agrippina into the sea. During the festival of Minerva, the Quinquatria, Nero invited her to dine at Baiae, treated her with great consideration, and later that night saw her on to the booby-trapped ship for the return to her villa at Bauli. At a given signal the roof collapsed, killing her friend Crepereius Gallus, but the ship did not break up as planned. Agrippina's friend, Acerronia Polla, called out that she was Agrippina, whereupon the oarsmen beat her to death. Agrippina herself, wounded but unrecognized, sprang into the water and swam until she was picked up by some small craft.[44]

Agrippina, feigning ignorance of the plot, sent word to Nero about her narrow escape. Nero, alarmed, sent for Burrus and Seneca, about whose prior knowledge Tacitus is uncertain. They realized that either Nero or Agrippina must die. Seneca suggested that the praetorians kill her, but Burrus refused, pointing out that the cohorts were bound by oath to the entire Domus. He suggested that Anicetus despatch her. To make it easier for Anicetus, Nero had Agrippina's messenger, Agerinus, arrested, having first taken the precaution of dropping a sword at Agerinus' feet as if he had tried to kill Nero on Agrippina's orders (*TA* 14.6.1–7.7). This was to be the justification for the murder.

Anicetus and his men forced their way into Agrippina's villa at Bauli. With two of his officers Anicetus burst into her bedroom. She declared, 'If you've come to visit me, report that I am better; if to kill me, I refuse to believe that it is on my son's orders'. The assassins closed around her bed. One of them hit her on the head. She bared herself, cried, 'Strike at the womb that bore him!', and died under a hail of blows.[45]

It was rumoured that Nero then rushed off to view her body, declaring that 'I did not know that I had such a beautiful mother', but Tacitus is sceptical.[46] The story may have been invented in order to rebut the suspicions of incest. At all events, Agrippina was cremated the same night with scant ceremony and was given an uncovered and unenclosed grave. Years before, astrologers had told her that Nero would become emperor but would kill his mother. This indomitable woman had replied, 'Let him kill me, but let him rule.'[47]

AFTER AGRIPPINA

Why did Nero do it? There is no simple answer. His own explanation, in a letter to the senate, that Agerinus had come to kill him and that Agrippina had paid for her complicity, was palpably untrue. That is why he tried to bolster it with a summary of her misdeeds over the years: she had sought a partnership in power, the allegiance of the praetorians, the humiliation of senate and people; she had opposed largesse for praetorians and plebs; she had arranged the deaths of distinguished men; only with difficulty had she been prevented from bursting into the senate-house and laying down the law to foreign nations; she had been responsible for all the mischief of Claudius' reign; good fortune was to be thanked for the shipwreck and for her final destruction (*TA* 14.11.1–3). This is too much for Tacitus, who indignantly asks how anyone but a fool could believe that the wreck was accidental, or that a shipwrecked woman had sent an assassin; Nero was a brute, but Seneca, who had drafted the letter to the senate, ought to have known better (14.11.3–4). Nevertheless, the official version had the desired effect. Thanksgivings were decreed; annual games at the Quinquatria were to commemorate the discovery of the plot; gold statues of Minerva and Nero were set up in the senate-house; Agrippina's birthday was declared a day of ill omen. As a final gesture of defiance, Nero recalled people whom she had driven into exile – Junia Calvina, Calpurnia, Valerius Capito, Licinius Gabolus, Iturius and Calvisius; and Lollia Paulina's ashes were brought home.[48] Whether he realized it or not, all this came perilously close to recognizing Agrippina as an associate in empire; *memoriae damnatio*, the eradication of someone's acts, was usually reserved for deposed rulers.

Nero might have persuaded some, but not everyone was impressed. The great Stoic, Thrasea Paetus, walked out of the senate in disgust. Lampoons circulated in profusion, proclaiming such messages as 'Nero, Orestes, Alcmeon – matricides all'. Datus, an actor in Atellan farces, mimed drinking and swimming in a song beginning, 'Farewell father, farewell mother!'[49]

Tacitus firmly believes that Agrippina's opposition to the proposed marriage with Poppaea was responsible for her death; she not only saw Poppaea as a threat to her own position, but also wanted to safeguard the interests of Octavia, her ally since her expulsion from the palace in 55. But the trouble is that it was only in 62, some three years after the murder, that Nero divorced Octavia and married Poppaea. Attempts to adjust the chronology so as to accommodate the belated marriage have not been very successful.[50]

It has recently been argued that the real obstacle to divorcing Octavia was not Agrippina, but two claimants to the throne, and it was only after getting rid of them that Nero felt free to proceed with the divorce and remarriage.[51] The two claimants are certainly prominent at this time. Faustus Sulla, Messalina's half-brother and husband of Claudius' other daughter, Antonia, was exiled to Massilia in 58 for raising a riot against Nero during one of the latter's nocturnal jaunts; in 62 Tigellinus had him killed because his proximity to the Rhine legions was viewed with apprehension by Nero. Rubellius Plautus, having survived his link with Agrippina, was asked in 60 to withdraw to his property in Asia; he was murdered in 62 when Tigellinus became aware of Nero's apprehensions in regard to his proximity to the eastern legions.[52] Tacitus in fact confirms the relevance of Nero's fears to the question of the marriage: 'Putting aside his fears, he prepared to expedite his marriage to Poppaea, hitherto deferred because of those fears, and to get rid of his wife Octavia' (*TA* 14.59.4). Tacitus adds that though Octavia behaved with propriety, Nero found her unacceptable because of her popularity as Claudius' daughter. He wrote to the senate denouncing Faustus and Rubellius, but saying nothing about their deaths; he added that the safety of the state was his prime concern. A thanksgiving was decreed and the senate went through the farce of expelling the two dead men from its ranks (14.59.5–6). Taking the senate's decree as approval of all his crimes, Nero divorced Octavia on the grounds of barrenness and married Poppaea (14.60.1). But this was not the end of the chapter for Octavia. For further light on the delay in marrying Poppaea we must look more closely at Claudius' unfortunate daughter.

OCTAVIA AND POPPAEA

The deaths of Faustus and Rubellius were not isolated events; they were part of a vast purge carried out by Nero in 62. Burrus had died, more probably from cancer of the throat than by poison, and had been replaced by two praetorian prefects – Faenius Rufus, whom Agrippina had advanced to the grain prefecture, and Ofonius Tigellinus, the evil genius of Nero's last six years. Burrus' death undermined Seneca, who was forced to withdraw from active politics and was driven to suicide three years later.[53] The domino effect continued: Seneca's removal weakened Faenius Rufus, now belatedly stigmatized as a friend of Agrippina. And only after that does Tacitus turn to Faustus and Rubellius.[54] It is against this background that we take up the further history of Octavia and Poppaea.

After noting the divorce and the marriage to Poppaea, Tacitus proceeds to elaborate. He says that Poppaea, dominating Nero as his wife as she had dominated him as his mistress, suborned one of Octavia's servants to accuse her of adultery with an Alexandrian flute player named Eucaerus (*TA* 14.60.2–6). Proof of adultery was, of course, not needed for divorce *per se*. But if adultery could be proved, it carried detractions from freedom, reputation and, above all, property which a bare repudiation did not carry. Poppaea wanted those consequences. She therefore arranged with Tigellinus to interrogate members of Octavia's household under torture. But most of the household maintained that Octavia was innocent, and from one of them, Pythias, Tigellinus got more than he had bargained for. Nero had to be content with a divorce on the grounds of barrenness. Octavia retained the right to her dowry, and Nero settled the claim by conveying to her Burrus' house and Plautus' estates.[55] Thus Burrus was already dead at the time of the divorce, but that does not invalidate Dio's statement that Burrus had opposed a divorce and had told Nero 'to give her back her dowry', which Dio takes to mean the empire which his marriage had brought him.[56] Clearly the divorce had been under discussion for some time; Burrus' death was a victory (or a windfall) for the pro-divorce lobby. The dilution of Faenius Rufus' power was another victory for Poppaea and Tigellinus. If Seneca also opposed the divorce,[57] the rearrangements of 62 become a clean sweep for the divorce lobby. The freedman Doryphorus, petitions secretary, was unwise enough to oppose Poppaea's marriage; he was poisoned in the same year (*TA* 14.65.1). Poppaea did not devote all her time to her toilet.

Faustus and Rubellius were thus only one factor, albeit the most conspicuous, in the equation. But on the specific question of the divorce Faustus was the more important. As the husband of Claudius' elder daughter, Antonia, he had a familial interest in the matter; and he was potentially the focus of a Claudian lobby which had pursued an erratic but vigorous course over the years following Britannicus' death.[58] Preventive action against Faustus preceded that against Rubellius by two years; he was sent away in the very year that saw the start of Nero's infatuation with Poppaea. Even before that, a mere year after Britannicus' death, Burrus and Pallas had been charged with promoting Faustus' claim to the throne (see Chapter 13, p. 198). We would very much like to know more about the part played by Faustus' wife, Antonia, in the affairs of the Claudian lobby. She was important enough in 65 to be scheduled to visit the praetorians in company with the conspirator Piso, in order to win popular support for him (*TA* 15.53.4). It is also said that after Poppaea's death she refused to marry Nero, whereupon he put her to death.[59] By proposing to marry Antonia, Nero had made a belated attempt to repair the damage caused by his divorce of Octavia. It is to that damage that consideration must now be given.

Nero, having got his divorce, might well have been content to leave it at that, but Poppaea thought otherwise. She realized that Octavia would be a focus for Claudian sentiment as long as she remained in Rome. It was undoubtedly at her prompting that Nero ordered Octavia to be moved to Campania under armed guard.[60] But Poppaea had miscalculated badly. The move sparked off a wave of popular demonstrations. It was rumoured that Nero had recalled Octavia, and this precipitated a more explicit demonstration. Joyful crowds flocked to the Capitol, threw down Poppaea's statues and carried those of Octavia on their shoulders, scattering flowers over them and placing them in the forum and the temples. There was even applause for Nero.[61] A noisy crowd invaded the palace, but were driven back by soldiers, and Poppaea's statues were reinstated. Always a good hater, she was now terrified of Nero's possible capitulation to mob violence. Throwing herself at Nero's feet, she strenuously denied that a crowd of Octavia's clients and slaves had the right to speak for the Roman people. Once they got a leader (*dux partium*?) Nero himself would be their target; even at a distance Octavia was manipulating them. What had she (Poppaea) done wrong? Was it because she was about to give the Domus a legitimate heir?[62] Would the Roman people rather have the child of an Egyptian fluteplayer? If that was what he wanted, let him take back the woman who dominated him, but let him do so of his own accord, not under coercion. Otherwise the mob would find her a new husband.[63]

Poppaea's arguments had the desired effect: Nero was both frightened and enraged. But the suspicions about the fluteplayer could not be substantiated; the examination of Octavia's maidservants had already shown that.[64] It was therefore decided to concoct a confession of adultery. The choice fell on Anicetus, who had murdered Agrippina but had got scant thanks for his pains (*TA* 14.62.3). Nero now promised him rich rewards, but threatened to kill him if he refused. Anicetus did even more than was required by his brief, inventing a stratagem by which he had violated Octavia's chastity. He was exiled to Sardinia, where he lived out his days in comfort.[65]

Nero proclaimed in an edict that Anicetus had been seduced by Octavia in order to win over his fleet. Forgetting his previous allegation of barrenness, Nero added that she had tried to hide her infidelities by an abortion, which he himself had verified (*TA* 14.63.1). Octavia was banished to Pandateria. Tacitus then writes a piece on the unfortunate Octavia which suggests that he had read Seneca's historical drama, *Octavia*.

> No exile ever earned more sympathy. The elder Agrippina and Julia Livilla were mature women whose miseries were alleviated by some memory of happiness. But Octavia's wedding day had been like a funeral and had brought her to a Domus which gave her nothing but sadness.[66] She was forced

to see her father poisoned, and then her brother; a slave-girl was raised above her; ruined by the marriage of Poppaea, she finally faced a charge more horrible than death.

(*TA* 14.63.2–4)

The comedy was nearly over. After a few days on Pandateria, Octavia received the order to die. She protested that she was no longer married, she was only a sister to Nero. She invoked the family name of 'Germanicus' and cited Agrippina. But the soldiers bound her and opened her veins (to make it look like suicide). Terror had, however, made her blood flow more slowly, so she was put in a hot bath and suffocated. As a final atrocity her head was cut off and taken to Poppaea. (There are too many of these macabre decapitations to be dismissed as fiction.) Tacitus observes in disgust that thanksgiving offerings were voted to the temples. He asks his readers to take it for granted in future that whenever an emperor ordered a banishment or an execution there was a thanksgiving to the gods (*TA* 14.64.1–5). The great historian was not opposed to the Principate as an institution, but he did not love the Julio-Claudians. After inspecting them through a special lens, we can hardly blame him.

Poppaea was not destined to enjoy her triumph for long. The birth of her daughter, Claudia, in January 63 brought both her and the infant the title of Augusta; and her hometown, Pompeii, may have been honoured by the status of a colony at about this time. When Claudia died less than four months later she was deified; Stoic opposition to the conferment of divine status on 'Poppaea's womb' was later remembered, and punished. But two years later Poppaea, again pregnant, was kicked in the stomach by Nero and died. She was not cremated in the Roman fashion, but was embalmed and buried in the mausoleum of Augustus. She was deified. The consecration aroused further Stoic resentment; C. Cassius Longinus, the leading lawyer of the day, spoke so openly that he was forbidden to attend her funeral and was exiled soon afterwards.[67] Poppaea's death was almost Nero's last attack on the women of the Domus. It was left only for Antonia to show that refusing to marry him was almost as dangerous as consenting.

THE SURVIVOR: STATILIA MESSALINA

Nero's third wife, Statilia Messalina, managed to break the dismal chain of domestic mayhem. In spite of her ominous *cognomen*, she survived him. Nor is there anything to suggest that she had to exercise special agility in order to do so. Great-great-grand-daughter of Statilius Taurus (cos. 37 BC), she had been married four times. That, allied to her natural intelligence and considerable erudition (including legal knowledge), had no doubt taught her how to negotiate the Neronian rapids.[68] Her erudition may have stood her in particularly good stead; it was the first time that Nero had been reminded of his mother on that level.

It is not certain, however, that Statilia herself had any greater regard for other people's lives than Agrippina had had. The death of her fourth husband, Vestinus Atticus, in April 65 is suspicious. Nero, whose mistress she had been since before her marriage to Atticus, was thought to have engineered the latter's death – by brute force as there were no charges that he could bring against him – and it was thought that one of the reasons was that Atticus had dared to marry Statilia although aware of her liaison with Nero.[69] This was followed in the same year by the death of Poppaea. People with suspicious minds may have felt that there was a connection. It is true that Statilia's marriage to Nero was not celebrated until about May 66,[70] but there must have been some point at which it dawned on Nero that he had enough trouble with the Pisonian conspiracy and its aftermath,[71] without complicating matters still further by a hasty marriage to Statilia which would add yet another charge of uxoricide to his dossier. By observing a quasi-*annus luctus* before remarrying he would give the story of Poppaea's accidental death time to consolidate. The deal proved to be to Statilia's advantage as well, for it sedated the one issue, the deaths of Atticus and Poppaea, on which she might have been identified with the excesses of the regime. As it was she kept her record unsullied, so much so that later on, after Nero's death, she was betrothed to Otho; and when he saw that the end of his ephemeral occupation of the throne was in sight, he commended his body and his memory to Statilia (Suet. *Otho* 10.2). Otho was evidently confident that Statilia was *persona grata* in all quarters and would be able to fulfil the trust without any interference from Vitellius.

CONCLUSION

One question calls for further comment. Was Agrippina really killed because she opposed the marriage to Poppaea, or was there another reason? Specifically, was there an ideological gulf between mother and son?

Opposition to the divorce of Octavia was by no means confined to Agrippina. For different reasons nearly everyone in the corridors of power was against it. The Principate was now a permanent institution, but its chronic instability was still a problem. There was a clear appreciation of the importance of imperial solidarity, hence Nero's identification with the Claudian connection, though he was not very consistent about it.[72] That identification had broad support, including that of Agrippina and Burrus.[73] But Agrippina and Nero did not see the Claudian connection in quite the same way. To her it meant a continuation of a situation in which she was the dominant figure; the only change was in the identity of the ruler whom she would control. But Nero could not accept that scenario. He had the insignia of Claudianism, but he was not a Claudian. Whether because of Seneca's influence or his innate disposition, he rebelled against subservience while unwillingly submitting to it. His rejection of maternal control came to a head in 55, and coincided with the start of a rejection of the Claudian connection. Not only was 'the last of the Claudians' brutally murdered, but the status of Divus Claudius was steadily diminished, if not annulled altogether (see n. 13 of this chapter). We conclude, then, that Agrippina's murder was not only prompted by her opposition to the divorce. It was, as Tacitus says, a crime long contemplated.[74] Seneca struck the first blow when he wrote the speech from the throne, abruptly throwing down the gauntlet to 'the best of mothers'. After that everything moved in the same direction. The advent of Poppaea was simply the final piece that caused everything to fall into place. Despite the drama in Tacitus' account, persuading Nero to oppose the movement centred on Octavia did not make great demands on her talents. She merely told him what he wanted to hear.

14

IN RETROSPECT

Looking back from our present vantage point, no longer harassed by the rigours of disputation and the tyranny of documentation, we ask ourselves two questions. What have we said? And have we said it successfully? Not all the matters discussed can be incorporated in our answer, but an overview of some of the highlights will present a fitting panorama of the breadth and sweep of women's historic role in Roman public life. Two themes will be covered: the politics of protest and the rise of the great political matron.

Our prediction that the Republic and the Julio-Claudian Princi-pate in tandem would offer the most cohesive picture has been fully confirmed. At every turn we have been confronted by echoes of the past, by later developments which were explicable and com-prehensible in terms of what had happened before. The poisoning trials of 331 BC with which the discussion opened were, as we interpreted them, the first manifestation of the politics of protest. Protest continued to be a significant theme over the centuries that followed. The cultists who dared to set up shop in the forum in the darkest days of the Second Punic War inherited the mantle, and so did the crowds of anxious women seeking news of casual-ties. Both *dramatis personae* and goals had changed, since women were now joined by men and matters affecting the community at large were being broached. But that simply confirms our forecast, that women would gradually expand the scope of their partici-pation. The abolition of *manus*-marriage had been mainly of interest to women, but war weighed heavily on everyone.

The demonstration against the *lex Oppia* showed that strictly feminist movements had not disappeared. On the contrary, they had assumed a new dimension in this unique example of direct women power; Cato learnt that fact of life to his cost. The climate of change in the post-war world inspired another kind of protest, the Bacchanalians and the endemic unrest that followed. The movement saw men and women from all levels of society joining together in a vast socio-economic upheaval that threatened the very foundations of society. The effects were still being felt in the Gracchan period; if the sources were more forthcoming we might find that under the guidance of Cornelia, mother of the Gracchi, a brake rather than an accelerator was applied by her sons.

Yet another example of the intensive reassessment that marks the second century is supplied by the Vestal revolt in the Gracchan period. The move was not entirely without precedent. The barbaric expiation inflicted on the Vestal Minucia had disgusted public opinion; the sequel was the protest-by-poison of 331. The atrocity had, however, continued to be used in the third century, until the Scipionic age discovered that hymn-singing maidens were just as acceptable to the gods. But although the past provided a general background, the Gracchan manifestation was on a different level. The whole basis of the institution was called in question. The immediate response was a modified – and differently motivated – version of the traditional remedy. The protest of 114 and the efforts of Licinia, who made a practice of challenging the rules, bore fruit, and in the first century the Vestals were able to play a part of some significance in mainstream politics. They were also able, when suspected of unchastity, to be given proper trial by regular courts in the open air, instead of by the Pontifex Maximus in some dark corner of the Regia.

Protests by women are not prominent in the late Republic. If we knew more about Sempronia, who helped Catiline, and about Catiline's wife, Aurelia Orestilla, we might have reason to revise that statement. But as it is the only documented protest is that by Hortensia in the triumviral period. The episode is, however, only imperfectly understood, because of our inability to define the *ordo matronarum* on whose behalf she spoke. Our parallel with the women's finance committee during the Second Punic War is a possible clue, the possibility of an official body for censorial assessments also helps, and so does the corporate identity that we have established for the Vestals. But that is as far as we can go. The fine print is lacking.

With the advent of the Principate the politics of protest assumes a different shape, although echoes from the past can still be heard.

The political activity of the imperial women is bifocal. On the one hand their attention is focused on the Domus in its purely internal, domestic aspects. On the other hand they break new ground by operating in the external sphere – *militiae* in contrast to *domi*. The main protest manifestations are on the domestic scene. The lead was taken by Augustus' daughter, Julia, whose *grex* displays some of the outward trappings of the Bacchanals – the *sacramentum* which bound Julia's group as the *coniuratio* had bound the cultists, uninhibited sexual attitudes, and the consumption of wine. We also recollect that when the people demanded Julia's recall from exile in AD 3 they threw blazing torches into the Tiber as the Bacchanals had done. But that is as far as the similarities go. The objectives of the two groups were very different; Julia and her friends did not have a social conscience. Good works were the concern of Livia, not of Julia; Livia was so noted for this that she nearly became *mater patriae*, but Livia was a pillar of the regime, not a protester. As for the cultural, avant garde side of *grex Iuliae*, it owed nothing to the Bacchanals, but it did have quite a lot in common with the Vestals of 114; and they in turn had simply intensified traits like wit and extravagance that had come down to them from Postumia in the fifth century, and no doubt from others. The Vestals also supplied, in the person of the *bon vivant* Veturius, the forerunner of some of Julia's friends.

The one matter on which it is not possible to relate the *grex Iuliae* to any earlier group is its objectives. The Bacchanals aimed to raise money by fair means or foul and, we may suppose, to use it to help the underprivileged. The Vestals of 114 hoped to break down the wall of tradition, and to a large extent they succeeded. But the Julian aims were essentially a product of the Principate. The target was Augustus' status as *pater patriae* and everything for which that status stood, especially the programme of mandatory marriage and moral reform. Literary personalities from Propertius to Ovid showed their dislike of the programme, and their sentiments were shared by their counterparts in the *grex Iuliae*. Oddly enough, the only one who had anything to show for his pains was Propertius. But he and his friends were favoured by the times; the Augustus of 27 BC was a far cry from the entrenched ruler of later years.

We turn now from the politics of protest to a topic of equal

213

importance, namely, the great political matron. The first fully credible woman in Roman public life is Verginia, the founder of the cult of Plebeian Chastity who struck a telling blow for parity (at the upper levels) between patricians and plebeians, and was also prominent in the drive for more equitable regulation of marriage and divorce. The names of the patrician prostitutes whom Fabius Gurges prosecuted have not been preserved, and little is known of Claudia, who staged a belated patrician backlash in the First Punic War, other than that incident.

Two or three names emerge in the Second Punic War. One of them is of special, almost unique, interest. She is Busa, the wealthy Apulian woman who enabled Scipio to stop the rot after Cannae. Totally without senatorial or equestrian connections, it is only by inference that she can even be assigned to the municipal aristocracy of Canusium; the determination of the town of Venusia not to be outdone by her suggests at least that much. Yet she was the only woman to be honoured by the Roman senate in all the long years of the war. By comparison with Busa, the nominally great Aemilia, wife of Scipio, can offer only wealth and ostentation. We have suggested that Aemilia might have had a hand in organizing the financial committee which handled contributions to Juno Regina (see Chapter 3, p. 28). But if there were any plebeian women like Busa domiciled within the stipulated ten miles of Rome, they would have been better suited to such a task than Aemilia. She is still, however, a likely sponsor, as she is of other important activities with which we have credited her. She was, after all, the mother of Cornelia. The third name, Claudia Quinta, is important only because of the myth which emphasizes the strong moral line taken by the Scipionic group in the closing stages of the war; as we have seen, that line probably included a law which partly anticipated the Augustan moral programme.

The Bacchanalian affair throws up two women of the people. One of them is Hispala, who betrayed the cult, thus becoming the first woman informer; her services were recognized by the senate. The other is Paculla Annia, the founder of the cult in its non-innocuous form. Three women are mentioned at a higher social level, but two of them, the patrician matron Sulpicia and her plebeian friend Aebutia, only have walk-on roles. The third, Aebutius' mother Duronia, is important. Her adherence to a cult that had very recently been given its new look by Paculla marks her out as a pioneer amongst its upper-class supporters. The first woman of her class to be associated with a politically significant cult since Verginia, she reflects the new thinking about popular sovereignty that was current in her day. Unlike Verginia, she crossed the class barrier.

The new thinking expanded the horizons of politically conscious women even more significantly later in the second century, when one Vestal, Claudia, mounted her famous challenge to the tribunes, and another, Licinia, claimed an independent right of dedication. Such thinking led, almost inevitably, to the Vestal revolt of 114 and the loosening of some of the shackles that followed. The Gracchan period witnessed something else that was even more important than Vestal emancipation, for it was then that the great political matron was born. The same intellectual ferment that had motivated the Vestals was responsible for the advent of Cornelia, mother of the Gracchi, but Cornelia was not a protester. She used her outstanding talents to stabilize rather than to change. Faced with a society on the point of collapse under the pressures – including the Bacchanalian movement – that conquest had brought in its train, Cornelia tried to awaken her sons to the need to defend the present by enlisting the best of the traditions of the past. Hence the position taken up in her letter to her younger son. Hence, too, her equation of her sons with the heroes of old. Her tragedy was that she was unable to perceive that a world empire could not simply revert to the institutions of a city-state.

The late Republic saw the flowering of the role that Cornelia had mapped out for political women. But the flowering included a slight mutation. The idealism of Cornelia was replaced in some cases by hard-headed pragmatism. Clodia was accused of many things, but issues of principle were not prominent amongst them. Even Servilia, the most accomplished female politican ever produced by the Roman Republic, was more interested in the fortunes of her family than in the welfare of the state. She influenced many public figures, but none, as far as our information goes, in the direction of social or economic reform. Again Sempronia and Aurelia Orestilla might strike a different note if we knew more about them, though it must be conceded that Sallust's unfavourable portraits of both women were not written by a man who lacked a social conscience. There are only two clear exceptions to the dominant theme of self-interest. Both Cato's wife, Porcia, and her aunt owed their true allegiance to the traditional *res publica* in the way that Cornelia had done. But strictly speaking they were not politicians. For the rest it was a question of self-interest all the way. But of course that is what the late Republic was all about, for men as well as women. Praecia and Chelidon, the 'fixers', merely made a business of what others more highly placed were doing less overtly.

The triumviral period saw some significant changes. The special situation of the dynasts opened new avenues for intervention by women, and Mucia and Octavia were able to exploit a talent for diplomacy that a Servilia had neither possessed nor needed. But the period belongs essentially to Fulvia. That astonishing woman foreshadowed the women of the emperor's house in so many ways, and in some respects went further than any of them would go. In her single-minded loyalty to one man she anticipated Livia; in her mastery of military matters she set a precedent that the elder Agrippina would follow, but on a more limited scale; she was also the inspiration for Plancina's review of the troops and the younger Agrippina's golden cloak; in her ability to influence the senate (L. Antonius' triumph) she was the direct descendant of Servilia; her skill at trading strategic moves with Octavian would, when inherited by Livia, be one of the qualities for which Tacitus specially commends the latter; her ability to bend both Clodius and L. Antonius to her will – in fact anyone except Antony – presaged Agrippina's domination of Claudius. (Were the Claudian men especially susceptible to strong-minded women? Clodius, Livia's first husband, Tiberius [twice], Germanicus, Claudius.) Earlier in the piece she had shown her mastery of both diplomatic and financial affairs in the matter of Deiotarus' restoration to his kingdom. Even on the bad side she was no more than a pace-setter; she may have been the first to collect decapitated heads, but she was not the last. Over and above all this she had a clear ideology, a more acute perception of the realities of power than any of her contemporaries. She was a confirmed Caesarian who knew that the traditonal *res publica* had had its day. If Antony had not driven her to despair, the shape of the Principate might have been very different.

Finally, the Principate. Many of the threads have been drawn together in previous chapters, and only a few matters of special interest need be raised here. That the succession was an ongoing problem from the outset, and continued to be so throughout the period, needs no further documentation. The women of the Domus knew it, Tacitus knew it, and we should know it. No other activity in which the women were engaged involved the same sharp break with the past. It occupied Octavia's full attention; and Livia made it her top priority, jointly with her commitments to Augustus. Julia presumably felt the same; her lighthearted remarks about her sons' legitimacy might suggest her lack of dedication to this particular cause, but as the first to exploit the divine blood of Augustus she must be credited with more than a casual interest. The subject continued to be of prime importance, to Agrippina in Tiberius' reign, to Messalina and Agrippina under Claudius, to Octavia and Poppaea under Nero. And as competition for the prize intensified, so those whose ancestry made them serious rivals were increasingly in danger of their lives, especially when Messalina's new politics uncovered the virtues of judicial murder.

The other prime consideration of imperial women was to maintain one's precarious foothold as the emperor's wife, and in some cases to press for constitutional status, for a partnership in power. The best example is Livia, not only for what she tried to become once Tiberius was on the throne, but also for what she did not try to become under Augustus. Did she refrain from pressing Augustus because she knew she could not succeed, or because she already had as much of a share as she wanted? In other words, as his constant adviser and confidante, to the extent of being consulted, even on public affairs, in preference to the members of his *consilium*, did this level-headed Claudian matron feel that this was as far as she need go? That is possible, but we cannot be sure without knowing whether she tried to secure from Augustus an official conferment of the titles of Augusta and *mater patriae*. We know that she acquired the one, though not the other, after his death, but had both been in the forefront of her mind before that? It certainly was not a woman unaccustomed to the exercise of power who took control when Augustus died and held the fort until Tiberius arrived.

If there is an epic in our period, it is the story of the elder Agrippina and the *Partes Agrippinae*. Whatever Tacitus thinks of her excitability and ungovernable temper, this indomitable woman did what no woman had done before. In defence of what she considered the inalienable rights of the Julian family against the usurping Claudians, she not only stood up to Tiberius and his sinister servant, Sejanus, she also put together, probably for the first time in Roman history, a political organization with a cohesive identity and identifiable goals. In the short term the purpose was to destabilize the regime, primarily in order to bring down the group's sworn enemy, Sejanus. That done, the next step would be to consolidate the succession claims of her sons, so as to ensure the reversion of the throne to the divine blood of Augustus. What more need she have done in order to be acknowledged not only as a fully fledged politician, but also as one of the most courageous politicians of our entire period?

There is not much to be added to what we have already said about Caligula. We need repeat only that Drusilla is most unlikely to have been an unwilling victim in her relationship with him. The divine blood of Augustus was a theme propagated by women members of the Domus even more vigorously than by men.

One of our most important findings for Claudius' reign is the changed perception of the Domus by both Messalina and Agrippina. Messalina, using a keen political intelligence that the lurid spotlight on her private life tends to obscure, realized that the Claudian Domus was not a mere continuation of what had gone before. Claudius, the Claudian who did not even enjoy Tiberius' adoptive Julianism, the man who had been elevated in order to nullify the coup which had temporarily abolished the Principate, did not have a secure grip on power. He needed all the help he could get, and for eight years much of that help was provided by Messalina. Her methods were unorthodox, cruel, and palpably self-interested, but her discovery of the potential of judicial murder played a significant part in repelling threats to the throne.

Of Agrippina's many contributions to the history of the reign, one that is often neglected is her abandonment of that Julian article of faith, the divine blood of Augustus. Once Nero became a Claudian by adoption, Agrippina threw herself wholeheartedly into promoting the new link, and redoubled her efforts when she herself was given the title of Augusta. Although technically this did not make her a Claudian – she was not adopted as Livia had been by Augustus (in his will) – it did strengthen the bond. In a certain sense she was simply returning to her origins, since her father had been a Claudian until his adoption by Tiberius and the latter's interlocking adoption by Augustus. But genetic reality seldom coincided with dynastic semblance in the Julio-Claudian labyrinth.

Having forged a Claudian link to her son's advantage, Agrippina reinforced his position (and also her own) after his accession by springing to the defence of Divus Claudius, the god who was now Nero's father. In this she showed herself better versed in the nuances of propaganda than the much vaunted Seneca. But when her own position came under threat Agrippina did not hesitate to turn the Claudian link against Nero. She espoused the cause of his 'brother' Britannicus, and when Nero countered that move by fratricide she allied herself to Octavia. By an astonishing feat of prestidigitation she began supporting the 'genuine' Claudians against the spurious occupant of the throne, even trying to revive her mother's party – with a Claudian logo instead of a Julian one. The purpose was, of course, to exert pressure on Nero to restore her partnership in power, but history had caught up with her. More's the pity. In spite of her many unpleasant qualities, one cannot help feeling a certain admiration for Julia Agrippina, the last of the really great Julio-Claudian matrons.

NOTES

1 INTRODUCTION

1 Livy probably reflects at least the substance of what was said by Valerius and Cato in 195 (see Chapter 4, p. 31). But even if the statements were invented by Livy they would still be a guide to Roman attitudes. The same goes for Appian's account of Hortensia's speech (see Chapter 7, p. 81).

2 On the general position of women see Balsdon 1962: 45–62; Herrmann 1964: *passim*; Finley 1968; Zinserling 1973: 48–53; De Riencourt 1974: 120–7; Pomeroy 1975: 150–89; Hallett 1984: 3–61; Peppe 1984: 14–16 and *passim*; Gardner 1986: *passim*; Cantarella 1987: 113–34. Some Greek women magistrates are noted by Cantarella, 91 but there is no trace of a Roman counterpart. On whether a woman was a *civis Romana* see Peppe 1984: 14–16, rightly concluding that she was. If any support for that finding is needed, the ingenious second-class citizenship known as *civitas sine suffragio* was by definition devoid of the right to vote or hold office, but was still *civitas*. 'Romulus' had traditionally given the Sabine women citizenship (L 1.14), but not the vote.

3 Balsdon (1962: 13) hints at women being powerful 'not always behind the scenes', but does not develop the idea beyond that hint.

4 See p. 10 of this chapter.

5 The sources for the regal period and the early Republic offer a generous supply of named women, but except for the Vestals, who got into the tradition through the pontifical chronicles, the credentials of many of them are suspect.

6 For the English equivalent see Beryl Atkins *et al.*, *Collins-Robert French-English Dictionary*, 2nd edn, Paris 1987: 177. See also Marshall 1990a.

7 Given the educational level of mid-second century women like Cornelia, Claudia and Laelia, and the questioning of tradition by at least Claudia (Chapter 5, pp. 42, 45), predecessors at the turn of the third century are likely enough, though direct evidence is lacking.

8 The decline was a gradual one right down the first century AD, from the new electoral arrangements for consuls and praetors in AD 5 to

the last known law of the popular assembly in Nerva's reign (Bauman 1989: xxv, 296).

9 The increasing importance of municipal aristocracies in the Principate would no doubt furnish a new focus of inequality, but that belongs mainly to a later period of the Principate than the one with which we are concerned.

10 Bauman 1989: 307. Whether the Julio-Claudian dynasty was in fact one entity, or two as argued by Wiseman 1982, will be discussed in due course.

11 It is sometimes asserted that one should be slow to give technical meanings to terms used in literary texts. But such texts are our main source for the law of the Republican period.

12 We do not know enough about Cato's *Origines* to say whether he used the conceptual approach. No doubt Sallust's monographs fall under that category, but the mainstream annalistic tradition certainly does not.

13 Bauman 1983: 10–11.

14 L 2.40.1 is not sure whether the deputation was officially authorized or was due to women's anxieties: *id publicum consilium an muliebris timor fuerit parum invenio*. Plut. *Coriol*. 33.3 has them intercede 'as women to women, not under a senatorial decree or consular edict'. DH 8.39.1 criticizes them for 'laying aside the proper custom of keeping to their homes'.

15 L 1.46.6, 1.48.5, 1.47.6; Sall. *Cat*. 25.1.

16 L 39.5–40.12; Plut. *Coriol*. 31–7; DH 8.37–56; L 3.48.8.

17 L 5.47–55; Diod. 14.116.9; Serv. ad *Aen*. 1.720.

18 [Cic.] *Herenn*. 4.23: as an adulteress she feared her husband and parents and had a motive to kill them; as a poisoner her motive must have been lust. Cf. *QIO* 5.11.39, citing a judgment of Cato; Sen. Rhet. *Contr*. 7.3(18), 6. On wine see *PNH* 14.89–90.

2 WOMEN IN THE CONFLICT OF THE ORDERS

1 On the conflict of the orders see the various papers in Raaflaub (1986), especially J. von Ungern-Sternberg, pp. 353–77.

2 Gaius 1.111: *filiae locum optinebat*. This is typical of the language used by Roman jurists in drawing an analogy. She was not his daughter, but the legal consequences of that relationship followed. Buckland (1963: 118) is even more forthright: '*Manus* made her the sister of her own children.'

3 L 8.18; VM 2.5.3; Oros. 3.10. On the nature of the punishment – death or a fine – see n. 14.

4 That the twenty were tried by ordeal is argued by Reinach 1908. The voluminous literature (Tomulescu 1974) has not produced a consensus on ordeal in Roman law.

5 Most scholars accept the essential accuracy of Livy's account. E.g., Kunkel 1962: 26–7, 58 n. 216; Herrmann 1964: 47–8; Palmer 1974: 122; Bauman 1974b: 255–7; Schumacher 1982: 39–42; Monaco 1984: 2013–4; Garofalo 1989: 128–34. But Münzer (*RE* 2A, 1923: 1721), is

worried because the two named women, Cornelia and Sergia, suggest a mid-century tract against the leaders of Catiline's conspiracy. Gagé 1963: 262–4 rejects Livy completely.

6 A progressive wing amongst the patricians needs no documentation. The Valerii are in the forefront all the way from L. Valerius Potitus (cos. 449), to L. Valerius Flaccus (cos. 195). The family competed vigorously with the Porcii for priority in *provocatio* legislation (Bauman 1983: 170–1). Fourth-century examples are the Minucii and the Claudii Marcelli, both liberal patrician families before making the transition to plebeian status.

7 Cf. Palmer 1974: 122, 132, 134. He does not say specifically that Rullianus was still aedile, but when Rullianus' son built a temple to Venus Obsequens after an analogous prosecution he did so as curule aedile (L 10.31.8–9).

8 They were *univirae* and were held in special esteem.

9 Wissowa (1912: 207) rejects Rullianus' foundation of a patrician sanctuary because he thinks a shrine of Fortuna Virgo was meant. But Palmer (1974: 123–5 and *passim*) finds Livy ultimately acceptable. The mid-fifth century elements of *conubium*: the ban in the XII Tables; the *lex Canuleia* of 445 which repealed the ban; the trouble at Ardea in 443. See Ogilvie 1965: 522–7, and, in Raaflaub (1986), see J. von Ungern-Sternberg pp. 357, 85, R. E. Mitchell p. 172, J. Linderski pp. 249, 259–61, W. Eder p. 296.

10 *Confarreatio* (available only to patricians), *coemptio, usus* (prescription following an informal marriage). See Raaflaub 1986, s.v. *confarreatio, coemptio, usus, usurpatio trinoctii*. See also, on *trinoctium*, Corbett 1930: 71–90, 108–12; Watson 1967: 19–31; Gardner 1986: 11–15, 18–19. For Wilms' theory that the three nights' absence had to take place during the *Lemuria* and at no other time, see A. Watson, in *Maior Viginti Quinque Annis*, Assen 1979: 195–7.

11 Bauman 1983: 22, 21–66.

12 A similar conclusion is reached on different grounds by J. Linderski, in Raaflaub 1986: 259. It cannot, of course, be suggested that 'Aulus' could have been the *praenomen* of a Volumnius. On the *praenomina* of the *gens* see M. Deissmann-Merten in *Kl.P.* 5.1329.

13 On the family court see Bauman (1984). As for the presiding magistrate in this case, *MRR* 1.143 entrusts the investigation to the consuls. But only the curule aedile is mentioned by Livy, and he is *prima facie* the presiding functionary. Cf. Kunkel 1962: 26–7, 58, n. 216; Bauman 1974b: 255–7; Garofalo 1989: 128–34. See also n. 14.

14 This raises the question of whether the penalty in the poisoning trials of 331 was capital. L 8.18.10 says *damnatae*, and adds that this was the first *quaestio de veneficiis* at Rome. The penalty in all the special commissions known to us was capital, and it is generally assumed to have been so in this case. See references in n. 5 (except Münzer and Gagé). But if, as has been rightly supposed (Garofalo 1989: 128–34), the curule aediles had jurisdiction because the danger to public health fell squarely within their jurisdiction, was not the case on all fours with Gurges' exaction of fines from prostitutes? Where did Rullianus get

the money for his shrine from? There is, however, a simple answer. Confiscation was a regular adjunct in capital cases, and the special *quaestio* created by *lex* in the Rullianus case gave him capital jurisdiction. Consequently the condemned lost their properties as well as their lives.

15 Cf. Balsdon 1962: 31. Palmer (1974: 134, n. 72) thinks *stuprum* here means adultery by married women, but the large sum raised looks more like an exaction from prostitutes. Gardner (1986: 123) claims that the women had neither committed adultery nor traded as prostitutes; they were guilty of 'nothing more than disorderly and uninhibited behaviour . . . after boozy festivals'. This peculiar suggestion cannot be allowed to stand. *Stuprum* usually means illicit sexual intercourse, but even when it occasionally means 'dishonour, shame' it is still remote from conviviality (*OLD* s.v.; A. Ernout & A. Meillet, *Dictionnaire étymologique de la langue Latine*, 3rd edn, Paris 1951, s.v.). Even more to the point L 10.31.9 says that 'Gurges assessed a fine and the matrons were convicted of *stuprum by the people*. This is an example of the parallel to the tribunes' jurisdiction which was a feature of the aediles' jurisdiction (Bauman 1974b). The tribune or aedile proposed a penalty, and the assembly adjudicated on it. The assembly sat as a court only in weighty matters; it did not spend time disciplining the drunk and disorderly.

16 On the enmity see Bauman 1983: 49, 58, 63–5.

17 Palmer 1974: 121–5, 134.

18 For Minucia's trial see L. 8.15.7–8, with Münzer 1937: 53–5, 64–5, also Mommsen 1887: 3.567, n. 2; Koch 1958: 1744; Ogilvie 1965: 98. On the Vestals in general see Koch 1958; Beard 1980; Cornell 1981; Schumacher 1982: 14–19. Graphic descriptions of burial alive can be found in Plut. *Num.* 10.4–7; *PE* 4.11 (see also Chapter 5, n. 36). Prior to Minucia, Oppia was punished in 483 and Orbinia in 472 (L 2.42.11; DH 8.89.5, 9.40.3). They were presumably buried alive as Dionysius (but not Livy) says, though Livy rather curiously notes the exact location of Minucia's interment and adds that the Polluted Field got its name from her unchastity (L 8.15.8). This looks like a notice of an innovation, but that may put too much weight on Livy's words.

19 Münzer (1937: 64–5) dates Minucia's induction to c. 367, shortly after the Licinio-Sextian laws. But that is too early. As a Vestal could leave the order after thirty years (Plut. *Num.* 10.1–2), her trial would have taken place in the very year when she became *emerita*, thus presupposing a sudden upsurge of conservative opposition after having accepted the plebeian appointment for nearly thirty years. It would also mean that Minucia, having observed the required standards of propriety for most of her tenure, altered her pattern of behaviour when she was very close to becoming a free agent. The plebeian breakthrough into the Vestal order should be seen as a by-product of Publilius Philo's laws of 339.

20 It could also arise in plebeian-with-plebeian marriages. But patrician women had to marry formally by *confarreatio* or *coemptio*, and the breaking of the *manus* bond needed another formality – *diffarreatio* or

remancipatio (Corbett 1930, chs 5, 9; Buckland 1963: 121; Watson 1965; M. Kaser, *Römisches Privatrecht*, 9th edn, Munich 1976: 235–6; Gardner 1986: 81–95; Linderski in Raaflaub 1986: 256).

21 The shrines of Pudicitia were not a state observance (Palmer 1974: 122).

22 Palmer (1974: 124) thinks the shrine was restored by Livia as part of Augustus' programme of moral reform. But he does not challenge the earlier position as attested by Livy.

23 On divorce see the references in n. 20.

24 On Appius and Volumnius see Bauman 1983: 21–65 (*passim*).

25 The grounds of divorce decreed by 'Romulus' were extended in c. 235, when Carvilius Ruga justified himself to the censors on the grounds that he had divorced his wife for barrenness. See Watson 1965; Bauman 1984: 1284–6 (arguing that even if the censors absolved him, as they may have done, the retardatory effect on his career was considerable). Although divorce without cause was still valid, failure to place an acceptable reason before the family council brought a censorial *nota*, as it had done in Annius' case. Verginia had set an important chain of reforms in motion.

26 Sources and discussion in Bauman 1967: 27–9.

27 A patrician Claudius does not reappear in the consular *fasti* until C. Claudius Nero in 207. The plebeian aediles had effectively ended the strong mid-third-century presence of the family, as represented especially by Ap. Claudius Russus (cos. 268), and Ap. Claudius Caudex (cos. 264), on whom see MRR 1. 199–200, 202–3.

3 WOMEN IN THE SECOND PUNIC WAR

1 The casualty list covers Servilia, buried alive in 273; Caparronia, who hanged herself when accused in 266; an unnamed victim who killed herself in 236; Tuccia, who is said to have proved her innocence in c. 230 by carrying water in a sieve. Sources in Münzer 1937: 208, n. 67, 203–9; Cornell 1981: 28, n. 5. Münzer rejects the case of 236 because it reminds him of the saga of Lucretia. But Caparronia's case would also have reminded him of that if we did not have her name.

2 Herrmann (1964: 52) completely ignores the evidence for the costly contributions laid down by the senate for men (L 22.1.17) when she asserts that only women were charged with the expiation.

3 On the struggle between Minucius and Fabius over the dictatorship, and the long confrontation between Flaminius and the oligarchs, see MRR 1.243, 242: Bauman 1967: 31; Scullard 1973: *passim*; M. Crawford, *The Roman Republic*, London 1978: 59–61. Flaminius was killed at Lake Trasimene shortly after the offerings.

4 L 22.52.7, 54.2–4. Scipio, although a private citizen, was enabled to levy *milites tumultuarii* (Bauman 1990: 344–5).

5 L 22.57.2–3. Münzer (1937: 210–14) points to the annalist's uncertainty as to which of the two Vestals committed suicide and which was buried alive; he is also worried about the variant name Florentia in the Livian epitome (*Per.* 22) and the punishment of an earlier Vestal, Opimia

(Oppia) in 483. In the same aftermath of Cannae a Gaul, a Greek and their wives were buried alive in the Forum Boarium (L 22.57.4–6). See A. Fraschetti, in *Le Délit réligieux dans la cité antique*, Rome 1981: 51–115. On the (possible) difference between an act of Vestal unchastity and a prodigy see Cornell 1981: 29–33.

6 L 22.55.1–56.5; VM 1.1.15, portraying the women as *coactae* and possibly reflecting contemporary criticism.

7 L 22.60.1–2, 61.3. B. O. Foster (Loeb edn of Livy, vol. 5, p. 396, n. 1) notes that men stood in the Comitium and women in the adjoining forum, but the latter was sometimes thought of as including the Comitium.

8 L 34.1.3; VM 9.1.3; Zonaras 9.17. Other sources in Culham 1982: 786, n. 2.

9 As far back as 420 a charge of unchastity was brought against the Vestal Postumia. She was, says Livy, innocent, but had aroused suspicion by dressing more elegantly and expressing herself more freely than was proper for a Vestal. She was acquitted, but was told by the Pontifex Maximus to moderate her witticisms and to dress more soberly in future (L 4.44.11–12).

10 The annalists noted the discrepancy between the ounce of gold here and the half-ounce under the *lex Oppia*. They solved the problem by having the tax of 210 accepted voluntarily, *without a decree of the senate* (L 26.36.8). This explanation makes it unnecessary to deal with the argument of Culham 1982: 787–8.

11 L 27.27.1–15. On the episode see Boyce (1937: 159–66), though she mistakenly has the pontiffs drop out of the picture after the gifting of the golden basin to Juno Regina. The decemvirs, far from taking full charge after that, as asserted by Boyce, were simply the executors of the original pontifical decree. Indeed on pp. 160–1 and 171 Boyce herself says as much. Andronicus was later honoured for having composed such a propitious hymn (Boyce, p. 159).

12 On Licinius Crassus, and on the Vestal of 206 see Bauman 1983: 92–110, 97. On the prodigies of the year see L 28.11.1–7. There was another birth of hermaphrodites in 200, when a chorus of twenty-seven maidens again sang a hymn, composed by P. Licinius Tegula (L 31.12.9–10). Tegula's relative, Licinius Crassus, was still Pontifex Maximus. There were further hymn-singings in 134, 119, 97, 92 (Boyce 1937: 158).

13 On the importation of Cybele see H. Graillot, *Le Culte de Cybele*, Paris 1912: 25–69; also Balsdon 1962: 32, 41; Herrmann 1964: 58–9; Toynbee 1965: 2.383–8; Gallini 1970: 71–2. The Scipionic group's insistence on moral purity is important (see Chapter 9, p. 107).

4 THE POLITICS OF PROTEST

1 It was, as is well known, a period of great social and economic dislocation. Despite occasional lapses, the exposition of that theme by Toynbee (1965) cannot be bettered.

2 L 34.1–8; VM 9.1.3; Zonaras 9.17.1. Short notices in *TA* 3.33.4; *Vir. Ill.* 47.6; Oros. 4.20.14.

3 Discussion in Briscoe (1981: 39–63), concluding that Cato's speech is a free composition by Livy. For other views see the citations in Bauman 1983: 158, n. 69. To the sceptics add Astin 1978: 25–7; Culham 1982, n. 13. Peppe (1984: 44–8) makes the surprising suggestion that Zonaras (9.17.1–4) is more accurate than Livy. My own view is that though authenticity is doubtful, Livy has supplied a useful source for the thinking of many Romans.

4 Not always skilfully. E.g., L 34.5.8, where Valerius cites Cato's *Origines*, a work which was in fact written in Cato's old age (Nepos, *Cato* 3.3).

5 Cf. the quotation at the head of Chapter 1.

6 Zonaras (9.17.1–4) has Valerius say, as a joke, that the women should be admitted to the assembly. They take him seriously and rush in, stay while the repeal is approved, put on some jewels and dance out. Zonaras had decided to improve on Cato's forebodings (at the head of Chapter 1).

7 There have only been a few discussions of the broader background to the affair. On Scullard's view see below. Culham (1982: 789–91) touches on two questions: a link between increased religious activity and displays of wealth by women; and (following Duckworth, Buck and others) an even more significant link between the repeal and Plautus (*Aulularia* 474–536), given that the play may date to 195–4. I here develop an idea which I briefly outlined in Bauman 1983: 159.

8 L 34.4.18–19 (Cato); 7.11–13 (Valerius).

9 Two sources of legal advice are possible: Sex. Aelius Paetus and the (still anonymous) women lawyers who were beginning to be active precisely in this period (see Chapter 5, p. 45). As to whether Cato (himself a lawyer) or Valerius' advisers had correctly analysed the position, one can only offer a general observation. The primary purpose of the *lex Oppia* was simply the imposition of temporary restrictions on feminine luxury. But as so often happens, the law had a secondary consequence, whether intended by the legislator or not, in the shape of an encroachment on *manus* and *patria potestas*. Valerius was probably correct when he claimed that the law was only an emergency wartime measure and should have been repealed along with all the other temporary expedients (L 34.6.10–18). It followed, then, that in fact the legislator could not be credited with having intended an encroachment on family law.

10 Scullard 1970: 188, 1973: 113. Cf. Pomeroy 1975: 180; Culham 1982: 788.

11 On their association with the Scipionic group see Bauman 1983: 92–110, 121–48.

12 Cf. Culham (1982: 791–2), though basing herself more on the religious aspect than the legal. On the latter see Chapter 5, p. 45. There is room for both aspects.

13 Cf. Bauman 1983: 159–60.

14 I was previously inclined to follow Steinwenter (*RE* 12, 1925: 2418–23),

though with reservations, when he said that Cato's main purpose in promoting the *lex Voconia* was in order to further his opposition to the emancipation of women which was gathering momentum as marriage without *manus* became more common; thus the ban on the institution of women as heirs was the main purpose of the law, and the restrictions in the law which also applied to men were a concession to the feminists (*Die Frauenpartei*). The difficulty was, and still is, the confinement of the restriction on women to the first census class. On the theories of Scullard, Astin and Kienast see Bauman, 1983: 177–8, and on the allegedly unscrupulous use of the *lex* by a woman in the first century, see Chapter 6, p. 66.

15 It is so seen by Herrmann 1964: 68–79, especially 74–6. Her view has not attracted much support. See for example Gallini 1970: 30–2.

16 Sources: L 39.8–19; *s.c. de Bacchanalibus* (*FIRA* 1.240–1); Cic. *Leg.* 2.37. Other sources in Rousselle 1982: 161, nn. 12, 13. On the allusions in Plautus see Gallini 1970: 47, n. 5. On support for a hard core of fact see Gallini, p. 12; Turcan 1972: 13–14; Rousselle pp. 4–19. On scepticism see Festugière 1954; Toynbee 1965: 2.394.

17 The summary of Livy's version that follows is an abbreviation of Bauman 1990: 334–8.

18 L. 39.8.4, 13.9, 14.4, 14.6, 15.6, 15.12, 16.4, 16.10.

19 The speech is a mixture of things that had been said, things that could have been said, and things said by Cato, who did deliver a speech on the Bacchanalian suppression.

20 L 39.18.6. There is no suggestion that the families exercised the decision-making power; that rested with the consuls in this matter. But the dividing line between public and private jurisdiction was not always so clearcut (see Bauman 1984: 1297–8).

21 At Sipontum in Apulia and Buxentum in Lucania he found Roman colonies founded as recently as 194 deserted (L 39.23.3).

22 She thus gained access to a category which women could not reach by inheritance.

23 She was not released from the perpetual tutelage to which all women were subject, but choosing one's guardian gave security against fraud.

24 L 39.17.6–7 lists as the high priest and founders of the cult (Paculla Annia's revised version) her sons Minius and Cerrinius, together with Marcus and Gaius Atinius of the Roman plebs and the Faliscan L. Opicernius. Duronia's husband, T. Sempronius Rutilus, was related to C. Sempronius Rutilus, plebeian tribune in 189. The two Atinii look like a subordinate branch of the Atinii family, which had recently become prominent. Cf. Gallini 1970: 34; Bauman 1990: 341–2. The Sempronii and the Atinii were connected, for Ti. Sempronius Longus (cos. 194) was a patron of the Atinii (A. E. Astin, in *Hommages à Marcel Renard*, Brussels 1969: 34–9.) Significantly, C. Sempronius Rutilus got no further than the tribunate, and the Atinii went into a 40-year decline after 186. Just what one would expect of families tainted by a link with the cult.

25 For the demonstration that all the common-law crimes attributed to

the cult by Livy were part of a single criminal enterprise, raising funds for the cult, see Bauman 1990: 342–3.

26 L 39.41.5–6. Livy's language apropos of the condemnations is important: *ad duo milia hominum*. It is hardly necessary to point out that *homines* does not mean only men; it implies 'persons' (*OLD* s.v.). Both men and women were involved. If it had been only women Livy would have used *feminarum* or *mulierum*, not *hominum*.

27 On forgery as one of the Bacchanalian crimes according to Livy, see Bauman 1990: 342–3.

28 The reason for saying this is that praetors were not yet involved in regular criminal jurisdictions. That would only start happening in 149, when the first permanent jury-court for *repetundae* was created.

5 WOMEN IN GRACCHAN POLITICS

1 The theme is broached by Peppe (1984, ch. III) in the course of his discussion of '*La donna nel diritto publico*'. The extent to which I agree with, differ from, or expand significantly on his brief remarks, appears below. Neither Herrmann (1964) nor Gardner (1986) is aware of women lawyers. For important discussions in shorter works see n. 28.

2 Her mother is called Aemilia Tertia by VM (6.7.1), but his picture of an obedient wife patiently tolerating her husband's liaison with a female slave does not square with the splendid matron whom we know as Scipio's wife. VM has given Aemilia Tertia either the wrong husband or the wrong tolerance.

3 On Cornelia see Münzer 1901; Herrmann 1964: 87–9; Bernstein 1978: 42–5, 48–50, 54–5; Stockton 1979: 22–6. The main sources are Plut. *TG* 1.2–5, 8.5, *CG* 19.1–3; App. *BC* 1.20.83 (on her daughter); Cic. *Brut.* 104, 211; *QIO* 1.1.6; Tac. *Dial.* 28; VM 4.4, 6.7.1; *PNH* 34.31; Plut. *CG* 4.3; *CIL* 6.31610.

4 Cic. *Brut.* 211. He probably saw them in published form, but that is not essential. The point is that they were collected. Quintilian also saw them despite Münzer 1901. *QIO* 1.1.6: 'We are told that the eloquence of the Gracchi owed much to their mother Cornelia, whose learned style has been transmitted to posterity by her letters.' Cornelius Nepos also saw them.

5 On the scope of the controversy see Instinsky 1971. Genuine: Münzer 1901; Stockton 1979: 26 and n. 17; A. Gratwick, *Cambridge History of Classical Literature*, vol. 2, Cambridge 1982: 145–6. Forged: Herrmann 1964: 88 and n. 4; Bernstein 1978: 44, n. 78. But see especially Horsfall (1987) arguing that Nepos (or a predecessor) adapted his material without destroying its essential veracity. It is not quite clear whether Horsfall thinks that the adaptation was made by Nepos or by Optimate circles either in the Gracchan period or in c. 100. He inclines towards F. Coarelli (*Le Dernier Siècle de la république Romaine*, Strasbourg 1978: 13–15, 25–6), who argues that the adapted excerpts and the dedication on Cornelia's statue both originated in c. 100. This raises the question of how far denigration of the Gracchi justified Saturninus' death in 100. The need to justify that could have been more acute in

63 at the time of C. Rabirius' trial, when Nepos was writing. But in any case Cornelia's importance in the public sphere was such that she would have been a symbol to be reckoned with at all material times – 133–121, 100, 63. Horsfall's theory of an essentially true adaptation by Nepos carries conviction.

6 But some are not convincing. E.g. VM 4.4: She showed her love for her children by telling a bejewelled Capanian woman that 'My jewels are my children'. See also n. 8.

7 On temples as worthy tombs see Plut. CG 19.1–3; Sen. Ad Marc. 16.3, Ad Helv. 16.6; Oros. 5.12.9; VP 2.7.1. For her complaint about what she was called see Plut. TG 8.5. For the tutors, her identification with the programme, and Aemilianus' death see VM 4.4; Plut. TG 8.5; Cic. Brut. 104; CD fr. 83.8; App. BC 1.20.83; Oros. 5.12.10.

8 Plutarch deduces from coded statements in her letters to Gaius that she assisted his sedition by sending mercenaries to Rome disguised as harvesters (CG 13.2), but this must be treated with caution. We are told by Diodorus as well as Plutarch that when Gaius proposed that anyone deposed from office by the people be barred from seeking office again, Cornelia persuaded him to drop the proposal although it was aimed at M. Octavius, the tribune who had tried to block Tiberius' agrarian bill (Diod. 34.25.2; Plut. CG 4.1).

9 Bauman 1967: 133.

10 PNH 34.31; Plut. CG 4.3; CIL 6.31610. On the possible date of the statue see n. 5.

11 On Scipio Africanus' ideas see Scullard (1970: 239), who acknowledges his repeated procurement of commands by the wishes of the people, but denies that this was unconstitutional or made him disloyal to his class. That may be so, but the repeated reliance on popular sovereignty is indicative of a distinct questioning of traditional assumptions. On Cornelia's sympathy with the programme, Plut. TG 8.5 suggests that her wish to be called mother of the Gracchi was a definite call to action. On the Gracchan crisis see E. Badian 1972: 668–731; Bernstein 1978: 71–101; Bauman 1983: 249–55.

12 On Cornelia's role in appointing Diophanes and Blossius see Herrmann 1964: 87; Stockton 1979: 25. Contra Bernstein 1978: 45–6. On Blossius' ideology see Bauman 1983: 251–5. On Mucianus' legal and cultural interests see ibid. 245–9, 303–12.

13 E.g. the disapproval of P. Mucius Scaevola in Bauman 1983: 285–8.

14 Iuris peritus and iuris consultus are not very clearly differentiated. To some 'one learned in the law' simply means 'a lawyer, jurisconsult'. So OLD s.v. iuris peritus. But others, e.g., A. Guarino (Labeo 97, 1981: 436) draw a distinction. Yet both (i) being learned and (ii) giving responsa are attested for iuris peritus. Thus (i) Cic. Brut. 102, Clu. 107; Agennius Agrim. p. 27; (ii) Cic. Q. Rosc. 56, Top. 28; Phaedrus 4.15.4; D 31.88.17 (cavere rather than respondere). AG (4.2.2, 13) has books written by both iure consulti and iurisperiti.

15 On Titinius see Daviault 1981: 31–7, 91–140 (fragments and discussion); also H. J. Rose, Handbook of Latin Literature, London 1936: 80; S. Weinstock, RE 6, 1937: 1540–46; H. Bardon, La Littérature Latine

inconnue, vol. 1, Paris 1952: 39–43; E. Vereecke, *Ant. Class.* 40, 1971: 156–85.

16 Fragment in Daviault 1981: 108, 110. That *res* can mean a court case needs no documentation.

17 Cf. Daviault 1981: 91, 108–9.

18 Marshall (1989: 39–40) rejects the theory that *Iurisperita* reflects 'an effort by Roman women of the second century BC to invade the men's preserve of the legal profession'. But E. Costa (*Il diritto privato romano nelle commedie di Plauto*, reprinted Rome 1968) has shown just how much information about legal matters can be gathered from Roman comedy. Nor are historians unaware of the dramatic impact of even a single word in other contexts, such as the classic example of whether Augustus possessed superior *dignitas* or superior *auctoritas*. See also n. 28 below. Peppe (1984: 84–5) refers to the Titinius *Iurisperita* only cursorily in his discussion of the link between women's legal knowledge and custom. On women's presumed ignorance of the law see n. 30 below, and the text there.

19 See Peppe 1984: 114–17; Garofalo 1989: 125–7, 148; also Bauman 1974b: 253; ibid. *Index* 5, 1974–5: 39, 41. Peppe argues that *Manilia ad tribunos plebi provocavit* in Gellius does not mean technical *provocatio*; he thinks that in fact she appealed for a tribunician veto. Leaving aside the question of whether *provocatio* originally meant anything more than an appeal for tribunician intervention, the distinction between *provocatio* and *appellatio* is not nearly clear enough to support a firm conclusion. Besides, Gellius says he got his information from the eminent Augustan jurist, Ateius Capito, *On Public Criminal Courts*. If Capito said *provocavit* he meant *provocavit*.

20 VM 5.4.6; Cic. *Cael.* 34; *ST* 2; CD fr. 74; Oros. 5.4.7.

21 The specific proof that there was a clash of legal doctrines is supplied by Suetonius: A Vestal accompanied her brother ('father', correctly, in other sources) in order to make it an act of sacrilege (*ne fas esset*) for any of the tribunes to interpose a veto (*ST* 2). The fact that other sources stress the filial piety aspect rather than the constitutional in no way implies that there was not a clash of legal doctrines. They have merely chosen to emphasize a different aspect. The clash between *patria potestas* and *maiestas* in 232 (Cic. *Inv.* 2.52) was also no doubt describable as lack of *pietas* on a son's part, but that did not detract from the constitutional significance of the incident. On Vestal sanctity and the tribunician veto see also Bauman 1981: 174–8, 1983: 301. There can be no doubt that Claudia showed a keen appreciation of the legal issues.

22 On Laelius and Scaevola see Bauman 1983: 253, 267–70, 312–14.

23 For *elegantia* as a lawyer's attribute see F. Schulz, *History of Roman Legal Science*, Oxford 1946: 335–6; P. Stein, *The Character and Influence of the Roman Civil Law*, London 1988: 3–17; Bauman 1985: 19–20, 25–6. On Laelius' matter-of-fact style see Cic. *Brut.* 83, 86. On Quintilian on Laelia see *QIO* 1.1.6. On education of daughters by fathers, see Hallett 1984: 338–40. On legal education of sons see Bauman 1983: 152, 227, 248.

24 On Q. Scaevola's thinking see Bauman 1983: 314–20. On C. Laelius' thinking see Bernstein 1978: 46, 52, 242–3; Stockton 1979: 27, 33, 70, 90. On Cicero's ambivalence see Bauman 1983: 233–5, 297, 303–4, 313–14, 316.

25 The accused was not Equitius trying to pass himself off as a citizen. He was an ally of L. Appuleius Saturninus, the populist leader whom we may safely identify as the browbeating tribune. For Metellus' rejection of Equitius' claim to citizenship see *Inscr. Ital.* 13.3.16b; Cic. *Sest.* 101; VM 3.8.6, 9.7.1; [Auct.] *Vir. Ill.* 62.1. On false claims to citizenship see Bauman 1983: 366–71. On the censor's dereliction of duty see L 43.16, 44.16.8, 45.15.8; Cic. *Rep.* 6.2; VM 6.5.3; [Auct.] *Vir. Ill.* 57.3; Fest. 360 L. On enmity between Metellus and Saturninus see Cic. *Sest.* 101; App. *BC* 1.126; Oros. 5.17.

26 L 8.18.9, 22.60.1–2, 34.2.2, 8; DH 8.39.1.

27 Note *in conspectu habita quaestione* in VM 8.2.3. The fact that the case was held 'in full public view' was specially noticed because a woman was appearing in person. Fannia gave a new slant to the *actio rei uxoriae* (Watson 1967: 69).

28 Marshall (1990a: 56–8) dates the case to the aftermath of the Social War, when social dislocation deprived her of male defenders. But this is to give the case a priority and a uniqueness to which it is not entitled in the light of Fannia's case. Afrania (below) did not appear in person because she lacked advocates. But Marshall's date, as such, is reasonable. The case is certainly later than the turn of the century; there were no public appearances by women in court cases before Sempronia. As for the particular court by which Maesia was tried, Marshall's aftermath of the Social War in fact gives a clue that he has missed. Maesia of the Umbrian city of Sentinum is a logical candidate for the *lex Varia maiestatis* of 91/90 BC, which established a jury-court to try those 'by whose assistance and advice the allies had taken up arms against the Roman people'. On that law see Bauman 1967: 59–68. The Varian court was notorious for its witch hunts, which makes Maesia's ability to persuade the jury even more noteworthy.

29 The litigious matron's name is twice given as 'C. Afrania' in VM. A. H. J. Greenidge (*The Legal Procedure of Cicero's Time*, Oxford 1901: 147) concludes that the 'Carfania' of the Digest is in fact Gaia Afrania. If so, she might have been a descendant of L. Afranius, the poet who followed Titinius in composing *fabulae togatae* and was a contemporary of Terence (VP 1.17.1). But the reading 'C. Afrania' is dubious. A feminine *praenomen* in the Republic is most unusual. In any case it would mean that Ulpian misread the name in the edict – not an easy inference for one of the great commentators on that document. Marshall (1989: 43–6) suggests that 'Carfania' could be a lapse of the pen by Justinian's compilers, but he does not press the point. I do not take his point about the Ulpian fragment not showing that women had in fact represented others before the praetor's ban. The casuistic Roman lawyers did not legislate for things that had not happened. For some interesting comments on the name of Bucco, the husband of Afrania/Carfania, see Marshall, p. 43, n. 23.

WOMEN AND POLITICS IN ANCIENT ROME

30 On ignorance of the law see *D* 22.6.8. Cf. 22.6.9 (pr, 48.5.39.4, CJ 1.18.10. On ignorance of court procedures see Ulp. XI.1. On *sexus infirmitas, inbecillitas* see *D*. 16.1.2.2, 22.6.9 pr. On *imperitia*, want of skill see *D*. 2.8.8.2. These phenomena were fully in place long before the Severan jurists, from whom the aforegoing Digest excerpts come. See, e.g., Cic. *Mur*. 27; *Gai*. 1.44. For discussions of these phenomena see Beaucamp 1976; Dixon 1984; Marshall 1990a.

31 For Chelidon and Clodia see Chapter 6, pp. 66 and 69; Livia and Urgulania Chapter 10, p. 135. For Celsus see Bauman 1989: 221.30, 180–4. He is a better guess than his father, also a jurist but not known as a court practitioner, whereas the son had the flamboyance of an orator – quite exceptionally amongst the jurists of the time. The alternative, that Juvenal is referring to Cornelius Celsus, the rhetorician known to Quintilian, is unlikely. He was earlier than Gallio (*QIO* 3.1.21), and Gallio was a brother of Seneca. On women's consultations of the chancellery see L. Huchthausen, *Klio* 56, 1974: 199–288; T. Sternberg, *Klio* 67, 1985: 507–27.

32 On this supposition see Münzer 1920: 243; Miltner, *RE* 13, 1926: 497; Marshall 1985: 196.

33 She passed out of her father's *potestas*, ceased to be an intestate heir, had no intestate heirs of her own, was free of agnatic guardianship, and had the full disposition of her property. She was, in the felicitous phrase of Hopkins (1983: 18), 'an honorary man'. But the extinction of the tie of piety is a moot point. See Bauman (1984: 1292–4) on Manlius Torquatus and his son.

34 See Chapter 3, n. 1 and p. 27. As there pointed out, the closing years of the war saw the abandonment of Vestal interment. See also, on the cases of 206 and 178, Münzer 1920: 173–7, 243–5.

35 More than one Licinia in a Vestal order comprising six women in all (Münzer 1920: 243) would strain coincidence too far. Sources for the trials: Greenidge & Clay 1960: 58–60; *MRR* 1.536, and below *passim*.

36 See the accounts of Vestal interment in Plut. *Num*. 10.4–7, *PE* 4.11: the Pontifex Maximus conducts the Vestal, in a covered litter which muffles her cries, to a small underground room in which are placed a couch, a lamp and a small quantity of food so that a consecrated life be not destroyed by hunger. The Pontifex Maximus utters certain ritual prayers and the Vestal then descends the steps leading to the room; the steps are removed and earth is piled over the entrance.

37 The evidence for a permanent secular court, created either under Peducaeus' law or in the early first century, will be considered in Chapter 6, p. 61.

38 Asconius' strictures on Cassius Longinus' conduct of the trial do not include any suggestion that *res iudicata* was rejected or even pleaded.

39 See Oros. 5.15.20–2; Obseq. 37: The virgin daughter of a Roman knight, P. Elvius (or L. Helvius), was struck by lightning while riding a horse; the bolt stripped her naked and scattered her clothes, which the soothsayers said portended disgrace for both Vestals and knights. A temple to Venus Verticordia was built. Plut. (*RQ* 83) adds that Gallic and Greek couples were buried alive in expiation of the prodigy,

but this is a doublet of an incident in the Second Punic War (see Chapter 3, n. 5).

40 Dio mentions a knight only in connection with Marcia, but other references could have dropped out of the *Excerpta Valesiana*. The role of the slave informer is in both Dio and the derivatives. There are some obvious similarities between Dio and the great Vestal scandal in Domitian's reign: a knight, Crispinus, was prominent; Domitian's chief Vestal, Cornelia, was acquitted and rearraigned; four Vestals were implicated. But most of the 'Domitianic' features in Dio's account are also found in Asconius and the Livian derivatives (see below). The only 'Domitianic' item not so found is Dio's assertion that the activities of 114 were concealed for a very long time; cf. Suet. *Dom.* 8.3. But a long delay in 114 is confirmed by Plut. *RQ* 83. On the Domitianic affair see Bauman 1989: 154–7.

41 Asconius (40 St.) says that Cassius also condemned several others – *et praeterea complures alias*. This means either other Vestals or lay-women. One MS has *alios* (Marshall 1985: 197). But what '*other* men' have been referred to, of whom *alios* could be a continuation?

42 Traditionally it took ten years to train a novice, ten years of active performance of her duties, and ten years for her to train others (Plut. *Num.* 10.1).

43 On faction fighting see Marshall 1985: 196–7. On expiation for Cato's defeat by the Scordisci see Cornell 1981: 28, n. 6. On machinations of families trying to create vacancies for their daughters see Hallett 1984: 87.

44 VM 3.7.9, 6.8.1; Cic. *Brut.* 122, *Inv.* 1.80.

45 *SA* 31.3; CD 55.22.5, 56.10.2; *TA* 4.16.6; L. 1.20.3.

46 This is not to imply that a Vestal was a cloistered nun. She attended triumphs, state funerals, inaugurations, the theatre, the games, and dined out and received visitors (Koch 1958; Beard 1980). But the evidence of dissatisfaction is there. Despite Hallett (1984: 87), one does not see families competing relentlessly for vacancies as late as 114. Inauguration was by seizure (*captio*) by the Pontifex Maximus when a girl was between 6 and 10 years old. She had very little say in the matter. The office may have been sought after in earlier times (Minucia, p. 17), but increased sophistication brought disenchantment. Something similar happened to the once highly prized decurionate.

47 There would be a return to barbarism under Domitian (*PE* 4.11). The reasons for that need not be gone into here.

6 THE POLITICAL STRATEGISTS OF THE LATE REPUBLIC

1 Watson 1967: 146–54; Pomeroy 1975: 150–5; Gardner 1986 chs 2 and 3.

2 On Fabia see Ascon. 70 St.; Cic. *Brut.* 236; Plut. *Cat. Min.* 19.3; Sall. *Cat.* 15.1, 35.1; also Münzer 1920: 96, n. 1. On Licinia see Plut. *Crass.* 1.2.

3 On a permanent court see Rawson 1974: 208. There is good evidence to support her. Plut. (*Crass.* 1.2) has Licinia prosecuted by a certain

Plotius; *diōkontos* suggests a technical accuser, not merely someone who informed the pontiffs. Plutarch also has Crassus acquitted by jurors (*dikastai*).

4 On *captio* by him as the method of induction into the Vestal order see Koch 1958; Beard 1980.

5 He was either inducted but removed, or nominated but never inducted. The latter is more likely. L.R. Taylor, *CP* 36, 1941: 113–16; Bauman 1983: 409–11.

6 *MRR* 2.23–4 with n. 11, 25 n. 12; L.R. Taylor, *AJP* 63, 1942: 385–412. But Szemler (1978) makes Metellus Pius the only certain member of the college at this time.

7 They are Fabia and Licinia who would be acquitted of unchastity in 73, together with Perpennia and Fonteia (*MRR* 2.24–5, 135, 137). On Fabia and Licinia see further below. The statement by VM (3.4.5) that Perpennia's grandfather was expelled from Rome for illegally assuming Roman citizenship is discounted in *MRR* (2.19 n. 1), but without good reason. Nothing useful is known about Fonteia.

8 Sources and full discussion in Moreau 1982. Caesar's position in the whole affair was equivocal. Despite the suspicion that Clodius had broken in in order to make love to Caesar's wife, Pompeia, Caesar took no action against Clodius, and though he divorced Pompeia, he denied that he had done so for adultery. Moreau (pp. 39–40) denies that Caesar said, 'Caesar's wife should be above suspicion and beyond reproach'. Whether Dio (37.45.2), *SJ* (74.2), and Plut. (*Caes.* 110.9, *Cic.* 29.9, *Apophth. Reg. Imper.* 206a) can be dismissed as easily is a moot point. It would be a pity to jettison such a well-known apophthegm.

9 There was no reaction to the scandal from the consulars in the senate, but the matter was raised by an ex-praetor, Q. Cornificius (Cic. *Att.* 1.13.3).

10 Moreau (1982: 63–5) thinks the pontiffs consulted the Vestals unofficially, but Cic. (*Att.* 1.13.3) quite clearly has them named in the senate's decree and participating in the ruling.

11 Despite the general belief (Scheid 1981: 131–3; Moreau 1982: 83–9), the charge was not *incestum*. It was framed by analogy with *incestum: de ea re non aliter quam de incestu quaereretur* (*Schol. Bob.* 89 St.). Cf. Cic. *Har.Resp.* 12. Moreau (pp. 139, 168) rejects the cumulation of charges attested by Dio (37.46.1) and Plut. (*Cic.* 29.4), on the grounds that only a single charge could be received by a *quaestio*. But special *quaestiones* not created under any of the public criminal laws were an exception. E.g. the charges received by the *Quaestio Mamiliana* in the Jugurtha scandal (Sall. *Jug.* 40.1).

12 In response to the narrow acquittal, by 31 votes to 25, Cicero said that twenty-five jurors had risked their necks, but thirty-one were moved more by hunger than by reputation (*Att.* 1.16.5).

13 Plut. *Cic.* 20.2–3. Cicero's house was used because it was customary to use the house of a magistrate with *imperium*. Cicero of course spent the night elsewhere, as Caesar did in 62.

14 Cic. *Fam.* 14.2.2, *Mur.* 73. On Cicero's support for Murena see Bauman 1985: 15–27.

15 That the *démarche* to Sulla was the first instance of collegiate Vestal action is unlikely. One thinks of the ruling on Licinia's unauthorized dedication in 123 (Chapter 5, p. 52). But Cic. (*Dom.* 136) only has the senate refer the question to the pontiffs.

16 On Catulus see Syme 1939: 21, 22, 25; H.G. Gundel in *Kl.P.* 3.793.

17 In AD 22 Tiberius allowed a funeral oration for Iunia, wife of Cassius and sister of Brutus, but forbade any display of the tyrannicides' images (*TA* 3.76).

18 Balsdon (1962: 53) glibly dismisses her as 'a woman of no breeding at all'. Whether or not she had 'breeding', her only crime was to make an impression on the political scene.

19 A certain Precianus (Bauman 1985: 68) who may have been related to her before his adoption.

20 Pursuant to the praetorian criterion of *bonum et aequum*, he could quite properly have based himself on the fiction that the testator had been enrolled by the censors, and in the first class, in order to defeat the *fraus legis* perpetrated by the testator.

21 Its dating to the aftermath of the Social War by Marshall (1990) is persuasive.

22 He is included in Cicero's list of *boni* who answered the call against Saturninus in 100 (*Rab. perd.* 21) and was praetor under Sulla, probably in 80 (*MRR* 2.80).

23 Balsdon (1962: 48) claims that Sempronia is not depicted as playing any part in 'the actual conspiracy'. But Sallust insists that she was indispensable to the meeting with the envoys (*Cat.* 40.5), and if that was not part of 'the actual conspiracy' then nothing was.

24 On her murky past see Sall. *Cat.* 15.2, 35.3; Cic. *Cat.* 1.14; VM 9.1.9; App. *BC* 2.2. She did not even forfeit her dowry, as Gaius Gracchus' wife, Licinia, had done in 121 (Bauman 1983: 286–8). One cannot exclude the possibility that her lenient treatment was the result of a compromise between Cicero and Caesar. There was a good deal of hard bargaining in the Catilinarian affair. Caesar, whose vote against the defendants remains a mystery, may have stipulated for a concession for Aurelia Orestilla, who was related to him through his mother.

25 Most writers make Gaius Gracchus her father (Münzer 1920: 272–3; Herrmann 1964: 103; W. Eder in *Kl.P.* 5.103, with reservations). Tuditanus is favoured by M. Ciaceri, *Atti. R. Accad. Arch. Lett. Bell. Art. Napoli* 11, 1929: 217–30. The case for Gaius Gracchus is not persuasive. Sempronia's father-in-law, Decimus Brutus Callaicus, had supported Opimius against the Gracchans in 121. Marriage into a family which had helped to destroy her father is highly unlikely for Sempronia.

26 Sall. *Cat.* 23.3–4, 26.3, 28.2; App. *BC* 2.3; Plut. *Cic.* 16.2; Flor. 2.12.6.

27 On the cases in which criminal charges by women were permitted see Mommsen 1899: 369 and n. 4. Women laying information in criminal cases perhaps go back to the *ancilla* who reported the poisonings of 331 (Chapter 2, p. 13), but Hispala is the first named example

(Chapter 4, p. 35). On women generally in court situations see Schroff, *RE* 14.2304; Peppe 1984; Marshall 1989, 1990.

28 Some would identify her as the Fulvia who took part in an orgy in 52 at which the guests included the consul Metellus Scipio (VM 9.1.8). But this depends on emending the MS of VM, [*Flaviam*] <*Fulviam*>, and on making that Fulvia the informer of 63. The identification has been made by Balsdon, 1962: 49; H.G. Gundel in *Kl.P* 2.633. But see Herrmann 1964: 103–4. Florus describes the informer as 'a worthless prostitute' (2.12.6), but her good character is vouched for by Sallust, Appian and Plutarch (n. 26).

29 The spelling 'Clodia' reflects P. Clodius' transfer to plebeian status. It is usually used for this sister as well, though in writing to her husband in 62 Cicero refers to her as *Claudia*. On the use of the alternative spelling see Skinner 1983: 282, n. 25.

30 *QIO* 8.6.53; Plut. *Cic.* 29.2; Cic. *Cael. passim*. On acceptance of all or some of the rumours see Münzer 1900; R. G. Austin, *Cicero: Pro Caelio*, 3rd edn, Oxford 1960: viii; Gardner 1958: 400; Balsdon 1962: 54–5; McDermott 1984. For an inconclusive view see Deroux 1973. Ramage (1984, 1985) concentrates excessively on esoteric interpretations of Cicero's speech. The most sustained attack on the traditional picture of Clodia is that mounted by Skinner 1983.

The general identification of Lesbia as Clodia is challenged by T. P. Wiseman, *Catullus and his World*, Cambridge 1985, *passim*, but the argument is not persuasive.

31 On Skinner's findings see n. 42.

32 Cicero refers to the subscriber as 'my friend Clodius' who had a record as an unsuccessful litigant (*Cael.* 27). No brother of Clodia was 'my friend' to Cicero, least of all the man who had driven him into exile in 58. Sources for the exile: *MRR* 2.195–6.

33 On the driving force see Münzer 1900; Balsdon 1962: 54; Gardner 1958: 405. On a subordinate role see Dorey (1958) in a paper making some useful points but also some wildly improbable claims: Cicero will have hated Clodia because she had tried to marry him, plundered his house during his exile, and humiliated him at Baiae. The record is set straight by Skinner 1983: 283–4. Skinner herself (282, n. 23) thinks she testified at the trial only in order to oblige her brother.

34 *D* 22.5.3.5. Cf. Mommsen 1899: 403, n. 1; Dorey 1958: 178, n. 3.

35 Except to note the view of Moreau (1982: 68–72), that the allegations of incest originated at the trial of P. Clodius in 61. For a detailed analysis of Cicero's thrusts see Ramage 1984, 1985. Charges of incest usually provoked a *tu quoque*. Clodius retaliated in 61 by accusing Cicero of incest with his daughter (CD 46.18; Ps.-Sall. *In Cic.* 2).

36 The further ground, an innuendo 'by which the person could be recognized', was only added in the Principate (Bauman 1974: 25–51).

37 Not *Quadrantaria* as in Quintilian.

38 Gardner (1958: 494–7), citing Plut. *Cic.* 29.4.

39 The trained advocate was P. Clodius; the reference to his lack of success as a litigant (Cic. *Cael.* 27) is as much a recognition of his extensive court practice as a jibe. He is Cicero's learned friend. As

Cicero mentions him last of the accusers, it is a safe guess that he spoke on the same two 'Clodian' charges as Cicero. Thus the strongest accuser and the strongest defender locked horns on the matters in which Clodia was directly interested. He was connected with her family in some way, perhaps as a client or freedman.

40 Both Catullus and Caelius were her juniors. If Bestia was tribune in 62 (*MRR* 2.541) he will have been younger than a woman born in c. 94. We do not know whether he reached the praetorship after his attack on Caelius. For that matter, we are not told the outcome of the trial. Gardner (1958: 405) assumes an acquittal in the light of Caelius' later career.

41 Münzer 1900; Balsdon 1962: 55. There is not much direct evidence. Catullus (5.1, 7.2, 43.7, 57.6, 58.1–2, 75.1, 79.1, 83.1, 86.5, 87.2, 92.1–2, 107.4) tells us much more about his complaints against Lesbia than about her qualities.

42 Skinner (1983) attempts to assess Clodia's influence on the basis of Cicero's letters rather than of *Pro Caelio*. She has Clodia devoted to her brother's interests, even to the extent of antagonizing her husband. But acts of Clodia against P. Clodius' interests lead Skinner to postulate a breach between brother and sister. The proof is said to be the apparent absence of Clodia's name from the list of those who wished to avenge his death. But the breach is highly speculative. Clodia's inclusion on the list might have gone up in flames when Sex. Cloelius destroyed public records (Cic. *Cael.* 78). Skinner is on safer ground when she has Clodia intercede with her husband in an attempt to heal the breach between Cicero and Metellus' relative, Metellus Nepos (Cic. *Fam.* 5.2.6). The attempt failed, but it confirms Clodia's political awareness. Nevertheless, if it were not for *Pro Caelio* we would hardly be able to portray Clodia as the political strategist.

43 There is no reasonable doubt as to Servilia's involvement in the crisis of the terminal date. She was on terms of close friendship with the jurist Servius Sulpicius Rufus, and Servius supported Caesar on the issue (Bauman 1985: 34–7, 14, 26, 32–3, 48). Servilia was in close touch with Servius in this matter.

44 R. Y. Tyrrell and L. C. Purser, *The Correspondence of M. Tullius Cicero*, vol. 5, Dublin 1915: 334; D. R. Shackleton Bailey, *Cicero's Letters to Atticus*, vol. 6, Cambridge 1967: 259. Contra Münzer 1923, 1820.

45 Cic. *Ad Brut.* 1.18 (i.e. Cary, No. 26). Münzer (1923, 1820) infers Servilia's conduct of the proceedings in parliamentary form from Cicero's careful choice of words: *at illa rettulit quaesivitque, quidnam mihi videretur*.

46 Her second husband, D. Iunius Silanus (cos. 62) had died in 60, and Caesar had divorced Pompeia at the time of the Bona Dea scandal. Münzer (1923, 1819) thinks the pearl necklace was an earnest of Caesar's intention to marry her, but the 18-year-old Calpurnia was better placed than the 40-year-old Servilia to give him the son that he wanted. The story that Caesar was Brutus' father (Plut. *Brut.* 5.1–2 *et al.*) is of course not true.

47 For Servilia's opposition see Cic. (*Att.* 13.22.4) with Münzer 1923, 1818; Hallett 1984: 53.
48 Plut. *Brut.* 13.2–6, 15.3–6, 53.4–5; *Cat. Min.* 25.2–4, 73.4; VM 4.6.5; CD 44.13.1–14.1, 47.49.3; App. *BC* 4.136. Plutarch's otherwise inexplicable failure to mention Servilia at all in the period after Caesar's death, despite his access to Cicero's correspondence with Brutus (*Brut.* 21.3, 23.1, 53.5), is best explained by his reliance on memoirs of Porcia's son Bibulus (by her first marriage) which contained a wealth of family material (cf. *Brut.* 13.2).
49 That Cato exempted her second husband, D. Iunius Silanus, from the prosecution for corruption which Cato and Servius launched against Murena in 62 (Bauman 1985: 16–17), was simply a family favour (cf. Plut. *Cat. Min.* 21.3–4). That Servilia instigated the prosecution of Scaurus in 54 (Marshall 1985: 151, 153, 155) is not provable. Servilia is supposed to have hated Pompey because of the murder of her first husband in 78; and her father, Q. Servilius Caepio (pr. 90?) had spent a large part of his life fighting cases against Scaurus' father (cos. 115). A not unimpressive *casus belli*, but whether Servilia is hidden behind the throng of twenty-three men connected with Scaurus' trial (Marshall, pp. 150–5) is a moot point.
50 On the friendship with Atticus see Cic. *Att.* 15.11.2; Nepos *Att.* 11. On asylum see Nepos, *op. cit.*, asserting that Atticus, having saved prominent men from the proscriptions, generally succoured the afflicted, including Servilia, to whom he showed the same consideration after Brutus' death as he had at the height of her prosperity (cf. Hallett 1984: 52).
51 Münzer 1923 takes Cicero's *ut appareret noctem et nocturnam deprecationem intercessisse* (*Att.* 2.24.3) as a pointer to Servilia's intervention.
52 CD (44.13.1–14.1) says that Porcia was the only woman privy to the plot. This means that someone had raised the question of Servilia's complicity.
53 Livius Drusus, the brother of Servilia's mother, Livia, was a conservative demagogue (Syme 1939: 87) who might be seen as an influence pointing Servilia towards Caesar's populism. But her father was a bitter opponent of Livius Drusus, as he had been of Saturninus (V. Fadinger in *Kl.P.*5.141–2).
54 On *humanitas* see Bauman 1980, 174–6.

7 THE TRIUMVIRAL PERIOD: DIPLOMACY, ORATORY AND LEADERSHIP

1 The death of Antony in August 30 is as good a date as any for the end of the triumvirate (since Lepidus' deposition in 36 a duumvirate). On the lead-up to the 'Restoration of the Republic' in January 27 see Judge 1974.
2 Veturia (see Chapter 1, p. 9) would no doubt be something of a precedent if her deputation to Coriolanus were true.
3 On the date of the Asian governorship see E. Badian, *Ath.* 34, 1956: 104–23; Bauman 1983: 386–67. Contra J. P. V. D. Balsdon (*CR* 51,

1937: 8–10), dating it to c. 98. R. M. Kallett-Marx (*CP* 85, 1989: 305–12) is not even aware of the full case for 95–4 and adds nothing to the debate. On the semi-divine honours see D. Magie, *Roman Rule in Asia Minor*, Princeton 1950: 1.174, 2.1064, n. 48; Bauman 1983: 383, 385.

4 On the tangled skein of Mucia's connection with the Metelli see Marshall 1985: 231–2. The alternatives in the text are probable in the order given.

5 *SJ* 50.1. He was said to have received reports of her misconduct while he was away, but to have ignored them (Plut. *Pomp.* 42.7). The true reason for the divorce was Pompey's arrangements with Caesar.

6 For Caesar's part in the manoeuvres see J. Ungern-Sternberg, *Unters. z. spätrepublikanischen Notstandsrecht*, Munich 1970: 110, n. 125, 123–5.

7 For Nepos' moves see *MRR* 2.174. Our suggestion is only a tentative one. Nepos had reasons not connected with Mucia for joining Pompey. Cf. Syme 1939: 32.

8 In 52 a *viator* entertained the consul Metellus Scipio at an orgy, setting up a brothel and prostituting 'Munia and Flavia' (VM 9.1.8). The names are usually emended to read 'Mucia and Fulvia', but is any emendation necessary? At least one 'Munius' is known, Munius Lupercus, who commanded a legion (TH 4.18.1, 22.1, 61.2). In any event, would Mucia have prostituted herself to Metellus Scipio, her relative by adoption, Pompey's latest father-in-law, and consul with Pompey in 52? A message to Pompey in such a bizarre form would have attracted more attention than a casual mention by Valerius Maximus. A second attack claims that 'Maecilia', who is said by Catullus to have had two intimates in Pompey's first consulship (70 BC) and two thousand in his second (55 BC), should read 'Mucilla', the diminutive of Mucia. So Pleitner on Cat. 113, cited by K. Quinn (*Catullus*, London 1970: 451–2) and accepted by Münzer (*RE* 16.450), though he does not insist that it is our Mucia. Most editors of Catullus reject the emendation: W. Kroll, 7th edn, Teubner 1968: 285; Quinn, *op. cit.*; R. A. B. Mynors, Oxford 1958: 103; C. J. Fordyce, Oxford 1961: 113. Rightly so; in 55 Mucia's divorce from Pompey was 6 years old.

9 App. *BC* 5.71.299; CD 48.36.1.

10 Julia in App. (*BC* 5.72.303), but mistakenly, unless, as surmised by Münzer (*RE* 10.895) the name is right but the description is wrong, since it may have been Antony's mother Julia. Three intermediaries are quite possible.

11 VM 8.3.3.; App. *BC* 4.32–34; *QIO* 1.1.6.

12 The speech is authentic, in substance even if not verbatim. *QIO* 1.1.6. says it is still read, and not merely as a compliment to Hortensia's sex (cf. VM 8.3.3). Also Münzer, *RE* 8.2481–2; Herrmann 1964: 111–15; Peppe 1984: 18–26. Balsdon (1962: 56) believes that it was a memorable speech but does not address the question of Appian's veracity. Pomeroy (1975: 175) has doubts about Appian but concedes that the 'rhetorical exercise' may include some genuine material. The slight inconsistency between Livy and Hortensia *ap.* Appian in regard to women in the

Second Punic War (Pomeroy, p. 178) could be due to Hortensia rather than to Appian.

13 What is known of the Matronalia, the matrons' festival celebrated on 1 March, does not go much further than the cult aspects (S. Weinstock, *RE* 14.2306–10; Latte 1960: 95; J. Gagé, *Coll. Lat.* 60, 1963). The custom of matrons giving gifts to their maidservants during the festival might have required some way of deciding the appropriate size of the gifts, but these *apophoreta* (Suet. *Vesp.* 19.1) may have been small 'take-home' presents, although the two million sesterces that Caligula gave Eutychus (*SG* 55.2) was more than that. *Conventus matronarum*: at such a meeting Agrippina was scolded and slapped by Galba's mother-in-law for setting her cap at him (Suet. *Galb.* 5.1.), but whether this was an organized morals court or a casual meeting cannot be determined. Ferrero (1911: 11), in one of his frustratingly undocumented pronouncements, speaks of 'a kind of woman's club, which called itself *conventus matronarum* and gathered together the dames of the great families'. Sirago (1983: 121) does not take it any further. Purcell (1986: 81–4, n. 33) has some interesting observations.

14 W. Waldstein, *SZ* 106, 1989: 657. On a bid for the franchise see Herrmann 1964: 114; Peppe 1984: 18–26, though his interpretation is unclear.

15 So Münzer, *RE* 8.2481–2.

16 That L. Valerius was effectively *ad idem* with Cato in the Oppian debate, as far as the exclusion of women from office is concerned, is strongly argued by Peppe 1984: 18–26. But he mistakenly implies from L 34.7.8–9 that Hortensia accepted the position adumbrated by Valerius.

17 *Phil.* 2.95, 5.11; *Att.* 14.12.1. It is only in the letter to Atticus, which is private, that Cicero identifies Fulvia by name. Cf. Chapter 6, p. 71 on Clodia.

18 CD 47.8.1–5. Dio's account should not simply be rejected. There was a strong tradition for violent expressions of red rage against enemies (Bauman 1974a: 215–17).

19 Hinard (1985: 439–40) suggests that Antony did recognize Rufus but pretended not to do so. Perhaps he wanted to spare Fulvia some of the ignominy by implying that the victim was not anyone of consequence. On her treatment of Cicero's head see n. 18.

20 In particular, Ligarius' wife, who hid her husband only to see him betrayed by a slave, followed his head as it was carried away, calling on the executioners to kill her as well, went to the triumvirs and accused herself, but got no reaction and starved herself to death (App. *BC* 4.23.93–5).

21 On L. Iulius Caesar see CD 47.8.5. For Octavian's propaganda see, e.g., Martial (11.20), preserving some lines penned against Fulvia by Octavian himself, which make up in obscenity for what they lack in literary merit. Also, the obscenities on the slingshots which Octavian's troops hurled into Perusia (*CIL* 11.6721.3, 4, 5, 14). For an interesting analysis of these 'Perusian acorns' see Hallett 1977. The gravamen of Octavian's 'poem' was that Fulvia had threatened to fight him unless

he made love to her. On abuse of the proscriptions see, e.g., a certain Fulvius who was betrayed by a former mistress because he had married someone else (App. *BC* 4.24). Despite the similarity of names, there is nothing to connect Fulvia with the incident.

22 On the legal principles involved see Bauman, *Athenaeum* 51, 1973: 270–93.

23 Cf. Babcock 1965: 5.

24 On this project cf. Bauman 1985: 92–103.

25 Specifically on appearing before soldiers, only the elder Agrippina, though her daughter did involve herself in military politics. Outside the Domus, Plancina, wife of Cn. Piso, was prominent in this respect (see Chapter 10, p. 141).

26 App. *BC* 5.14, 19, 21, 33, 43, 59, 62; CD 48.5.1–4, 6.4–7.1, 10.1–4; L *Per.* 125; VP 2.74.2; Plut. *Ant.* 28.1; Florus 2.16.5; Oros. 6.18.17–18. Syme (1939: 207–12) makes the main features of the operation reasonably clear.

27 References in n. 21. It is not essential to establish the accuracy of Martial's attribution of the obscene verses to Octavian. The point is that *someone* condemned Fulvia's military pretensions.

28 CD 48.6.4–7.1; App. *BC* 5.19.

29 CD 48.10.3–4; App. *BC* 5.19; VP 2.74.2–3; Florus 2.16.2(5); L. *Per* 125.

30 For the sacrifice story see Bauman 1982b: 105–7. For Fulvia's flight see App. *BC* 5.50, 52. VP (2.76.2) says Octavian gave her safe conduct and an escort. But to VP it is still 'womanish flight'.

31 App. *BC* 5.55, 59, 62; CD 48.28.3.

32 Münzer 1912: 284. Recent writers are less perceptive. Thus Balsdon (1962: 49): 'This Amazon of a woman . . . a virago'; Herrmann (1964: 119): 'L'odieuse Fulvia'; Pomeroy (1975: 185): 'The evil wife'; B. Perrin (Loeb edn of Plutarch): 'She redeemed a dissolute (*sic*) life by her passionate devotion to Antony.'

33 Münzer 1910: 284; H. A. Grueber, *Coins of the Roman Republic in the British Museum*, London 1910: 1.570, 575, 2.499; Plate LVI, 1, 10.

34 VP 2.74.3. Cf. CD 48.10.4; Florus 2.16.2(5). The androgyne syndrome again.

8 THE FOOTHILLS OF THE PRINCIPATE

1 Another Octavia, known as Octavia Major, was a half-sister of this Octavia and Octavian (see for example Syme 1939: 112).

2 E.g., Pompey and Caesar's daughter, Octavian and Fulvia's daughter.

3 On the Octavia coin and her priority over Fulvia, see Hammond 1937: 1860–1. Also the references in Chapter 7, n. 33.

4 On happiness see App. *BC* 5.76; Plut. *Ant.* 33.3. On deification see Sirago 1983: 62, n. 16.

5 On Octavia's diplomacy see App. *BC* 5.76, 93–5; Plut. *Ant.* 33.3, 35.1–4; CD 48.54.1–5. Cf. Singer 1947. Antyllus was executed after Actium, but Dio thinks that the betrothal was never seriously intended (CD 48.54.4). See also Hammond 1937: 1861–2.

6 Hammond (1937: 1862) with catalogue references.

7 Plut. *Ant.* 53, 54.1–2; CD 49.32.4–5, 33.3–4, 50.3.2.

8 CD 49.15.5–6. The grant came eight years after an unsuccessful attempt by Octavian to be elected as tribune, apparently without giving up his patrician status (Bauman, 1981: 170, n. 27).

9 Caesar had received a similar grant in 44 (Bauman 1981: *passim*).

10 CD 49.38.1. See also n. 12 below.

11 On statues see Cornelia, Chapter 5, p. 44. On release from tutela see Hispala, Chapter 4, p. 36.

12 Strictly speaking what was granted was not tribunician sacrosanctity, but an analogous position (Bauman 1981: 167–72). But convenience dictates its description as 'tribunician sacrosanctity'.

13 On opposition see Bauman 1989: 32–4. On Vestal sanctity Bauman 1981: *passim*. Also Chapter 5, p. 47.

14 *SA* 69.1; CD 48.44.2. On the Pontifex Maximus' 'reward', see n. 16 below.

15 CD 48.44.1–5; *TA* 5.1.3, with the notes of Furneaux and Koestermann; *SA* 62.2; *ST* 4.3. Carcopino (1958: 65–82) subjects the chronology to a clinical examination in order to defend the reputations of Octavian and Livia, but people could hardly be blamed for suspecting the worst. *SC* (1.1) notes the possibility that Octavian was Drusus' father. Balsdon (1962: 68) thinks they 'lived together' until Drusus' birth and were 'formally married' three days later. But Tacitus' *penatibus suis gravidam induxerit* (*TA* 5.1.3) implies a *deductio in domum*. And what was the point of asking the pontiffs *an necdum edito partu rite nuberet* (*TA* 1.10.4) if they were only planning concubinage?

16 Octavian refused the people's demand that he transfer the priesthood from Lepidus to himself (App. *BC* 5.131). That the concession was in return for services rendered is a possible explanation. There is also reason, however, to think that if conservative lawyers had not insisted on his retaining the post, Lepidus would have been deposed (Bauman 1989: 33–4).

17 *SA* 70. Suetonius describes Antony's action as spiteful (*amarissime*), and does not pass on the names. He probably did not have them. A predecessor had taken up the cudgels on behalf of Octavian. But Suetonius does quote the lampoon, from which a useful chronological inference can be drawn.

18 For the Capitoline banquet see CD 49.15.1. On Augustus' adoption of Apollo see Bauman 1989: 40–2.

19 CD 48.31.4; Plut. *Ant.* 31.3; VM 9.15.2.

20 On Willrich's belief that the precedent for Octavia and Livia was Vestal sanctity, and for a refutation thereof, see Bauman 1981: *passim*. The point made in the text reinforces that refutation.

21 CD (44.5.3, 49.15.5–6) makes this clear. On other passages in Dio, and in the Latin sources, see Bauman 1974a: 2–10.

22 Ollendorf 1926: 906; R. Hanslik in *Kl.P.* 3.688; Sirago 1983: 36–7.

23 Specially as such. It continued to be conferred separately even after the full *tribunicia potestas* became the *summi fastigii vocabulum* (*TA* 3.56.2) (Bauman 1981: *passim*).

24 On the oath see A. von Premerstein, *Vom Werden und Wesen des Prinzipats*, Munich 1937: 26–8, 36–8, 47–52; also EJ 315; *CIL* 11.5998a; *OGIS* 797; *ILS* 190; *SG* 15.3; CD 59.9.2; Philo *Leg. ad Gai.* 5; *TA* 14.7. On the subsumption of insults under the *lex maiestatis* see Bauman 1974a: 25–51.

9 WOMEN IN THE AUGUSTAN PRINCIPATE

1 The name by which he was known prior to becoming 'Augustus'. He is 'Octavian' in the previous chapter.

2 On the highly controversial 'restoration' see, for example, Syme 1939: ch. 22; F. Millar, *Journal of Roman Studies* 63, 1973; 50–67; W. K. Lacey, ibid. 64, 1974: 176–84. No assessment of the problem can be complete without referring to Judge 1974. Nothing of value is offered by P. Cartledge, *Hermathena* 119, 1975: 30–40; he has never heard of comparative law.

3 See Bauman 1967: 198–245; 1974a: 3, 9, 13–15, 74, 79, 131, 186. Livia's 'violation and diminution' is noticed by Tacitus in Tiberius' reign, but will serve as a general characterization of her position. See, however, Chapter 10, p. 133.

4 Who so much as remembers the names of Sulla's wives, or thinks of Marius' Julia as anything but Caesar's aunt? Mucia is a major figure in her own right (Chapter 7, p. 78), but is better known as a relative of the Metelli than as Pompey's wife. Calpurnia is little more than a voice prophesying doom on the Ides of March. Even Servilia's high profile owes relatively little to her link with Caesar. Cornelia had certainly been a charismatic figure, but it was due as much to her own efforts as to the reflected glory of her sons.

5 See Bauman 1967: 198–245.

6 On 'the divine blood of Augustus' see Chapter 9, p. 112.

7 Hammond 1937: 1862.

8 For Marcellus' acceleration see *TA* 1.3; CD 53.28.3–4; *PNH* 19.24. For the bypassing of Marcellus see CD 53.30.1–2, 31.1, 4; VP 2.93.1. On his death see CD 53.40.4–5; Prop. 3.18.1–10; Verg. *Aen.* 6.860–86.

9 Plut. *Ant.* 87.2–3. See also Roddaz 1984: 311.

10 CD 54.6.5, 12.5; *RG* 1.6. See also Salmon 1968: 19–20; Levick 1976: 29–30, 233, n. 26; Roddaz 1984: 351–81.

11 Agrippa's wife in 32 was Atticus' daughter, Caecilia. Atticus' biographer lays great stress on his close links with Augustus and the role of the Tiberius-Vipsania betrothal in cementing the friendship (Nepos *Att.* 19.2–20.3).

12 Despite VP (2.93.1–2), *SA* (66.3) and *ST* (10), it is probably an exaggeration to claim that Agrippa's resentment was the reason for his withdrawal to the east, though he was not too pleased about it. Cf. Syme 1939: 344–9; Roddaz 1984: 317–18. Agrippa did, however, deputize for the absent Augustus at the Julia-Marcellus wedding (CD 53.27.5).

13 So Levick (1976: 27), dating the marriage to 20 or 19 when Vipsania was of marriageable age. Roddaz (1984: 317, n. 44) thinks it took place before the Julia-Marcellus marriage. Cf. Syme 1939: 345.

14 On Octavia motivated by revenge see Balsdon 1962: 73–4. On Livia's promotion of Proculeius see R. Hanslik, *RE* 23.72–4.

15 CD 54.35.4; L *Per.* 140. The alternative date of 10–9 in *SA* 61 is wrong Hammond (1937: 1864). B. Perrin (Loeb edn of Plut. *Ant.*) inexplicably makes it 4 BC.

16 On the propaganda see Bauman 1974a: 25–51, 221, n. 195. Some of the material is discussed in Chapter 10, p. 133. On Agrippa's banishment see Bauman 1974a: 30–1. On the plotting to reinstate him see Norwood 1963. A full bibliography on this matter is not necessary for our purpose. Agrippa is touched on in this chapter, p. 120 in connection with the younger Julia.

17 On this legislation see Corbett 1930: 133–46; Last 1952: 443–52; Kunkel 1974: 91–2, 135–44; Finley 1968: 135; Bauman 1968, 1984; Thomas 1970; Brunt 1971: 562–6; Cantarella 1972; Csillag 1976; Raditsa 1980: 296–7, 310–19; Hopkins 1983: 95–6, 242–3; Galinsky 1981; Des Bouvrie 1984: 106–7; Gardner 1986: 117–38. Further references in Raditsa 1980; Des Bouvrie 1984. There is much of value, in addition to this legislation, in Villers 1982.

18 This fairly reflects the majority view of the writers cited in n. 17. Of the dissenters, the theory of Galinsky (1981) that Augustus wanted to demonstrate to conquered peoples that it would be to their advantage to be ruled by a superior race completely fails to convince. The role postulated by Galinsky had been efficiently performed by *maiestas populi Romani* since ancient times (Bauman 1967: ch. 1; 1978). That role was certainly not relegated to laws carrying sub-capital penalties. On Augustus and *pater patriae* see this chapter, p. 113.

19 On the censor Metellus, see L *Per.* 59; *SA* 89. On Cicero see *Leg.* 3.7; *Marc.* 23. On Horace see *Carm.* 3.6, 24; *Carm. Saec.* 17–20, 45–8; *Ep.* 2.1.2–3. On Ovid see *Fast.* 5.17–29. For 'Romulus' see DH 9.22.2, 2.15. On ancestral models see *RG* 8; *SA* 34.1. On Pudicitia see Palmer 1974: 137–9. See also Chapter 2, p. 15.

20 Prop. 2.7.1–3: *Gavisa est certe sublatam Cynthia legem/qua quondam edicta flemus uterque diu/ni nos divideret.*

21 On the law passed and repealed, see Jörs 1893: 4–28; Gardthausen 1896: 1.902. On the proposal dropped see Mommsen 1899: 691, n. 1; H. Last, *Cambridge Ancient History* 10.441, n. 3; Besnier 1979.

22 Badian (1985), arguing that Propertius is merely referring to a triumviral law imposing a tax on the unmarried which Augustus repealed in 28 BC.

23 Sulla's law need not, however, have created the *quaestio perpetua*, or permanent jury-court for adultery which we know under Augustus' law. It was quite possible for a crime to be defined by a public criminal law, but for trials to be referred to the family court. E.g. Appuleia Varilla in AD 17 (*TA* 2.50.4). The passage in Sallust to which Plutarch refers has not survived in the extant fragments of his *Historiae*. Although that work only covered events from 78 to 67 BC, a reminiscence of Sulla on a moral issue would not be surprising in Sallust.

24 On this law and its date see Kunkel 1962: 123, n. 449. He does not accept Sulla's law (Kunkel 1974: 62), but Rotondi (1912: 359–60) does.

On the whole question raised by Badian, see the difference between the matrimonial and adultery laws noted by Bauman 1968: 75, n. 63.

25 So Brunt 1971: 560; Hopkins 1983: 95.

26 On Augustus' gradual utilization of the full potential of the tribunician power see Bauman 1989: 30–1. On opposition to the programme later in the reign see this chapter, p. 122.

27 Sources: *TA* 1.53.1–2, 3.24.2, 4.44.3–5, 6.51.2; VP 2.93.2, 96.1, 100.2–5; Sen. *Ben.* 6.32.1–2, *Brev. Vit.* 4.5; *SA* 19.2, 63–5, 101.3; *ST* 7.2–3, 10, 11.4, 50.1; CD 54.35.4, 55.2, 4, 55.9.7, 55.10.12–16, 55.13.1, 56.32.4; Macrob. *Sat.* 1.11.17, 2.5; *PNH* 7.45, 7.149, 21.8–9.

28 *SA* 65.2, 101; *ST* 50; CD 56.32.4.

29 E.g., T. Vinius' wife, whom she saved from the proscriptions (CD· 47.7.4–5; App. *BC* 4.44; *SA* 27.2).

30 VP 2.100.5. Crispinus had been consul in 9 BC, Ap. Claudius was a great-nephew of Fulvia and P. Clodius, Gracchus was a descendant of the reformers of 133–121 BC and Scipio was a grandson of Scribonia.

31 VP 2.100.5; Sen. *Clem.* 1.10.3.

32 The solution to be offered was worked out, as far as the legal aspects are concerned, in Bauman 1967: 198–245. The present solution is geared more specifically to the politics of the question. The main thrust of the legal basis as previously worked out is embodied here without further discussion, but there are some additions in that regard as well.

33 The collection is accepted without comment by Carcopino 1958: 88–9; Balsdon 1962: 83–4; Meise 1969: 20. Sattler (1969: 517, n. 75) notes earlier attacks on *Sat.* 2.5.9, but finds the anecdote acceptable.

34 If, as seems likely, Julia was born in 39, and began going grey in, say, her mid-thirties, the anecdote will date to c. 4 BC.

35 6 BC is favoured by Carcopino 1958: 115–8; Sattler 1969: 502, n. 40. But Levick (1976: 37) points out that where relations had still been good enough in 9 for Julia to join Livia in entertaining senators' wives to celebrate Tiberius' ovation, Julia was not present at the celebration of his triumph in 7. Carcopino's explanation of why she was not there is not convincing.

36 *ST* 10; VP 2.99.2, 100.2–5; CD 55.9.7.

37 On denigration of the Claudii Nerones see Levick 1976: 37, 42. On Tiberius' lineage see *ST* 3.1. Levick vacillates between Julia having claimed superiority for her own lineage and having done so for that of Ap. Claudius.

38 Carcopino 1958: 118–23. The blackening of Tiberius' name will have been done by Julia getting her lover Gracchus to help her with a letter to Augustus. That there was such a letter is established by *TA* (1.53.5), but without any indication of content or occasion. Sattler (1969: 511) goes part of the way with Carcopino. But she surely did not write to tell Augustus that Tiberius had refused to supersede Gaius and Lucius.

39 Descent from Venus Genetrix had been invented by Caesar in 68 (*SJ* 6.1; Cic. *Fam.* 8.15.2; also D. Wachsmuth in *Kl.P.* 5.1178). On Augustus' *de facto* tenure, and the numinous nature of the status see Bauman 1967: 235–6.

40 *PNH* 21.8–9; CD 55.10.12–16; *TA* 3.24.2–3. On the Tacitus passage

see Bauman 1967: 199, 201, 205–6, 212, 228, 233, 242. See also below.

41 *Palam facta* appears to have prompted Carcopino (1958: 128–34) to invent a nocturnal meeting in the forum for purely conspiratorial purposes, at which Catilinarian-type mixtures of wine and blood were drunk and oaths to kill Augustus were sworn. Carcopino is unaware of the legal implications of *TA* 3.24.3. Cf. n. 40 above.

42 So Groag 1919: 84–8; H. Dessau, *Gesch. d. röm. Kaiserzeit*, Berlin 1924–30: 1.466–7; Groebe, *RE* 1.2584; Syme 1939: 426–7; Balsdon 1962: 86; Levick 1972: 798–801; 1976, 41–2; Sirago 1983: 65. One of the few voices raised against this view is Sattler 1969: 514–15. Meise (1969: 24–7, 44–7) has a useful discussion but makes the charge of adultery a smokescreen for one of conspiracy, thus falling victim to the endemic 'dummy charges' favoured by Rogers 1931. If it were suggested that there had to be some explanation for the discriminatory treatment of Iullus Antonius, I would add to what I have already said (Bauman 1967: 241–2) that there can be no question of Iullus having been charged with conspiracy while the others were charged with adultery. Even Dio, on whom the conspiratorial view largely depends, makes the factual basis nocturnal revels and drinking bouts (*kōmazein kai sympinein*) and says that it was because of this (*touto praxas*) that Iullus was suspected of monarchical ambitions (CD 55.10.12–16).

43 Discussion in Bauman 1967: 201–6, 227–30, 225–42.

44 In the basic sense of 'a swearing together'. It should be noted that Pliny alleges a plot in quite a separate passage from that referring to Augustus' edict.

45 On Gracchus see Furneaux 1.249, n., citing Ovid *Pont.* 4.16.31; *TA* 1.53.4. On Iullus see Hor. *Carm.* 4.2 with E. C. Wickham, *The Works of Horace*, 3rd edn, Oxford 1896: 1.288.93. On Crispinus (pr. 2 BC) see CD 55.10.11. On Julia's Crispinus see VP 2.100.5. On Scipio see Prop. 4.11.55. On Demosthenes see Sattler 1969: 517. On Ap. Claudius see T. P. Wiseman, *HSCP* 74, 1968: 220. It is sometimes suggested that Julia's mother, Scribonia, should be added to the list, because Augustus had wronged her by a brutal divorce as soon as Julia was born. Hence, it is said, her presence with Julia on Pandateria. But she was about 68 at the time of the scandal (Leon 1951: 168–9), had anything but the light touch appropriate to the circle (*SA* 62.2), and while still Augustus' wife constantly reproached him about his liaison with Livia (*SA* 69.1). She would not have approved of the *grex Iuliae*. She went to Pandateria because she was Julia's mother. Griffin (1984: 155–60) has an interesting piece on the literary opposition to Nero. It would be even more interesting if she had been aware of the literature relating to the Augustan and Tiberian precedents.

46 *Revocatio in servitutem* for ingratitude is first attested for Claudius, who decreed it against a freedman who had laid a charge against his patron (*D* 37.14.5). Despite Buckland (1963: 71), this need not have been the first case.

47 On the analogy with *patria potestas* see Strabo 6.4.2, p. 288C; Sen. *Clem.* 1.14.2; CD 53.18.3. Cf. Bauman 1967: 236–7. On Messalla and

Augustus see *SA* 58.2. On the literary chorus see Bauman 1967: 238, n. 124. On the final achievement see *RG* 35.1.

48 If Juvenal (6. 308–13) is any guide to the nocturnal activities of imperial Rome, it is not surprising that Augustus' letter to the senate gave only the general thrust of the circle's preoccupations.

49 On Apollo as the protoype jurisconsult under whose aegis Augustus placed his programme of law reform see Bauman 1989: 40–2. That reform was closely bound up with his legislative programme. See *ibid.* 56–8 on the link between the *ius respondendi* and the *lex Papia Poppaea*. On Marsyas see *ibid.* 41, n. 89. The legend about the musical contest between Apollo and Marsyas (H. von Geisau in *Kl.P.* 3.1051) describes one area of rivalry between the two entities; the chaplet on Marsyas' statue describes another. Another part of the night's activities, at 'the very Rostrum from which her father had proposed his adultery law', lacks any further detail, but one would not be surprised if it had something in common with the nocturnal frolics in Juvenal's Rome (Juv. 6.306–48). For Levick's theory regarding the Marsyas statue see n. 85.

50 That Augustus' personal life fell far short of the standard that he demanded from others is well known. See p. 125 on Livia's role in that regard.

51 On what follows the most help has been derived from Thibault 1964. But the theory concerning book 3 of *Ars Amatoria* is original. It was foreshadowed in Bauman (1989: 51–3), and is here developed in greater detail.

52 Thibault 1964: 33; G. P. Goold, Loeb edn of *Ars Amatoria*, 2nd edn, 1979: x. Syme (1978: 13–20) thinks there was a first edition in c. 9 BC and a second in 1 BC. But this applies only to books 1 and 2.

53 Ovid T. 3.5.45, 5.47–8; Ovid P. 2.9.67–71. T. 3.5.49, 2.103–4. T. 2.103–8.

54 For discussion of these speculations see Thibault 1964: 50–4. Texts: ibid. 24–7, 143, nn. 73, 74.

55 Sources: *TA* 4.71.6–7, 3.24.2–7; *SA* 65.1, 72.3, 101.3; Scholia (2) ad Juv. 6.158; *SC* 26.1. For discussions see Norwood 1963; Bauman 1967: 242–3, 1974: 30–1; Meise 1969: 35–48; Syme 1978: 206–11.

56 On AD 1 see E. Hohl, *Klio* 30, 1937: 323–42. On AD 6 see Norwood 1963: 153. Syme (1978: 210–11) denies that Paullus was executed at all; he was exiled and survived until 14, being the member of the Arval Brethren who died that year (*ILS* 5026). But this cannot be. A criminal conviction against a priest meant expulsion from the order. (Bauman 1983: 398). Syme (1978: 208) correctly has Paullus alive at the time of the adultery condemnation. Thus the conspiracy would have come later.

57 Meise 1969: 44–7, 223–35. Whether failure to pass on information was culpable is a moot point. It is probably covered by *D* 48.4.1.1: *cuius opera consilio <dolo> malo consilium initum erit*. It was indictable in Macedonian law (Bauman 1990b: 131). But the penalty under *D* 48.4.1.1 was capital.

58 Thibault 1964: 21 – correctly.

59 Cf. W. Krause, *RE* 18, 1942: 1933–4 and in *Kl.P.* 4.384.

60 Despite Krause 1942; Hollis 1977: xiii; Henderson 1979: xi. It is guesswork either way, but if – as cannot be disputed – Ovid thought about a third book only after completing the first two, we do not know enough about his speed of composition to estimate how long he needed for book 3. Hollis (xi-xii) allows him ten years for the first, five-book, edition of *Amores*. And it was only after another ten years' reflection, while working on other poems, that he identified the parts of *Amores* that were not worth retaining in the second edition.

61 So Bauman (1989: 51 and n. 141), tentatively having him trained by Labeo at the Proculian School.

62 See Bauman (1968: 76) on the *ad hoc* procedure for clearing a backlog of cases in c. 27 BC.

63 On *lex Papia Poppaea* see Last 1952: 452–6; Brunt 1971: 560–6. On the amendment by Tiberius see Bauman 1989: 56–8.

64 As the marriage ordinance is the only law expressly attested as having been introduced and amended during Augustus' reign (the five years' prescription for adultery in 2 BC was presumably by *lex*, but we do not have the name of the proposer), we have no control by which to check whether the laws of 18–17 were specially made Julian (in preparation for the Secular Games of 17?), leaving all amendments to be proposed by others. The laws of 18–17 were not, of course, the only Julian laws in the reign (Bauman 1989: 44, 219), but we are here concerned only with amendments.

65 On *Amores*, cf. Hollis 1977: xii, 150–1.

66 *TA* 1.3.3, 1.5.1, 2.43.5, 2.77.6, 2.82.2; CD 53.33.4, 55.10a.10, 56.30.1–2; Sen. *Marc.* 2.5.

67 VM 6.1 pr.; Sen. *Marc.* 4.3; *TA* 5.1.5.

68 CD 56.46.2 against *TA* 1.14.3. Cf. Bauman 1981: 175 and n. 60.

69 Despite Willrich (1911: 54–5), the sacrosanctity of 35 BC and the *ius liberorum* of 9 BC (CD 55.2.5–6) were not based on Vestal precedents (see Bauman 1981: 175 and n. 62). The Vestals did not receive the *ius liberorum* until the time of the *lex Papia Poppaea* (CD 56.10.2). The only borrowing from the Vestals in Livia's dossier is the release from perpetual guardianship (CD 49.38.1; *FIRA* 1.37).

70 On the tradition see *SA* 71.1; *TA* 5.1.5. On the canard, see Ollendorff 1926: 903.

71 On checks on luxury in food and clothing see Ferrero 1911: 58–62; Ollendorff 1926: 904.

72 Ollendorff 1926: 904, citing this in support of Ferrero's theory about Livia's role in the marriage and morals programme.

73 For a survey of the literature see Sattler 1969: 499–502. For other discussions see Gardthausen 1896: 1.2.1028, 1.3.1101; Meise 1969: 5–34.

74 Sen. *Marc.* 4.3; *SA* 84.2. Cf. Ollendorff 1926: 904.

75 Of the two dates, 16–13 BC (Sen. *Clem.* 1.9.2–12), AD 4 (CD 55.14–22), Seneca's is to be preferred, though it still has problems. But Dio's date has more (Bauman 1967: 196–7).

76 The metaphor probably originated with Livia and is thus one of the few memorable sayings associated with her name. Another is the statement about virtuous women and statues (Chapter 8, p. 97).

77 It might be argued at a pinch that Augustus had deliberately arranged to summon his *consilium* and then cancelled it in order to let it be known that a new entity, the *amica principis*, had been created. But in view of our position on Livia and official status under Augustus (this chapter, p. 128) such a possibility must be ruled out.

78 Sen. *Marc.* 4.3; *TA* 3.34.12; *SA* 24.1. Despite Ollendorff (1926: 905), Livia did not accompany Augustus to Gaul over 16–13 BC. Dio says that Augustus went there in order to live with Maecenas' wife, Terentia, away from prying eyes (CD 54.19.2). This is one of the difficulties confronting Seneca's date for the conspiracy of Cinna. But as already observed, Dio's date is worse.

79 Ollendorff 1926: 906–7; EJ p. 95, no. 127; *CIL* 10.7464, 10.7340, 11.3076; Ollendorff, *op. cit.* 914.

80 See my 'Tanaquil-Livia and the Death of Augustus' (*Hist.* 43 (1994)).

81 But see p. 128 below.

82 Especially 'Our search for models of virtue will be better when you take on the role of first lady' (tr. Purcell 1986).

83 Purcell (1986) himself cites Ovid's Princeps Femina (*Pont.* 3.1.125). Also in point: Livia alone is worthy to share the bed of mighty Jupiter; she restored the temple of Bona Dea in order to imitate and follow her husband in everything; no husband but the *pater patriae* deserved Livia (*Fasti* 1.649, 6.637, 5.157; T. 2.157–64 is also relevant to the *de facto* status of *mater patriae*).

84 On *Livia Augusti dea* see Furneaux: 1.172. On eventual deification see Ov. *Fast.* 1.536. On other honours see n. 69 above. Sacrosanctity, release from tutelage and statues went back to 35, before anyone was Princeps, and in any event were given to Octavia as well as to Livia.

85 Levick (1972: 798–801, 1976: 41–2) makes the background to the trials of 2 BC a family faction centred on Scribonia and having a populist ideology. Levick supports the theory by quite a different interpretation of the Marsyas incident from that which we have advanced. The garlanding will have been a tribute to the free city, and the inclusion of a tribune amongst Julia's lovers will be connected with the tribunician agitation of 2 BC. The circle stood for an alliance of palace and people against the austere oligarch, Tiberius. The plan to marry Julia to Iullus Antonius had become urgent, because Augustus would soon consider Gaius and Lucius capable of standing on their own feet, thus dispensing with the need to have Iullus as a husband and a guardian. The hypothesis is not convincing. If Julia wanted to secure her sons' rights, why did she need Iullus if Augustus was about to do it for her? As for the democratic alliance against Tiberius, not much of an alliance was needed against Tiberius at this time. The populist ideology of 'the alliance' is refuted by the previous occasion on which indignities had been inflicted on the statue; the tribunes had refused to intervene on behalf of the perpetrator (*PNH* 21.8–9). As for the tribunician agitation (CD 55.9.10), what has it got to do

with Julia? In any case it was settled amicably. Moreover, only one of the ten tribunes belonged to the *grex*. Furthermore, there is, unlike the popular demonstrations in AD 3 (see this chapter, p. 118), no trace of any popular protest at the time of her condemnation. The revelations of what she had done had shocked the plebeian conscience much more than that of the upper ranks of society. That is why Augustus, urged on in all probability by Livia, had 'revealed what he should have concealed' (Sen. *Ben.* 6.1–2).

10 TIBERIUS, LIVIA AND AGRIPPINA

1 *Noverca* (stepmother in *TA* 1.33.5, but carrying such terms back a step was not unusual (Furneaux: 1.225, n.).

2 On the suggestion see A. von Premerstein, *Vom Werden und Wesen des Prinzipats*, Munich 1937: 269. On the refutation see De Martino 1972–4: 4.447.

3 Gaius and Lucius, for example, were Caesars. But nobody other than the emperor was an Augustus. Even that was not entirely favoured by Tiberius. He reacted ambivalently to the title of 'Augustus' conferred on him by the will (*SA* 101.2; *ST* 26.2; *CD* 57.2.1, 8.1).

4 Cf. Chapter 9, p. 126. There were in fact two proposals, *parens patriae* and *mater patriae*, both of which Tiberius forbade (*TA* 1.14.2; *CD* 57.12.4). There was only *parens patriae* in *ST* 50.3. There was a difference: *parens*, as a common noun, would equate Livia more closely with the male rulers, *mater* would put her on a somewhat lower level. Alföldi (*Museum Helveticum* 10, 1953: 106–14) regards Caesar's *parens patriae* as the lineal ancestor of Augustus' title, but that leaves the insistence on a difference in the sources very much up in the air.

5 *TA* 1.14.2; *ST* 50.2 (both *Augusti filius* and *Liviae filius* were to be part of his nomenclature, but he was already *divi f.*, which took care of the Augustan side of it). *CD* (57.12.4) thinks that he was to be called only after his mother, in contrast to the Greek practice.

6 *TA* 1.14.2–3, including the veto of a lictor. Contra *CD* 56.46.2. Perhaps she was allowed a lictor only for her priestly function, not for public appearances in general. On October see *ST* 26.2. See also n. 9.

7 If her supporters are to be identified by reference to their friendship with her but not with Tiberius, only one or two names spring to mind, e.g., Q. Haterius Arippa, C. Fufius Geminus. Cf. this chapter, pp. 134, 137. Her close women friends like Urgulania and Plancina no doubt influenced men to support her, as Mutilia Prisca influenced Fufius Geminus (this chapter, p. 137). But Tacitus does not speak of a Party of Livia, as he does of Agrippina. Livia's differences with Tiberius were not a clarion call. *ST* (51.2) attests a general attack on her friends after her death, but specifies only a knight. *TA* (5.2) has Tiberius condemn 'womanish friendships', but only Geminus suffers.

8 *TA* 1.14.3; *ST* 50.2.

9 He refused *pater patriae*, warning the senate in ominous terms of the dangers of the status (*ST* 67.2–4). Cf. *ST* 28; *TA* 1.72.2, 2.87.2; *CD*

57.8.1, 58.12.4. He would not allow his name to be given to September (*ST* 26.2).

10 EJ 102a, 102b; *TA* 4.13.2; 4.37–8; Bauman 1974a: 77–9.
11 In the east she monopolized a sizeable share of the pantheon (Ollendorff 1926: 917–8; Seager 1972: 145–6). Even in the west she was 'Mother of the World' (Spain), 'Ceres' (Gaulus near Malta), 'Juno' (Africa) (EJ 123, 126, 127). As priestess of Augustus see below *passim*.
12 *TA* 5.2.1; CD 58.2.2, 6. The senate took it upon itself to order a year's mourning by women, but softened the blow by expressing approval of Tiberius' conduct in not attending the funeral because of public business. The senate also voted an arch recognizing her good deeds, but Tiberius promised to pay for it himself; however, he simply allowed it to fall into abeyance. Whether someone who appropriated imperial *maiestas* to herself (Chapter 9, p. 99) actually declined deification ahead of time is a moot point.
13 Bauman 1974a: 103. On the institutionalizing power of the *crimen maiestatis*, see *ibid. passim*, especially on the compulsory celebration of the birthday of Divus Julius, ibid. 74.
14 On the rash of anonymous (and pseudonymous) pamphlets see Bauman 1974a: 25–51, 221, n. 195. The translation of the example from *ST* 59.1 is by Robert Graves, *Suetonius: The Twelve Caesars*, Penguin 1957. See also *TA* 1.72.5. On the demands for payment see *TA* 4.57.5; CD 57.3.3.
15 Falanius was also alleged to have included a statue of Augustus in the sale of a property, and in the same year a certain Rubrius was charged with swearing a false oath by Augustus, and Granius Marcellus was charged with substituting Tiberius' head for Augustus' on a statue (Bauman 1974a: 71, 76). Livia may well have been involved in those matters as well, but there is no direct link as there is in the case of the suspect cultist.
16 Bauman 1974a: 62–5.
17 She was the grandmother of Urgulanilla, at one time the wife of Livia's grandson, Claudius.
18 CD (57.12.5), wrongly installing the dedicated statue in Livia's house.
19 *ST* 50.2–51.2. Her controversial attempt to have the new citizen made a juror had a parallel in Augustus' reign. When Livia sought a consulship for a Gaul, Augustus refused to cheapen the citizenship and gave only exemption from tribute (*SA* 40.3).
20 CD 57.12. The letters bearing both names could be a generalization from the Archelaus case, but the other items are likely enough.
21 *ST* 51.2; *TA* 5.1–3, 6.10.1; CD 58.2.1–3a, 4.5–7.
22 *SG* 23.2. The attempt by Purcell (1986: 79) to have Caligula comparing the *stola* with the *toga* in a constitutional sense is forced.
23 CD (58.2.1) says she was 86; *PNH* (14.8.60) makes it 82. Dio is probably right.
24 *ST* 50.1 says that Tiberius first showed his hatred of Drusus by producing a letter in which Drusus had raised the question of compelling Augustus to restore the Republic. Levick (1976: 32–3) doubts the hatred

but not the letter. Tacitus obviously knew of the letter and extrapolated suspicions against Germanicus from it.

25 But his basic facts, including the Rhine Bridge, are genuine. He specially cites the elder Pliny's lost work on the German Wars for the latter. (*TA* 1.69.2). This is Tacitus' only citation of that work. The matter was so important that he wanted it verified. Modern authors do not make enough of the incident. Syme (1958: 1.276) merely notes the citation. Levick (1976: 153–4) is slightly more expansive. So is Seager 1972: 80. But Kornemann (1960) does not notice it at all.

26 Although there is no tradition for Fulvia as a populist, she appears to have been on fairly comradely terms with Antony's veterans, whose cause she championed. Even Octavian's troops at Perusia injected a note of bawdy familiarity into the slingshots that they hurled at her. Cf. Chapter 8, n. 21.

27 She might well have questioned the double standards that sanctioned similar conduct on Agrippina's part.

28 For Tacitus' references to her high birth see *TA* 1.40.3, 2.43.5–7, 2.71.6, 4.52.4. On Mitylene see Furneaux 1.348; EJ 95.

29 *TA* (3.3.1–3) insinuates that Antonia stayed away either because of ill-health, or because of her deep grief, or because Livia and Tiberius kept her away as a cover for their own absence. But it was not for nothing that Tacitus made the intervention of Livia and Tiberius his last choice. He knew that the senate had voted honours for Germanicus, and had stipulated that the list be approved by Tiberius, Livia, Drusus, Antonia and Agrippina (*TA* 2.83; *Tabula Siarensis*, in *ZPE* 55, 1984: 55–100). Except for the omission of Claudius, the Domus still presented a superficially united front.

30 As he had agreed to do for Livia's other friend, Urgulania. Cf. this chapter, p. 135.

31 *TA* 3.15.1–3, 3.16.5–7, 3.17.3–8, 3.18.1–2. In *TA* (6.26.4) Tacitus describes the offences which cost Plancina her life as 'notorious crimes' but gives no details. If it means the murder of Germanicus it raises the awkward question of double jeopardy. Dio rather strangely says that Tiberius hated Plancina, 'not on account of Germanicus but for another reason' (CD 58.22.5). Dio was worried about double jeopardy but had no details.

32 *TA* 3.33. Caecina had, as legate of Lower Germany at the time of the mutiny, lost his nerve, sparking off the panic which Agrippina quelled (*TA* 1.32–7, 48–9, 64–9). Thus he had a grudge against service wives. Cotta's initiative three years later resulted in a definitive regulation of the situation with gubernatorial entourages (*TA* 4.20.3). This appears, however, to be the decree which the lawyers date to AD 20 (*D* 1.16.4.2; EJ 41). Raepsaet-Charlier (1982: 61, n. 42) thinks the mistake in the date lies with the Digest rather than with Tacitus. For an interesting analysis of the decree see Fanizza 1977.

33 *TA* 3.29, 3.56–7, 4.12.2–7. *TA* 4.4.1–3, 4.3, 4.8.1, 4.11.4; EJ 52.

34 For a discussion of Wiseman's theory that there was no such thing as a Julio-Claudian dynasty (a theory with which I largely agree), see Chapter 11, n. 22.

35 Not, however, to the public courts, that is, the permanent jury-courts. The increasing role of the senate as a criminal court, applying the public criminal laws but behind the closed doors of the senate, made it a suitable venue. Augustus had not allowed the senate to deal with his supreme crisis (Chapter 9, p. 113 and Bauman 1967: 203–4, 231–3), but Tiberius referred most cases to the senate. His exercise of personal jurisdiction (on Capri) was exceptional (Bauman 1989: 135).

36 On that crime see this chapter, p. 147.

37 CD 57.24.1; TA 4.17.1–3. On Drusus and Asinius Gallus see Shotter 1989: 148.

38 As enunciated by Rogers (1931) and more briefly in his *Criminal Trials*, Middletown 1935: 75–6, 102. He sees a continuous conspiratorial line from the elder Julia to Agrippina, who is said to have inherited her mother's ambitions and to have pursued them relentlessly, with a short break over 19–23. The argument does not convince. Was she conspiring over the fourteen years of her marriage to Germanicus? If so, was she acting with him or against him? Moreover, if she was pursuing a Julian line (which she undoubtedly was), in what way was that an inheritance from her mother? Are we to believe that the elder Julia pursued a Julian line against Augustus? Agrippina's line was a response to a post-Julia development, the Claudian domination of the two-tier system through Tiberius and Germanicus.

39 The mutiny was in Lower Germany.

40 On the rule against magisterial accusers see Bauman 1966: 422–4. On Varro's father and Silius see TA 3.43.4. The claim by TA (4.19.1) that Varro used his father's feud with Silius as a pretext in order to gratify Sejanus is not one of Tacitus' best deductions.

41 Tacitus ingenuously says that while both Silius and Sosia were clearly guilty of *repetundae*, the case was conducted on the basis of *maiestas* (TA 4.19.5). Somehow the relatively 'normal' practice of fleecing the provincials had been blown up, by the malice of the accuser, into treason. But Tacitus knows better than this. As he himself tells us, the prosecution alleged that Silius had connived with Sacrovir and had delayed taking steps to suppress the revolt (TA 4.19.4). In fact *repetundae*, in its most common sense of extorting money from provincials, did not figure in the case at all. Tacitus himself notes that no provincials lodged claims against Silius (TA 4.20.1). Here, *repetundae* is used in its more general sense of the improper receipt of money, namely bribes from Sacrovir. That is the meaning of the accuser's claim that Silius had besmirched his victory by greed – *victoria per avaritiam foedata* (TA 4.19.4). For republican parallels see Bauman 1983: 85–7, 392–6.

42 On confiscation against Silius see Bauman 1974a: 117–19. On the concession to Sosia see TA 4.20.2–3.

43 Stein, *RE* 10, 1918: 796. Cf. TA 3.40.2. Furneaux, 1.441 thinks it was Caesar or Augustus, but the result is the same.

44 See below. Chelidon (Chapter 6, p. 66) was *de facto* patron of her 'clients', but there is no question of a formal *clientela*. Nevertheless the germ of the notion was there.

45 For the legions' offer and the emphasis they placed on her name and lineage see *TA* 1.35.3, 1.40.3, 1.41.3, 1.69.

46 On Serenus and Cornutus see *TA* 4.28. On Suillius see *TA* 4.31.5–6.

47 *TA* 4.39–40. The letters are queried by Syme 1958: 1.404, 2.702. But no queries are raised by Koestermann *ad loc.*, Seager (1972: 195–7) or Shotter (1989 *ad loc.*). It should be noted that Tacitus does not purport to give the exact words of the letters: 'The gist of the document was' – *eius talis forma erat* (*TA* 4.39.1).

48 *TA* 4.3, 4.8.1, 4.10–11; *ST* 62.1; *CD* 58.11.6–7; *PNH* 29.20.

49 It has been noticed, for example, that Drusus had nearly died (from natural causes) two years earlier, when Clutorius Priscus signed his own death warrant with his own pen. Meise (1969: 49–90) distinguishes a number of motifs, including Tiberius' suspicion that Gemellus, the surviving twin son of Drusus and Livilla, was illegitimate. Meise infers that this was used to justify Tiberius' choice of Caligula as his successor. But Josephus specifically makes Gemellus 'the son of his son' (*Ant.* 18.211, 219). On these issues see also Seager 1972: 181–5; Hennig 1975: 33–40.

50 On her *atrocitas* see Shotter 1989: 183. On her excitability see *TA* 1.33.5, 2.28.3, 2.72.1, 3.1.1, 4.3.2, 4.52.3, 6.25.3.

51 Syme (1958: 271, n., 277–8) points out that the only cases where Tacitus acknowledges his source are *TA* 1.69.2 (the elder Pliny on the Rhine Bridge) and the marriage request. But although Syme discounts the large attributions to the memoirs favoured by some scholars, he does not exclude the possibility of some unacknowledged citations.

52 Marsh 1931: 179, n. 4; Hennig 1975: 82, 104, n. 87; Shotter 1989: 21, 183.

53 *TA* 1.12.6, 1.13.2, 2.35, 2.36, 3.11.2, 3.19.4, 4.7.1, 6.23.1, 6.25.1–2; *CD* 57.2.5, 58.3.1–6.

54 Their shared *cognomen* suggests the possibility of a family link, though how far the *cognomen* is a reliable guide in the early Principate is a moot point. See Bauman, 'Personal Names, Adoptions and Families of the Roman Jurists', *SZ* 108, 1991: 1–20.

55 Whether because of Livia's domination or Agrippina's tactics, or for any one of a dozen other reasons, cannot be determined. Kornemann (1960: 180) thinks it was the cumulative pressure of four widows.

56 *TA* 4.68–70; *CD* (58.1b–3) adds the story of Sabinus' dog that stayed with him throughout, finally leaping into the river with his body; *PNH* 8.145; *ST* 61.2.

57 In what follows I adopt, with amplifications and modifications, the attack on Tacitus' chronology of the episode mounted by Meise 1969: 237–44. Specific references for the major steps in the argument will be given in the notes at appropriate points.

58 *TA* (5.3.3–4.2) locates everything under AD 29, in the preliminaries to the final *dénouement* of that year. One reason for removing it from 29 is because it offers a solution to the problem raised by *SG* (10.1), according to which Caligula at first lived with his mother, but after she was relegated went to live with Livia. So Meise 1969. This can only be reconciled with the assertion that Livia protected Agrippina

as long as she lived (*TA* 5.3.1) if the relegation referred to by Suetonius was, as a sub-capital penalty, acceptable to Livia, who will only have been concerned to afford protection against capital penalties. Meise's change of date may also help to make sense of *PNH* (8.145), where it is said that Sabinus was punished 'in the aftermath of Nero's case', though this is not so certain. Pliny seems to be referring to the case in 29 which sent Nero into definitive exile.

59 Her internment at Herculaneum is reliably deduced from Sen. *De Ira* 3.21.5: Caligula destroyed the villa where his mother had been incarcerated.

60 *TA* 4.67.5–6. Augustus' statue had been used as a place of asylum ever since his deification (Bauman 1974a: 85–92).

61 *TA* 4.67.6; *ST* 53.2.

62 In view of *PNH* (8.145, n. 58) we cannot be sure that Sabinus was eliminated before the relegation of Agrippina and Nero in 27. Yet both happened in the same year, except for the formal verdict against Sabinus on 1 January 28.

63 *TA* (5.3.1) makes Livia's death a watershed; only after that did crushing despotism emerge.

64 *TA* 5.3.2. In a letter to the senate just before this Tiberius had attacked 'womanish friendships', by which he meant Livia's sponsorship of Geminus (*TA* 5.2.2).

65 Bauman 1974a: 25–51. The arrival on the scene of pamphleteering drives the final nail into the coffin of the idea that Tiberius' original complaints of homosexuality and insubordination had any part in the final stage. At that stage it was unmistakably sedition under the treason laws. Neither homosexuality nor insubordination had anything to do with that.

66 Philo *Flacc.* 19.158, 125, 185–8. He was exiled and later put to death by Caligula.

67 *PNH* 8.145; *ST* 54.2, *SG* 7; CD 58.8.4. He died before the fall of Sejanus.

68 For the trials on Capri see Bauman 1989: 135. On Agrippina tried by the senate, Marshall (1990b: 345) thinks the case was initiated in the senate but then subsumed under Tiberius' personal *cognitio*, no doubt because of *TA* 5.5.1: *integra tamen sibi cuncta postulavit*. But this could simply mean that he wished to clarify the position before remitting the case to the senate. In Cn. Piso's case he summoned his *consilium* and gave a hearing to both the prosecution and the defence before sending the case back to the senate (*TA* 3.10). He did this because of the malicious rumours about himself (3.10.5), that is, that Piso had had secret instructions from Tiberius to dispose of Germanicus. If personal considerations caused him to prefer the senate in that case, the same should hold good for Agrippina. There had been no attempt to curb the senate's authority in the cases of her friends, Sosia and Pulchra – despite his non-disclosure of the Sacrovir scandal to the senate until it was all over.

69 *ST* 53.2; *SG* 15. On her death see *TA* 6.25.1. Tacitus notes that she might have been denied food to make her death look like suicide. *ST*

(53.2) does not mention this. On the androgynous evaluation see *TA* 6.15.2–3. On the senate's vote see *TA* 6.25.4–5, *ST* 63.2.

70 The legal rule is stated by *TA* (6.10.1) apropos of Vitia who mourned the death of her son, Fufius Geminus: because women could not be charged with aiming at supreme power, they were accused for their tears.

71 Bauman 1974a: 25–51.

72 Cf. again the demonstrators' cheers for Tiberius.

73 For the lurid details of his end see *TA* 6.23.4–24.4. On the law applicable to his case see Bauman 1989: 78–9.

74 *TA* 6.23.5; *ST* 65.2; CD 58.13.1.

75 Marsh (1931: 197, n. 2) thinks it possible and holds that it would have made Drusus joint emperor. Kornemann (1960: 207); Hennig (1975: 97); Seager (1972: 221) note the evidence without comment. Levick (1976: 211) discusses the false Drusus, but does not suggest that it had anything to do (which it did not) with the fall of Sejanus. For some recent theories on the fall of Sejanus and one or two suggestions see Bauman 1989: 80–2.

76 Cornutus was in charge of fund raising in the Sacrovir affair. The same can possibly be said about Titius Sabinus, but is not certain.

11 CALIGULA'S SISTERS

1 On the aforegoing see Meise 1969: 92–9; Bauman 1974a: 204–10, 106; 1981: 174–8; Barrett 1989: 60–2 with notes.

2 On the sources see Barrett 1989: xx–xxiii. There is not much to be gained from J. P. V. D. Balsdon, *ANRW* II 2, 1975: 92–4. I do not argue for Caligula's sanity (see n. 12). But some of the record needs to be set straight.

3 On complete rejection of the item see Meise 1969: 99–100; Barrett 1989: 62. On Antonia and Tiberius see Jos. *Ant.* 18.179–86. On Herod Agrippa see *ibid.* 18.183–6, 236.

4 Some attributions have no merit. E.g., that Caligula poisoned Antonia or drove her to suicide (*SG* 23.2, CD 59.3.6) is sheer fantasy.

5 *SG* 15.3; CD 59.3.4. Meise (1969: 98) thinks they were also included in the vows for the state, but that was quite separate from the vows for the emperor (Furneaux 1.512; Shotter 1989: 148).

6 Meise 1969: 99; Barrett 1989: 62–3.

7 References in n. 6.

8 A. O'Brien Moore, *RE* Supp. 6, 1935: 711.

9 The numerous decrees of the senate that have been preserved epigraphically (*FIRA* 1.240–300) do not assist; they do not record the formula pronounced by the proposing consul.

10 So Nony 1986: 230.

11 Barrett 1989: 63 and fig. 15 (*BMC* 36–7). Cf. Nony 1986: 230–1. The figures are in standing postures accompanied by their names. The centre position is occupied by Drusilla, which enables her name to be placed horizontally above her head. Agrippina on the left and Livilla on the right have their names recorded vertically.

12 For a summary of current clinical diagnoses see Barrett 1989: 214–7.

13 Jos. *Ant.* 19. 204; *SG* 24.1; CD 59.22.6; Eutrop. 7.12.3; Vict. *Caes.* 3.10, *Epit.* 3.4; Hieron. *ap.* Eus. 178; Schol. Juv. 4.81; Oros. 7.5.9. Cf. Barrett 1989: 85, 274, n. 48; also Nony 1986: 275.

14 On his own showing, however, Suetonius must be treated with caution after *SG* 21. With *SG* 22 he ends his account of Caligula the emperor and starts on Caligula the monster. Not all the 'monster' section is suspect, but care must be taken.

15 So *SG* 24.1. But CD (59.11.1) makes it her second husband, Aemilius Lepidus. For some reason Suetonius does not notice the Lepidus marriage at all (*SG* 24.3, 36.1; *SC* 9.1).

16 *SG* 24.1: *in modum iustae uxoris propalam habuit*. The implications of the language here have not been explored before. Suetonius is not saying that a lawful marriage, *iustae nuptiae*, existed between them. *In modum uxoris habuit* is not his usual expression for a formal marriage. He nearly always uses *duxit uxorem*: *SJ* 1.1, 21, 52.3; *SA* 62.1; *ST* 7.2; *SG* 12.1; *SC* 26.2; *SN* 35.1; occasionally *in matrimonium accepit*: *SA* 62.2; *SC* 26.2. Here he intends to convey that it was *analogous* to a formal marriage, but was not one. The evidence available to him revealed that Caligula had done all the things that would normally be evidence of lawful marriage, such as *deductio in domum, affectus maritalis* – living together in the man's house and behaving towards each other as man and wife. On these see Corbett 1930: 92–4.

17 *SG* 24.1–3; CD 59.11–12.1. See also R. Hanslik in *Kl.P.* 1.1015–6; Herz 1981; Nony 1986: 273–5, 289–97; Barrett 1989: 32, 34, 44, 77, 89, 94–5, 166–7, 86–9.

18 *SG* 24.2; Sen. *Polyb.* 18.4–5.

19 Fully stated by Ferrero 1911: 222–38. See also Colin 1954; Köberlein 1962; R. Hanslik in *Kl.P.* 1.1016; Salmon 1968: 149–50 and other references in Barrett 1989: 307, n. 21. Nony (1986: 289–97) writes interestingly about the deification. Barrett (1989: 220, 85) rejects the tradition for incest because it was back in the past, and the purity of the bloodline could hardly have benefited from Drusilla's two husbands and Caligula's four wives. But Antonia's house merely saw the start of the liaison. As for the diluting marriages, in Suetonius he abducts her from her first husband, after the death of his first wife.

20 Herz 1981. Too much time is spent investigating Old Egypt by Köberlein 1962. There are some pre-Hellenistic strands, notably the possibility that Diva Drusilla's appellation, Panthea, was a common cult name of Isis (Barrett 1989: 88). But finally it is a question of what the Greek-speaking Ptolemies and Cleopatras were doing.

21 On the reaction against Antium see Jos. *Ant.* 19. 30; *SG* 23.1, 26.3: CD 59.20.1. Barrett (1989: 220–1, 96) does not effectively dispose of this evidence. On the genuine importance of Antony in Caligula's thinking see Colin 1954: 400–3; P. Herz, *Bonner Jahrbücher* 181, 1981: 110. It is worth noting that Cleopatra Selene, the daughter of Antony and Cleopatra who was brought up by Octavia, had a daughter named Drusilla (*TH* 5.9.3).

22 Wiseman (1982) holds that there was no such thing as a Julio-Claudian

dynasty; there was only the Julian dynasty, to which Claudius did not belong, but once his usurpation was over the Julian line was resumed by Nero. The argument is basically sound, despite Tacitus' assertion that the reigns of Tiberius, Caligula and Claudius were analogous to the inheritance of a single family (*TH* 1.16). On that passage see Bauman 1989: 307–8. On the Claudian 'usurpation' see Chapter 12, p. 166 below. But despite its technical inaccuracy, convenience dictates the retention of the expression 'Julio-Claudian dynasty'.

23 *SG* 24.1: *heredem quoque bonorum atque imperii aeger instituit*. Levick (1990: 46) dismisses Suetonius out of hand. But elsewhere (*ibid*. p. 44) she assumes the existence of the will and wonders if it was the only one that Caligula made.

24 E. Kornemann (*Doppelprinzipat*, Leipzig 1930: 59) argued that the idea of dual sovereignty was extended to women by making Livia an Augusta and the end result was Agrippina under Nero. But Livia was only made Augusta by Augustus' will. If, despite *SC* (11.2), Antonia used the title of Augusta when it was offered by Caligula, or even if it was used officially without her acquiescence (SMW No. 3: 8), there is some basis for Kornemann. But Caligula may have known that Antonia was not going to live much longer and may have made an honorific gesture rather than a serious attempt at a co-regency. But with Drusilla it was different.

25 CD 59.1; Philo *Leg. Gai*. 23. Cf. Mommsen 1887: 2.1135, n. 5. One of the consuls who helped Caligula to invalidate the will was Cn. Acerronius Proculus. It is only with reluctance that I have rejected him as the Proculus who headed the Proculian law school (Bauman 1989: 120–3, 125, 133). Barrett (1989: 51), whose book appeared at the same time as mine, identifies Acerronius as that Proculus. It is a pity that the identification cannot be driven home, for Acerronius had close links with the younger Agrippina (Bauman: 122, 129). Barrett (p. 52) makes the interesting point that Caligula was able to pay the legacies despite the setting aside of the will because Tiberius' property came to him as emperor after the cessation of the will. Levick (1990: 45) thinks the will was annulled under a *querela inofficiosi testamenti*, but that is not possible.

26 See, e.g., Bauman 1989: 130–40.

27 For some reason Barrett (1989: 82) attaches importance to this link.

28 She paid for it in 36, when she was charged with adultery with a slave and committed suicide (*TA* 6.40.4).

29 So Nony 1986: 276. There is no specific information on the date, but this is as good a guess as any.

30 On these respective dates see Barrett 1989: 77; Nony 1986: 276. I do not pretend to understand Suetonius' statement that he divorced her after a few days (*SG* 25.1), or Dio's that it was within two months (CD 59.8.7). Still less do I understand the assertion that when he divorced his third wife, Lollia Paulina, because she was barren, he commanded her not to have intercourse with any man (*SG* 25.2; CD 59.12.1, 23.7). Meise (1969: 104–5) thinks a similar ban was imposed

on Livia Orestilla. But the scholiast on Juv. 5.109 might have been confused. One can hardly blame him.

31 *SG* 24.3. Augustus was said to have seduced women in order to keep track of his enemies' designs (*SA* 69.1).

32 On no more than adultery see Simpson 1980: 252–3. Sources: CD 59.22.8; *TA* 14.2.4; Rutil. 1.303.

33 For a critical account see Barrett 1989: 101–13; also Meise 1969: 108–15. J. P. V. D. Balsdon (*The Emperor Gaius*, Oxford 1934: 75) glibly assumes Agrippina's participation without bothering about the evidence. He later had doubts: 1962: 117.

34 Adopting, purely for the sake of argument, the overworked conspiracy theory that we have been repelling ever since the elder Julia.

35 Barrett 1989: 110. On Vinicius' survival skills see Bauman 1989: 83.

36 Bauman 1974a: 130–4.

37 Tacitus' language regarding Albucilla's group, *conscii et adulterii eius* (sc. *Albucillae* – *TA* 6.47.2) is strikingly similar to Suetonius' *adulteras et insidiarum adversus se conscias* with reference to Agrippina and Livilla (*SG* 24.3).

38 Just how the entanglement took place is beyond recovery. But the sources are unanimous about there having been something.

39 He is said to have prostituted Agrippina and Livilla to old roués – *exoleti* (*SG* 24.3).

12 MESSALINA, AGRIPPINA AND CLAUDIUS

1 *SC* 25.5, 29.1. Cf. *TA* 12.1.1; CD 60.2.4–5.

2 CD 60.4.1; *SC* 12.1; *SN* 6.3–4. Cf. Meise 1969: n. 58.

3 *SC* 11.2–3; CD 60.5.1.

4 *SC* 11.2; CD 60.5.2.

5 Herz 1981: 326–35. But the level-headed Claudian would not have wanted to adopt the full Julian panoply.

6 Despite Griffin 1984: 288, n. 13.

7 Though she was not the first Diva. That honour belonged to Drusilla. Mottershead (1986: 35, 51) points out that the date of Livia's consecration, 17 January 42, coincided both with the centenary of her birth and with her marriage to Augustus.

8 On Divus Augustus and the *lex maiestatis* see Bauman 1974a: 71–108. Drusilla was given the protection after her death but before her consecration. CD (59.11.2–4) wrongly dates to after the consecration the capital sentence imposed on the man who sold hot water (Bauman, pp. 105–6). But it indicates Dio's expectation of protection for all Divi/ae.

9 Mottershead 1986: 36.

10 Mottershead 1986: 158–9. On Urgulania see Chapter 10, p. 135.

11 On her marriage see Ehrhardt 1978: 56 (summer 37); Mottershead 1986: 107 (early 39); Syme 1958: 437, n. 5 (shortly before 41). On her birth see A. Esser, as cited by Ehrhardt 1978: 55, n. 26 (AD 3); R. Geer, *TAPA* 62, 1931 (AD 26). A. von Domaszewski (*Gesch. d. römischen Kaiser*, Leipzig 1909: 2.36) makes her 'elderly' in 48. Syme 1958:

437, n. 5 (before 20). Ehrhardt 1978: 55 (specifically 20). Herzog-Hauser and Wotke 1955: 246 (25). Meise 1969: 152, n. 122 (24 at the latest).

12 A magisterial pronouncement by Syme (1958: 437, n. 5, 150, 179), based on the assumed death of her father by 20 and the fact that her half-brother, Faustus Sulla, was consul in 52.

13 Despite Balsdon (1962: 104) discussing only a fraction of the evidence. Sources: Juv. 6.115–32 with *scholium*, also 10.329–45, 14.329–31; *PNH* 10.172, 29.8; CD 60.14.3, 18.1–2, 22.4–5, 27.4, 28.2–5, 31.1–5; *TA* 11.26.1, 35.4–7, 36.1–5. On the emergence of 'the new woman' see especially Ferrero 1911: 252–6. Her portrayal by Scramuzza (1940: 90.261, n. 32) as 'a tool in the hands of older . . . evildoers' is unrealistic. Suetonius is the one significant omission from the list of condemnatory sources. His references to Messalina are surprisingly restrained (*SC* 17.3, 26.2, 27.1, 29.3, 36, 37.2, 39.1; *SN* 6.4; *Vit.* 2.5).

14 Juv. 6.120–32; *PNH* 10.172, 29.8; *TA* 11.35.4–7, 36.1–5; CD 60.18.1–2, 31.1–5.

15 Sources and discussions: Fitzler, *RE* 10.939; Meise 1969: 140–2. See also Herzog-Hauser and Wotke 1955: 249–50; Ehrhardt 1978: 61; Mottershead 1986: 119. Livilla was also involved with that evil genius of Nero's reign, Tigellinus, if *'Iulia'* instead of *'Fulvia'* is read in Schol. Juv. 1.155, p. 16W. On Seneca's part see Koestermann on *TA* 12.8.3, 13.41.4–5. The *crimine incerto nec defensione ulla data occidit* of *SC* 29.1 is often criticized, e.g., by Koestermann on *TA* 12.8.3; Meise, *op. cit.* p. 140. But manifest guilt was a substitute for the suspended *lex maiestatis* throughout Claudius' reign (Bauman 1974a, *s.v.* Manifest Guilt, *Crimine nullo* procedure). On Livilla's interment see SMW No. 87. It was after Messalina's death.

16 CD 60.12.5; SMW No. 98; *SC* 27.2 (with the wrong date of birth – Mottershead 1986: 112–13).

17 At first sight Dio's assertion that Drusilla had been given all the honours that Livia had received (CD 59.11.2) seems to include 'Augusta'. So Hoffsten 1939: 57 and n. 40. But Temporini 1978: 29–30 points out that in inscriptions she is only Diva Drusilla, not Diva Drusilla Augusta.

18 The technique of creating new institutions through the criminal law was used quite often (Bauman 1974a: *passim*).

19 When included in vows for Claudius' safety she is *Valeriae Messalinae Aug.* (SMW No. 99a). But the abbreviation stands for *Augusti.* Cf. SMW No. 99b: *Messalina Augusti.* As for *Sebastē* (*BMC* Pontus, p. 154, No. 14), Meise (1969: 150, n. 110) thinks it is false. It would probably be hazardous to suggest that it was a flattering expression of gratitude by Mithridates, to whom Claudius had granted Bosporus (CD 60.8.2) with, arguably, her help.

20 CD 60.22.2; *ILS* 1664, 1781.

21 Meise (1969: 140–1) takes it as a case of *aemulatio*, a similar struggle for power and influence to that between the elder Agrippina and Claudius' sister, Livilla. A more specific interpretation is offered in the text.

22 Meise (1969: 141) arguing that the charge of adultery was simply a

synonym for 'political linkage'. On a more specific role for that charge see n. 23.

23 With *prima facie* evidence of adultery in his hands, an accuser got access to the evidence of the defendant's slaves and might hope to uncover something more serious known to the domestic slave (Bauman 1974a: *passim*).

24 Cf. the trial of Valerius Asiaticus.

25 T. A. Dorey, *Das Altertum* 12, 1966: 147.

26 One never ceases to be surprised at the chronic inability of the sources to give detailed information about conspiracies. Though the conspiracy of Catiline ought to make us more tolerant of the sources' inadequacies. With full coverage by Cicero and Sallust, scholars still cannot make up their minds as to what really happened.

27 *SC* 37.2; CD 60.14.2–4, with Bauman 1974a: 196–7.

28 On that tenebrous episode see M. Swan, *AJP* 91, 1970: 149–64; Bauman 1974a: 197–200; Wiseman 1982: 61–3. Meise (1969: 147 and n. 100) underestimates the relevance of Silanus' case. Scramuzza (1940: 47–8) dismisses Scribonianus with an anecdote. McAlindon (1956: 117–18; 120) has some useful comments. See also Ehrhardt 1978: 63 and n. 78; Syme 1986: 165; Levick 1990: 58–60.

29 *PE* 3.16.6; *TA* 16.34.3; CD 60.16.6. On Vibia see *PE* 3.16.9. The outcome of Arria's example to her husband is not certain. CD (60.16.6) says she was wounded, but TA (16.34.3) implies that she died. *PE* (3.16.10) has her son-in-law, Thrasea Paetus, urge her not to commit suicide, whereupon she dashes her head against the wall but survives. 'Vibia' in *PE* 3.16.9 is the usual supplement for a corrupt text. Syme (*Hermes* 92, 1964: 415, n. 2) reads 'Vinicia'. Contra Koestermann 3.197.

30 On Catonius' case see CD 60.18.2; [Sen.] *Apocol.* 13 – henceforth cited without the putative author's name as I have no strong views on Seneca's authorship or non-authorship. See, however, Chapter 13, n. 13. On Julia's case see *TA* 13.32.5, 43.3; *SC* 29.1; CD 60.18.4; *Apocol.* 10.4, 13.5; Sen. *Oct.* 944–6. Messalina got her regular prosecutor, P. Suillius Rufus, to charge Livia, but allegedly (and quite feasibly if there was manifest guilt) without preferring formal charges. It is a safe guess that Suillius also led the attack on Catonius.

31 Cf. Meise (1969: 143–4) and Erhardt (1978: 65–6 and n. 10) identifying Catonius' colleague as the Rufius Pomfilius of *Apocol.* 13.5. A link between Catonius and Julia is inferred from Catonius' presence on Drusus' staff in 14. Cf. *TA* 1.29.2 with Furneaux's note.

32 On these alliances see Ehrhardt 1978: 58, 67–8. Cf. McAlindon 1956: 126–8; Meise 1969: 144 and n. 84; Wiseman 1982: 64; Mottershead 1986: 112, 119.

33 She had of course favoured, and presumably arranged, the match. But after her death he was destroyed.

34 CD 60.29.6a. How did Dio, in his state of ignorance, know that the charges were false?

35 *Apocol.* 11.2, 5 with Meise 1969: 145–6.

36 Syme, having absolved Messalina of responsibility in 1958: 259, condemned her in 1986: 183. Wiseman (1982: 65) puts it all down to 'the

false smile of the "Claudian peace" ' as presented by Calpurnius Siculus. But once Claudius had allowed Magnus to use the dangerous *cognomen* that Caligula had forbidden him to use (CD 60.5.8–9), where did Magnus (and his family) go wrong?

37 CD 60.27.4 tries to involve Livilla's widower, M. Vinicius, who died in 46, in Messalina's net. She will have poisoned him because she feared a backlash from her murder of his wife, and because he refused to have sex with her. This is not Dio at his best. The sexual rejection is a threadbare stereotype, the sudden fear of a backlash four years after the event is nonsense, and poison without even a semblance of judicial proceedings was not Messalina's way.

38 *TA* 11.1–3, 13.43.3, 5; CD 60.29.4–6a. When Messalina leaves the room to dry her tears, Tacitus adds that she had left in order to complete the destruction of Poppaea. He does not mean, however, that this was done that very day. It is more in the nature of a footnote by Tacitus prior to returning to the main trial (see below). Dio gives great prominence to Vitellius' assumption of the role of defence counsel, saying that it was just in time to stop Claudius from acquitting Asiaticus. He also says that the charges were false and were instigated by Messalina.

39 Claudius' absent-mindedness is too well attested to be ignored (cf. Bauman 1974a: 185). The 'threat of imprisonment' that drove Poppaea to suicide (*TA* 11.2.5) meant, of course, incarceration for the purpose of being strangled in the common dungeon. Cf. Furneaux, 2.3.

40 CD 60.22, 28; *TA* 11.36.

41 The *intra cubiculum* procedure used against Asiaticus has been examined by Kunkel 1974: 197–200. He holds that Vitellius' submission on Asiaticus' behalf let in the doctrine of *confessus pro iudicato est*, a confession dispensing with the need for a trial. Therefore it was not a trial. Claudius and Vitellius as consuls were simply holding a preliminary enquiry to decide whether to refer the case to the senate. The *liberum arbitrium mortis*, the free choice of death, was not a sentence, but an inducement to Asiaticus to avoid a trial in order to save his name and property. But Kunkel himself concedes that it was a recognized death sentence in AD 66. (*TA* 16.33.2–3; *D* 48.19.8.1). And Dio says specifically that Asiaticus was tried before Claudius and came close to an acquittal (CD 60.29.4). Tacitus is to a similar effect. Claudius consults about absolution – *consultanti super absolutione* – which suggests consultation of his *consilium*, not merely of his fellow-consul (*TA* 11.3.1). Two points are decisive. First, how did Messalina get hold of the Gardens of Lucullus if there was no decree of confiscation followed by a forced sale? Far from saving his property by his suicide, Asiaticus lost it. Second, after the condemnation of the two Petrae the senate voted rewards to accusers; one of the recipients was Sosibius, co-accuser with Suillius at Asiaticus' trial (*TA* 11.4.5–6).

42 *TA* 11.4.1: Suillius proceeded to add to the list of accused (the two Petrae). This is introduced by *vocantur post haec patres* – after Asiaticus' case the senate was summoned. Other names not noticed by Tacitus are thus possible. The evidence is not conclusive, but the military force that was sent to arrest Asiaticus suggests more than one defendant.

43 The tears need not, of course, be a Tacitean embellishment. The whole purpose was to work on Claudius' sympathies.

44 For a possible reconstruction of his activities see Levick 1990: 61–4.

45 She died there (this chapter, p. 177). Forced sales at low prices went back to Caesar and Servilia (Chapter 6, p. 75).

46 In any case *TA* (11.6.5) reduces Suillius' role as the only subject of the attack. Tacitus puts a plea for leniency into the joint mouths of Suillius, the equally notorious Cossutianus Capito, and 'others like them'.

47 *SC* 28; Sen. *Ad Polyb.* 8.2, 11.5. Cf. R. Hanslik in *Kl.P* 4.982–3; Millar 1977: 75–6.

48 Herzog-Hauser and Wotke 1955: 251.

49 Did Messalina also raise money by non-forensic means? CD (60.17.5–6) attests a thriving trade in citizenship by Messalina and the freedmen. But this is merely part of the tradition satirizing Claudius' citizenship policy (cf. *Apocol.* 3). There were no doubt some individuals on whose behalf Messalina interceded with Claudius. But of a thriving trade there is no sign. Messalina's gateway to politics was through the criminal law.

50 Sources: *Apocol.* 11.1, 5, 13.4–5; *PNH* 29.8, 20, 10.172; Jos. *Ant.* 20.149; Sen. *Oct.* 257–72, 950–1; Juv. 6.116–32, 10.329–45 with *schol.*; Vict. 4.6–12; *Epit. de Caes.* 4.5–6; CD 60.31.2–5; *SC* 26.2, 29.3, 36, 39.1. And, first and foremost, Tacitus as above. Literature: the facts are well summarized by Herzog-Hauser and Wotke 1955: 251–8. There is still much good sense in Furneaux, 2.40–3. The best analytical account is Meise 1969: 123–69. On the legal issues see Bauman 1974a: 177–88. In general see Ferrero 1911: 251–65; Scramuzza 1940: 25, 90, 261, nn. 32–6; Syme 1958: 348, 375, 407, 539; Colin 1956; A. Momigliano, *Claudius*, 1961: 76, 120; T. A. Dorey, *University of Birmingham Historical Journal* 8, 1961: 1–10; W. Allen, *Numen* 9, 1962: 99–109; Balsdon 1962: 97–107; Koestermann, 3.85–108; Mottershead 1986, ad *SC loc. cit.*; Levick 1990: 64–7.

51 On the validity of the marriage see n. 56.

52 *TA* 11.32.5, 6. The Vestal came into it because of her link with Claudius as Pontifex Maximus.

53 *TA* 11.35.3–36.5; CD 60.28.2. Six of the knights not named by Tacitus are named by *Apocol.* 13.4. See also n. 55.

54 Narcissus did not necessarily mislead the tribune. Claudius' inconsistencies were notorious (Bauman 1974a: 185). My wife, a speech pathologist, suggested when that work was in preparation that Claudius suffered from cerebral palsy and that inconsistent behaviour was a feature of the condition.

55 *TA* 11.37–8. She was executed without trial under the doctrine of manifest guilt; the senate's *abolitio imaginum*, only a partial adoption of the disabilities usually imposed on a *hostis*, was voted independently of what Claudius (and/or Narcissus) ordered against her (Bauman 1974a: 182–6). That the proceedings at the camp were not trials is less certain (*ibid.* 186–8).

56 See the review of modern opinions by Meise 1969: 127–69. Also Mehl 1974: 50–95; Guarino 1975; Mottershead 1986: 108, 127–8; Levick

1990: 64–7. On the legitimacy of the marriage, both parties were patricians, and thus eligible for the religious ceremony of *confarreatio*. There are some suggestive details: ten witnesses, an *auspex*, bridal veil and nuptial couch, a sacrifice to the gods, a banquet, Messalina's refusal to marry except in due form (*legitime*), and the signature of a formal contract (*TA* 11.26.7, 27.1; Juv. 10.333–38; *SC* 26.2). But in fact *confarreatio* is not possible. It required the presence of the Pontifex Maximus, and Claudius was not there. But the essentials of a non-religious formation of *iustae nuptiae* were present: *deductio in domum* (*TA* 11.27.1–2); *affectus maritalis*, or intention to create a permanent union (*TA* 11.27.1 – 'as if for the purpose of procreation'). Messalina had not been formally divorced by Claudius, but that may not matter. The second marriage was a tacit repudiation of the first (Herzog-Hauser and Wotke 1955: 253). Contra perhaps Robleda (1976), but 'Don't you know that you're divorced?' (*TA* 11.30.5) guarantees that this was a case of automatic dissolution. Guarino (1975: 14, 18) is not quite sure what he thinks.

57 Meise 1969: 148–61. Cf. Ehrhardt 1978: 68. Mehl (1974: 65, n. 353, 74–9) is sceptical.

58 The sources were worried by the absence of any indication that she had attempted direct action against Agrippina. Hence the story that she had in fact sent men to strangle Nero, only to be thwarted by a snake which darted out from under his pillow (*SN* 6.4; *TA* 11.11.6).

59 The fact that Claudius subsequently allowed Britannicus to be passed over in favour of Nero is beside the point; that would never have happened had Messalina remained in the box seat.

60 Suet. *Vit.* 2.5; *TA* 12.5.2–6.5.

61 *TA* 11.26.1. On this passage cf. Mehl 1974: 59.

62 *TA* 12.65.4, 14.2, 14.9.5, 12.37.6.

63 *TA* 12.1.4–2.3. Which came first in the literature of the early second century, Juvenal's 'turbot' *consilium* (4.75–81) or Tacitus' parody?

64 *TA* 12.1.1; *PNH* 9.117–8; Schol. Juv. 4.81; Suet. *Life of Passienus Crispus; SN* 6.3; Hieron. *Chron. ad Abr.* 2054; Suet. *Galb.* 5.

65 If, with Furneaux (2.64–5) and Koestermann (3.111) one reads *familiae Iuliae Claudiaeque* for *familiae Claudiae quae* in *TA* 12.2.3, Wiseman's denial of a Julio-Claudian dynasty (1982) strikes a snag. But neither A. J. Church and W. J. Brodribb nor M. Grant recognize *Iuliae* in their translations: 'a link to unite the descendants of the Claudian family'; '(to) unite two branches of the Claudian house.'

66 Bauman 1989: 86, 127–30. The note by Levick (1990: 209, n. 4) was anticipated by the aforegoing.

67 *TA* 12.3.2–4.5, 8.1. Junia Calvina was recalled by Nero after Agrippina's death (Bauman 1989: 94).

68 As Nero was *sui iuris*, Claudius adopted him by the legislative procedure known as *adrogatio*. *SC* (39.2) credits the observation about a Claudian 'first' to Claudius. Syme (1958: 316, 707) thinks Tacitus transferred the remark to the lawyers in deference to 'the dignity of history'. Contra Mottershead 1986: 132. Either is possible. The lawyers had a special interest in *adrogatio*, but Claudius, like Tiberius, was a lawyer.

69 A point in favour of Wiseman 1982.

70 On these see Griffin 1984: 29.

71 As *adrogatio* was an act of the people (n. 68), Agrippina's implied threat was to prosecute Britannicus (see this chapter, p. 183).

72 *TA* 12.41.6–8. In *SN* (7.1) Britannicus calls him 'Ahenobarbus' and Nero himself complains to Claudius, but Tacitus is to be preferred. The essential part of the adoption was the change in the *nomen gentilicium*, Domitius.

73 Claudius' own interest in literature is a factor here. Agrippina had more to offer him than either Aelia Paetina or Lollia Paulina.

74 *TA* 12.22.3, 14.12.3; CD 60.33.2b. Her exile is dated to 49 by Tacitus, to 50 by Dio's editors.

75 On Augusta: see *TA* 12.26.1; CD 60.33.2a; SMW 100–2a. On the *carpentum* see *TA* 12.42.3; CD 60.33.2[1]; SMW 102b. This honour is dated to 51 by Tacitus, to 49 by Dio's editors. On the cloak see *PNH* 33.63; CD 60.33.3. The contrast with the attire of Claudius and Nero appears only in Dio. Pliny notes that Tarquinius Priscus celebrated a triumph wearing a golden tunic. The near miss was a feature of the age. Cf. Trimalchio's ring, which hinted at equestrian status (Petronius *Satyricon* 32).

76 *TA* 12.27.1–2; *PNH* 4.106; *CIL* 9.1584, 14.208.

77 *TA* 12.37.5, 42.3; CD 60.33.7, 12. Dio cites the great fire to which she accompanied Claudius. Tiberius had considered something similar a usurpation by Livia (*ST* 50.3).

78 *TA* 12.42.1–2, 14.11.1, 14.7.5; CD 60.33.6a. See also Chapter 13, p. 202.

79 SMW 128b, 139, 141; CD 60.33.1.

80 Bauman 1974a: 1–24, 25–51, 143–6, 194–204 and *passim*. Contra P. A. Brunt, in *Sodalitas*, Naples 1984: 469–80.

81 On the insulting salutation see *TA* 12.41.6–8. On Vitellius see *TA* 12.42.4–5.

82 Details in Bauman 1989: 127–30.

83 CD 60.33.3a, noting that Callistus had died.

84 *TA* 12.57.4–5; CD 60.33.5.

85 *TA* 12.59. Occult practices were not *maiestas* (Bauman 1974a: 59–69).

86 Mehl (1974: 158 and n. 541) notes the similarities between the cases of Statilius and Asiaticus, but distinguishes them by the fact that Agrippina had no part in the actual trial of Statilius. Scramuzza (1940: 97–8) presents evidence for Statilius' establishment of a mystery cult, but argues that the real motive for the prosecution was the needs of the aqueduct system, not Agrippina's covetousness. But see n. 87.

87 Disapproval of Agrippina: they hated the informer so much that they expelled him in spite of Agrippina's intrigues on his behalf (*TA* 12.59.4). On the start of a reaction see Koestermann, 3.210. If she had been acting in the public interest (aqueducts) she would not have lost ground.

88 For details of the prodigies see *TA* 12.64.1–3; *SC* 46; CD 60.35.1; *PNH* 2.25, 23, 92. Furneaux (2.114 n.) observes that until *TA* 12.43 Tacitus does not notice portents. Furneaux thinks that the trigger is the danger to the Domus through Nero's adoption.

89 *TA* 12.64.4; *SC* 43; CD 60.34.1; Jos. *Ant.* 20.151.
90 On the reinstatement of Britannicus see also this chapter, p. 187.
91 Oost (1958: 121) thinks Narcissus was Claudius' own (manumitted) slave. He will have known Aelia Paetina when she was Claudius' wife, hence his support for her candidacy. Oost should have added that when Narcissus put her name forward he made a special point of her devotion to the well-being of Britannicus and Octavia (*TA* 12.2.1).
92 She was thus a typical latifundist. On the significance of that in this period see Bauman 1989: 104–5, 107.
93 *TA* 12.66.1–2, 13.1.4; CD 60.34.4. Tacitus dates Narcissus' death to the start of Nero's reign. Similarly Dio. But the ill-treatment while imprisoned was in Claudius' reign.
94 Cf. n. 98. There is no third alternative; not even speculation can conjure up a deal promising Narcissus his life if he destroyed the documents.
95 *SC* 44.2–6; *SN* 33.1; *TA* 12.66–7; CD 60.34.2–4, 35; Sen. *Oct.* 164–5, 31–2, 44, 102; Mart. 1.20.4; Juv. 5.147, 6.620–1; *PNH* 2.92, 11.189, 22.92. Not sure are Jos. *Ant.* 20.151 and Philostr. 5.32. Other sources in Meise 1969: 185, n. 58.
96 See the resumé of opinions in Meise 1969: 185, n. 58. Add Warmington 1969: 19–20 (sceptical); Griffin 1984: 32 (non-committal); Levick 1990: 76–7.
97 Mottershead 1986: 141.
98 *SC* 44.1. One of Suetonius' throwaway lines: 'He was cut short by Agrippina, who besides that was being accused of many other crimes both by her conscience and by informers.' But see n. 99.
99 *TA* 12.69.5; CD 61.1.2. Tacitus is following a Julian source here; his reason for the concealment of the will is fatuous unless it confirms that Britannicus was instituted as co-heir.

13 AGRIPPINA, NERO AND THE DOMUS

1 *TA* 13.2.5–6; *SN* 9; SMW 106, 107, 141.
2 Far from being an admirable character, CD (61.6.4–5) says he practised extortion in his province on an extensive scale. He was a descendant of Augustus. Caligula had called him 'the Golden Sheep' (*TA* 13.1.1–3).
3 *PNH* (7.58) makes Nero privy to the poisoning. But that would not affect the point made in the text.
4 It was a special exception when Tiberius allowed the senate to try L. Capito, procurator of Asia, for exceeding the authority given to him by the emperor (Bauman 1974a: 117, n. 42). In 57 P. Celer, who had killed Silanus, was charged with extortion in the same province of Asia. Nero tried the case personally. He could not acquit Celer, but delayed the trial until he died of old age (*TA* 13.33.1–2).
5 *TA* 13.2.1–5, adding that though Nero was disgusted with Pallas' arrogance, he publicly honoured his mother. A confused tradition asserts that because Nero often rode with her in her litter, therefore he left all public and private business in her hands (*SN* 9; CD 61.32). But Zonaras (11, 12, p. 37.29–38.3 D) infers the mandate without the shared litter.
6 So Griffin 1984: 39–40.

7 *TA* 12.69.1–3; Jos. *Ant.* 20.152. On the prefecture see Chapter 12, p. 183. Burrus did, however, retain his loyalty to Agrippina to a large extent. Cf. this chapter, p. 202, with nn. 26–8.

8 *TA* 13.4.1–3; CD 61.3.1.

9 Bauman 1989: 137. The law which Claudius amended was not a *lex imperfecta*, despite Griffin 1984: 251, n. 60.

10 For Livia's attempts on behalf of Divus Augustus, see Chapter 10, p. 133. The *graphē paranomōn* of Athenian law (Bauman 1990b: *passim*) had no Roman counterpart.

11 Furneaux (2.159) and Koestermann (3.242–3) mistakenly hold that she opposed only the quaestorian law.

12 *TA* 13.5.1–2. On the library, see Mommsen 1887: 3.929 and n. 3.

13 *Apocolocyntosis*, 'The Pumpkinification of Claudius', can possibly be seen as an attack on Agrippina as priestess; it will have been more topical at the end of 54 than later. But an attack at that time depends largely on whether the piece was composed by Seneca, who was at odds with Agrippina from the start. His authorship is accepted by Kraft, *Hist.* 15, 1966: 96–122; Griffin 1984: 96–7. Contra B. Baldwin, *Phoenix* 18, 1964. Griffin rejects a political purpose; it was 'a farce in which nothing except the young Princeps is treated seriously'. Baldwin makes it a squib not published before 58; it will have favoured Britannicus' cause. To Kraft it was an attack on the Claudius-Britannicus party which in late 54 and 55 threatened Nero's position. *Quot homines tot sententiae*. According to Suetonius, Claudius' divine status was neglected and eventually cancelled (*abolitum*) by Nero; specifically, Nero almost totally destroyed the temple to Divus Claudius on the Caelian, which had been begun by Agrippina. Claudius' status was restored by Vespasian (*SN* 45; *Vesp.* 9.1). Griffin (1984: 98) argues that although Nero's interest declined as time went on, the honour was never actually cancelled. But how, then, did Vespasian make the restoration? If, as Griffin says, Nero simply cleared the ground for the Domus Aurea without intending any slight to Claudius, are we to suppose that Vespasian merely built Claudius' temple somewhere else? If so, where? If Nero at first called himself *Divi filius* but abandoned it after 56 (Griffin, *op. cit.*), this is more of a deliberate change than casual neglect. Moreover, the Domus Aurea was not put under way until 64, ten years after Claudius' death. Thus Nero's neglect of Claudius' temple ran for five years after Agrippina's death, before he discovered that he needed the site.

Griffin overestimates the retention of *Divus Claudius* in the Acts of the Arval Brethren and in documents of officials in Egypt and Rome just after Nero's death. Countless citations in Justinian retain the *Divus* of pre-Christian emperors' decrees; legal conservatism was stronger than any need to salve the Christian conscience. In other words, *Divus* was retained even though it no longer meant anything.

14 *TA* 13.12.1–2; *SN* 28.1; CD 61.7.1; *CIL* 11.1414.

15 In 58 Nero renounced the friendship of the future emperor Otho for casting aspersions on Acte. She was still close enough to him in 59 to be able to furnish information to Seneca that may have forestalled

Nero's commission of incest with Agrippina. After his death she deposited his ashes in the family tomb of the Domitii (*TA* 13.12.1, 46.4–5, 14.2.2–3; *SN* 50).

16 *TA* 13.13.1–4. CD 61.7.1 has Agrippina lose her pre-eminence in the palace because of Acte, whereupon she resorts to admonitions, violence and threats. On the threats, as more adequately described by Tacitus, see below p. 195.

17 Syme (1958: 277) thinks this foreshadowed her memoirs. The date of the composition of the memoirs is placed by Griffin (1984: 23) in the latter part of Claudius' reign. In that case she could not have included the poisoning of Claudius in that work. *TA* (13.14.4), which attests the threat to tell all, is dated to AD 55. At best that threat is one that was only used as a pressure point; it was never carried out.

18 Again no reference to the divine blood.

19 *TA* 13.15–27; *SN* 33.2–3; CD 61.7.4. For an account of the episode see Walter 1955: 79–82. On Nero's guilt and Seneca's knowledge see Griffin 1984: 73–4, 254, n. 35.

20 *TA* 13.2.3, 14.1, 18.3. Cf. Chapter 10, p. 154 on *Partes Agrippinae*.

21 Despite Koestermann, 3.234. She did have an association with a prominent Stoic in the person of Rubellius Plautus, but that does not mean that P. Celer was her Stoic mentor. Nor does it mean that Agrippina was motivated by Stoic principles in what was no more than an attempt to reassert control over Nero. The considerations that moved the Stoic opposition to Nero (Bauman 1989: 112–21) would not have had a prominent place in Agrippina's thinking.

22 She is said to have been the Drusilla who was a granddaughter of Antony and Cleopatra. So Hanslik in *Kl.P.* 1.413. Contra H. Heubner, *P. Cornelius Tacitus: Die Historien*, vol. 5, Heidelberg 1982: 134. If she was so descended, her husband could never have been considered for Agrippina's party. For other friends of Agrippina see below on the attempt to charge her.

23 *TA* 13.18.4–5; CD 61.8.4–5. That Titius Sabinus was the last of her mother's clients (Chapter 10, p. 150) suggests that Sejanus may have deliberately cut off her support in the same way as Nero would do to the daughter.

24 He did revive it three years later (Bauman 1974a: 143–5).

25 He learnt from Fabius Rusticus, a former protégé of Seneca, that Nero wrote a letter appointing Caecina Tuscus, the son of Nero's old nurse, as Burrus' successor, but was persuaded by Seneca to allow Burrus to stay on. But according to the elder Pliny and Cluvius Rufus, a consular in Nero's reign, Nero had no doubts about Burrus' loyalty.

26 *TA* 13.20.2–21.2. 'Tampering with the praetorians' was Agrippina's cultivation of tribunes and centurions in her moves to form a party. 'Undermining the loyalty of the provinces' comprised contacts with Asia, where Plautus had extensive interests. If the *maiestas* law had been revived against her, this would not have been in conflict with our postulate of the non-availability of a charge of aspiring to supreme power against a woman (Chapter 1, p. 12). That was not what Agrippina was alleged to have done.

27 The reason, says Tacitus, is that to have raised a defence would have conceded that there was a charge to meet, to have spoken about benefits would have been to reproach him (*TA* 13.21.9). The Romans knew that a point *in limine* must, as in modern law, be taken before entering a plea.

28 *TA* 13.21.9–22.3. The accusers were guilty of *calumnia* for attempting to prosecute a non-existent crime (Bauman 1974a: 212–13). Walter (1955: 88) would be less critical of Tacitus if he had borne this in mind.

29 He would be put to death in 62, after having been banished to his estates in Asia in 60 (Bauman 1974a: 111–12).

30 *TA* 14.51.5, 14.57.1, 13.22.1–2.

31 *TA* 13.23.1–4. On Burrus' vote see Bauman 1974a: 213. The vote is misunderstood by Griffin 1984: 75.

32 See this chapter, pp. 192, 202. The exact position of Burrus at any given time is not easily determined. Even Tacitus had trouble. Cf. n. 25.

33 *TA* (13.31.1), commenting acidly on 'historians who like to fill their pages with praise of the beams in Nero's amphitheatre, which is not the serious stuff that history should be made of and is fit only for the official gazette'. Tacitus is criticizing *PNH* 16.200.

34 The suggested link with Agrippina emanates from Cizek 1982: 60–1. On the fiscal reforms attempted in 58 (not 57–8) see *TA* 13.50–1 with M. A. Levi, *Nerone e i suoi tempi*, Milan 1949, 141–4; Walter 1955: 96–8; Garzetti 1974: 152, 154. The rebuff to Nero was unusual, but no names of senators are known. The abortive fiscal reform was probably devised by Phaon who succeeded Pallas as financial secretary. Cf. Bradley 1978: 275.

35 *TA* 13.32.3–5. Furneaux (2.195–6) argues that if the foreign superstition was Christianity the charge might have been adultery, which was often thought to be encouraged by Christian rituals; a charge of adultery would fit in with the referral to the domestic tribunal (cf. Syme 1958: 2.532; Koestermann 2.297). But this argument fails for three reasons. Tacitus says that the charge was capital – *de capite famaque coniugis cognovit* – which adultery was not. The domestic court was not restricted to cases of adultery (Bauman 1984). And the Romans did not need a euphemism for adultery.

36 For the Arval records see SMW 19, 21. On the rift see Balsdon 1962: 122.

37 Each of the years 54 and 55 occupies as much space in Tacitus as 56 and 57 combined: 150 lines of Furneaux's text, 228, 92, 40. Dio is similar.

38 Suetonius notices Poppaea only incidentally in his *Nero*, and not in connection with Agrippina's death at all. His definitive notice of her is in *Otho* 3, where she helps to put Otho in a favourable light. The emperor for whom Suetonius' father had fought in the civil war (*Otho* 10.1) was not to be linked to a woman involved in matricide.

39 *PNH* 37.50, 28.183, 33.140; Juv. 6.462; CD 61.28.1.

40 *TA* 13.46.1–2. Nero's initial link with Poppaea is the subject of a confused tradition. In one version Nero fell in love with her while

she was still Crispinus' wife, but through fear of Agrippina got Otho to pretend to marry her, intending to reclaim her after divorcing Octavia (*TH* 1.13.3; Suet. *Otho* 3.1–2; Plut. *Galb.* 19.2; CD 61.11.1–3). Syme (1958: 290) thinks the *Annales* version reflects Tacitus' better acquaintance with the facts than he had in *Historiae*.

41 *TA* 13. 46.3–4. Who had the greater influence over Nero at this time, Agrippina or Acte? The sources give more exposure to Agrippina, but every now and then Acte is presented as the dominant factor. Bradley (1978: 202) takes *Otho* 3.2 to mean that Agrippina's power was far from completely broken by her removal from the palace in 55. One can unhesitatingly agree with that assessment despite Warmington 1969: 47. All in all, Agrippina should be awarded the palm. If she had already been displaced by Acte there would have been no need to kill her. The view in n. 43 below does not overturn the assessment expressed here.

42 There is no way of verifying Plut. (*Galb.* 19.5, 20.1), where it is claimed that Otho was saved from death by Seneca, in contrast to his wife and sister, who were put to death because of his marriage to Poppaea.

43 Bradley (1978: 163), though he doubts an independent contribution by Acte. Syme (1958: 377, n. 1, 744) considers Acte's role an anachronism. But why? She was involved enough to build a shrine to Ceres in the hope of preventing Nero's marriage to Poppaea (Henderson 1903: 62–3), and to bury Nero. Agrippina's rage at the advent of Acte was not invented by Tacitus.

44 On the collapsible ceiling see *SN* 34.2. On the collapsible ship see *TA* 14.3.5–5.7; *SN loc. cit.* On Acerronia Polla and Agrippina see Bauman 1989: 120, 122.

45 *TA* 14.8.3–6; CD 61.13.5; Sen. *Oct.* 368–72.

46 *SN* 34.2–4; CD 61.12.1–13.4; *TA* 14.9.1.

47 *TA* 14.9.2–5. CD (61.2.1) dates the declaration to the first year of the reign. The astrologer may have been Ti. Claudius Balbillus, who may be the man who became prefect of Egypt when Agrippina's friends were rewarded after her acquittal (Koestermann, 4.43; Bradley 1978: 219–20).

48 *TA* 14.12.1–2, 5–6, 12.22. Tacitus adds that Junia Silana had died at Tarentum, after returning from exile when Agrippina's malevolence either subsided or became ineffective.

49 *TA* 14.12.1–2; *SN* 39.2–3.

50 The *start* of the liaison is dated to late 59, after Agrippina's death, by Walter 1955: 131–2; and to 62 by Warmington 1969: 47.

51 Griffin 1984: 98–9. Partly anticipated by Koestermann, 4.144; Meise 1969: 172.

52 *TA* 13.47, 14.57.1–6, 14.22.5, 57.5.

53 *TA* 14.51, 52.1, 56.6, 52–56 *passim*, 15.61–4. On the aforegoing, and also on the ideological struggle which also reached flashpoint in 62, see Bauman 1989: 102–7, 111–13, 119–27.

54 *TA* 14.57.1. When we note that Rubellius was actually destroyed as one of the Stoics whose wealth was even more offensive than their

philosophy (Bauman 1989: 111–12), we begin to wonder how far Nero's fear of Faustus and Rubellius can be seen as a special phenomenon isolated from the contemporary scene as a whole.

55 *TA* 14.60.5; *SN* 35.2. Presumably the deceased owners had bequeathed the properties to Nero, who then passed them over to Octavia. One would not like to contemplate the alternative of confiscation by the Fiscus and appropriation for Nero's private commitments. But it is not impossible.

56 *TA* 14.60.4–5; *SN* 35.2; CD 62.13.4, 62.13.1–2 (misunderstood by Garzetti 1974: 611).

57 So W. C. McDermott, *Lat.* 8, 1949: 252–3.

58 On the place of the Claudian connection in Nero's propaganda see especially Meise 1969: 171–215.

59 *SN* (35.4) attesting a charge of attempted revolution. It was a competent charge against a woman.

60 The whole tenor of Tacitus at this point stresses Poppaea's domination of Nero.

61 That Nero was rumoured to have recalled Octavia is the accepted meaning of the crux in *TA* 14.60.6 (Furneaux, 2.308; Koestermann, 4.147). On the applause for Nero, compare the applause for Tiberius at the comparable demonstration on behalf of Agrippina and Nero (Chapter 10, p. 152).

62 Balsdon (1962: 126) argues from TA (14.61.5) and Sen. (*Oct.* 181–8, 590–2) that Poppaea's pregnancy started before the marriage; Nero will have delayed the marriage to make sure that she was able to bear children. Cf. Meise 1969: 200, n. 122. Griffin (1984: 99) criticizes Tacitus for only hinting that she was pregnant at the time of the divorce, but could that not be because he was not sure? Griffin herself (259, n. 86) postulates a very narrow margin: she conceived by the end of April 62 and the child was born by 21 January 63. This makes conception after the wedding quite possible, especially if the child was premature. It died within less than four months (*TA* 15.23.4).

63 *TA* 14.60.5–61.7 with Furneaux's adoption of Andresen's punctuation.

64 *TA*14.62.1: *elusa erat*. Careless disregard of the pluperfect leads both Church and Brodribb and M. Grant to give the impression in their translations that the examination of the *ancillae* was held at this point.

65 *TA* 14.62.1–6, *SN* 35.2.

66 Cf. *SN* 35.1: when Nero's friends criticized him for neglecting Octavia, he replied with a crude pun: 'Let her be satisfied with the insignia of wifehood (*uxoria ornamenta*).'

67 On the colony see Griffin 1984: 102–3. On the infant's deification see Bauman 1989: 88. On Poppaea's death see *TA* 16.6.1; *SN* 35.3; CD 62.27.4; Schol. Juv. 6.462. Tacitus notes an alternative tradition which has her poisoned, but rather unexpectedly rejects it 'because it is malevolent rather than truthful, for Nero wanted children and loved his wife'. Suetonius says he kicked her because she scolded him for coming home late from the races. On the consecration see *TA* 16.6.2; SMW 25, 148–9. On Cassius see Bauman 1989: 88, 107–13.

68 *TA* 15.68.5 with Furneaux's note; *SN* 35.1. On her erudition see Juv.

6.434–56 with Schol. ad 6.434. On the identification of the person there referred to as Statilia see C. W. Stoker, *The Satires of Juvenal and Persius*, London 1839, ad loc.; L. Friedlander, *D. Iunii Juvenalis Saturarum Libri V*, Leipzig 1895, ad loc.; R. Hanslik in *Kl.P.* 3.1241. E. Stein (*RE* 2208–10) is dubious. So is E. Sikes, *Cambridge Ancient History* 11.723 (by implication). Balsdon (1962: 128), E. Courtney, *A Commentary on the Satires of Juvenal*, London 1980, ad loc. and Winkler 1983: 184 do not express an opinion.

69 *TA* 15.68.3–5; *SN* 35.1. Cf. Bauman 1974a: 147.

70 Griffin (1984: 194), also discussing his attempt to marry Antonia. Griffin appears to imply that he did not make up his mind to marry Statilia until there was no longer any prospect of a favourable response from Antonia. That is one possible explanation for the delay. For another see below p. 209.

71 For an account of this conspiracy see Griffin 1984: 166–70.

72 On imperial solidarity see Bauman 1974a, 99–104. On Nero's Claudianism see Meise 1969: 176–87; Griffin 1984: 96–9.

73 Seneca did not share their views, though his own stance was far from consistent. The funeral oration for Claudius that he wrote for Nero was laudatory, but the speech from the throne was not (*TA* 13.3.1–2, 4). One wonders just how much of Nero's confusions and vacillation was due to Seneca, the man for all seasons.

74 Cf. Warmington 1969: 47: '[Nero had to] liberate himself from the psychological domination of his mother and enjoy . . . the fruits of autocratic power.' See also Garzetti 1974: 608–9.

SELECT BIBLIOGRAPHY

Works not frequently cited and, with a few exceptions, ancient sources and articles in standard reference works are sufficiently identified in the notes and the abbreviations and are not listed here.

Allen. W. (1941) 'The political atmosphere of the reign of Tiberius', *TAPA* 72: 1–25.

Astin, A. E. (1978) *Cato the Censor*, Oxford.

Babcock, C. L. (1965) 'The early career of Fulvia', *AJP* 86, 1–32.

Badian, E. (1972) 'Tiberius Gracchus and the Roman revolution', *ANRW* I (1): 668–731.

—— (1985) 'A phantom marriage law', *Philologus* 129: 82–98.

Balsdon, J. P. V. D. (1962) *Roman women: their history and habits*, London (repr. 1975).

Barrett, A. A. (1989) *Caligula: the corruption of power*, London.

Bartels, H. (*post* 1962) *Studien zum Frauenporträt der augusteischen Zeit*, Munich.

Bauman, R. A. (1966) 'Tiberius and Murena', *Hist.* 15: 420–32.

—— (1967) *The Crimen Maiestatis in the Roman Republic and Augustan Principate*, Johannesburg (repr. 1970).

—— (1968) 'Some remarks on the structure and survival of the *Quaestio de Adulteriis*', *Antichthon* 2: 68–93.

—— (1969) 'The Duumviri in the Roman criminal law and in the Horatius legend', *Hist.: Einzelschriften* 12.

—— (1974a) *Impietas in Principem: A Study of Treason against the Roman Emperor with special reference to the first century A.D.*, Munich.

—— (1974b) 'Criminal prosecutions by the aediles' *Lat.* 33: 245–64.

—— (1976) 'The Gracchi and Saturninus', *Journal of History* 7: 53–68.

—— (1978) 'Maiestatem populi Romani comiter conservanto', in *Essays in Honour of Ben Beinart*, Cape Town, 1: 19–36.

—— (1980) 'The "Leges Iudiciorum Publicorum" and their interpretation in the Republic, Principate and later Empire', *ANRW* II (13): 103–233.

—— (1981) 'Tribunician sacrosanctity in 44, 36 and 35 BC', *RhM* 124: 166–83.

—— (1982a) 'The resumé of legislation in Suetonius', *SZ* 99: 81–127.
—— (1982b) 'Hangman, call a halt!', *Hermes* 110: 102–10.
—— (1983) *Lawyers in Roman Republican Politics*, Munich.
—— (1984) 'Family law and Roman politics', in *Sodalitas: Scritti in onore di Antonio Guarino*, Naples, 1283–300.
—— (1985) *Lawyers in Roman Transitional Politics*, Munich.
—— (1989) *Lawyers and Politics in the Early Roman Empire*, Munich.
—— (1990) 'The suppression of the Bacchanals: five questions', *Hist.* 39: 334–48.
—— (1990a) *Political Trials in Ancient Greece*, London: Routledge.
Beard, M. (1980) 'The sexual status of Vestal Virgins', *Journal of Roman Studies* 70: 12–27.
Beaucamp, J. (1976) 'Le vocabulaire de la faiblesse feminine dans les textes juridiques romains du troisième au quatrième siècle', *Revue historique de droit français et etranger* 54: 485–508.
Bernstein, A. H. (1978) *Tiberius Sempronius Gracchus*, Ithaca.
Besnier, R. (1979) 'Properce (Elégies II, VII et VIIA) et le premier échec de la législation démographique d'Auguste', *Revue historique de droit français et étranger* 57: 191–203.
Boyce, A. A. (1937) 'The expiatory rites of 207 B.C.', *TAPA* 68: 157–71.
Bradley, K. R. (1978) *Suetonius' Life of Nero*, Brussels.
Briscoe, J. (1981) *Commentary on Livy xxxiv–xxxvii*, Oxford.
Brunt, P. A. (1971) *Italian Manpower 225 BC–AD 14*, Oxford.
Buckland, W. W. (1963) *A Text-Book of Roman Law from Augustus to Justinian*, (3rd edn rev. P. Stein), Cambridge.
Cantarella, E. (1972) 'Adulterio, omicidio legittimo e causa d'onore in diritto romano', in *Studi Scherillo* 1:243–74, Milan.
—— (1987) *Pandora's Daughters*, Baltimore.
Carcopino, J. (1958) *Passion et Politique chez les Césars*, Paris.
Cassola, F. (1968) *I Gruppi Politici Romani nel III Secolo A.C.*, Rome.
Ciccotti, E. (1895) *Donne e politici negli ultimi anni della Roma repubblicana*, Milan (repr. 1965).
Cizek, E. (1982) *Néron*, Paris.
Classen, C. J. (1973) 'Ciceros Rede für Caelius', *ANRW* I (3): 60–94.
Colin, J. (1954) 'Les consuls du César-Pharaon Caligula et l'héritage de Germanicus', *Lat.* 13: 394–416.
—— (1956) 'Les vendanges dionysiaques et la legende de Messaline', *Les Etudes classiques* (Namur) 24: 25–39.
Corbett, P. E. (1930) *The Roman Law of Marriage*, Oxford (repr. 1969).
Cornell, T. J. (1981) 'Some observations on the "crimen incesti" ', in *Le délit religieux dans la cité antique*, Rome, pp. 27–37.
Courtney, E. (1980) *A Commentary on the Satires of Juvenal*, London.
Csillag, P. (1976) *The Augustan Laws on Family Relations*, Budapest.
Culham, Ph. (1982) 'The *Lex Oppia*', *Lat.* 41: 786–93.
Daviault, A. (1981) *Comoedia Togata: Fragments*, Paris.
Della Corte, F. (1982) 'Le *leges Iuliae* e l'elegia romana', *ANRW* 30 (1): 1539–58.
De Martino, F. (1972–4) *Storia della Costituzione Romana*, Naples, 4 vols.

De Riencourt, A. (1974) *Sex and Power in History*, New York.

Deroux, C. (1973) 'L'Identité de Lesbie', *ANRW* I (3): 390–416.

Des Bouvrie, S. (1984) 'Augustus' legislation on morals – which morals and what aims?' , *Symbolae Osloenses* 59; 93–113.

Dixon, S. (1984) 'Infirmitas sexus: womanly weakness in Roman law', *Tijdschrift voor Rechtsgeschiedenis* 52: 343–71.

Dorey, T. A. (1958) 'Cicero, Clodia and the *Pro Caelio*', *Greece and Rome* 27: 175–80.

Ehrhardt, C. (1978) 'Messalina and the succession to Claudius', *Antichthon* 12: 51–71.

Eisenhut, W. (1964) 'Ceres', *Kl.P.* 1: 1113–15.

Fanizza, L. (1977) 'Il senato e la prevenzione del crimen repetundarum in eta tiberiana', *Labeo* 23: 199–214.

Ferrero, G. (1911) *The Women of the Caesars*, New York.

Festugière, A. J. (1954) 'Ce que Tite-Live nous apprend sur les mystères de Dionysos', *Mélanges d'archéologie et d'histoire* 66: 79–91.

Finley, M. I. (1968) 'The silent women of Rome', in *Aspects of Antiquity*, London, pp. 129–42.

Fitzler (1917) 'Iulius (Iulia)', *RE* 20: 896–906.

Gagé, J. (1963) 'Matronalia. Essai sur les devotions et les organisations culturelles des femmes dans l'ancienne Rome', *Coll. Lat.* 60.

Galinsky, K. (1981) 'Augustus' legislation on morals and marriage', *Philologus* 125: 126–44.

Gallini, C. (1970) *Protesta e integrazione nella Roma antica*, Bari.

Gardner, J. F. (1986) *Women in Roman Law and Society*, London.

Gardner, R. (1958) 'Cicero *Pro Caelio*', Loeb edn (rev. 1965).

Gardthausen, V. (1896) *Augustus und seine Zeit*, Leipzig.

Garofalo, L. (1989) *Il processo edilizio*, Padua.

Garzetti, A. (1974) *From Tiberius to the Antonines*, tr. J. R. Forster, London.

Greenidge, A. H. J. and Clay, A. M. (1960) *Sources for Roman History, 133–70 BC* (2nd edn E. W. Gray), Oxford.

Griffin, M. T. (1984) *Nero: The End of a Dynasty*, London.

Groag, E. (1919) *Studien zur Kaisergeschichte* III: 'Der Sturz der Iulia', *Wiener Studien* 40: 150–67, 41: 74–88.

Guarino, A. (1975) 'In difesa di Messalina', *Labeo* 21: 12–26.

Hallett, J. P. (1977) 'Perusinae Glandes and the changing image of Augustus', *American Journal of Ancient History* 2: 151–71.

—— (1984) *Fathers and Daughters in Roman Society*, Princeton.

Hammond, M. (1937) 'Octavius (Octavia)', *RE* 17: 1859–68.

Henderson, A. A. R. (1979) *P. Ovidi Nasonis: Remedia Amoris*, Edinburgh.

Henderson, B. W. (1903) *The Life and Principate of the Emperor Nero*, London.

Hennig, D. (1975) *L. Aelius Seianus*, Munich.

Herrmann, C. (1964) 'Le rôle judiciaire et politique des femmes sous la république romaine', *Coll. Lat.* 67.

Herz, P. (1981) 'Diva Drusilla: Agyptisches und Römisches im Herrscherkult zur Zeit Caligulas', *Hist.* 30: 324–36.

Herzog-Hauser, G. and Wotke, F. (1955) 'Valeria Messalina', *RE* 8A: 246–58.
Heurgon, J. (1964) *Daily Life of the Etruscans*, tr. J. Kirkup, London.
Hinard, F. (1985) *Les proscriptions de la Rome républicaine*, Rome.
Hoffsten, R. B. (1939) *Roman Women of Rank of the Early Empire*, Diss. Philadelphia.
Hollis, A. S. (1977) *Ovid: Ars Amatoria Book I*, Oxford.
Hopkins, K. (1983) *Death and Renewal*, Cambridge.
Horsfall, N. (1987) 'The "Letter of Cornelia": yet more problems', *Athenaeum* 65: 231–4.
Instinsky, H. U. (1971) 'Zur Echtheitsfrage der Brieffragmente der Cornelia, Mutter der Gracchen', *Chiron* 1: 177–89.
Jolowicz, H. F. and Nicholas, B. (1972) *Historical Introduction to the Study of Roman Law* (3rd edn), Cambridge.
Jörs, P. (1893) 'Die Ehegesetze des Augustus', in *Fschr. Mommsen*, Marburg.
Judge, E. A. (1974) '*Res Publica Restituta*: A Modern Illusion?', in *Polis and Imperium*, Toronto, pp. 279–311.
Kaplan, M. (1980) '*Agrippina semper Atrox*', in Deroux (ed.) *Studies in Latin Literature and Roman History*, Brussels, pp. 410–17.
Köberlein, E. (1962) *Caligula und die agyptischen Kulte*, Meisenheim am Glau.
Koch, C. (1958) 'Vesta', *RE* 8A: 1717–76.
Knobloch, F. S. (1978) 'An ephemeral city-name', *Journal of the Society of Ancient Numismatics* 9: 35.
Kornemann, E. (1960) *Tiberius*, Stuttgart.
Krause, W. (1942) 'Ovidius Naso', *RE* 18: 1910–86.
Kunkel, W. (1962) *Untersuchungen zur Entwicklung des römischen Kriminalverfahrens in vorsullanischer Zeit*, Munich.
—— (1974) *Kleine Schriften*, Weimar.
Laikeit (1917) 'Iulius (Agrippina)', *RE* 10: 909–14.
Last, H. (1952) 'The social policy of Augustus', *Cambridge Ancient History*, (1st edn), pp. 425–56.
Latte, K. (1960) *Römische Religionsgeschichte*, Munich.
Leon, E. F. (1951) 'Scribonia and her daughters', *TAPA* 82: 168–75.
Levick, B. M. (1972) 'Tiberius' retirement to Rhodes in 6 BC', *Lat.* 31: 779–813.
—— (1976) *Tiberius the Politician*, London.
—— (1990) *Claudius*, London.
Little, D. (1982) 'Politics in Augustan poetry', *ANRW* II (30.1): 254–370.
McAlindon, D. (1956) 'Senatorial opposition to Claudius and Nero', *AJP* 77: 113–32.
McDermott, W. C. (1984) 'Clodia and Ameana', *Maia* 36: 3–11.
Malcovati, E. (1945) 'Donne di Roma antica', *Quaderni di Studi Romani* 8.1.
Marsh, F. B. (1926) 'Roman parties in the reign of Tiberius', *American Historical Review* 31: 233–50.
—— (1931) *The Reign of Tiberius*, Oxford.
Marshall, A. J. (1989) 'Ladies at law: the role of women in the Roman

civil courts', in Deroux (ed.) *Studies in Latin Literature and Roman History*, Brussels, pp. 35–54.

—— (1990a) 'Roman ladies on trial: the case of Maesia of Sentinum', *Phoenix*, pp. 46–59.

—— (1990b) 'Women on trial before the Roman senate', *Classical Views* 34: 333–66.

Marshall, B. A. (1985) *A Historical Commentary on Asconius*, Columbia, Miss.

Mehl, A. (1974) *Tacitus über Kaiser Claudius*, Munich.

Meise, E. (1969) *Untersuchungen zur Geschichte der Julisch-Claudischen Dynastie*, Munich.

Melmoux, J. (1978) 'La lutte pour le pouvoir en 51 et les difficultés imprévues d'Agrippine', *Lat.* 37: 350–61.

Millar, F. (1977) *The Emperor in the Roman World*, London.

Mommsen, T. (1887) *Römisches Staatsrecht* (3rd edn, repr. Basel 1952).

—— (1899) *Römisches Strafrecht* (repr. Graz 1955).

Monaco, L. (1984) '*Veneficia matronarum*: Magia, Medecina e Repressione', in *Sodalitas: Scritti in onore di Antonio Guarino*, Naples, pp. 2013–24.

Moreau, P. (1982) *Clodiana Religio: Un procès politique en 61 avant J.C.*, Paris.

Mottershead, J. (1986) *Suetonius: Claudius*, Bristol.

Münzer, F. (1900) 'Clodia', *RE* 4: 105–7.

—— (1901) 'Cornelia', *RE* 4: 1592–5.

—— (1910) 'Fulvia', *RE* 7, 281–4.

—— (1920) *Römische Adelsparteien und Adelsfamilien*, Stuttgart (repr. 1963).

—— (1923) 'Servilia', *RE* 2A: 1817–21.

—— (1937) 'Die römischen Vestalinnen bis zur Kaiserzeit', *Philologus* 92: 47–67, 199–222.

Nony, D. (1986) *Caligula*, Paris.

Norwood, F. (1963) 'The riddle of Ovid's relegation', *Classical Philology* 58: 150–63.

Ogilvie, R. M. (1965) *A Commentary on Livy*, Oxford.

Ollendorf, L. (1926) 'Livius (Livia)', *RE* 13: 900–27.

Oost, S. I. (1958) 'The career of M. Antonius Pallas'. *AJP* 79: 113–39.

Palmer, R. E. A. (1974) 'Roman shrines of female chastity from the caste struggle to the papacy of Innocent I', *Rivista Storica dell' Antichità* 4: 122–59.

Peppe, L. (1984) *Posizione giuridica e ruolo sociale della donna romana in età repubblicana*, Milan.

Pomeroy, S. B. (1975) *Goddesses, Whores, Wives and Slaves*, London.

Purcell, N. (1986) 'Livia and the womanhood of Rome', *Proceedings of the Cambridge Philological Society* 32: 78–105.

Raaflaub, K. A. (ed.) (1986) *Social Struggles in Archaic Rome*, Berkeley/Los Angeles/London.

Raditsa, L. F. (1980) 'Augustus' legislation concerning marriage, procreation, love affairs and adultery', *ANRW* II (13): 278–339.

Raepsaet-Charlier, M.-Th. (1982) 'Epouses et familles de magistrats dans les provinces romaines aux deux premiers siècles de l'Empire', *Hist.* 31: 56–69.

Ramage, E. S. (1984) 'Clodia in Cicero's *Pro Caelio*', in *Studies in Honour of C. R. Trahman*, Scholars' Press, pp. 201–11.

—— (1985) 'Strategy and methods in Cicero's *Pro Caelio*', *Atene e Roma* 30: 1–8.

Rawson, E. (1974) 'Religion and politics in the late second century BC at Rome', *Phoenix* 28: 193–212.

Reinach, S. (1908) 'Une ordalie par le poison à Rome', *Revue Archéologique* 2: 236–53.

de Riencourt, A. (1974) *Sex and Power in History*, New York.

Ritter, H.-W, (1972) 'Livias Erhebung zur Augusta', *Chiron* 2: 313–38.

Robleda, O. (1976) 'Cic. De Orat. 1, 40, 183; 56, 283 y el divorcio de Mesalina', *SDHI* 42: 424–30.

Roddaz, J.-M. (1984) *Marcus Agrippa*, Rome.

Rogers, R. S. (1931) 'The conspiracy of Agrippina', *TAPA* 62: 141–68.

Rotondi, G. (1912) *Leges Publicae Populi Romani*, Milan (repr. 1962).

Rousselle, R. J. (1982) *The Roman Persecution of the Bacchic Cult*, Diss. State University of New York.

Salmon, E. T. (1968) *A History of the Roman World from 30 BC to AD 138* (3rd edn), London.

Sattler, P. (1969) 'Julia und Tiberius: Beiträge zur römischen Innenpolitik zwischen den Jahren 12 vor und 2 nach Chr.', in W. Schmitthenner (ed.), *Augustus*, Darmstadt, pp. 486–530.

Schachermeyr (1932) 'Tanaquil', *RE* 4A: 2171–3.

Scheid, J. (1981) 'Le délit religieux dans la Rome tardo-républicaine', in *Le délit religieux dans la cité antique*, Rome, pp. 117–69.

Schumacher, L. (1982) *Servus Index*, Wiesbaden.

Scramuzza, V. M. (1940) *The Emperor Claudius*, Cambridge, Mass.

Scullard, H. H. (1970) *Scipio Africanus: Soldier and Politician*, London.

—— (1973) *Roman Politics 220–150 B.C.* (2nd edn), Oxford.

Seager, R. (1972) *Tiberius* Berkeley/Los Angeles.

Shotter, D. C. A. (1989) *Tacitus: Annals IV*, Warminster.

Simpson, C. J. (1980) 'The "conspiracy" of AD 39', *Coll. Lat.* 168: 347–66.

Singer, M. W. (1947) 'Octavia's mediation at Tarentum', *Class. Journ.* 43: 173–7.

Sirago, V. A. (1983) *Femminismo a Roma nel Primo Impero*, Catanzano.

Skinner, M. B. (1983) 'Clodia Metelli' *TAPA* 113: 273–87.

Stockton, D. (1979) *The Gracchi*, Oxford.

Syme, R. (1939) *The Roman Revolution*, Oxford.

—— (1958) *Tacitus*, 2 vols. Oxford.

—— (1978) *History in Ovid*, Oxford.

—— (1986) *The Augustan Aristocracy*, Oxford.

Szemler, G. J. (1978) 'Pontifex', *RE* Supp. 15: 331–96.

Temporini, H. (1978) *Die Frauen am Hofe Trajans*, Berlin/New York.

Thibault, J. C. (1964) *The Mystery of Ovid's Exile*, Berkeley/Los Angeles.

Thomas, J. A. C. (1970) 'Lex Julia de Adulteriis Coercendis', *Etudes Macqueron*, pp. 637–44.

Tomulescu, C. St. (1974) 'Les ordalies, le *sacramentum* et la *Lex Pinaria*', *RIDA* 21: 323–34.

Toynbee, A. J. (1965) *Hannibal's Legacy*, 2 vols, Oxford.

Turcan, R. (1972) 'Religion et politique dans l'affaire des Bacchanales', *Revue de l'histoire des religions* 91.

Villers, R. (1982) 'Le mariage envisagé comme institution de l'Etat dans le droit classique de Rome', *ANRW* II (14): 285–301.

Walter, G. (1955) *Néron*, Paris.

Warmington, B. H. (1969) *Nero: Reality and Legend*, London (repr. 1981).

Watson, A. (1965) 'The divorce of Carvilius Ruga', *Tijdschrift voor Rechtsgeschiedenis* 33: 38–50.

—— (1967) *The Law of Persons in the Later Roman Republic*, Oxford.

Willrich, H. (1903) 'Caligula', *Klio* 3: 85–118, 288–317, 397–470.

—— (1911) *Livia*, Leipzig/Berlin.

Winkler, M. M. (1983) *The Persona in Three Satires of Juvenal*, Hildesheim.

Wiseman, T. P. (1982) 'Calpurnius Siculus and the Claudian civil war', *Journal of Roman Studies* 72: 57–67.

Wissowa, G. (1912) *Religion und Kultus der Römer* (2nd edn), Munich.

Zinserling, V. (1973) *Women in Greece and Rome*, tr. L. A. Jones, New York.

GENERAL INDEX

INDEX TO SOURCES

185, 265–6 nn. 88–9; 65: 186, 264
n. 62; 66: 266 nn.93, 95; 69: 266,
nn. 99, 7; **XIII** 1: 266 nn. 93, 2;
2: 197, 266 nn. 1, 5, 268 n. 20;
3: 272 n. 73; 4: 192, 267 n. 8; 5:
194, 267 n. 12; 6: 194; 8: 194;
12: 267 nn. 14–15; 13: 195, 268
n. 16; 14: 195, 268 n. 17; 15–27:
268 n. 19; 17: 195; 18: 156, 268
n. 23; 19: 146, 196–7; 20: 268
n. 26; 21: 268–9 nn. 27–8; 22:
269 n. 30; 23: 269 n. 31; 31: 269
n. 33; 32: 261 n. 30, 269 n. 35;
33: 266 n. 4; 41: 260 n. 15; 42:
175; 43: 175, 261–2, nn. 30, 38;
45; 200; 46: 267 n. 15, 269–70
nn. 40–1; 47: 270 n. 52; **XIV** 1:
200–1, 268 n. 20; 1–7: 202; 2:
201, 259 n. 32, 264 n. 62, 267
n. 15; 3: 201; 3–5: 270 n. 44; 7:
243 n. 24, 265 n. 78; 8: 270 n. 45;
9: 259 n. 32, 270 nn. 46–7; 11:
203; 12: 265 n. 74, 270 nn. 48–9;
18: 268 n. 20; 22: 270 n. 52; 51:
269–70 nn. 30, 53; 52: 270 n. 53;
52–6: 270 n. 53; 56: 270 n. 53;
57; 269–70 nn. 30, 52, 54; 59:
204–5; 60: 205, 271 nn. 55–6, 61;
60–1: 271 n. 63; 61: 271 n. 61;
62: 207, 271 nn. 64–5; 63:
207–8; 64: 208; 65: 206; **XV** 23:
271 n. 62; 53: 206; 68: 271–2
nn. 68–9; **XVI** 6: 271 n. 67; 33:
262 n. 41; 34: 261 n. 29;
Dialogus: 28: 228 n. 3;

Historiae: **I** 13: 269 n. 40; 16:
257 n. 22; 73: 11; **IV** 18: 239
n. 8; 22: 239 n. 8; 61: 239 n. 8;
V 9: 257 n. 21
Terence: *Hecyra* 198: 36

Ulpian: **XI**.1: 232 n. 30

Valerius Maximus: **I** 1.15: 225 n. 6;
II 5.3: 221 n. 3; 9.2: 18; **III** 4.5:
234 n. 7; 5.3: 84; 7.9: 233 n. 44;
8.6: 49, 231 n. 25; **IV** 4: 228–9
nn. 3, 6; 6.5: 238 n. 48; **V** 2.1:
82; 4.6: 230 n. 20; **VI** 1 pr.: 248
n. 67; 5.3: 231 n. 25; 7.1: 228
nn. 2–3; 8.1: 233 n. 44; **VIII** 2.3:
231 n. 25; 3: 50, 82, 239 n. 11;
IX 1.3: 225–6 nn. 8, 2; 1.8: 236
n. 28, 239 n. 8; 1.9: 235 n. 24;
5.4: 85; 7.1: 231 n. 25; 15.2: 242
n. 19
Velleius Paterculus: **I** 17.1: 231
n. 29; **II** 7.1: 229 n. 7; 16.3–4:
83; 36.3: 11; 74.2: 241 n. 26;
74.2–3: 241 nn. 29, 34; 76.2: 11,
241 n. 30; 88.3: 11; 93.1–2: 243
nn. 8, 12, 245 n. 27; 96.1: 245
n. 27; 99.1: 103; 99.2: 245 n. 36;
100.2–5: 245 nn. 27, 31, 36;
100.3: 113; 100.4: 109; 100.5:
246 n. 45; 104.1: 104; 121.1:
105; 123: 108
Vergil: *Aeneid* 6.860–86: 243 n. 8

Zonaras: 9.17: 225–6 nn. 8, 2–3, 6;
11, 12, p. 37.29–38.3 D: 266 n. 5